Wittgenstein and His Interpreters

Wittgenstein and His Interpreters

Essays in Memory of Gordon Baker

Edited by Guy Kahane,
Edward Kanterian,
and Oskari Kuusela

Blackwell
Publishing

© 2007 by Blackwell Publishing Ltd

Chapter 7, Part II adapted from Adrian Moore, *Points of View* pp. 126–36. Oxford: Oxford University Press, 1997. By permission of Oxford University Press.

BLACKWELL PUBLISHING
350 Main Street, Malden, MA 02148-5020, USA
9600 Garsington Road, Oxford OX4 2DQ, UK
550 Swanston Street, Carlton, Victoria 3053, Australia

The right of Guy Kahane, Edward Kanterian, and Oskari Kuusela to be identified as the Authors of the Editorial Material in this Work has been asserted in accordance with the UK Copyright, Designs, and Patents Act 1988.

First published 2007 by Blackwell Publishing Ltd

1   2007

Library of Congress Cataloging-in-Publication Data

Wittgenstein and his interpreters : essays in memory of Gordon Baker / edited by Guy Kahane, Edward Kanterian, and Oskari Kuusela.
    p. cm.
    Includes bibliographical references and index.
    ISBN 978-1-4051-2922-0 (hardback : alk. paper)
1. Wittgenstein, Ludwig, 1889–1951.   I. Kahane, Guy, 1971–
II. Kanterian, Edward.   III. Kuusela, Oskari.
    B3376.W564W5545 2007
    192–dc22

                                                              2007001491

A catalogue record for this title is available from the British Library.

Set in 10/12.5pt Galliard
by SNP-Bestset Typesetter Ltd, Hong Kong
Printed and bound in Singapore
by Markono Print Media Pte Ltd

The publisher's policy is to use permanent paper from mills that operate a sustainable forestry policy, and which has been manufactured from pulp processed using acid-free and elementary chlorine-free practices. Furthermore, the publisher ensures that the text paper and cover board used have met acceptable environmental accreditation standards.

For further information on
Blackwell Publishing, visit our website:
www.blackwellpublishing.com

Contents

Notes on Contributors

Alice Crary is Associate Professor of Philosophy at the New School for Social Research. She has published articles on moral psychology, ethical theory, meta-ethics, philosophy and literature, feminist theory, animals and ethics, J. L. Austin, Wittgenstein and other issues and figures. She is author of *Beyond Moral Judgment* (2007). She is also co-editor of *The New Wittgenstein* (2000) and *Reading Cavell* (2006) and editor of *Wittgenstein and the Moral Life: Essays in Honor of Cora Diamond* (2007). She is currently writing a book on ethics and animals.

Hans-Johann Glock is Professor of Philosophy at the University of Zurich. Prior to that he was Professor of Philosophy at the University of Reading and Junior Research Fellow at St. John's College, Oxford. He also held visiting positions at Queen's University, Kingston, the University of Bielefeld and Rhodes University, Grahamstown. Glock is the author of *A Wittgenstein Dictionary* (Blackwell 1996), *Quine and Davidson* (2003) and *What is Analytic Philosophy?* (2007). He has edited *The Rise of Analytic Philosophy* (Blackwell 1997), *Wittgenstein: A Critical Reader* (Blackwell 2001), *Strawson and Kant* (2003) and is the co-editor of *Wittgenstein's Philosophical Investigations* (1991), *Wittgenstein and Quine* (2005) and *Wittgenstein and Analytic Philosophy* (2009).

P. M. S. Hacker is a Fellow of St John's College, Oxford. He co-authored five books with Gordon Baker: the first two volumes of the monumental multi-volume *Commentary on the Philosophical Investigations* (Blackwell 1980, 1985), *Frege: Logical Investigations, Language, Sense and Nonsense* (Blackwell 1984), and *Scepticism Rules and Language* (Blackwell 1984). In addition, he has written *Insight and Illusion* (Blackwell 1972/1986), *Appearance and Reality* (Blackwell 1987) and the remaining two volumes of the *Commentary* (Blackwell 1990, 1996), as well as the epilogue *Wittgenstein's Place in Twentieth Century Analytic Philosophy* (Blackwell 1996). More recently, he has written, together with Max Bennett, *Philosophical Foundations of Neuroscience* (Blackwell 2003). His next book is entitled *Human Nature: The Categorial Framework*.

Guy Kahane is Deputy Director of the Oxford Uehiro Centre for Practical Ethics at Oxford University. He works in meta-ethics, value theory, practical ethics, and the philosophy of neuroscience. He holds D. Phil. and B. Phil. degrees in Philosophy from Oxford University and a B.A. degree in Philosophy and Psychology from Tel Aviv University.

Edward Kanterian is a lecturer in philosophy at Trinity College and Jesus College, Oxford. Previously he held lecturerships at St Catherine's College, Oxford and the University of Reading. He works in semantics and meta-physics, is the author of *Analytic Philosophy* (2004) and has a forthcoming book on Frege. He holds a D. Phil. degree from Oxford University and an M.A. degree from Leipzig University.

Oskari Kuusela is an Academy of Finland Postdoctoral Fellow at the Department of Philosophy, University of Helsinki. His research interests include Wittgenstein, ethics and a variety of 'metaphilosophical' topics. He has published articles on Wittgenstein and Kant and is the author of *Wittgenstein and the Concept of Philosophy* (forthcoming). He holds a D. Phil. in Philosophy from Oxford University.

Marie McGinn is a senior lecturer in the Philosophy Department at York University. She is the author of *Wittgenstein and the Philosophical Investigations* (1997) and *Elucidating the Tractatus: Wittgenstein's Early Philosophy of Logic and Language* (2006).

Ray Monk is Professor of Philosophy at the University of Southampton. He studied philosophy at the universities of York and Oxford, writing his postgraduate thesis on Wittgenstein's philosophy of mathematics. He has written biographies of Wittgenstein (1990) and Russell (1999) and is working on a biography of the physicist Robert Oppenheimer. He is also the author of the book *How to Read Wittgenstein?* (2005). His current philosophical research interests are the philosophy of biography and Wittgenstein's philosophy of mathematics.

A. W. Moore is Professor of Philosophy at the University of Oxford and a Fellow of St Hugh's College, Oxford. He is the author of *The Infinite* (2nd edition 2001), *Points of View* (1997) and *Noble in Reason, Infinite* *in Faculty: Themes and Variations in Kant's Moral and Religious Philosophy* (2003). He is also the editor of *Meaning of Reference* (1993), *Infinity* (1993) and Bernard Williams' posthumously published anthology *Philosophy as a Humanistic Discipline* (2006).

Katherine Morris is a supernumerary fellow in philosophy at Mansfield College, Oxford University, where she has been since 1986; she completed an M. Phil. in Medical Anthropology at Oxford in 2005. She is the co-author, with Gordon Baker, of *Descartes' Dualism* (1996) and the editor of *Wittgenstein's Method: Neglected Aspects* (Blackwell 2004), a collection of the later Baker's essays on the later Wittgenstein. She has written numerous articles on Sartre and Merleau-Ponty and is writing a book on Sartre for Blackwell's Great Minds series.

Stephen Mulhall is Fellow and Tutor in philosophy at New College, Oxford. He was previously a Prize Fellow of All Souls College, Oxford, and a Reader in Philosophy at the University of Essex. His research interests include Wittgenstein, Heidegger and Kierkegaard. He is the author of *On Being in the World: Wittgenstein and Heidegger on Seeing Aspects* (1990), *Inheritance and Originality: Wittgenstein, Heidegger, Kierkegaard* (2001), *Philosophical Myths of the Fall* (2005) and *Wittgenstein's Private Language: Grammar, Nonsense and Imagination in Philosophical Investigations, 243–315* (2006).

Alois Pichler is the Director of the Wittgenstein Archives at the University of Bergen. He has co-edited with the Wittgenstein Archives *Wittgenstein's Nachlass: The Bergen Electronic Edition* (2000), and with Georg Henrik von Wright Wittgenstein's *Vermischte Bemerkungen/Culture and Value* (1994; Blackwell 1998). His other publications are mainly in the field of Wittgenstein scholarship: *Wittgenstein's Philosophische Untersuchungen: Vom Buch zum Album* (2004) and *Wittgenstein: The Philosopher and His Works* (2006), co-edited with Simo Säätelä, and in the field of Humanities Computing, where he relates his work on Wittgenstein to the digital turn, as in 'Encoding Wittgenstein: Some remarks on Wittgenstein's *Nachlass*, the Bergen Electronic Edition, and future electronic publishing and networking' (2002).

Hilary Putnam is Cogan University Professor Emeritus in the Department of Philosophy at Harvard University. He has written extensively on issues in metaphysics and epistemology, philosophy of science, philosophy of language, and philosophy of mind. In recent years he has also written extensively on the relations between scientific and non-scientific knowledge and on American pragmatism. His book *Ethics Without Ontology* (2004) deals with many of these topics.

Joachim Schulte teaches at the University of Zurich. He has published a number of articles and four books on the philosophy of Wittgenstein: *Experience and Expression* (1993), *Wittgenstein: An Introduction* (1992), *Chor und Gesetz: Wittgenstein im Kontext* (1990) and *Wittgenstein: Leben Werk Wirkung* (2005). He is co-editor of critical editions of Wittgenstein's *Tractatus Logico-Philosophicus* (1989) and *Philosophical Investigations* (2001). In recent years, he has chiefly worked on Wittgenstein's middle period.

David G. Stern is Professor of Philosophy at the University of Iowa. He is the author of *Wittgenstein's Philosophical Investigations: An Introduction* (2004) and *Wittgenstein on Mind and Language* (1995), and co-editor of *Wittgenstein Reads Weininger*, with Béla Szabados (2004) and *The Cambridge Companion to Wittgenstein*, with Hans Sluga (1996).

Acknowledgements

This volume is dedicated to the memory of Gordon Baker, distinguished interpreter of Wittgenstein and our former supervisor at Oxford. We are indebted to Katherine Morris for encouraging us to pursue this project and for much helpful advice. We are also grateful to P. M. S. Hacker and Rupert Read for useful comments on the introduction as well as to Jakob A. Bertzbach, William Child, Steven Hall, and Jonathan Witztum for their advice and assistance. We also want to thank our publisher, in particular Nick Bellorini and Gillian Kane.

Abbreviations

Works by Wittgenstein

The following abbreviations are used to refer to Wittgenstein's published works, listed in chronological order.

TLP   *Tractatus Logico-Philosophicus.* Translated by Ogden, C. K. London: Routledge & Kegan Paul, 1951.

BB   *Preliminary Studies for the "Philosophical Investigations," Generally Known as the Blue and Brown Books.* Edited by Rhees, R. Oxford: Blackwell, 1958.

NB   *Notebooks 1914–1916.* Edited by Anscombe, G. E. M. and von Wright, G. H., translated by Anscombe, G. E. M. Oxford: Blackwell, 1961.

TLP   *Tractatus Logico-Philosophicus.* Translated by Pears, D. F. and McGuinness, B. F. London: Routledge & Kegan Paul, 1961.

RFM   *Remarks on the Foundations of Mathematics.* Edited by Anscombe, G. E. M., Rhees, R., and von Wright, G. H., translated by Anscombe, G. E. M. Oxford: Blackwell, 1956. 2nd edition 1967, 3rd revised edition 1978.

Z   *Zettel.* Edited by Anscombe, G. E. M. and von Wright, G. H., translated by Anscombe, G. E. M. Oxford: Blackwell, 1967.

EPB   "Eine Philosophische Betrachtung." In *Schriften*, Vol. 5, 117–282. Edited by Rhees, R. Frankfurt am Main: Suhrkamp, 1970.

PT   *Prototractatus, An early version of Tractatus Logico-Philosophicus.* London: Routledge & Kegan Paul, 1971.

PG   *Philosophical Grammar.* Edited by Rhees, R., translated by Kenny, A. Oxford: Blackwell, 1974.

PR   *Philosophical Remarks.* Edited by Rhees, R., translated by Hargreaves, R. and White, R. Oxford: Blackwell, 1975.

RPPi   *Remarks on the Philosophy of Psychology*, Vol 1. Edited by Anscombe, G. E. M. and von Wright, G. H., translated by Anscombe, G. E. M. Oxford: Blackwell, 1980.

BBB   *Das Blaue Buch, Eine Philosophische Betrachtung (Das Braune Buch).* Edited by Rhees, R. Frankfurt am Main: Suhrkamp, 1984.

OC   *On Certainty.* Edited by Anscombe, G. E. M. and von Wright G. H., translated by Anscombe, E. and Paul, D. Oxford: Blackwell, 1993.

LE   "Lecture on Ethics." *Philosophical Review* 74 (1965): 3–12. Reprinted in PO, pp. 37–44.

PO   *Philosophical Occasions 1912–1951.* Edited by Klagge, J. and Nordmann, A. Indianapolis: Hackett Publishing, 1993.

DB   *Denkbewegungen, Tagebücher 1930–1932/1936–1937.* Edited by Somavilla, I. Innsbruck: Haymon, 1997.

PI   *Philosophical Investigations*, 2nd edition. Edited by Anscombe, G. E. M. and Rhees, R., translated by Anscombe, G. E. M. Oxford: Blackwell, 1997.

CV   *Culture and Value*, revised edition. Edited by von Wright, G. H. in collaboration with Nyman, H., revd. edn. by Pichler, A., translated by Winch, P. Oxford: Blackwell, 1998. First edition 1980.

PIKr   *Philosophische Untersuchungen, Kritisch-genetische Edition.* Edited by Schulte, J., Nyman, H., von Savigny, E. and von Wright, G. H. Frankfurt am Main: Suhrkamp, 2001.

BT   *Big Typescript: TS 213.* Edited by Luckhardt, C. G. and Aue, M. Oxford: Blackwell, 2005.

Wittgenstein's *Nachlass*

References to Wittgenstein's *Nachlass* (as cited in the von Wright catalogue; von Wright 1982/1993a) are by MS or TS number followed by page number.

BEE   *Wittgenstein's Nachlass, The Bergen Electronic Edition.* Edited by the Wittgenstein Archives at the University of Bergen. Copyright by Oxford University Press, the University of Bergen, the Wittgenstein Trustees, 2000.

Lecture Notes by Others, Conversations and Correspondence

LC   Barrett, Cyril, ed. *Lectures & Conversations on Aesthetics, Psychology, and Religious Belief. Compiled from notes taken by Yorick Smythies, Rush Rhees and James Taylor.* Berkeley: University of California Press, 1966.

EL   Engelmann, Paul. *Letters from Ludwig Wittgenstein. With a Memoir.* Oxford: Blackwell, 1967.

WVC   McGuinness, Brian, ed. *Wittgenstein and the Vienna Circle: Conversations Recorded by Friedrich Waismann.* Translated by Schulte, J. and McGuinness, B. Oxford: Blackwell, 1979.

AWL   Ambrose, Alice, ed. *Wittgenstein's Lectures, Cambridge 1932–35.* Oxford: Blackwell, 1979.

LWL   Lee, Desmond, ed. *Wittgenstein's Lectures 1930–1932. From the notes of John King and Desmond Lee.* Oxford: Blackwell, 1980.

DC   Drury, M. O. C. "Some Notes on Conversations with Wittgenstein." In R. Rhees, ed., *Recollections of Wittgenstein,* 1984, pp. 76–96. Oxford: Oxford University Press. Also in R. Rhees, ed., *Ludwig Wittgenstein – Personal Recollections,* 1981, pp. 91–111. Oxford: Blackwell. And in 'Conversations with Wittgenstein', in R. Rhees ed., 1981, pp. 112–189. See also *The Danger of Words and Writings on Wittgenstein.* Edited by Berman, D., Fitzgerald, M. and Hayes, J. Bristol: Thoemmes Press, 1996.

BC   Bouwsma, O. K. *Wittgenstein: Conversations, 1949–1951.* Indianapolis: Hackett, 1986.

LFM   Diamond, Cora, ed. *Wittgenstein's Lectures on the Foundations of Mathematics, Cambridge 1939, From the Notes of R. G. Bosanquet, Norman Malcolm, Rush Rhees, and Yorick Smythies.* London: Harvester, 1976 / Chicago: Chicago University Press, 1989.

VW   Wittgenstein, Ludwig and Waismann, Friedrich, *The Voices of Wittgenstein, The Vienna Circle, Ludwig Wittgenstein and Friedrich Waismann.* Edited by Baker, G. London: Routledge, 2003. (For abbreviations of Waismann's works, see below.)

Introduction

Guy Kahane, Edward Kanterian, and Oskari Kuusela

In what way, if any, is interpreting Wittgenstein different from interpreting other great philosophers? Are there any special difficulties relating to Wittgenstein interpretation? With some philosophers, we face straightforward obstacles. Take the example of Socrates. The only remaining record of Socrates' thought is its representation in Plato's dialogues and a handful of reports from other ancient sources. Indeed, to vividly illustrate the difficulty in accurately ascertaining what the historical Socrates really thought, Gregory Vlastos once suggested that we imagine that all that we knew of Wittgenstein's later philosophy were scattered reports and the writings of a close student (Vlastos 1991, 98).[1] Vlastos's choice of Wittgenstein as an object of comparison is probably not accidental. During Wittgenstein's lifetime the only sources of information about Wittgenstein's later philosophy were rumour and hearsay, the articles of some of his students, and manuscripts of dictations to students that were circulated from hand-to-hand. But Wittgenstein's death was followed by the publication of the *Philosophical Investigations*, the primary statement of his later views, and the decades that followed saw the publication of many collations of earlier and later writings: *The Blue and Brown Books*, *Remarks on the Foundations of Mathematics*, *Culture and Value*, *Remarks on the Philosophy of Psychology*, and others. More recently, Wittgenstein scholars have been granted electronic access to Wittgenstein's *Nachlass*, his literary remains. Those who embark today on the project of attempting to understand Wittgenstein's philosophy thus have a wealth of writing to study. One might think that by now there should be no difficulty in putting together an accurate picture of Wittgenstein's views – that the contrast between our understanding of Wittgenstein and of Socrates couldn't be greater. The irony is that the opposite is true.

Wittgenstein interpretation is a fertile project. His work has been the subject of thousands of articles, collections and books. Yet from all the wealth of available evidence there has emerged, not a single clear portrait, but a series of competing and often wildly contradictory Wittgensteins. It is still common for interpreters to claim that all prior readings of Wittgenstein have got things fundamentally wrong.[2] Disputes over numerous points of detail, as well as over the very aim of Wittgenstein's philosophy, continue.

What explains this situation? What does it tell us about the project of Wittgenstein interpretation? On what aspects of Wittgenstein's philosophy is there general consensus, and what remains under dispute? The essays collected in this volume, written by some of the leading Wittgenstein scholars today, discuss these and related questions. Starting out from a range of distinct and often opposing perspectives, the contributors consider various aspects of Wittgenstein interpretation: the relation between our understanding of his conception of philosophy and our reading of specific passages and remarks; the intimate connection between the substance and style of Wittgenstein's singular mode of philosophical writing; the usefulness of associating Wittgenstein's work with specific schools of thought or philosophical traditions; and related matters. Many of the essays touch on various aspects of the work of the late Wittgenstein scholar Gordon Baker, to whom this volume is dedicated. This is more than appropriate, since in his rich career Baker made an essential contribution to the painting of not one, but at least three of the dominant competing interpretations of Wittgenstein's philosophy.[3]

The essays in this volume certainly do not add up to any unified portrait of Wittgenstein. What we do hope, however, is that the juxtaposition, in a single volume, of these snapshots from different interpretative angles will offer an accurate and much needed view (or, to borrow a term of Wittgenstein's, an *Übersicht*) of the current state of Wittgenstein interpretation.[4]

In this introduction, we attempt to provide a framework for the discussion. We shall proceed as follows. *Section I* sketches a brief history of Wittgenstein interpretation, and in the course of doing so, highlights the main exegetical approaches. In *Section II* we try to identify some main points of contention, and to trace the way these have changed over time. *Section III* turns to look at various aspects of Wittgenstein's writings – his view of philosophy, and the way that view is expressed in the unique style and mode of his writings – and consider the ways that these make interpreting Wittgenstein so challenging. Finally, *Section IV* presents the papers in the volume.

I   Main Approaches to Wittgenstein Interpretation

Within the mass of work on Wittgenstein, it is possible to identify several broad patterns of assumptions and methods shared by groups of interpreters. It is important, however, to note that our list of interpretative approaches is drawn for a particular purpose: to serve as a guide for orientation in the vast body of writing on Wittgenstein. As such, it inevitably plays down important differences between the figures grouped together as well as interesting affinities between figures placed under opposing headings. We shall give most attention to approaches to Wittgenstein within the English-speaking or analytic tradition, though we end by mentioning some readings of Wittgenstein in relation to so-called continental philosophers or readings of him in a 'continental context'. Although our focus is on scholarly work that explicitly aims to interpret Wittgenstein's writings, we shall not ignore attempts to apply his philosophy in various areas; such attempts implicitly embody an interpretation of Wittgenstein, and they often bring to light the implications and commitments of a given reading.

1   Initial responses

Writings referring to and discussing Wittgenstein appear from the 1920s onwards – mainly by the members of the Vienna Circle, by Oxford and Cambridge philosophers or in texts about logical positivism.[5] The early/ mid 1950s, however, really mark the beginning of a steady accumulation of articles *on* Wittgenstein.[6] The details of the *Tractatus* conception of language and the world were now discussed in journals and edited volumes.[7] With the posthumous publication of the *Philosophical Investigations* in 1953, general attention was drawn to Wittgenstein's later philosophy. Among the earliest responses to that work were the reviews by Norman Malcolm, Peter Strawson and Paul Feyerabend (see Pitcher ed. 1968). Fierce debates followed, and several of Wittgenstein's closest students assumed the role of explaining as well as defending Wittgenstein's later work. A famous example of this trend is Rush Rhees's dispute with Ayer on the interpretation of Wittgenstein's discussion of private language (Rhees 1954, Ayer 1954, both reprinted in Pitcher ed. 1968).

The first book-length treatises on Wittgenstein appeared in the late 1950s and early 1960s.[8] Wittgenstein's work now became an object of scholarly study. Anscombe's, Black's and Stenius's books from this period on the *Tractatus* still retain the status of standard commentaries, and their basic approach to the *Tractatus* remained unchallenged until fairly recently (see §3 below). Certain persisting types of Wittgenstein commentary also emerged around this time. One natural way to respond to Wittgenstein's style of writing is a remark by remark commentary, as exemplified by Black in the case of the *Tractatus*. Thirteen years later the same format was employed by Hallet (1977) in a commentary on Wittgenstein's *Philosophical Investigations* as well as in the 1980s by von Savigny (1988; 1989) and most famously by Baker and Hacker (see §2 below). A second widely employed format is first to discuss Wittgenstein's early philosophy and then move on to his later philosophy, often through an examination of his later criticism of his early thought. Again a basis can be found in Wittgenstein's writings themselves, especially in his suggestion in the preface to the *Philosophical Investigations* that his later work should be studied by juxtaposing it with the *Tractatus*. This form readily invites questions concerning the continuity of Wittgenstein's philosophy, a topic addressed explicitly, for instance, in Kenny (1973).[9]

The earliest readers perceived a sharp contrast between the *Tractatus* and the *Philosophical Investigations*, presenting Wittgenstein as holding, at different points, two radically opposing philosophies. As Wittgenstein's intermediate writings became available, it became clear that his route from his early to the later views was gradual. Nevertheless, the conception of Wittgenstein's philosophy as divided into early and late periods has persisted. What remains an object of dispute in later readings is the nature of Wittgenstein's route to his later thought and how exactly to understand the relation between his early and later philosophy – or perhaps his early and later *philosophies*.

2   The 'orthodox' interpretation

Wittgenstein interpretation reached a high point of scholarly detail in Gordon Baker and Peter Hacker's comprehensive commentary on the *Philosophical Investigations*, published in four volumes from 1980 onwards. Baker and Hacker's interpretation of Wittgenstein is continuous with earlier work, most notably that of Anscombe (1959), Malcolm (1954), Stenius (1960), Black (1964), Ambrose (1966), Pears (1971), Kenny (1973; 1984) and Fogelin (1976), but their interpretation is worked out in greater detail, making careful use of Wittgenstein's *Nachlass*.[10] More recent interpreters following a similar approach include Hans-Johann Glock (1991; 1996), Oswald Hanfling (1989; 2004), Richard McDonough (1986), Joachim Schulte (1992; 1993), Severin Schröder (2006), and to an extent Stephen Mulhall (1990) and David Stern (1995).[11] This reading dominated the field from the 1970s until the 1990s. It has recently been labelled 'orthodox' by its opponents.

Although there are many important differences between the above authors,[12] they share a broadly similar approach to Wittgenstein's early and later philosophy insofar as they attribute substantial views and arguments to Wittgenstein. To take Baker and Hacker as a representative example, they view the *Tractatus* both as a reaction to and culmination of a representational conception of the relation between language or thought and reality that had dominated European philosophy for centuries, a model which reached Wittgenstein through his immediate predecessors Frege and Russell, and which he refined in the picture theory of meaning. According to the picture theory, language mirrors the world, propositions are descriptions of states of affairs consisting of names that stand for objects in the world, and language connects to reality via mental acts relating names to their meanings. Thus, the *Tractatus* is understood as offering a subtly worked out version of the representational model, articulating a theory of the essence of any possible language, the metaphysical structure of the world, and their interrelation. The theory delimits what can be said from what cannot be said but at most shown, where the latter includes the very essence of language and the world. This leads to the paradox of the *Tractatus*, since its propositions must be themselves nonsensical, given that they are trying to say what cannot be said but can only be shown. While this paradox has suggested to orthodox interpreters that something is awry with the *Tractatus* conception of language, they do not believe that everything in the book needs to be rejected. For instance, Wittgenstein's criticism of Frege's and Russell's conceptions of logic, and his own positive contribution to the clarification of the nature of logical propositions, stand firm. Similarly, his discussion of the problem of intentionality contains insights fundamental to his later solution (see Hacker 1996, Ch. I). Finally, the *Tractatus*' programme for future philosophy as a non-cognitive, elucidatory discipline is significant and an important connection to the later work.

The *Philosophical Investigations*, by contrast, is understood by the 'orthodox' interpreters as a rejection of the Tractarian model of the language-world relation, and through it, of the tradition behind it. In particular, the book propounds an explicit anti-metaphysical view: philosophy is not taken to consist in the pursuit of the sempiternal and hidden structure of language and the world. Language can still be said to have essential features, but they lie in plain view and need only to be made perspicuous by way of describing the uses of words or by tabulating the rules by which language is governed (see PI §92). Many of these features are not immutable, however, but belong to changing linguistic practices. The world, on the other hand, is no longer viewed as an object of *a priori* philosophical speculation, but only of empirical scientific investigation. The logical syntax of language does not mirror the hidden structure of the world, but is simply a means of representing the world. The study of language will thus not uncover any hidden metaphysical features of reality, since there are none. The traditional conception of the aims of philosophy, shared by the *Tractatus*, is taken to be the result of a misunderstanding of the relation between language and the world by (i) sublimating the essence of our language, and (ii) mistaking features of our linguistic representation of the world for features of the world. What previous philosophers took to be metaphysical truths about the nature of reality are in fact no more than 'shadows cast by grammar' (Baker and Hacker 2005, 97). Therefore, we need to discard this idealised model of language and give a systematic account of the language-games in which concepts are used and thus make our conceptual framework explicit in order to resolve philosophical problems. Since such problems arise when we use expressions 'in a language-game other than the one appropriate to it' (Kenny 1973, 164), bringing 'words back from their metaphysical to their everyday use' (PI §116) will do away with these problems.

Accordingly, the *Philosophical Investigations* is seen as engaging in both a positive and a negative task: on the one hand in the tabulation of grammar and the interrelations of concepts such as meaning, rule, understanding, knowledge, thinking, the inner and the outer, etc., and on the other hand, in dispelling confusions brought about by misunderstanding these concepts and the network of conceptual relationships in which they are embedded. For example, the later Wittgenstein is taken to argue that since language is a rule-governed practice (positive result), the idea of a private language is incoherent (negative result). Reading Wittgenstein as providing an overview of grammatical rules that will dissolve philosophical problems and confusions, this interpretation sees his later work as largely continuous with the work of Oxford philosophers such as Ryle, Austin and Strawson.

Concerning the *Philosophical Investigations* the interpretative method employed by orthodox interpreters consists in a systematic reading of the main text by establishing interconnections between remarks, often based on tracing individual remarks to their earlier contexts. In addition, in many cases orthodox readers interpret Wittgenstein's arguments as direct responses to, and thus to some extent as engaging with, the argument of other philosophers such as Frege, Russell and Moore. The orthodox interpretation attributes to Wittgenstein a concern with a methodical account of philosophically relevant concepts for the therapeutic purpose of releasing us from deep-seated confusions, but not primarily an ethical interest in philosophy, as certain other interpreters do (see below). Consequently, the hermeneutic task is seen as consisting in working out his nuanced and complex arguments and analyses, both positive and negative. On this approach, then, interpreting Wittgenstein need not be fundamentally different from the interpretation of other major philosophers.

3 *The new interpretation of the* Tractatus

It is characteristic of both the early readings of the *Tractatus* and the 'orthodox' interpretation that they attribute to the early Wittgenstein theories such as logical atomism or the picture theory of language.[13] The remarks in the *Tractatus* to the effect that its propositions are to be considered nonsensical (TLP 6.54) did, of course, catch the attention of Russell, Ramsey and others of the very earliest commentators. Nevertheless, the problem of the self-proclaimed nonsensicality of the book did not become a main focus of the interpretation of the book. This approach to the *Tractatus* was challenged from the 1980s onwards by an alternative interpretation developed by Cora Diamond, James Conant, and others.[14] The proponents of this type of reading are sometimes referred to as the 'New Wittgensteinians', following the publication in 2000 of *The New Wittgenstein*, an influential collection of articles representing this approach. This interpretation of the *Tractatus* is also described as *resolute*, and contrasted with the *ineffability* reading defended by orthodox interpreters. The debate about the interpretation of the nonsensicality of the *Tractatus* dominated Wittgenstein scholarship from the late 1990s onwards.

Diamond and Conant reject the 'orthodox' attribution to the *Tractatus* of ineffable doctrines and claim that it should be read as engaging in a therapeutic activity whose goal is to make its reader turn away from philosophical theorising. Wittgenstein aims to achieve this by adopting an alternative method of philosophising designed to help its reader to come to see how doctrines which at first sight appear to make sense collapse into nonsense upon closer examination.[15] It would be mistaken to conceive of the *Tractatus* as seeking to draw a limit to language by appealing to a nonsensical theory or a set of nonsensical arguments. The *Tractatus* does indeed seek to draw such a limit, but it aims to do so simply by relying on the reader's pre-theoretical comprehension of what makes sense. On this view, the method of the *Tractatus* is perhaps better compared to Kierkegaard's ironic style than to argumentative philosophical texts such as those of Aristotle and Kant. Also, rather than arguing for any particular 'fixed' readings of the remarks of the *Tractatus*, Conant and Diamond see themselves as articulating a programme for reading the book. Ultimately it is up to the individual readers of the *Tractatus* to work their way through the book and experience the collapse of its sentences (Conant and Diamond 2004, 47).

One apparent advantage of this reading is that it avoids portraying the *Tractatus* as straightforwardly self-undermining. After all, on the orthodox interpretations, the statements of the book are thought by Wittgenstein to be at once true (Preface) and nonsensical (TLP 6.54), at once trying to say what can only be shown and insisting that it cannot be said. Diamond and Conant too believe that the *Tractatus* ultimately fails to advance a philosophy without doctrines. But they portray this failure as less straightforward than the early and 'orthodox' readings. In their view, the project of the *Tractatus* ultimately fails because the method of philosophical clarification as logical analysis which the book advocates has built into it a doctrine about the essence of language (Conant and Diamond 2004).[16]

The new interpretation of the *Tractatus* also raises anew the question of the continuity of Wittgenstein's philosophy. This question had been posed earlier when, for example, interpreters wondered whether Wittgenstein retained a version of the picture theory in his later philosophy (see Stenius 1960; Kenny 1973), or even aspects of his conception of philosophy (see Kenny 1973; for a similar, more recent account, see Hacker 2005, 303–6). The New Wittgensteinians claim that there are even stronger affinities between Wittgenstein's early and later philosophy (see Conant 2004).[17] This raises the stakes in the interpretation of Wittgenstein's later philosophy, because it now becomes harder to explain why the later Wittgenstein rejected his earlier work.

4   *Therapeutic readings of Wittgenstein's later philosophy*

Although this dispute about the *Tractatus* continues to excite much attention, the debate has partly shifted to the interpretation of Wittgenstein's later work. Here too recent work has challenged the received interpretations by placing a very different emphasis on the *therapeutic* aspect of Wittgenstein's later work.[18] Accordingly, Wittgenstein's later philosophy is not to be understood as trying to convince the philosopher's interlocutor with the force of arguments or facts about ordinary language use.

Rather, Wittgenstein's aim is to release us from disquietude and puzzlement due to philosophical pictures or ways of looking at things we have adopted and which entangle us in philosophical problems, and to replace such disruptive conceptions with more helpful ones.[19] It is thus of the very nature of the therapeutic interpretation that it does not converge on a set of shared doctrines attributed to Wittgenstein. Instead of making philosophical assertions, Wittgenstein is thought to employ, for instance, analogies and rules as objects of comparison to make relevant aspects of language use perspicuous. Readings of this type thus tend to pay more attention to the details of Wittgenstein's style (for more on this, see §4 below).

Although this therapeutic interpretation has until fairly recently been on the margins of Wittgenstein scholarship, it has its roots in some of the earliest readings of Wittgenstein: those of John Wisdom (1953), O. K. Bouwsma (1961 and BC)[20] and Friedrich Waismann, who was Wittgenstein's collaborator in the 1930s (see Waismann 1997 and VW). In the United States, this reading is associated especially with Stanley Cavell (Cavell 1976; 1982; 2005) and Burton Dreben, and in Britain, with the later work of Gordon Baker (2004).[21] Further criticism of the orthodox view that is in line with the therapeutic approach emerged in the 1990s, focusing on Wittgenstein's method (Pichler 2004; Stern 2004; see also §3 above).[22]

An extreme form of the therapeutic approach was advocated by Burton Dreben, whose interpretation of Wittgenstein is captured in the aphorism attributed to him, 'Philosophy is garbage, but the history of garbage is scholarship'.[23] On his reading of Wittgenstein (drawn perhaps more from the *Tractatus* than the *Philosophical Investigations*), there are no positive moves left to make in philosophy. All that remains is the critical dissection of classical philosophical texts, always aimed at demonstrating the points at which their authors crossed the boundaries of meaningful utterance and fell into nonsense.

Another unique voice in Wittgenstein interpretation is Stanley Cavell, who reads Wittgenstein as a modernist author grappling with the plight of a self-conscious modern subject who can no longer take for granted common conventions of history. A central theme in Cavell's aesthetic-ethical reading of the *Philosophical Investigations* is the tension between the deep human need to transcend the ordinary and the common, and the ultimate futility of any such attempt.[24] Cavell accordingly resists orthodox interpretations that portray Wittgenstein, for example, as conclusively dissolving scepticism by appeals to fixed rules of language (Cavell 1976,

Ch. IX; 1982).[25] In his many writings, Cavell has applied Wittgensteinian ideas to ethics, literature, music and film.[26]

A different version of the therapeutic approach was developed by Gordon Baker from the late 1980s onwards, arising out of dissatisfaction with his earlier interpretation of the *Philosophical Investigations* co-authored with Peter Hacker (see Baker 2004). Characteristic of the later Baker's work is detailed attention to Wittgenstein's language, such as his use of modal expressions. Rather than seeking to articulate doctrines about language, the aim of the later Wittgenstein is to articulate pictures and conceptions employed for the purpose of dissolving philosophers' 'thought cramps'. Baker emphasised Wittgenstein's comparison between philosophy and psychoanalysis (see MS 109, 174; also Hacker in this volume): he saw Wittgenstein's philosophy as concerned with problems which *particular* individuals have in *specific* historical contexts – whereby it is not assumed that such problems could not be shared by many, but only that the 'medicine' that works for one might not necessarily work for everyone. G. H. von Wright, the editor of many of Wittgenstein's works, also stressed the relativity of philosophical problems and clarifications to particular historical contexts, although von Wright is probably not best characterised as a therapeutic interpreter in Baker's sense (see von Wright 1982, 216).

It's worth noting that although the therapeutic approach to the later Wittgenstein might invite comparisons with the 'resolute' reading of the *Tractatus*, it shouldn't be assumed that the two necessarily go together: Baker, for example, held on to a more or less orthodox reading of Wittgenstein's earlier work.[27]

5   *Wittgenstein interpretation and mainstream analytic philosophy*

Most of the interpreters we've discussed so far are not interested only in establishing the correct interpretation of Wittgenstein's views, but also see themselves as *followers* of Wittgenstein – accepting in the main Wittgenstein's later philosophy, as they interpret it, if not that of the *Tractatus*.[28] These readings of Wittgenstein are presented, then, from what is sometimes called a *Wittgensteinian* point of view. There are however also interpretations of Wittgenstein that aren't developed from an explicitly Wittgensteinian standpoint.[29] The most famous and influential example of such a reading is Saul Kripke's discussion of Wittgenstein's remarks on rule-following and private language (Kripke 1982), but in fact many contemporary mainstream analytic philosophers who could by no means be described as followers of Wittgenstein often invoke his name and claim to present an account of his views. Some of these authors, of course, merely draw on some conventional understanding of what Wittgenstein supposedly said (an understanding that broadly corresponds to what we called the "Orthodox Interpretation"). But others clearly aim to give a more or less novel, and more or less sympathetic, account of Wittgenstein's views on this or that matter, and relate them to contemporary discussions of first-person authority, sensation language, necessity and normativity, meaning and use, and many other topics. These accounts are naturally very diverse, but what they have in common is that they try to extract and assess particular theses or arguments they purport to find in Wittgenstein's texts, to state them in contemporary jargon, and to assess them by contemporary methods and standards.[30]

Thus Kripke claimed to find, in the remarks on rule-following in the *Philosophical Investigations*, a powerful argument that leads to a troubling sceptical paradox. Kripke then claimed to find in these remarks a sceptical solution to the paradox. But although this struck many Wittgenstein scholars as a thoroughly misguided reading of the text,[31] Kripke was in fact only following in the footsteps of the first reader of Wittgenstein's earliest work. Russell's introduction to Wittgenstein's *Tractatus* notoriously questioned the self-destructing pronouncements that bracket that text and thus found in it, against the apparent wishes of its author, a range of substantive philosophical theses and arguments. Kripke's is, therefore, an interpretative dilemma (or temptation) that confronted readers of Wittgenstein's work from the very start (see Mulhall in this volume).

This interpretative dilemma is due to the apparent chasm between Wittgenstein's conception of philosophy and that held by many mainstream analytic philosophers. Despite significant disagreement about Wittgenstein's conception of philosophy, the majority of his interpreters agree that Wittgenstein's view of philosophy is radically at odds with a traditional conception of philosophy as a form of positive theoretical inquiry into the nature of world, mind and language. And although mainstream analytic philosophers of the last fifty years or so also have opposing views of philosophy, they mostly share, at least in broad outline, this traditional conception of philosophy.[32] The problem, then, is that when a philosopher treats Wittgenstein's writings as a repository for philosophical theses or theories, or for arguments for such theses or theories, he is wilfully ignoring what Wittgenstein himself claimed to be doing (cf. PI, §128).

There are several ways of dealing with this conundrum. One approach, pursued most vigorously by Michael Dummett and later on by Crispin Wright, is to decline to take Wittgenstein's remarks about his own work seriously: to insist that despite his repeated disavowals, Wittgenstein does traffic in substantive philosophical theses, such as, for example, a use theory of meaning or behaviourist view of sensation language (see Dummett 1959; 1978; Wright 1980; 1986; 2001).[33] Note however that to take this route is to commit oneself to substantive exegetical claims about a tension inherent within Wittgenstein's philosophy, something that most mainstream readers of Wittgenstein have declined to do.[34]

A different version of this strategy is to claim to accept Wittgenstein's conception of philosophy at least in broad outline, but to understand its implication for philosophical method more liberally than Wittgenstein himself and most Wittgensteinians. John McDowell, for instance, follows Wittgenstein in seeing philosophy as having exclusively critical and therapeutic aims, but is rather more sceptical about the possibility of achieving these aims through the assembly of reminders about everyday language use. He thus sees greater room for internal engagement with traditional and contemporary philosophy, employing their own idiom in the service of a more satisfying 'diagnostic deconstruction' of philosophical problems (see McDowell 1994),[35] and this also shapes his reading of Wittgenstein's texts.[36]

Yet another approach is to simply dismiss such worries of fidelity to the authors' intentions. In line with the impatience that some analytical philosophers still have regarding questions of history and interpretation, it might be claimed that it simply doesn't matter what Wittgenstein had in mind when he wrote the *Philosophical Investigations*. What matters is rather whether certain propositions and arguments – whatever their source – are philosophically interesting or defensible. Indeed Kripke's attitude to the exegetical question is revealing. He employs a device that has also been taken up by others: instead of explicitly attributing the argument he sets out in his book to Wittgenstein, he presents it as an argument that *struck* him while reading the *Philosophical Investigations*. Hence the common label of 'Kripkenstein' to the imaginary philosopher who raises a sceptical paradox about rule-following. Those who take this approach are obviously positioning themselves outside the orbit of the project of Wittgenstein *interpretation*, and indeed, the voluminous mainstream discussion of rule-following has increasingly detached itself from any explicit consideration of Wittgenstein's texts.[37]

It's worth remarking, however, that similar problems arise, as we have seen, *within* the circle of avowedly Wittgensteinian interpreters. For although most of these interpreters decline explicitly to ascribe to Wittgenstein *philosophical* theories and theses, or arguments *for* such theses (as opposed to clarificatory statements, or arguments such as *reductio* arguments intended to make perspicuous the logical consequences of philosophical views), it is still very much in dispute among them what counts as ascribing to Wittgenstein theses and arguments in the first place. For, as we saw earlier, on some therapeutic readings of Wittgenstein's later philosophy, to read his remarks on, say, the intelligibility of a private language as a *reductio ad absurdum* argument, as many interpreters have done, is a gross misunderstanding of the text that is no better than finding in it a sceptical paradox.[38]

6 Connections to the continent

Mainstream readings of Wittgenstein in the English-speaking world have tended to locate his work in relation to the founding figures of analytic philosophy, Frege, Russell and Moore, or to later figures within this tradition, such as Carnap, Quine, Austin and Ryle (Hacker 1996; Glock 2004; Biletzki 2003). But we've already noted readings on which Wittgenstein's philosophy is thought to echo continental figures such as Kant[39] or Kierkegaard (see Creegan 1989; Mulhall 2001). Not very surprisingly, readings that interpret Wittgenstein in the light of continental approaches have mostly been spearheaded by adherents of continental philosophy in the English-speaking world. We thus find comparisons between Wittgenstein's philosophy and that of Nietzsche, Heidegger, Merleau-Ponty and Derrida.[40]

In the continent itself, attitudes to Wittgenstein's work tend to be more cautious, as Wittgenstein has often been taken to belong to the opposing analytic tradition. In France, for example, Wittgenstein's work was mostly ignored by major figures such as Foucault and Derrida.[41] Perhaps the first to write about Wittgenstein in France was Pierre Hadot,[42] reading Wittgenstein as continuous with ancient ethics, with its emphasis on philosophy as a way of life. Hadot was followed by others such as Jacques Bouveresse, who attempted to relate Wittgensteinian ideas to the present concerns of French philosophy (see Bouveresse 1987; 1995), and Jean-François Lyotard, who has made controversial use of Wittgensteinian notions in several of his writings (Lyotard 1984; 1988; 1993). In Germany, Jürgen Habermas (Habermas 1988; 1998) and Karl-Otto Apel (Apel 1973; 1992) drew on Wittgenstein in their attempts to establish a foundation for critical theory and ethics.

Within this tradition, Wittgenstein's views on Freud have received special attention. Wittgenstein's relation to Freud presents a challenge to interpreters. On the one hand, we find positive references such as Wittgenstein's remark to Rhees that he is 'a disciple of Freud' and 'a follower of Freud' (LC, 41). On the other hand, Wittgenstein also voices criticisms of Freud's view of psychoanalysis as a science. According to Wittgenstein this understanding of psychoanalysis involves a confusion between the concepts of cause and reason, and Freud is better understood as having invented a new way of describing phenomena, rather than making factual, scientific claims. In the context of the discussion of Wittgenstein's relation to Freud some authors have been concerned with elucidating Wittgenstein's method of philosophy by focusing on his comparison between philosophy and psychoanalysis (see Wisdom 1953; McGuinness 2002, Ch. 20; Baker 2004, chs. 8, 10), while others have sought to make use of Wittgenstein's ideas in a critical examination of psychoanalysis. Readings of Wittgenstein have thus also played a role in debates about psychoanalysis, both on the continent and in the English speaking world (see Cioffi 1969; 1998; McGuinness 2002, Ch. 20).[43]

7   Other interpretations

Let us end this section by briefly mentioning readings of Wittgenstein that do not fit neatly any of the broad patterns of exegesis that we've considered so far. These include interpretations of Wittgenstein as a pragmatist, sometimes argued on the basis of Ramsey's influence on Wittgenstein (cf. Putnam 1995), or as a common sense philosopher in the style of G. E. Moore (cf. Stroll 1994). Jaakko Hintikka, partly in collaboration with Merrill B. Hintikka, proposed an interpretation of Wittgenstein according to which Wittgenstein maintained throughout his career a commitment to the ineffability of semantics and the privacy of experience, and which sees the development of Wittgenstein's philosophy centring on a move from giving primacy to phenomenological language in the *Tractatus* to giving primacy, in his later philosophy, to everyday reference to physical objects, made possible by the practices involved in various language-games (Hintikka and Hintikka 1986; Hintikka 1996). Finally, John W. Cook developed a controversial reading on which in both the early and later work Wittgenstein was a reductionist empiricist committed to a phenomenalist understanding of language (Cook 1994; 1999; 2005).

II   Themes and Controversies

Our overview of approaches to Wittgenstein interpretation highlighted a number of radically divergent accounts of Wittgenstein's early and later philosophy. But discussion of Wittgenstein's philosophy has also centred on particular themes and disputes. These are often interpretative disputes about the significance or intent of aspects of Wittgenstein's texts – some disputes have focused on a single obscure remark – as well as disputes about the correctness of Wittgenstein's claims. In this section we will survey, roughly in chronological order, several of the key disputes that dominated Wittgenstein interpretation from the publication of the *Philosophical Investigations* onwards.[44]

In early readings of the *Philosophical Investigations*, special attention was given to Wittgenstein's use of notions such as **language-game**[45] and **family resemblance**[46] – notions that have since gained currency outside academic philosophy as well – and there was much debate about their meaning and status. Discussion of the notion of a **criterion**, a notion that appears throughout the *Philosophical Investigations*, exemplifies this form of exegetical controversy. Wittgenstein contrasted criteria with what he called symptoms, a term he uses to refer to inductive evidence for the presence of a phenomenon. An inflamed throat is a symptom of angina, but a groan or withdrawal of one's hand from a fire are, according to Wittgenstein, not symptoms but criteria for a person's being in pain (see BB, 24–25). Wittgenstein thus takes criteria to mark a relation between two phenomena that isn't merely empirical, but there was much dispute about the exact nature of this relation, as well as about the role that it plays in Wittgenstein's understanding of mind, language and scepticism. For example, several readers influenced by Michael Dummett's anti-realism, such as the early Gordon Baker and Crispin Wright, have taken Wittgenstein's remarks on criteria to offer the foundation for an anti-realist semantics based on assertion-conditions, as opposed to a realist semantics based on truth-conditions (Baker 1974; 1977; Dummett 1978; Wright 1982).[47] Opposing readings have denied that the notion of criterion has any such theoretical import and take Wittgenstein's use of it to be continuous with everyday use, merely marking a grammatical distinction between empirical evidence and conceptual yet defeasible connections between phenomena (Kenny 1972; Canfield 1986; Hacker 1986; 1990).

The view that criteria provide non-inductive evidence for the truth of statements was seen by early readers such as Rogers Albritton and Norman Malcolm as the basis for a definitive refutation of scepticism, and in particular of scepticism about other minds (Albritton 1959; Malcolm 1954).[48] Albritton and Malcolm held that when, for example, certain behavioural criteria are met, we can know with certainty that someone is in pain, leaving no logical space for sceptical doubt. An alternative interpretation, associated with Stanley Cavell, sees this as a misunderstanding of Wittgenstein's attitude to scepticism. On this reading, criteria do not determine the certainty of statements but have to do with the applicability of the concepts employed in statements (see Affeldt 1998; Cavell 1982).[49]

Whereas some controversies revolved around the significance of key notions used by Wittgenstein, others focused on the interpretation of central passages in the *Philosophical Investigations*. One of the very first disputes following its publication was about the interpretation of Wittgenstein's discussion of a ***private language***. A private language, as Wittgenstein defines it in PI §243, is a language whose words refer to immediate, private sensations that can be known only to the speaker. In remarks that came to be known as the 'private language argument', Wittgenstein suggests that such a private language is impossible because meaning cannot be assigned to the words of a language that in principle cannot be understood by others. There has been much disagreement about the details and intended conclusion of the argument, as well as about its soundness.[50] In early discussion of the argument a central question was whether Wittgenstein is to be read as holding that language is possible only when embedded in an *actual* community – a reading known as the 'Community View' – or whether he is to be rather read as holding the weaker claim that it must be possible only *in principle* that others would be able to understand the meaning of the words of a language.[51] Other disputes concerned the supposed role in the argument of verificationism or scepticism about memory,[52] and even, following Kripke, the suggestion that the crucial part of the argument actually takes place in Wittgenstein's earlier remarks on rule-following (see below).[53]

Many interpreters have taken Wittgenstein's discussion of private language to have momentous consequences for epistemology, the philosophy of language and the philosophy of mind. Orthodox interpreters have disagreed about the details of the argument, but they generally agree that it amounts to a general refutation, by way of a *reductio ad absurdum*, of Cartesian dualism, phenomenalism, solipsism, idealism and empiricist views that seek to ground language in immediate experience. Early discussion focused on whether the upshot of Wittgenstein's argument amounts to a form of behaviourism, a reading now widely rejected by most interpreters.[54]

More recent disagreement focused on the aim of the argument – and on whether the relevant passages are even best understood as an *argument* of any kind. Thus according to a reading recently pressed by therapeutic interpreters such as Gordon Baker, Wittgenstein's remarks on private language are to be understood, not as a *reductio* argument that has as its target an entire philosophical tradition initiated by Descartes and Locke, but as having a more limited and specific purpose and as aimed only at specific contemporaries of Wittgenstein, such as Russell.[55]

From the 1980s onwards the interpretative focus turned to Wittgenstein's remarks on *rule-following*, remarks that raise questions about what it is to follow a rule – how a rule can set an objective standard of correctness and determine in advance the correctness of a potential infinity of possible applications. The main trigger for this shift of exegetical interest was the publication of Saul Kripke's influential monograph which portrayed Wittgenstein as raising a sceptical paradox about the possibility of rule-following and consequently about meaning in general (Kripke 1982).[56] Although Kripke was cautious not to present this reading as a straightforward interpretation of Wittgenstein, it evoked an almost unanimous rejection from Wittgenstein scholars both as a reading of Wittgenstein and on substantive philosophical grounds (see for example Baker and Hacker 1984; Winch 1987, Ch. 5), though Kripke's arguments continue to shape much of the discussion of rule-following in mainstream analytic philosophy (see Boghossian 1989; Hale 1997).[57]

This common rejection of Kripke's reading did not prevent Wittgenstein scholars from having disagreements of their own. An example of one such controversy relates to the role of a social practice in following a rule, a controversy that continued the earlier discussion of the Community View. Whereas Malcolm (with Kripke) took the position that rule-following presupposes actual communal agreement, Baker and Hacker defended the weaker view that it merely requires the possibility of such agreement (Baker and Hacker 1985; 2001; Minar 1991; 1994; Malcolm 1995, Ch. 11; Canfield 1996).

Many of Wittgenstein's reflections about rule-following were made in the context of his extensive remarks on *necessity* and the *philosophy of mathematics*, remarks whose interpretation remains a source of great controversy.[58] Wittgenstein's view of mathematics has been interpreted in turn as a form of conventionalism, constructivism, anti-realism or finitism. Such interpretations seem to accommodate various aspects of Wittgenstein's remarks on the subject, but they have also met much resistance. Although this discussion has a long history, it is only more recently, however, that Wittgenstein's writings on mathematics have been treated in volume-length studies (see, for instance, Wright 1980; Shanker 1987; Puhl 1993; Frascola 1994; Marion 1998).

Another form of controversy is exemplified by attempts to determine the significance of Wittgenstein's philosophy for subjects on which he wrote only little, such as *religion* (Cook 1988; 2005; Malcolm 1993; Hudson 1975; Nielsen 1967; Phillips 1970; 1976; 1986; 1993) and *aesthetics* (Hagberg 1995; Lewis 2004; Cavell 2005; Gibson and Huemer eds. 2004; Read and Goodenough eds. 2005). One such subject that received much attention is *ethics*. Although the *Tractatus* contains remarks on ethics and value, and although Wittgenstein delivered an early lecture on ethics (see PO, Ch. 5), evidence for his later views on the subject depends largely on a few scattered remarks in the *Nachlass* and reported conversations. This relative silence has not been seen as a reason not to engage in a debate over the implications of Wittgenstein's work for ethics. Some of the earliest work on this was by Rush Rhees (1969; 1999). By now a large body of work in moral philosophy defends a Wittgensteinian approach to ethics (see Anscombe 1981; Cavell 1982; Lovibond 1983; Diamond 1991; Phillips 1992; McDowell 1998a; 1998b; 1998c; Gaita 1998; 2004; Crary 2007). Wittgenstein's thought has also played a role in the rise of virtue ethics (for example, McDowell 1998c; Lovibond 2002) and particularist views in ethics (see Hooker and Little 2000 eds.; McDowell 1998c), as well as in discussions of the relation between philosophy and literature in the context of ethical thought (see Diamond 1991, Ch. 15). Wittgenstein's ideas have been similarly influential in debates within meta-ethics. The scarcity of direct evidence for his views, and the general lack of interpretative consensus, have meant, however, that Wittgenstein's thought has been taken by different philosophers to support wildly opposing meta-ethical views – whether relativism, realism or anti-realism.[59]

There has also been disagreement about the implications of Wittgenstein's philosophy for subjects on which he wrote or said virtually nothing, such as *political philosophy*. Wittgenstein's views have sometimes been interpreted or criticised as expressive of a conservative worldview (see Adorno 1982, 42; Marcuse 1964, 173; Nyíri 1981; Bloor 1983), but more recently it has also been used to develop critical (Habermas 1988; 1998; Apel 1973; 1992), Marxist, postmodernist and feminist approaches to politics.[60]

Most recently – since the 1990s – discussion of Wittgenstein has increasingly centred on his conception of the *nature of philosophy*, a focus also reflected by many of the papers in this volume (see Hilmy 1987; Glock 1991; 2004; Kienzler 1997; Baker 2004; Ammereller and Fischer eds. 2004; Baker and Hacker 2005). As we saw earlier, a major area of heated controversy relates to the interpretation of the *Tractatus* and the role of nonsense in that book. In this context questions have also been raised regarding the continuity of Wittgenstein's philosophy, for instance, whether the *Tractatus* might not be seen as practising a form of 'philosophical therapy' that is not as far removed from Wittgenstein's later philosophy as maintained by the orthodox interpretation (see, for instance, Crary and Read eds. 2000). It is sometimes asked whether there are only one, two, three, or adding up various suggestions, even five 'Wittgensteins' (philosophical authors with distinctive philosophical outlooks), a question that has recently been discussed, for example, in connection with Wittgenstein's *On Certainty* and other later writings which are receiving increasing attention from Wittgenstein scholars (see Moyal-Scharrock 2004 ed.; McManus 2004 ed.; Conant 2007).[61]

III Questions of Style and Method

One challenge to Wittgenstein's interpretation is the unique way in which his texts are written. His two major works, the *Tractatus* and the *Philosophical Investigations*, are not structured in chapters and subchapters displayed by a list of contents. The texts themselves do not seem to advance in a linear and transparent manner, with a thesis or counter-thesis being proposed and then argued for or refuted, or with quotations and explicit references to works of other philosophers.[62] In the *Tractatus* the prose is condensed to a bare minimum, eliminating any redundancy, with many sentences exhibiting the character of definitive oracular pronouncements, ordered by means of a weighted system of numeration. The *Philosophical Investigations*, by contrast, contain numerous thought experiments, examples, metaphors, analogies, rhetorical questions, irony, fragments of monologues and dialogues. But in the *Investigations* there is also no unbroken 'narrative' or immediate transparency of the author's intentions. What the reader finds is rather an 'album', 'a number of sketches of landscapes', of 'loosely connected remarks' (Preface).[63]

This manner of writing seems partly due to Wittgenstein's way of practising philosophy. He sought primarily to clarify problems for himself, rather than to explain his views to an audience. As he put it towards the end of his life: 'Nearly all my writings are private conversations with myself.'[64] But the difficulty of understanding him is also due to the fact that he developed his own, highly original *style of writing*, presumably intended to meet, like the style of several other twentieth-century philosophers (e.g. Adorno, Benjamin, Derrida, Heidegger), strict literary and systematic requirements. Broadly speaking, we can distinguish between two aspects of this issue. One is to see style as a *personal* and *cultural* trait representative of Wittgenstein the man, his artistic views and taste, and his epoch. The other is to see it as an element pertinent to his *philosophical method*.[65]

It is noteworthy that in the Preface to the *Philosophical Investigations* Wittgenstein acknowledges a certain failure concerning the *Bemerkungen* (remark) style of the book: 'The best that I could write would never be more than philosophical remarks; my thoughts were soon crippled if I tried to force them in any single direction against their natural inclination.' But he adds that the fragmentary style is connected with the very nature of his investigation, which requires him to criss-cross a wide field of thought.[66] He thus viewed the book's style both as a shortcoming, but also as grown out of philosophical necessity. In what follows we shall review various attempts to account for Wittgenstein's style.

1   Externalists

One immediate reaction to Wittgenstein's style is to be struck by its originality, but to consider it to be characteristic of the *man* Wittgenstein. On this view, his style is external to method and content, and the latter can be extracted from his writings without any loss of substance. Let us call interpreters endorsing this view 'externalists'. A good example is Peter Strawson's early review of the *Philosophical Investigations* (Strawson 1954). Right from the start Strawson points out the difficulty of understanding the book given its structure and style. And he briefly considers the possibility that some may argue that we should not attempt to present Wittgenstein's view in a conventional form. But Strawson immediately dismisses this as a 'very specialised view of the nature of philosophical understanding' (Strawson 1968, 22) and proceeds to discuss and engage with Wittgenstein's views topic by topic, as he would do with any other philosopher. Note that in doing so, Strawson does not think he is dismissing what he takes to be Wittgenstein's method, but only what he calls the 'idiosyncrasies of style and form' (Strawson 1968, 64). What Strawson understands by method is the piecemeal assembly of reminders of how we use words on particular occasions in order to dissolve metaphysical confusions. This therapeutic method is not a matter of choice, but dictated by language itself, the very source of philosophical problems. Style, by contrast, is something peculiar to Wittgenstein the author which we don't need to share, even if we share his method.

Strawson's approach was subsequently endorsed by many other inter-preters, whether implicitly or explicitly. It is explicitly shared by Wittgen-stein scholars such as Hintikka, Hilmy, Fogelin, Rundle, von Savigny and Glock, to mention but a few.[67] This hermeneutic approach is also implic-itly shared by the wide majority of 'mainstream' analytic philosophers who view Wittgenstein's texts simply as a repository of arguments relevant for various contemporary debates, arguments to be evaluated by standard procedures, but otherwise treat his writing style either as purely idiosyn-cratic (maybe even as eccentric), 'simply a stylistic and literary prefer-ence',[68] or as an aspect of his anti-theoretical attitude to philosophy, both of which are not to be followed (see Dummett 1978, 453).

But there are also interpreters who view the matter of style as relevant to, indeed as a consequence of, Wittgenstein's philosophical outlook. For them method and style are internally related to each other. Let us call these interpreters 'internalists'. We can distinguish between *moderate* and *strong internalists*.

2   Moderate internalists

Moderate internalists claim that style has an important function for Witt-genstein's method, indeed that it is derived from the latter and serves to express it in a distinctive way. But they maintain that since his philosophi-cal method consists in putting forward positive arguments, in rejecting false arguments and providing us with a correct representation of our conceptual framework, his style ultimately serves *argumentative* ends.[69] Style is thus subservient to method, answers to its needs, but does not exhaust the latter. That the form of the *Investigations* cannot uniquely determine the content is given precisely through the fact that the form is expressly *chosen*, that Wittgenstein had *reasons* to select a certain manner of composition. These reasons, philosophical reasons, must themselves be therefore independent of and prior to the application of a certain style, and they are expressible without employing the style which they justify. On this account, the justification of Wittgenstein's style is derived from his method, making the latter distinct and systematically prior to the former.

Moderate internalists are interpreters such as Malcolm, Kenny, the 'second' Baker, Hacker, Kienzler, Schulte (1990) and Schroeder. One good example of this is Kienzler's study of Wittgenstein's turn from his early to his later period. Kienzler provides evidence that one of the main catalysts for this turn was Wittgenstein's thorough re-reading and re-thinking of *Frege's* theories in 1930–1932. Wittgenstein had already come to reject important aspects of Frege's logic and philosophy of language and the new reading made him reject even more such aspects (see Kienzler 1997, 179). Nevertheless, Frege became a strong influence for the later Wittgenstein in one crucial respect, namely style, be it through the preference of the former for clear and concise formulations, incisive pictures and metaphors, or exaggerated talk and parody.[70] But like Frege's, Wittgenstein's style is a function of philosophical arguments and thus not a replacement of the latter.[71] This is what distinguishes this use of style from its employment as mere literary style and aesthetic effect. Parody, for instance, has in both Frege and Wittgenstein the purpose of providing a survey of fundamental concepts *ex negativo*, of demonstrating false philosophical assumptions and of clarifying categorial mistakes.[72]

Similar arguments have been employed to explain the partly dialogical structure and the album-type character of the *Philosophical Investigations*.[73] Accordingly, a large number of interpreters have taken such fragments of dialogue to serve an argumentative purpose, displaying an opposition between the voice of the enlightened philosopher and that of a tempted and mistaken philosopher.[74] Indeed, Jane Heal has argued not only that the *Philosophical Investigations* is an argumentative work, but that Wittgenstein employed the dialogical form precisely in order to pursue traditional philosophical questions in a discursive-rational way (see Heal 1995). On these interpretations, the later philosophy consists to a large extent in resolving conceptual confusions, and Wittgenstein must therefore pick up *some* thinker's concrete confusions, often those of the author of the *Tractatus* himself, as an example to demonstrate this method (§133). This makes the dialogue form an important option (Schroeder 2006, 124f.). Equally, the album-type character of the *Investigations* is explained by the fact that Wittgenstein intends to attack and correct a whole array of interrelated conceptions and presuppositions in both his former and in traditional philosophy. This is due (a) to the nature of philosophical concepts, which stand in multiple relations to each other and cannot be reduced to some more basic level of analysis, and, following this, (b) to the nature of any deep philosophical error, which develops numerous ramifications across the conceptual network.

Moderate internalists do not ignore the fact that Wittgenstein regarded his book as fragmentary, indeed, from the point of view of its composition even as a failure. What they deny is that this implies a lack of unity and systematicity in his views and methodology. On the contrary, as Baker and Hacker have argued, the fact that he struggled for sixteen years with the composition of the book as a whole and agonised over the formulation and arrangement of particular remarks shows that he had a rationale for that composition, albeit a rationale that is not directly visible and needs to be reconstructed. The commentary by Baker and Hacker takes precisely this as its explicit goal, making extensive use of the *Nachlass* to retrace the complicated origin and fuller context of individual remarks and the underlying arguments.[75] We must view the *Philosophical Investigations* like 'a sketchbook of a master-artist who could not produce a finished canvas' (Baker and Hacker 2005, 34). Nevertheless, through this sketchbook the intended canvas of the *Investigations*, its unity and integrity, can be reconstructed, at least in its major features. Thus this approach acknowledges that a certain aspect of Wittgenstein's style, namely the album-type character, is indeed of importance for the *Investigations*. But it also reveals that the initial appearance of fragmentariness of the book, the sequence of more or less connected remarks, is an illusion and that the content of the book is both argumentative and systematic in character (see Hacker 1996, 124).[76] To use a slightly different analogy with art, we could say that here the understanding of style is like the understanding of some abstract artwork, e.g. Jackson Pollock's *Autumn Rhythm*. It is an understanding that consists in realising the complex rationale behind some apparently unconnected patches and lines (in Pollock), sentences and remarks (in Wittgenstein). But unlike mere artistic style, Wittgenstein's album-type style draws its rationale from a whole range of interrelated arguments, which, as the very practice of Baker and Hacker's commentary is meant to show, can be stated independently of that style.[77]

3   *Strong internalists*

Strong internalists, by contrast, reject both the idea that the content of the *Investigations* is argumentative and that it is really separable from the style of the book. The book has a wholly therapeutic purpose, aiming at particular, unnamed individuals and their craving for a metaphysical point of view. The therapy does not aim to make general claims, but to make the afflicted individuals give up this craving and become new persons. A given survey of the grammar of a language may be adequate in one case, i.e. is therapeutically successful, but not in another (Baker 2004, 194f.). Consequently, interpreters following this line of thought claim that the fragmentary method of the *Investigations* is matched by its fragmentary style, indeed that the former is not detachable from the latter. In its most consequential form, as represented, for instance, by Gordon Baker, this approach maintains that the book does not contain any merely rhetorical elements, but that every aspect of Wittgenstein's prose, including possibly even his use of italics (see on this Baker 2004, Ch. 11), must be counted as part and parcel of his method.

Other strong internalists do single out certain aspects of Wittgenstein's style as inessential, but claim that other aspects, such as the *Bemerkungen-* style and the dispersed dialogues, are constitutive of Wittgenstein's method. Examples of the more qualified version of strong internalism are Stanley Cavell's aesthetic-ethical and David Stern and Alois Pichler's polyphonic readings of the *Philosophical Investigations*. As early as 1962 Cavell argued against treating Wittgenstein's unconventional style as a mere idiosyncratic trait (Cavell 1976, Ch. 2). There is a 'voice of temptation' and a 'voice of correctness' in the book, but neither of them represent Wittgenstein's actual views. Instead, both voices are only part of a larger dialogue, a confession which does not intend to convince, but to make us see things in a different way. More recently, Cavell has pointed out that the 'literariness' of the *Investigations* is no mere ornament, but rather essential to the book, as there is no 'aesthetic concern of the text that is separate from its central work' (Cavell 2001, 250). To understand the book we therefore need a matching aesthetic effort.

Cavell exemplifies this approach by considering the notion of perspicuous representation. In Wittgenstein's book we have not only the articulation of certain philosophical problems, but also a certain existential pathos typical of the modern subject, i.e. 'torment, perverseness, disappointment, suffocation, illness, strangeness, etc.' (Cavell 2001, 257). To this Wittgenstein opposed the aesthetic experience of complete clarity, perspicuousness and beauty he came to have in ordering ordinary language in his own prose, an experience which he had first encountered with mathematical proofs. It is noteworthy, however, that although Cavell denies that there is a system in the *Investigations*, he does admit that there is systematicity and argumentation, 'or something of the sort' (Cavell 2001, 250, 264). Also, he does not deny that there is another strand in the book that does correspond to the concerns of mainstream analytic philosophy.

The recent interpretations by Pichler and Stern suggest that the *Philosophical Investigations* does not have a simple dialogical structure.[78] Instead, the book is claimed to have a polyphonic character, with various voices competing with each other and no ultimate authorial authority. Pichler argues that we can distinguish an indefinite number of voices (e.g. 'the voice of the quotation of Augustine's text', 'the voice of the translation of Augustine's text', 'the voice of the deliberately twisted interpretation of the quotation', etc.), which do not compete for a final verdict, but rather deny, precisely through their multiplicity, any 'dogmatism'. Wittgenstein's real intention is to contribute to liberation from particular philosophical problems in particular contexts (see Pichler 2004, 219f.). The argument for this is to a large degree philological: Pichler claims that the form of the *Philosophical Investigations* is not due to a personal shortcoming of the author, but instead to his explicit decision to drop the linear and systematic composition technique still employed in the *Brown Book* and adopt instead the album-type form in November 1936.[79] David Stern also stresses the plurality of voices in Wittgenstein's book, although he identifies only three of them, which sometimes overlap with each other. There is the voice of 'Wittgenstein's narrator' and that of the 'interlocutor'. In addition, there is the voice of the 'commentator', providing ironical remarks, rhetorical questions, and jokes on the exchange between the previous two voices, thus ultimately dismissing any definitive view. This third voice, Stern claims, is the closest one to Wittgenstein (Stern 2004, 21ff.). The commentator is neither a realist nor an idealist, neither a behaviourist nor a psychologist, etc. All these doctrines are equally nonsensical and all Wittgenstein really does is to occasionally make this 'serio-comedy' patent by means of similes and platitudes (Stern 2004, 25).

IV   The Articles in This Volume

The first six articles in this volume discuss, from different perspectives, some fundamental general questions in Wittgenstein interpretation, often with reference to Gordon Baker's own distinctive later approach. The rest of the volume turns to more specific problems and debates about Wittgenstein's early and later writings, relating to questions about transcendental idealism, the metaphysics of the *Tractatus*, private language, philosophy of mathematics, and ethics.

   In 'Perspectives on Wittgenstein: An Intermittently Opinionated Survey', Hans-Johann Glock provides a critical overview of attempts to interpret Wittgenstein's philosophy. He first sketches a brief history of the reception of Wittgenstein's work from the publication of the *Tractatus* to the present. In the remaining sections he elaborates on certain general parameters of disagreement between Wittgenstein's interpreters, critically discussing the question of continuity vs. discontinuity in Wittgenstein's thought, immanent vs. genetic approaches to his texts, rationalist vs. irrationalist interpretations, and finally intrinsic vs. extrinsic motives for studying him. For instance, Glock pleads for the traditional distinction between the early and the later *work* of Wittgenstein, rejecting the idea that we must speak of distinct *thinkers*. He also argues for an interpretation of Wittgenstein which attributes to him claims, reasons and arguments, arguing that opposing therapeutic interpretations fail on several grounds, including hermeneutic and argumentative inconsistency. Finally, Glock rejects what we earlier called 'internalist' interpretations, arguing that no philosophical substance is lost if we discount Wittgenstein's style and rephrase his arguments in a more conventional manner.

In her 'Wittgenstein's Method: Ridding People of Philosophical Prejudices', Katherine Morris discusses three different types of readings of Wittgenstein (all represented by Baker at various points of his career). Morris suggests that comparison between these readings and the employment of the notion of 'intellectual prejudice' in Nietzsche and Merleau-Ponty will help us explain certain difficulties encountered by 'analytic' philosophers in interpreting Wittgenstein. Morris's primary aim is illumination by way of contrast. On the one hand, these three conceptions of Wittgenstein are meant to illuminate each other. On the other hand, they are intended to help to bring to view differences between two groups of philosophers, one of which takes 'prejudice' as simply another word for an erroneous view to be refuted, whereas the other seeks to treat prejudices in a manner analogous to psychotherapy.

The next essay takes a different stance on this latter issue. In 'Gordon Baker's Late Interpretation of Wittgenstein', Peter Hacker first tells the tale of his lengthy collaboration with Baker, which resulted in three books and numerous articles on Wittgenstein. However, in the late 1980s Baker came to repudiate much of Hacker's and his own former approach to Wittgenstein, formulating his criticism in various articles (see Baker 2004). In the second part of his essay Hacker addresses this criticism for the first time, explaining how their disagreement grew and why he thinks Baker's later position was mistaken. In particular, he takes issue with Baker's characterisation of Wittgenstein's later philosophy as modelled on Freudian psychoanalysis and with Baker's reliance on Waismann's late writings as a key to Wittgenstein's thought. In this context, Hacker critically discusses several key notions relied upon not only by Baker, but by most adherents of the therapeutic reading, such as 'dogmatism', 'picture', 'metaphysical use of words' and 'therapy'. He also argues that, *pace* Baker, Wittgenstein *was* engaged in arguing against philosophical doctrines, concluding that, contrary to Baker's claims, Wittgenstein, like Ryle, had no qualms about identifying category mistakes and category confusions as a source of philosophical error, or about characterising his endeavours as plotting the logical geography of concepts for elucidatory purposes.

Alois Pichler's 'The Interpretation of the *Philosophical Investigations*: Style, Therapy, *Nachlass*' is an examination of different approaches to the interpretation of Wittgenstein's *Philosophical Investigations*. Pichler draws a contrast between interpretations (such as those of the earlier Baker, Hilmy and von Savigny) that attribute to Wittgenstein philosophical theses and theories supported by linear arguments, and interpretations (such as those of Cavell and the later Baker) that see Wittgenstein as dissolving philosophical problems through philosophical therapies that need not be systematically related. On the basis of observations relating to Wittgenstein's style, and in particular, to inconsistencies and tensions found in the text, Pichler develops an argument in favour of a therapeutic approach to the *Philosophical Investigations*. Another interpretative contrast Pichler addresses is the role of Wittgenstein's *Nachlass* in the interpretation of the *Investigations*. He asks whether the book should be read immanently or contextually, drawing general lessons about a methodologically sound employment of the *Nachlass* in interpreting the *Philosophical Investigations*.

Two articles are devoted to commentary on Baker's controversial reading of a key passage in the *Philosophical Investigations* where Wittgenstein describes his method as bringing 'words back from their metaphysical to their everyday use' (PI §116). Many interpreters have taken the key phrase here to be 'everyday use', understanding Wittgenstein to claim that philosophers fall astray when they use words in ways that violate the conventions that govern everyday language use. On this interpretation, Wittgenstein's philosophical method is seen as broadly continuous with the 'ordinary language philosophy' of Austin and Ryle. In his paper 'Wittgenstein on Metaphysical/Everyday Use' (Baker 2002), Baker challenged this reading, claiming that the word that 'wears the trousers' here is 'metaphysical', where this word is understood to have a traditional sense of referring to essence, necessity and nature. Instead of reading 'metaphysical' to mean 'deviating from everyday use', Baker suggested we read 'everyday use' to simply mean 'non-metaphysical'. If Baker is correct, then a dominant interpretation of Wittgenstein may be based on a serious misreading.

In his 'Ways of Reading Wittgenstein: Observations on Certain Uses of the Word "Metaphysics"', Joachim Schulte further investigates Baker's suggestion. Emphasising the nuances of the German meaning of phrases used by Wittgenstein, Schulte examines a number of passages where Wittgenstein uses the word 'metaphysical', and suggests a picture of its meaning that is more complex than that suggested by Baker, and which doesn't attribute to Wittgenstein any clear-cut distinction between 'metaphysical' and 'everyday' use. Schulte's article is an example of how the 'textual archaeology' of the genesis of Wittgenstein's remarks – the way Wittgenstein changed his wording in different versions and in changing contexts – may be used to resolve exegetical disputes.

Hilary Putnam's 'Metaphysical/Everyday Use: A Note on a Late Paper by Gordon Baker' provides a different perspective on Baker's interpretation. Although Putnam shares Baker's doubts about interpreting Wittgenstein's philosophy as continuous with 'ordinary language' philosophy, he is also sceptical about Baker's way of drawing the contrast between metaphysical and everyday use. Putnam suggests that Baker takes a too narrow view of the range of philosophical confusions that Wittgenstein is interested in. As he points out, many of the most important philosophical disputes in late twentieth-century philosophy can't be made to fit Baker's contrast between metaphysical and non-metaphysical, yet clearly these are debates on which Wittgenstein would have had much to say.

In his essay 'Wittgenstein and Transcendental Idealism', A. W. Moore addresses a much debated exegetical question (e.g. see Anscombe 1981; Malcolm 1982; Williams 1983). In the first part Moore argues that the early Wittgenstein was, in some sense, a transcendental idealist. Distinguishing between *limits* and *limitations*, where the former are indicative of essential features, and the latter rather of features which exclude certain possibilities, Moore argues that transcendental idealism is present in the *Tractatus* in two respects. First, through Wittgenstein's indulging the human temptation to transcend the limits of thought and language, and thus to mistake limits for limitations set by the subject, thereby succumbing to transcendental idealism. Second, through Wittgenstein's urging us to counter this very temptation, a move which itself appears to involve the exclusion of certain possibilities and thus another misidentification of limits with limitations. In the second part of his essay Moore defends the contrasting view that there is no transcendental idealism to be found in the works of the later Wittgenstein, since questions leading to such idealism, such as 'What are the limits of the world?', are dismissed as nonsense. Nevertheless, Moore goes on to argue that transcendental idealism has an important place in the exegesis of Wittgenstein's later work, since there are significant passages in which he struggles with the temptation to fall back into transcendental idealism, passages which resist any simple resolution.

Another central interpretative debate is addressed by Marie McGinn in her 'Simples and the Idea of Analysis in the *Tractatus*': does Wittgenstein endorse a form of realist metaphysics in his early book? She argues, with Ishiguro, McGuinness and others, in favour of an anti-metaphysical interpretation, according to which Wittgenstein is engaged in an investigation that is internal to language and which refrains from reasoning from the system of representation to something outside it. McGinn defends this interpretation in view of what she takes to be its greatest challenge, namely Wittgenstein's remarks on simples in the *Tractatus*. She argues that there is a plausible reading of these that does not commit him to making claims about the ontological structure of a language-independent reality. Contrary to what he wrote in his *Notebooks*, according to her in both the *Tractatus* and the *Prototractatus* there is no talk of a direct correlation between names and objects outside of propositions. The talk about simples does not involve any claim about ultimate constituents of reality, but only a claim about necessary features of our symbolism. McGinn argues that this has important consequences for our understanding of the idea of logical analysis in the *Tractatus*.

Stephen Mulhall's 'Words, Waxing and Waning: Ethics in/and/of the *Tractatus Logico-Philosophicus*' aims to assess the readings of Wittgenstein's book associated with Diamond and Conant, with specific reference to its remarks on ethics. On the basis of a detailed examination of Wittgenstein's remarks, Mulhall argues that Wittgenstein's text at once enacts a certain therapeutic fall into nonsensicality, and aims to identify and exemplify a way in which one's language and form of life can nevertheless meet the challenge of articulating an ethical stance towards the world. Approaching the *Tractatus*' concluding methodological remarks in the light of its remarks on ethics, Mulhall is led to observations regarding Wittgenstein's conception of the role of moral philosophy and the book's ethical point. He concludes his engagement with the text of the *Tractatus* – including what he calls its 'non-propositional register' – by raising questions about the status of exegetical commentary on the *Tractatus*.

In 'The Uses of Wittgenstein's Beetle: *Philosophical Investigations* §293 and Its Interpreters', David Stern sets out to assess the far-reaching objections raised by Gordon Baker to traditional interpretations of Wittgenstein's famous remarks on private language (PI §243ff.) as a *reductio ad absurdum* of Cartesian dualism. Baker proposes a very different framework of interpretation, one on which Wittgenstein's primary aim in those sections of the *Investigations* was 'the elimination of prejudices that stand in the way of our noticing important aspects of what is perfectly familiar' (Baker 1998, 353). Stern's paper attempts to evaluate Baker's proposal by reviewing some of the leading interpretations of Wittgenstein's 'beetle in a box' argument (PI §293), usually construed as one of the principal expositions of such a *reductio ad absurdum*, starting with the early discussions by Strawson and Malcolm, and surveying the debate until the present.

In his essay 'Bourgeois, Bolshevist or Anarchist? The Reception of Wittgenstein's Philosophy of Mathematics', Ray Monk surveys the reactions to Wittgenstein's later philosophy of mathematics, from the 1930s to the present day. Monk argues that until recently most commentators have failed to appreciate how radical Wittgenstein's remarks on mathematics are, not realising the extent to which they must be read in the context of his later, therapeutical conception of philosophy. On Monk's reading, Wittgenstein shouldn't be interpreted as attempting to propose substantive doctrines about the nature of mathematics, e.g. finitism or conventionalism, contrary to what is claimed in Ambrose (1935) or Dummett (1959). Following Gerrard (1991), Monk suggests that Wittgenstein does not argue for (or against) the truth of a certain theory of mathematics which would itself have mathematical consequences. Since Wittgenstein advocates a strict separation between mathematics and the philosophy of mathematics, he intends to leave the practice of mathematics as it is. What Wittgenstein targets is rather the motivation behind branches of mathematics which are informed by confused pre-philosophical pictures, for instance set theory and transfinite number theory. The philosopher's task is to dispel these pictures by making us see mathematics under a different perspective – a therapeutic change of aspect which will put those questionable branches out of business.

In the final article, 'Wittgenstein and Ethical Naturalism', Alice Crary considers the relation between Wittgenstein and ethical naturalism. Focusing on the recent work of Phillipa Foot, Crary investigates the Wittgensteinian assumptions implicit in non-reductive naturalism in ethics, and argues that we can find in Wittgenstein's later philosophy the resources needed to defend it. Crary suggests that Foot's attempt to ground morality in practical reason lacks an account of the objectivity of meaning, and, following McDowell and Cavell, she argues that we can find such an account in Wittgenstein's remarks on rule-following. These remarks articulate a pragmatic view of language that should lead us to rethink the traditional fixation of moral philosophers – including Foot – on moral judgement, directing our attention to the sensibility that informs all of an individual's modes of thought and talk. Crary ends by suggesting that Wittgenstein's few and scattered remarks on 'ethical themes' can indeed be interpreted as an expression of the idea that ethics is distinguished by a concern, not with a particular region of discourse, but with a dimension of *all* of discourse.

Notes

1 Vlastos's concern, of course, is to highlight the problem of ascertaining the views of the historical Socrates on the evidence of the writings of Plato and Aristotle.

2 See Morris in this volume for discussion of three of the dominant competing portraits.

3 See again Morris in this volume and the Introduction to Baker (2004).

4 See also Bilezki's (2003) discussion of the project of Wittgenstein interpretation.

5 One important early interpreter was Frank Ramsey, who both published papers and lectured on the *Tractatus* in Cambridge (cf. Ramsey 1966). Ramsey's notes for his lectures have also survived. Ramsey's interpretation of the *Tractatus* has recently been studied and discussed by Peter Sullivan (cf. Sullivan 2005). Informed by extensive personal communication with Wittgenstein, Ramsey's engagement with the *Tractatus* may well deserve more attention than it has received so far.

6 See Frongia and McGuinness eds. (1990), a very useful source giving short summaries of articles and various indexes for tracking down topics of discussion and people.

7 For instance, Pears (1956). See also essays collected in Copi and Beard (1966).

8 Pole (1958), Anscombe (1959), Stenius (1960), Black (1964), Griffin (1964) and Pitcher (1964), who discusses both the *Tractatus* and the later philosophy.

9 Early examples of this form are Hallett (1967), Fann (1969), Bogen (1972), Hacker (1972) and Kenny (1973). For later discussions of the continuity of Wittgenstein's philosophy, see below.

10 See Baker and Hacker (1980; 1985), Hacker (1986; 1990; 1996; 2001).

11 However, Mulhall's and Stern's essays in this volume would not be correctly classified among 'orthodox' readings.

12 For instance, between Hacker and Pears on the issue of realism in the *Tractatus*, and between Baker and Hacker and Malcolm on rule-following.

13   Wittgenstein seems to ascribe a theory to himself in the manuscripts leading to the *Tractatus* (see e.g. MS 101, 52r, 64r, MS 102 57r, 123r, MS 104, 75), but interpreters disagree on the status of these passages as evidence for Wittgenstein's views at the time of the completion of the *Tractatus*.

14   See Conant (1990; 2002), Diamond (1991), Conant and Diamond (2004). The roots of this interpretation are to be found in the writings of Ishiguro (1969), McGuinness (2002, Ch. 8; first published 1981) and Winch (1969; 1987; 1993). Cf. also Diamond (2005) on Winch. Other proponents of this type or a similar reading include Ricketts (1996), Goldfarb (1997), Kremer (1997; 2001), McGinn (2001; 2006), Ostrow (2002), McManus (2006). See also essays in Stocker ed. (2004) and Mulhall in this volume. More radical versions have been articulated by Burton Dreben in his unpublished lectures, by Floyd (2002) and Read and Deans (2003). For critical replies see Hacker (2000; 2003), Proops (2001) and Mounce (2001). The latter is replied to by Read and Deans (2003).

15   See Mulhall's essay in this volume for a discussion of the *Tractatus'* remarks on ethics in this light and of its use of language.

16   It is important to note that the views of the so-called new readers are diverse. Marie McGinn and Denis McManus emphasise that the *Tractatus* does offer positive insights into the logic of language (McGinn 2006, McManus 2006) – even though it is not clear that the result of clarification in the *Tractatus*, as Conant and Diamond envisage it, could not be characterised as something positive, insofar as the result is meant to be the logic of language becoming perspicuous. Not all representatives of the 'new reading' accept that the *Tractatus'* failure lies in it putting forward a theory of any kind, even an implicit one. See Floyd (2002), Read and Deans (2003).

17   Indeed, on an extreme reading, such as that of Gerrard, there is only 'one Wittgenstein' (see Gerrard 2002). Such a 'strong continuity thesis' is not accepted by Conant (2002 and 2007).

18   See also the introduction to Crary and Read eds. (2000, 2).

19   Several authors see such an aim as making Wittgenstein's later philosophy akin to ancient Pyrrhonian scepticism. See Fogelin (1987), Stern (2005).

20   Fann (1969) might also be described as leaning towards this direction.

21   The interpretations of Goldfarb (1983), Winch (1987), Genova (1995), Phillips (1999), Savickey (1999) and Hertzberg (2001) could probably also be classified in this category.

22   Other therapeutic readers include Hagberg (2003) and Fischer (2006). Richter (2004) can perhaps also be included in this approach.

23   Dreben's aphorism is apparently a deliberate variation on a remark by Saul Liberman, who reportedly once introduced a 1940s lecture by the famous Kabbalah scholar Gershom Scholem with the words 'Nonsense is nonsense – but the history of nonsense is scholarship' (see Floyd and Shieh 2001, 429, fn. 9).

24 For examples of Cavell's approach to Wittgenstein, see Cavell (1962; 1976; 1982; 1995; 1996). Mulhall (1996) provides an overview of Cavell's approach to Wittgenstein and philosophy.

25 For discussion of Cavell's understanding of scepticism, see Stroud (2000, Ch. 5).

26 Cavell's writings include Cavell (1977; 1987; 1988; 1989; 1990; 1994).

27 Baker criticised the new interpretation of the *Tractatus* in an unpublished review.

28 Hanfling (1989) notes this state of affairs. Examples of interpreters who are strongly critical of Wittgenstein are Hintikka and Cook (see §7 below). Interestingly, their reading of Wittgenstein is also significantly at odds with most other interpreters.

29 It should go without saying that there is no sharp distinction between giving an interpretation of Wittgenstein and doing philosophy in Wittgenstein's spirit, nor one between Wittgensteinians and non-Wittgensteinians. That these are not sharp distinctions does not mean that they do not draw useful dividing lines.

30 A list of such readings would be very long. Let us just mention several examples: Blackburn (1984; 1990; 1993); McGinn (1984); Boghossian (1989); Pettit (1990); Millikan (1990); Brandom (1994, Ch. 1); Horwich (2005). For a recent examination of Wittgenstein's early and later views from a 'mainstream' standpoint, see Soames (2003a; 2003b).

31 Though there was an interesting dissenting voice: the qualified praise in Anscombe (1985).

32 Even analytic philosophers who see philosophy as continuous with natural science, and thus not as an *a priori* inquiry into the essential structure of reality, still view philosophical inquiry as a cognitive discipline.

33 From a very different perspective, see the ascription to Wittgenstein of radical doctrines in Hintikka and Hintikka (1986); Hintikka (1996); Cook (1994).

34 For discussion see the exchange between Wright (1995) and McDowell (1998d), as well as Wright (2001).

35 Richard Rorty can be read as adopting a broadly similar approach to Wittgenstein. McDowell criticises Rorty's understanding of 'Wittgensteinian quietism' in McDowell (1994, xxi, 142).

36 See the essays collected in part III of McDowell (1998).

37 See the essays collected in Miller and Wright (2002).

38 This was Gordon Baker's later view. On this, see Morris, Hacker, and Stern, this volume. See also Conant (2004). As Morris notes at the end of her paper, what is at stake here importantly depends on whether we take a narrow or permissive understanding of 'argument'.

39 For readings of Wittgenstein as a Kantian transcendental philosopher, see Hintikka (1981); Rossvaer (1981); Kannisto (1986); Garver (1994); Forster (2004). See also the essay by Moore in this volume.

40   Examples of such readings are Rorty (1980); Glendinning (1998); Mulhall
      (1990; 2001); Staten (1985); Stone (2000). See also Morris in this volume.
      Naturally, the purpose of such comparisons may sometimes be to throw light
      also in the other direction.

41   See the exchange in Mulhall (2001a) and Derrida (2001). Pierre Bourdieu
      is perhaps an exception. In an interview, he remarked that 'Wittgenstein is
      probably the philosopher who has helped me most at moments of difficulty'
      (Bourdieu 1990, 9).

42   See the editor's introduction to Hadot (1995).

43   Bouveresse (1995) is an attempt to recruit Wittgenstein in an attack on
      Lacanian psychoanalysis in France.

44   The interpretation of the *Tractatus* has also generated a number of disputes.
      We have earlier discussed the dispute between the orthodox and 'new' read-
      ings of the *Tractatus*. For discussion of two important controversies,
      see McGinn and Mulhall, this volume. Our survey of key controversies is
      of necessity selective. Important disputes we will not discuss include dis-
      cussion of the relation between meaning and use, Wittgenstein's response
      to scepticism, and the relation between his views and idealism and
      relativism.

45   For discussion of the notion of language-game, see Kenny (1973); Baker and
      Hacker (1980; 2005); Hilmy (1987, Ch. 3); Hintikka and Hintikka (1986);
      Rhees (1998).

46   For discussion of family resemblance, see Bambrough (1961); Ambrose
      (1966); Griffin (1974); Baker and Hacker (1980; 2005); Dilman (1978);
      Rundle (1990).

47   For Wright's later views, see Wright (1984).

48   For early criticism see Rorty (1973).

49   McDowell (1982) develops an influential alternative account of the notion
      of a criterion and its bearing on scepticism.

50   See for example Budd (1989, Ch. 3); Canfield (1986); Conant (2004); Fogelin
      (1987, Ch. 12); Hacker (1986, Ch. 9; 1990, essays I–X); McDowell (1998e);
      McGinn (1997, Ch. 4); Pears (1988, Chs. 13, 14, 15); Soames (2003,
      Ch. 2); Wright (1986); and Stern, this volume. A survey of various attempts
      to extract an argument from Wittgenstein's remarks is Schroeder (2006).

51   See especially the debate between Rhees (1954) and Ayer (1954).

52   For discussion see Kenny (1973, 191f.).

53   According to Kripke, the main argument appears in the discussion of
      rule-following starting around §138. As Kripke observes, the conclusion of
      the private language argument is stated in §202, well before the argument's
      traditional location. Kripke suggests that the sections following §243 are
      only a discussion of the purported counterexample of sensation language
      to a conclusion Wittgenstein's has argued for earlier. See Baker and Hacker
      (1984) for a reply.

54 Strawson's (1968) review of the *Philosophical Investigations* found such behaviourist implications (see Stern, this volume, for discussion). For a typical contemporary view of this issue, see Hacker (1990).

55 See Baker (2004, chs. 5–7); also Stern in this volume. For Russell's relevant views see Russell (1918).

56 Kripke's interpretation was anticipated in Fogelin (1976). An important early collection of papers on rule-following is Holtzman and Leich (1981).

57 For a recent collection of articles in this vein see Miller and Wright (2002).

58 For a few representative articles see Ambrose (1935; 1955); Dummett (1959; 1978; 1997); Stroud (1965); Wrigley (1977); Baker and Hacker (1985; Ch. VI), Hacker (1996, 255–64); Cassam (1986); Baker (1988); Diamond (1991, Ch. 7); Glock (1996; 1997); Putnam (2001); Monk in this volume.

59 Cf. Arrington (1989); Blackburn (1981; 1993); McDowell (1998a; 1998b); for expositions and discussions of Wittgensteinian ethics see Johnston (1989; 1999); Richter (2000); and papers in a 2002 Special Issue of *Philosophical Papers* devoted to Wittgenstein and ethics.

60 For the last three approaches see Pitkin (1972); Crary (2000); Scheman and O'Connor eds. (2002); Kitching and Pleasants eds. (2002); Heyes ed. (2003); Wallgren (2006).

61 The five Wittgensteins would be: the author of NB, that of the *Tractatus*, a middle Wittgenstein of late 1920s and early 1930s, the author of the PI, the author of the late remarks of which OC is composed.

62 The problem extends to other works by Wittgenstein, e.g. *The Big Typescript*. But there are more 'linear' works as well, e.g. 'Remarks on Logical Form', *The Brown Book* and the joint effort with Waismann leading to *The Principles of Linguistic Philosophy* (on the latter see Baker 1979, 245).

63 See Pichler (2004), 199f. for a more detailed list of what could count as stylistic elements. For an early analysis of Wittgenstein's style see Binkley (1973).

64 CV, 77e.

65 For the personal and cultural dimension of style see Schulte (1990); von Wright (1993); Schroeder (2006, 4.1).

66 And as he notes in 1937 (MS 118, 95v): 'I have often tried, in vain, to put [my remarks] into a satisfactory order or to thread them together in *one* string of words. The result was artificial and unsatisfactory, and my strength turned out to be far too slight to pursue the matter to its conclusion. The only presentation of which I am still capable is to connect these remarks by a network of numbers which will make evident their extremely complicated connections.'

67 Witness Hilmy: '[. . .] much of his style, especially the gross features which have tended to be emphasized in some of the secondary literature, is incidental to his method', where by the former Hilmy means the album-type

character of the book, while by the latter primarily the method of language-games (Hilmy 1987, 15). See also von Savigny (1988) for a similar attitude.

68   As Kripke comments on Wittgenstein's preference for dialogues in the *Philosophical Investigations*. See Kripke (1982, 5).

69   And where it serves only aesthetic purposes it is eliminable.

70   This is acknowledged by Wittgenstein himself. See Z §712.

71   This is why Wittgenstein can argue against Frege's views while adopting the latter's own style. See Kienzler (1997, 182).

72   This is acknowledged by Wittgenstein, for example when he comments on his own critical discussion of Skolem's proof of the associativity of addition: 'I parody a certain conception in order to point out a mistake in it. This method can be applied generally. (Frege against Cantor)' (MS 112, 64).

73   Wittgenstein, however, also expressed his dislike for the Socratic type of dialogue in CV, 21.

74   See for instance Kenny (2006, 12f.). For examples of this interpretation see Baker and Hacker (2005, 137f., 158f., 162, 167, 319).

75   See for instance the use of tree diagrams to display the interconnections between individual remarks in the *Investigations* in Baker and Hacker (2005, 44f., 94ff.).

76   For an earlier occurrence of this observation see Malcolm (1968, 65).

77   See the thematic overview of Wittgenstein's book in straightforward prose in Baker and Hacker (2005, 7–23).

78   Interestingly, they have been recently joined in this claim by Anthony Kenny, although he strongly opposes the 'new' reading of Wittgenstein at a general level. See Kenny (2006, xvf.).

79   See Pichler (2004, 12f.) and the strictly philological evidence he puts forward (2004, 231–63). Interestingly, Pichler stresses that even if his interpretation is correct, orthodox readers of Wittgenstein would still be entitled to extract philosophical theses from his work. They would just not be justified to attribute them to the man known by the name 'Ludwig Wittgenstein' (Pichler 2004, 18ff.).

Chapter 1

Perspectives on Wittgenstein: An Intermittently Opinionated Survey

Hans-Johann Glock

Wittgenstein himself only published one significant philosophical work, the *Tractatus*. Nevertheless, some fifty years after his death any attempt to provide even a superficial survey of the literature on Wittgenstein would be futile. A fairly comprehensive bibliography up to 1995 sports in excess of 9,000 entries (Philip 1996; see also Frongia/McGuinness 1990 and Shanker and Shanker 1986), and the stream of publications has not abated since then. In a poll among professional philosophers in North America, the *Philosophical Investigations* was ranked as the most important philosophical work of the twentieth century and the *Tractatus* came in fourth (Lackey 1999, 331–2). Both works have inspired analytic and continental philosophers alike. Indeed, Wittgenstein is a contested thinker between these two highly general trends in contemporary philosophy (Glock 2004). There are Wittgenstein societies in Austria, Germany, Hungary, Poland and North America. The Austrian society organizes an annual *Wittgenstein Symposion* in Kirchberg, Lower Austria, the area where he taught as a primary school teacher in the 1920s; the German society publishes the *Wittgenstein Studies*. The British journal *Philosophical Investigations* is also devoted predominantly to his work and his philosophical legacy. Finally, there are the Brenner Archives in Innsbruck as well as Wittgenstein Archives in Bergen, Cambridge and Helsinki. The Bergen Archives have not only produced an electronic edition of the complete *Nachlass*, they also publish a regular series of Working Papers and run a web-site (www.wittgenstein-portal.com) with links to most of the relevant electronic databases.

Wittgenstein has also become a cult figure outside of academic philosophy. He is the subject of at least four biographies (Bartley 1985; McGuinness 1985; Monk 1990; Schulte 2005), as well as of a movie and of several documentaries. He has inspired numerous novels, plays, poems, musical compositions and works of pictorial art. Finally, he is the only philosopher to have made it onto the *Times* list of the '100 most important people of the [twentieth] century' (www.time.com/time100/scientist).

In this essay I shall disregard Wittgenstein's impact outside of academia.[1] Even within the area of academic philosophy my survey is inevitably selective in the extreme. In at least one respect, however, it has a wider scope than might be expected. Whereas most Anglophone Wittgenstein commentators wouldn't be caught dead reading non-English texts by anyone other than Wittgenstein or Frege (at a pinch), I go as far as referring to important secondary literature in exotic languages like German, French and Italian.

The first section provides a very brief history of Wittgenstein scholarship. It will mention several specific exegetical disputes that have made philosophical headlines, e.g. whether the *Tractatus* is committed to empiricism or whether the so-called rule-following considerations amount to a form of Humean scepticism. In the sequel, however, I shall try to bring into focus some more general parameters of disagreement between serious commentators: continuity vs. discontinuity in Wittgenstein's thought (sct. 2), immanent vs. genetic approaches to his texts (sct. 3), rationalist vs. irrationalist interpretations (sct. 4), and intrinsic vs. extrinsic motives for studying him (sct. 5).[2]

I   The Story of Wittgenstein Reception

The *Logisch-Philosophische Abhandlung* was published in 1921, and the German-English edition entitled *Tractatus Logico-Philosophicus* in 1922. The first (anonymous) reviews followed hot on its heels. But the reception of Wittgenstein's ideas started even before the book was published. Of the first two lectures that make up 'The Philosophy of Logical Atomism', Russell stated that 'they are very largely concerned with explaining ideas which I learnt from my friend and former pupil Ludwig Wittgenstein' (1918, 160; see also 182). Russell's 'Introduction' to the *Tractatus* provides a more substantial reading, though one that Wittgenstein condemned as superficial and misleading, with partial justification. Russell commends the attempt to construct a theory of symbolism which clarifies the relation between language and reality. The book also converted him to the view that instead of describing the most general features of reality, logic and mathematics consist of tautologies and are hence rooted in language; this in turn inspired him to take an interest in the topic of meaning (1959, 108; see Monk 1997).

On the other hand, Russell criticized not only the cryptic constructivist philosophy of mathematics in the *Tractatus*, but also the mystical ideas and the notorious distinction between what can be said in meaningful propositions and what can only be shown.

Like Russell, Ramsey treated the *Tractatus* primarily as a contribution to the foundations of logic and mathematics (see sct. 5 below). He had participated in its translation and wrote the first important review of it (1923). His guiding ambition was to reformulate Russell's logicist foundations of mathematics on the basis of Wittgenstein's novel account of logic and of the nature of the proposition (1925, 164). It is also probable that Wittgenstein inspired the redundancy theory of truth for which Ramsey is now famous. In return, Ramsey put his finger on the colour exclusion problem that was to lead eventually to the unravelling of the *Tractatus* conception of logic as resulting from the truth-functional combination of logically independent elementary propositions (see Glock 2005). He also rectified a definite mistake in Russell's 'Introduction'. Wittgenstein is not just concerned with 'the conditions for a logically perfect language' (TLP, x), 'his doctrines apply to ordinary languages' (1923, 9). For Wittgenstein, 'all propositions of our everyday language, just as they stand, are in perfect logical order' (5.5563). What is needed is not an ideal *language* that replaces natural languages, but an ideal *notation* which brings out the underlying logical structure which sentences in the vernacular possessed all along. Unfortunately, this has not prevented countless later commentators from classifying the early Wittgenstein as an 'ideal language philosopher' together with Frege, Russell, Carnap and Quine. In fact, his position was much closer to the kind of formal semantics propagated by Montague, Davidson and Dummett, which detects formal calculi in natural languages.

In the meantime, the *Tractatus* had come to the attention of the Vienna Circle, a group of scientifically minded philosophers led by Moritz Schlick. It was recognized by some of them (Schlick, Carnap, Waismann) as a turning-point in the history of philosophy. But their grasp of it was partial (see Hacker 1996a, Ch. 3), for instance when they assimilated the account of mathematical equations to that of logical tautologies. The idea that metaphysical pronouncements are nonsensical pseudo-propositions appealed to their anti-metaphysical zeal, and they dismissed the suggestion that there are ineffable metaphysical and ethical truths. They harnessed the restriction of philosophy to the analysis of language, in particular of the propositions of science, to their conviction that science is the only source of knowledge and understanding. Wittgenstein himself found this scientistic view offensive, even though his restriction of meaningful language to the empirical 'propositions of natural science' (TLP 6.53) sold the ticket on which the logical positivists were travelling. As committed empiricists they welcomed the idea that necessary propositions are analytic, and hence do not express knowledge of reality. Unlike previous versions of empiricism (Mill, Mach), this logical empiricism promises to do justice to their necessity while avoiding both Platonism and the Kantian idea of synthetic *a priori* truths.

Schlick made contact with Wittgenstein, and although the latter did not take part in the weekly meetings of the Circle, he met a select few (Schlick, Waismann, and, initially, Carnap and Feigl). Together with the *Tractatus*, these discussions (recorded in *Wittgenstein and the Vienna Circle*) were formative influences on the development of logical positivism in the interwar years. In the course of these discussions, Wittgenstein developed the now notorious principle of verification, according to which the meaning of a proposition is the method of its verification. Like Schlick and Carnap he combined verificationism with a version of phenomenalism, thereby strengthening further the impression that the *Tractatus* had been an empiricist overture to logical positivism. This interpretation was initially propagated by Ayer (1936) and Popper (1934), and has more recently been revived by the Hintikkas (1986).

After Wittgenstein's return to Cambridge in 1929, his principal influence was through his teaching, and through the circulation of lecture notes and dictations like the *Blue, Brown* and *Yellow Book*. Wittgenstein's pupils and disciples began to spread his fame, often to his chagrin. He was offended by having been turned into a leading representative of the 'scientific world-view' of the logical positivists. He also had a protracted fallout with Waismann over the project – initially planned as a joint venture – of making Wittgenstein's post-*Tractatus* thought accessible, and he took umbrage at Ambrose's and Lazerowitz's application of his ideas (see Glock 2001; Baker 2003; Monk 1990, 346, 413). Later on Rhees, Anscombe and Malcolm expounded and emulated Wittgenstein's ideas and, in decreasing order of intensity, his literary style and intellectual demeanour. By contrast, Wittgenstein's most important pupil, von Wright, went his own philosophical way. Although as a literary executor he greatly contributed to Wittgenstein scholarship, notably through his catalogue of the *Nachlass*, he only discussed Wittgenstein's ideas in print long after leaving Cambridge.

Wittgenstein's influence through hearsay was decisively superseded by the posthumous publication of the *Investigations* in 1953. Given that its author died as a living legend, it is small wonder that a number of leading postwar analytic philosophers reviewed the book, in particular Feyerabend, Hampshire and Strawson. Just as the *Tractatus* had been associated with logical positivism, Wittgenstein's later work was associated with so-called 'ordinary language philosophy', a movement which flourished between the 1930s and the 1960s, especially at Oxford. For good reasons. Through his writings and/or personal contact Wittgenstein influenced major protagonists of what is more aptly called conceptual analysis, especially Ryle and Strawson (Hacker 1996a, Ch. 6.3). Like Wittgenstein, the conceptual analysts took a linguistic turn by regarding philosophical problems as conceptual and concepts as embodied in language. Again like Wittgenstein but unlike the logical positivists, they thought that traditional philosophical problems are to be solved or dissolved not by constructing artificial languages, but by describing the ordinary use of philosophically contested terms. Finally, like Wittgenstein most of them were suspicious of large-scale quasi-scientific theory-construction in philosophy.

Between the late 1950s and the late 1960s, respect for Wittgenstein's achievements was at its peak. The emphasis was on two topics. One was the later philosophy of language, especially the slogan that meaning is use and the idea of family resemblance, which were regarded as central to the proper conduct of philosophical analysis. The other was the philosophy of mind, especially the private language argument and the idea of a criterion, which were recognized as powerful challenges to Cartesian dualism, phenomenalism and scepticism about other minds.[3]

Wittgenstein's work was interpreted and exploited widely. For the first time after the war interest was not confined to Anglophone and Scandinavian countries. German and Austrian scholars started drawing attention to various continental contexts of Wittgenstein's work (e.g. Specht 1963; Haller 1988). Italian authors have made valuable contributions from the 1950s to the present (see Frascolla 1994; Marconi 1997). The reception of Wittgenstein's work in France was a slower process, the efforts of pioneers like Bouveresse (e.g. 1987) notwithstanding.

A more scholarly and philological approach to Wittgenstein was encouraged by the publication of important parts from the *Nachlass*, and by the appearance of the first commentaries on the *Tractatus*. While Anscombe (1959) stressed the logical aspects of the book and its indebtedness to Frege, Stenius (1960) put emphasis on the picture theory and the affinities with Kant. Black (1964) still provides an indispensable aid to the study of the text, even though its verdicts on the most vexed exegetical problems are problematic. Of equal importance is the collection of interpretative essays by Copi and Beard (1966).

David Pole's critical monograph on the later philosophy appeared as early as 1958. It was famously countered by Cavell (1962), but set a trend for later negative assessments (e.g. Findlay 1984; Cook 1994). In the 1970s Wittgenstein studies gradually became more scholarly. Ground-breaking studies of the whole of Wittgenstein's work and its development were provided by Kenny (1973), Pears (1971), Hacker (1972) and Fogelin (1976). But full-scale commentaries on the *Investigations* only got started in earnest after the Cornell microfilm version of the *Nachlass* became available in 1967. Hallett's commentary (1977) is helpful in providing background material from the *Nachlass* and delineating the intellectual background. But a far more substantial contribution to both the interpretation and assessment of the book is the four volume commentary by Baker and Hacker (1980 and 1985), completed by Hacker (1990 and 1996). On a momentous scale, it combines textual exegesis – often based on the emergence of passages in the *Nachlass* – encyclopaedic knowledge of the historical background, and analytic reconstruction of the structure and lines of argument. Von Savigny's commentary (1988–89/1994–96) is the only one in German. It agrees with Baker and Hacker on one important point: in spite of its desultory appearance the *Investigations* displays more argumentative structure than is commonly assumed. Both commentaries even discern chapters, continuous stretches of text devoted to a specific cluster of issues. Unlike Baker and Hacker, von Savigny deliberately forsakes appeal to previous versions of the text (see sct. 3). But as a meticulous native speaker, von Savigny pays unusually close attention to details of German wording and syntax, and makes plenty of important discoveries, e.g. concerning anglicisms in Wittgenstein's German prose. He also provides a useful survey of alternative readings of each passage, and is most keenly aware of the exegetical choices that arise at each juncture.

An entirely different approach was taken in Kripke's fascinating yet highly problematic discussion of Wittgenstein's so-called 'rule-following considerations'. Kripke does not purport to provide an accurate account of the primary texts, but to propound 'Wittgenstein's argument as it struck Kripke' (1982, 5). As regards its content, Kripke's interpretation is characterized by two features. First, like many other commentators, he adopts a *communitarian* reading according to which rule-following and language are inherently social; secondly, like Fogelin before him he portrays Wittgenstein as constructing a sceptical paradox in the style of Hume. Kripke's book continues to be highly influential in a debate about rule-following which has lost contact with Wittgenstein interpretation (see Wright/Miller 2002). As regards Wittgenstein studies proper, it placed rule-following at the centre of attention, leading for example to McDowell's communitarian yet non-sceptical reading (1998). It also helped to rekindle interest in Wittgenstein's philosophy of mathematics, for instance through Crispin Wright (1980; 2001). But it was vigorously contested by more orthodox interpreters like Baker and Hacker (1984).

Whether actual or perceived, this orthodoxy has come under vehement attack since the late 1980s from very diverse quarters. One theme unites its otherwise diverse enemies: the conviction that Wittgenstein was a singular thinker who should not be assimilated to either traditional or analytic philosophy of any kind, not even Kantian critical philosophy or conceptual analysis. In particular, there is a pervasive feeling that his hostility to theories and theses and his therapeutic aims make his work incommensurable not just with traditional metaphysics but also with any philosophy which conceives of itself as a cognitive discipline based mainly on rational argument (see sct. 4). Although there have been trenchant responses, especially by Hacker (2001), these 'unorthodox' voices are clearly in the ascendancy. In quantitative terms, they now constitute a new mainstream, not among analytic philosophers interested in or sympathetic to Wittgenstein, but within the smaller arena of Anglophone Wittgenstein studies. However, they have yet to produce interpretations of either the *Tractatus* or the *Investigations* to rival those of the orthodoxy in detail, comprehensiveness and sophistication. It also remains to be seen whether the erstwhile revolutionaries will become targets of an analytic backlash or of a further revolution.

II Continuity vs. Discontinuity

The first readers of the *Investigations* were struck by the sharp contrast to the *Tractatus*, especially if they had not had the privilege of witnessing the evolution of Wittgenstein's thought through personal contact. This gave rise to the idea that Wittgenstein was unique in the history of our subject in producing two philosophies which are at loggerheads with each other. In its most extreme form, this led to the postulation of two literary persona – Wittgenstein I or early Wittgenstein, author of the *Tractatus*, and Wittgenstein II or later Wittgenstein, author of the *Investigations* (Pitcher 1964; Stegmüller 1965).

Against this kind of dichotomy, scholars like Fann (1969) and Kenny (1973, Ch. 12) pointed to a whole catalogue of ideas that run through Wittgenstein's entire work, notably his conviction that philosophy is *toto caelo* different from science, and that it has to do with problems of language rather than matters of facts. Their hand was strengthened by the increasing availability of writings following Wittgenstein's return to Cambridge in 1929. These clearly display that his original intention had been to elaborate and modify some of the thoughts of the *Tractatus*. It dawned on him only slowly that a more radical rethinking was required.

However, instead of restoring to Wittgenstein a unified oeuvre, these discoveries lend succour to the idea of a distinct 'transition' or 'middle period' (e.g. Pitcher 1964, v–vi; Arrington 1983; Stern 1991; Glock 2001). The idea of a fundamental change between *Tractatus* and *Philosophical Investigations* persists, but it is acknowledged to be *gradual* and to have occurred some time *after* Wittgenstein's official resumption of philosophy. There are conflicting claims about what marks the turning-point from the transition period to Wittgenstein's mature later work (see Stern 2005, 172–5). Hintikka and Hintikka (1986) date it at the end of 1929 and identify it with the abandonment of the phenomenalism which they detect not just at the beginning of the transition period but already in the *Tractatus*. Schulte (1989/1992) and Pichler (2004) date it in 1936, with the start of work on the first version of the *Investigations*. In his exemplary study of Wittgenstein's *Wende*, Kienzler (1997) settles on 1931, for two reasons: at that stage the basics of the conception of philosophy propounded in the *Investigations* had been laid, and the date comports well with Wittgenstein's own remarks on how he changed his mind after the completion of the *Tractatus*. For what it is worth, I incline to the less committed verdict that the *Big Typescript* of 1933 at any rate marks the *end* of the transition period, since it already contains his mature views not just on the nature of philosophy, but also on meaning and intentionality.

Even more recently, the idea of yet another 'third' Wittgenstein has been launched, this one postdating the *Investigations* Part I (Moyal-Sharrock 2004). One possible rationale is that after the completion of the book Wittgenstein started to discuss philosophical psychology in its own right and in a more positive vein, rather than in connection with clearing up confusions about language and its connection to reality (e.g. see Schulte 1993). Another reason is the impact of *On Certainty*, a selection from Wittgenstein's last manuscripts which is increasingly hailed as a third stroke of genius, and one which adopts a distinct outlook (Stroll 1994).

At this stage we face an *embarassement de richesse*: four Wittgensteins – early, middle, late, latest – when two already proved an exegetical handful. One does not have to be a die-hard positivist or follower of Occam to sympathize with the maxim: *philosophi non sunt multiplicanda sine necessitatem*. Perhaps Stern is right to suspect that the very question of how many Wittgensteins there are betokens the kind of essentialism that Wittgenstein warned us against (2005, 170–2). On the other hand, there is nothing essentially essentialist in trying to distinguish *periods* in the work of a thinker. Such distinctions can be more or less helpful in understanding that work and its development, and for this very reason they are bound to be contentious in multiple respects.

By contrast, the heuristic device of distinguishing not just periods and lines of thought but different *thinkers* is not just potentially misleading, it also disguises important features of Wittgenstein's development. There are abiding ideas and themes (the difference between philosophy and science, and the importance of language, to stick to uncontentious cases). There are also numerous transformations in his oeuvre, along a variety of parameters ranging from methodological precepts through philosophical ideas and stylistic matters to the receding of certain topics – notably dropping the philosophy of mathematics – and the emergence of others – notably aspect-perception and epistemic questions – after 1944.

In addition to this fairly standard mixture of continuity and change, however, there is also a feature which *is* distinctive of Wittgenstein's philosophical development, and which might even be unique. There is a single decisive – though gradual – change of mind, namely the one which separates the *Tractatus* from the *Investigations*. This change is evident in numerous remarks from the *Nachlass* after 1929, as well as in lectures and in conversations. Between 1929 and 1945 Wittgenstein developed a philosophical outlook that is explicitly and sharply critical of his early work. This fact is most striking in the Preface of the *Investigations*. After all, the very rationale for publishing that work lies in its opposition to the *Tractatus*.

> Until quite recently, I had actually given up the idea of publishing my work in my lifetime . . . . Four years ago, however, I had occasion to reread my first book . . . and to explain its ideas to someone. It suddenly seemed to

> me that I should publish those old thoughts and the new ones together:
> that the latter could be seen in the right light only by contrast with and
> against the background of my old way of thinking. For since beginning to
> occupy myself with philosophy again, sixteen years ago, I have been forced
> to recognize grave mistakes in what I wrote in that first book.

By contrast, the reflections after 1949 nowhere *contradict* Part I of
Philosophical Investigations substantially, much less explicitly. Instead, they
extend some of its ideas to new areas, notably that of aspect-perception,
or, in a more substantial and important departure, to epistemological
issues like certainty and scepticism.

Add to this the fact that in the Preface the *Tractatus* proclaimed to
have solved the fundamental problems of philosophy, and that its author
abandoned philosophy between 1922 and 1928 (except for sporadic
exchanges with Ramsey). And now it appears that the contrast between
an early and a later work is fundamentally correct. Opponents of the
dichotomy willy-nilly confirm this impression by frequently speaking of
the early and the later Wittgenstein themselves.

It is salutary to compare Wittgenstein's case with that of Plato and of
Kant. The works of all three fall into distinct periods which are undeniably
important to understanding their ideas. In the case of Plato, there is an
easily discernible contrast between early, middle and late dialogues, but
no explicit announcement of a change of mind. In the case of Kant, there
is a self-professed transformation (aka awakening from 'dogmatic slum-
bers') which separates the critical from the pre-critical writings. But the
latter hardly rival the former in importance. In Wittgenstein's case, by
contrast, we have two powerful philosophical visions, distinct and self-
contained, except that the later work evolves partly out of sharp and
explicit criticisms of the early work.

III   Genetic vs. Immanent Hermeneutics

My second strategic conflict is one about the methods and indeed the
objects of interpretation. It concerns the *type of source* to which one can
appeal in making sense of Wittgenstein's two major works – the *Tractatus*
and the *Investigations*. This then spills over into a debate over whether
these two are even the *proper topics* of Wittgenstein interpretation.

Among Anglophone commentators, such hermeneutic debates have
only flared up sporadically, although they have played an important (if

not altogether happy) role in substantive exegetical quarrels. The standard sequence is roughly as follows: first one propounds readings of Wittgenstein's official works; next these readings are confronted with countervailing evidence; finally one establishes to one's own unbridled satisfaction that this evidence is quite unreliable or downright inadmissible because of the type of source from which it stems.

There are some exceptions to such ad hoc hermeneutics, notably the debate over whether Wittgenstein's later self-criticism is a reliable guide to the views of the *Tractatus*. Perhaps it is 'The Ghost of the *Tractatus*' rather than the book itself which provides the target (Kenny 1984). Or perhaps the later Wittgenstein was just very adept at extracting the important fundamentals of his earlier views from less important details (Hacker 1975).

But the only sustained debate of these issues has taken place in the wake of von Savigny's Commentary on the *Investigations* (1994; see also Raatzsch 2003). Following the increasing availability of material other than the *Tractatus* and the *Investigations*, the major interpretations were *genetic* or *source-oriented*. In dealing with difficult passages of the *Investigations*, in particular, commentators like Baker and Hacker have liberal recourse to *Nachlass* sources, as well as to Wittgenstein's other published and unpublished writings, lectures and conversations. This genetic approach often leads to a kind of passage hunting in the *Nachlass* jungle which is not just bothersome, but also fraught with risks. Obviously one cannot just take any of Wittgenstein's remarks from any period to shed light on remarks from other periods, because of the constant changes in his opinions. In order to overcome this problem one would need a picture of his overall development which would allow one to decide whether any changes occurred with respect to the topic at issue. Alas, such a picture could in turn emerge only as a result of interpreting the *Nachlass*, which alone documents his movements of thought between the publication of the *Tractatus* and the completion of Part I of *Philosophical Investigations*.

Furthermore, in view of the disorderly appearance, provisional character and (occasionally) unsatisfactory content of the *Nachlass* material, which Wittgenstein himself commented on, one must try to follow him in separating 'the wheat from the chaff' (MS 119, 79), an arduous task which, unfortunately, the selection policy of his initial editors has not fulfilled altogether happily.

Von Savigny avoids these vagaries by appeal to two interrelated hermeneutic principles. First, his approach is *reader-* rather than *author*-oriented. It assumes that the author's intentions are irrelevant, unless they are stated in the text. Secondly, and as a consequence, it is *immanent*. An interpretation should only take into consideration what a reader can understand by looking at the text itself. Consequently, other writings (whether by Wittgenstein or other authors) are taken into consideration only where the *Investigations* itself refers to them. Otherwise its passages are to be interpreted exclusively from their *context* in the *published text*.

Though rarely discussed in the Anglophone literature, the immanent approach marks an important vantage point within the landscape of Wittgenstein-exegesis. Immanentist attitudes often seem to fuel hostile or indifferent reactions to the genetic approach (e.g. Hanfling 1989). Furthermore, the immanent alternative throws into sharp relief two contrasting hermeneutic positions. Whereas von Savigny completely disregards author's intentions and biographical information, other commentators have maintained that in Wittgenstein's case, at least, the real prize is precisely to understand the author rather than the text, and that this reorientation is in line with his own intentions (Diamond 1991, 57, 64–5; 2000, 155–6; see sct. 5 below).

The general question of whether the intentions of an author or the context of writing can or must be taken into account in interpreting a text is beyond the scope of this essay (see Taylor 1998). But some of its repercussions are clearly important to Wittgenstein studies. For one thing, there is a middle ground between the aforementioned extremes. One must concede to the immanent approach that there is a difference between the project of understanding a text and the project of understanding the context of its production, the overall oeuvre of which it is a part, its author or even the latter's intentions. Accordingly, readers of the *Investigations* need not be *interested* in Wittgenstein or the *Nachlass*. But it does not follow that this work can be properly *understood* without taking the latter into consideration.

Some of the author's intentions concerning a text have at most an indirect bearing on its interpretation. But a text is after all a means of communication. In establishing how it should be understood, we therefore need to know at the very least *what its author intended to get across*. Of course, there remains a difference between *what a text says* and what its author *meant* to say or write. Furthermore, von Savigny is perfectly right to insist that to understand what a text literally says, one only needs to grasp the conventional meaning of its sentences, without understanding what the author meant to say.

He is also right to point out that an author can be *held responsible* not just for what she meant to say, but also for what she actually did say. But what that is depends on both the general linguistic conventions and the assumptions governing a specific genre *at the time of writing*. For any author of any period needs to take certain things for granted, without annunciating them explicitly. This means that at least *some* aspects of the context are directly relevant, not the economic conditions of the text's production, for instance, but the relevant linguistic conventions and those features which the author assumes to be familiar to readers.

Furthermore, we need *more* than nominal understanding of the literal content when it comes to either a work of art (see PI §§522–35) or a work of philosophy. As regards the latter, it is not just possible but probable that the author has not managed to convey her message in a clear and cogent fashion, and that her reasoning relies on numerous tacit assumptions. In that case it is important to establish what problem or view or line of reasoning she tried to get across.

These points apply to the *Investigations* with a vengeance. It was intended as an *instrument of philosophical clarification*. We understand it to the extent to which we understand the insights and arguments its author attempted to convey. For this reason an ideal interpretation should reconstruct the most powerful position which is compatible with the context of a passage and the overall corpus. It should look at obscure passages, and first formulate interpretive questions and philosophical objections. Next it should try to find answers to the questions and responses to the objections by considering all of the exegetical resources available, including *both* the context and the *Nachlass*.

There is an additional cluster of reasons why in the case of the *Investigations* looking at the 'genesis' of a passage is often helpful and sometimes indispensable. The final text rarely identifies its targets. Wittgenstein was interested in undermining not so much specific positions or theories, but rather paradigmatic ideas which inform a whole strand of philosophical thinking. This procedure has the disadvantage that it is often unclear what precisely he had in mind. The *Nachlass* as a whole, not just the immediate sources of a remark, often helps to identify the authors he was thinking of, and thus gives us a better idea of the paradigmatic positions he considered in the *Investigations*.

More generally, the way in which Wittgenstein composed the *Investigations* has aptly been labelled as 'the snippet-box manner of composition' (Hacker 1972, 177). It is the result of a constant revision of typescripts based on first-draft manuscripts. This revision involved the following elements: (i) inserting new remarks copied out from other drafts; (ii) pruning away others; (iii) rearranging their order; (iv) curtailing particular remarks; (v) changing specific phrases or words. These processes, in particular (ii)–(iv), had a tendency to condense the remarks. The text became stylistically more polished, but occasionally at the cost of diminishing its intelligibility. There is no better or more straightforward way of redressing this difficulty than by looking at the starting point of the condensation process.

At the same time, von Savigny rightly highlights a danger in the genetic approach, namely that editorial changes to a remark – notably condensing them or using them in a new context within a relatively ordered sequence of sections – can give them a completely new meaning. Of course, there is no reason to accept that every alteration *must* alter the content of a passage. As von Savigny himself points out, this would have the consequence that Wittgenstein's final text might completely depart from all of its previous versions (1994, 25), immediate predecessors included. This is conceivable, of course, but extremely improbable. Instead, the onus lies on someone opposing an otherwise plausible genetic interpretation. He has to demonstrate that the source of the remark is after all irrelevant, by showing for example that it contradicts clearly stated positions of the *Investigations*, or that the alteration is due to a change of mind on Wittgenstein's part. The latter cannot be done without consulting the *Nachlass* or Wittgenstein's biography. The ironic result of heeding von Savigny's warning, therefore, is that assessing genetic interpretations requires going beyond the interpreted passage itself.

In doing so, however, immanent evidence carries greater weight than external evidence. I submit that the order of importance is as follows:

- ❖ the immediate context of the interpreted passage;
- ❖ other passages of the same work;
- ❖ the direct sources (immediate or mediate) of the passage;
- ❖ the rest of the corpus;
- ❖ lecture notes;
- ❖ other biographical evidence.

Note finally that the *source* of evidence is *only one* consideration among many, and that it can be outweighed by the *nature* of the evidence. A clear and unambiguous statement from trustworthy notes of lectures or conversations trumps a speculative and precarious argument based on slender evidence from the text itself.[4]

A second challenge to the genetic mainstream has it that the *real inter-pretandum* of Wittgenstein exegesis should not be the manuscripts or typescripts he left us at all – whether authorized for publication or not – but rather the *whole* of the *Nachlass*, which constitutes a single 'hypertext' (Stern 1994; Pichler 2004, Ch. 2.2). According to one version, the *Nachlass* is a network of cross-referring 'scripts', and it is up to readers to reorganize the remarks from these scripts into 'texts', proper objects of interpretation.

In this respect, the hypertextualists share von Savigny's orientation towards the reader rather than the author. For it is certain that Wittgenstein himself did not *intend* to produce a hypertext. Instead, most of the post-1929 manuscripts and typescripts form an integral part of his avowed – if extremely troubled and occasionally aborted – endeavours to present the results of his later thinking in the form of a *book* (see PI, Preface; von Wright 1982, 111–36; Schulte 2005a). But as regards its readiness to move from official texts to other parts of the *Nachlass*, the hypertext approach is even further removed from the immanent approach than the genetic mainstream. I counsel against both extremes. For the purposes of rational reconstruction it may occasionally be advantageous to draw on Wittgenstein's work in a mix-and-match manner. But for the purposes of *interpretation*, one should draw on the *Nachlass* not just in the controlled manner advocated above, the exercise should also stand in the service of making sense of the texts Wittgenstein actually left us.

To steer a middle-course between the Scylla of immanentism and the Charybdis of hypertextualism one needs, among other things, certain points of orientation in the *Nachlass* – texts which manifest his considered ideas at certain stages of their development. This in turn leads to a question forcefully posed by Schulte: What is to count as a *work* by Wittgenstein? The *Tractatus* obviously qualifies by dint of having been published by Wittgenstein himself. As regards the *Nachlass*, Schulte suggests that a text must satisfy the following criteria (1991, Ch. I.3):

1 Wittgenstein's own assessment of it as a self-standing and suitable expression of his views at the time.
2 A detectable line of thought with claims, arguments, objections, etc.
3 A polished style and state of completion.

Schulte has recently opined that by these criteria only the *Investigations* Part I qualify (2005a). I am more inclined to follow his original verdict of including the *Philosophical Remarks*, the *Big Typescript*, and the prewar version of the *Investigations* as well. Be that as it may, Schulte himself is hesitant about *On Certainty*. It clearly fails (1): not only does the material hail from a first draft manuscript, it is a selection from that manuscript. At the same time *On Certainty* satisfies (2) and (3) to a degree that may even excel that of the *Investigations*. To me this observation suggests that the material he composed shortly before his death may actually be better for having escaped his editorial attentions. And this reinforces a more general lesson, namely that Wittgenstein's editing did not always change matters for the better.

IV   Rationalist vs. Irrationalist Interpretations

Wittgenstein and reason: as regards matters of content rather than method this is perhaps the most important topic of current Wittgenstein scholarship. Among the fundamental issues it is the most contested, and among the contested issues it is the most fundamental. There is no dearth of disagreement on, for example, the private language argument, the rule-following considerations or his philosophy of mathematics. But these topics are not as fundamental as Wittgenstein's attitude towards reason. For here we are dealing with the question of what kind of thinker Wittgenstein was. Was he a proponent of the claims of reason, of rational argument, justification and clarification? Or was he an enemy of such enlightenment ideals? Was he even a philosopher in the traditional sense, or rather a sage, prophet or guru?

Opinion on these matters divides roughly into two camps: *rationalist* and *irrationalist* interpretations. Although this division itself is a prominent feature of contemporary Wittgenstein studies, the terminology I have chosen requires explanation. First, I use the term 'rationalist' to include not just the continental rationalists with their emphasis on innate ideas and *a priori* knowledge, but any position which stresses that our beliefs should be subject to critical scrutiny and supported by argument, no matter whether these arguments invoke reason or experience. Similarly, I use the term 'reason' for the general ability to justify one's actions and beliefs by way of argument, and not in the narrow (and, in my view, misguided) sense employed by modern theories of rationality, in which it refers to a disposition to act exclusively in one's own interest.

Secondly, I do not distinguish between analytic and continental interpretations (cf. Biletzki 2003, Ch. 10). Explaining these general categories in a coherent manner is a substantial task in its own right (see Glock

2007). More importantly, the label 'continental' would be even more misleading in this specific context. Among the *bona fide* continental philosophers who first took up Wittgenstein there are irrationalists like Lyotard (1984). But there are also figures like Apel (1980) and Habermas (1988) who develop Wittgensteinian ideas in directions which are ultrarationalist, culminating in the idea that the preconditions of linguistic discourse will provide the elusive rational foundation for morality long sought by Kantians.

Still, there is a connection between rationalist interpretations and analytic philosophy. Originally, Wittgenstein's work was seen simply in the context of the logical and methodological debates with Frege, Russell, Ramsey and the logical positivists that he personally participated in. He was treated as a member of the analytic tradition, albeit a highly exotic and troublesome one. Since that tradition prides itself on its concern with argument and justification, and sometimes even defines itself by reference to this priority, it would seem that Wittgenstein was part of *The Dialogue of Reason* (the title of Cohen 1986; see also Føllesdal 1997). Later, through the efforts of Stenius, Pears, Hacker and Garver (1994), it was recognized that there is a strong Kantian element to both the early and the later work. But this did not threaten his image as either an analytic philosopher or a proponent of reason. Strawson and Bennett had sanitized the *Critique of Pure Reason*, and as a result the sage of Königsberg could be treated as an honorary analytic philosopher. In any event, Kant's critical philosophy is an eminently rationalist enterprise, namely the attempt of reason to establish its own nature and limits. In so far as Wittgenstein undertakes a linguistic transformation of this critical enterprise, he is committed to the claims of reason.

Irrespective of any specific philosophical pedigree, the aforementioned 'orthodox' commentators try to extract from both the *Tractatus* and the *Investigations* arguments relevant to philosophy understood as a rational enterprise, even if these arguments are mostly taken to be negative. In this they have the blessing of several striking passages. Thus Wittgenstein insisted that philosophy should provide arguments that are 'absolutely conclusive', and he described his own thought as the 'rejection of wrong arguments' which is open to those feeling a need for 'transparency of their own argumentation' (MS 161, 3; BT, 408, 421).

Irrationalist interpretations of Wittgenstein have been equally common. This is hardly surprising, given the mystical parts of the *Tractatus*, his later exhortations against philosophical explanations or justifications, and his 'quietist' claim that philosophy should leave everything as it is. Although there is a fair degree of overlap in both doctrine and personnel, one can distinguish the following variations on the irrationalist theme:

❖ existentialist interpretations: Partly fuelled by letters and by reports from personal friends like Engelmann (1967/EL) and Drury (1984/DC), the mystical, ethical and religious aspects of Wittgenstein's work are stressed and linked to existentialist thinkers like Kierkegaard, Tolstoy and Nietzsche (Janik/Toulmin 1973).[5]

❖ therapeutic interpretations: On account of the famous comparisons with psychoanalysis, it is held that the grammatical remarks of Wittgenstein's later work are not conceptual clarifications but only therapeutic attempts to make us abandon philosophical problems for the sake of intellectual tranquillity (Wisdom 1953; Bouwsma 1986).

❖ aspect interpretations: a related position developed by Baker from the early 1990s onwards. It holds that these grammatical remarks are not part of philosophical arguments that appeal to reason, but designed to effect a conversion in outlook analogous to the dawning of a new aspect in aspect-seeing (Baker 2004).

❖ nonsense interpretations, of which more anon.

❖ Pyrrhonian interpretations, according to which Wittgenstein does not just aim to overcome traditional, metaphysical philosophizing by a better 'critical' variety, but seeks to bring philosophy as such to an end (Fogelin 1976, Ch. XV; Stern 2004).

❖ genre interpretations: the idea that the *Philosophical Investigations*, in particular, must not be read as an academic treatise that contains if not theories or theses then at least some definite philosophical questions and arguments, but as an album or part of a "hypertext" that is meant to inspire and resonate in wholly diverse directions (e.g. Stern 1996; Pichler 2004).

❖ postmodern interpretations: a position inaugurated by Rorty (1980), according to which Wittgenstein, along with Heidegger and the pragmatists, paves the way for an 'edifying philosophy' in which the traditional concern with truth and objectivity is abandoned in favour of the hermeneutic attempt to keep a conversation going. According to Rorty, Wittgenstein supports Dewey's and Quine's attack on the idea that philosophy is a subject distinct from the empirical sciences (e.g. 1982, xviii, 28).

Irrationalist interpretations are not necessarily irrational. Postmodern irrationalism is indeed postmodern, that is to say, it is entertainingly ludicrous. In view of his anti-scientism and his insistence on the sui generis character of philosophy, the suggestion that Wittgenstein was keen to dissolve philosophy into science beggars belief.

By contrast to this fanciful distortion, the other versions of irrationalism all have at least some foundation in the texts and in Wittgenstein's life. There are also notable voices that advocate a compromise between rationalist and irrationalist readings. But they tend to lapse ultimately into irrationalism, because they resist the idea that Wittgenstein philosophized in a vein that is similar to or has points of contact with the kind of conceptual investigation one finds in Aristotle, Kant or so-called ordinary language philosophy.[6]

The irrationalist interpretation which has made most of a splash in recent years is the nonsense interpretation. It was inspired by Stanley Cavell and Burton Dreben, and is currently epitomized by Cora Diamond (1991; 2000) and James Conant (2001; 2002). Starting out from these American origins it has, under the title the 'New Wittgenstein' (Crary and Read 2000; see also McCarthy and Stidd 2001), led to a debate which is overheated, over-hyped and over here.

What sets the New Wittgensteinians apart from other irrationalist approaches are two points.[7] The first is a reading of the *Tractatus*. In the final sections, Wittgenstein condemns the propositions of the *Tractatus* itself as nonsensical (6.54–7). According to a standard interpretation, his reason was that these propositions try to express truths about the essence of language which, by Wittgenstein's own lights, cannot be expressed in meaningful propositions, but which show themselves in logical propositions and in empirical propositions properly analyzed.[8] According to the New Wittgensteinians, by contrast, the *Tractatus* is not meant to consist of illuminating nonsense that vainly tries to hint at logico-metaphysical truths, but of 'plain nonsense' (Diamond 1991, 181; Conant 1992, 198), nonsense in the same drastic sense as gibberish like 'piggly tiggle wiggle'. The purpose of the exercise is therapeutic. By producing such sheer nonsense, Wittgenstein tries to unmask the idea of metaphysical truths (effable or ineffable) as absurd, and to wean us off the temptation to engage in philosophy.

The second distinctive claim of the New Wittgensteinians is that Wittgenstein's conception of nonsense, both early and late, was 'austere' rather than 'substantial' (Crary 2000, 12–13; Diamond 1991, 111–12; Conant 2002, 380–3). There is just one kind of nonsense, namely plain nonsense, since it is illusory to suppose that nonsense – notably of the philosophical variety – could result from combining meaningful words in a way that transgresses the rules of logical syntax or grammar.

The 'plain nonsense' interpretation promises to rescue the *Tractatus* from the charge of being self-defeating. Alas, it has several fatal drawbacks (see Hacker 2001, Ch. 4; Glock 2006; Schroeder 2006, Ch. 2.5). It is at odds with the external evidence, writings and conversations in which Wittgenstein states that the *Tractatus* is committed to the idea of ineffable insights. Secondly, unlike the illuminating nonsense detected by orthodox interpretations, sheer gibberish cannot be in any way superior to the philosophical nonsense resulting from 'misunderstanding the logic of our language' (TLP 4.003). Consequently, if the pronouncements of the *Tractatus* were meant to be mere nonsense, Wittgenstein would have to be neutral between, for example, Frege's and Russell's idea that propositions are names of objects and the idea that they differ from names in saying something, or between their claim that the propositions of logic describe abstract objects and the claim that they are tautologies. In fact, however, Wittgenstein continued to defend the latter ideas even after abandoning the *Tractatus*. Finally, the nonsense interpretation employs hermeneutical double standards. On the one hand, it must reject as deliberate nonsense remarks which insist that philosophical propositions are attempts to say something that can only be shown. On the other hand, it must accept as genuine those remarks that provide the rationale for declaring philosophical pronouncements to be illegitimate. Yet these two types of remarks are inextricably interwoven. Furthermore, any concession that some parts of the book furnish the standards by which the *Tractatus* in particular and metaphysics in general qualify as nonsense reintroduces a distinction between illuminating and non-illuminating nonsense, a distinction which the New Wittgensteinians condemn as 'irresolute' or even a case of 'chickening out'. The only resolutely consistent *interpretation* is one which acknowledges *the text itself* to be resolutely *inconsistent*, because it consciously advances sentences which, by its own standards, cannot make sense.

Whereas most orthodox interpreters do not condone the position they detect in the *Tractatus*, the New Wittgensteinians not only ascribe the aforementioned views to Wittgenstein, they also *subscribe* to them. They endorse the austere conception of nonsense.[9] They also think that the statements of the *Tractatus* are indeed gibberish, yet nonetheless capable of establishing the futile nature of all philosophy.

How precisely this combination is to be effected remains unclear. For gibberish cannot state a reason for anything, least of all for dismissing a venerable intellectual enterprise that tackles fundamental questions through rational argument. Indeed, *if* Wittgenstein *had* intended to produce hokum and succeeded, this fact would provide a reason for abandoning *not* philosophy but the philosophical study of his writings.

Even less extreme irrationalists portray Wittgenstein as diverging radically from the rationalist mainstream of Western philosophy. They have invoked several points of irreconcilable contrast. One is the rejection of *systematic* philosophy, another the exclusively *negative* or critical aim of his project, a third the vision of an *end of philosophy*, a fourth the condemnation of *theories* and *theses*, and a final one the replacement of *argument* by *therapy*. Although these issues are standardly run together, it is important to keep them apart. Many conceptual analysts rejected systematic philosophy in favour of a piecemeal procedure, yet without restricting our subject to critique, let alone therapy. Conversely, even if the main task of philosophy is critical, it could be pursued in a systematic manner, as in Kant's Transcendental Dialectic, which provides an architectonic survey and demolition of metaphysical errors. Once more in the spirit of Kant, one might regard philosophy as a negative enterprise without either predicting or demanding its demise, on the grounds that the sources of philosophical error spring eternal. Finally, one can grant that Wittgenstein's project has a positive side, namely presenting an overview of grammar, yet insist that this is purely descriptive and no more involves arguments than his cure of confusions (e.g. Kenny 2004, 176).

The conflict over philosophical *theories* may be spurious, since Wittgenstein had a very restrictive conception of theory, confining it either to the deductive-nomological theories of the empirical sciences (PI §109; see Hanfling 2004) or to the attempt to provide an analytic definition of what he regarded as family-resemblance concepts (e.g. PG 119–20; RPP I §633).[10] Neither proscription rules out dealing with philosophical questions in a sustained and orderly fashion.

The dispute over philosophical theses is all the more real. There is no gainsaying Wittgenstein's claim that philosophy states only truisms that anyone would admit (PI §§126, 599; BT 412). But this is easily accommodated by rationalists: philosophy provides 'reminders' (PI §127) of patterns of linguistic use that competent speakers are perfectly familiar with outside of philosophy. Indeed, this procedure is blatantly incompatible with the Pyrrhonian refusal to advance claims *of any kind*, including the descriptions of the 'actual use of language' which Wittgenstein explicitly propagates (e.g. PI §124). Furthermore, if, his descriptivism notwithstanding, Wittgenstein had indeed adopted such a 'no position'-position, he would confront a fatal dilemma. Either his remarks conform to his 'no opinion'-methodology, then they cannot amount to a genuine contribution to philosophical or metaphilosophical debate. Or they do not, then his practice belies his stated methodological views. Furthermore, he would be propounding the (non-obvious) thesis that there are no (non-obvious) philosophical theses. In either case – incommensurability and inconsistency – his attacks on traditional philosophy would be self-contradictory and his conception of philosophy would be incoherent (Glock 1991).

Irrationalist interpreters might respond that Wittgenstein's project is a purely therapeutic one. 'Discussion is less a matter of constructing rigorous arguments from incontrovertible premises than of making propaganda for alternative points of view' (Baker 2004, 219, see 68). But such propaganda is philosophically immaterial. For its only criterion of success is the suppression of a certain intellectual urge. It cannot distinguish between achieving this goal by *extrinsic* means, such as threats, drugs or a knock on the head, and achieving it in the only way that is philosophically pertinent, namely through rational argument.

At this juncture rationalists like myself have been accused of succumbing to 'the prejudice according to which any form of persuasion that is not demonstrative is non-rational' (Morris 2004, 11). A curious complaint, since it is the explicit crux of my rationalism, at any rate, that Wittgenstein's 'undogmatic procedure' for resolving conceptual confusions (just like certain transcendental arguments) revolves around arguments that are *elenctic* rather than demonstrative (Glock 1996, 261–2, 297–8).[11] He tries to show that philosophical problems or propositions can get off the ground only by using words according to conflicting rules.

This leaves open the possibility that a new way of looking at a philosophical problem or concept, notably placing it in a novel context, constitutes yet another alternative to demonstration, 'a form of rational persuasion without the possibility of proof' (Baker 2004, 282–3). Unfortunately, from the fact that one *can* look at something in a certain way it does not follow that it is *correct* to look at it that way. Even if the idea of philosophical aspect-dawning is reformulated in a less subjectivist manner, namely as drawing attention to aspects which the object of investigation *actually possesses*, it does not follow that newly emphasized features are more important than previously noted ones.

Perhaps the proposal is that one *should* look at matters afresh because it dissolves philosophical problems. That begs the question, however, of whether dissolution is the appropriate response to these problems. That question is at least addressed by Wittgenstein's remarks to the effect that such problems rest on conceptual confusions. But these are precisely the aspects of his work that irrationalist interpreters tend to set aside.

It is true that the *Investigations* feature few explicit answers to Wittgenstein's numerous self-posed questions (see Kenny 2004, 78). But as von Savigny observed in conversation, many of the questions are *rhetorical*. In any event, even without the aid of the *Nachlass*, a line of reasoning can be extracted from much of the book. Again, Wittgenstein did not take sides in traditional disputes, but tried to undermine the assumptions common to the participants. He also tried to *dissolve* questions which lead to such misguided alternatives. But in doing so he sought the 'right question'. And he did provide answers to Socratic questions like 'What is understanding?', since doing so is a prerequisite of dissolving misguided questions and theories. What he rejects with respect to such Socratic questions is merely the insistence that they can only be answered by providing *analytic definitions* (BB 17–20; PI §§64–88).

But even where Wittgenstein rejects a traditional question as phrased, his remarks must nevertheless address an *underlying problem*. Otherwise he simply would not have anything to say on the topics at issue and his rejection would be no more than an expression of lack of interest, something those pursuing the question can ignore. Thus, when Wittgenstein dismisses questions like 'What is the ground of necessary truth?' he still addresses the philosophical problem of necessity by other questions like 'What is it for a proposition to be necessary?' Questioning a question in a philosophically relevant sense must involve taking up an underlying common problem in a more adequate way.

Wittgenstein suggested that philosophical illumination may arise from a book featuring nothing but jokes and questions and that we should respond to *all* philosophical questions not by giving an answer, but by asking a new question (RFM 147; Malcolm 1984, 27–8). In that very remark, however, he himself willy-nilly provides an *answer* to the question of what role questions play in philosophy. This rejoinder sounds bloody-minded only because it has to match the obstinate silliness of seriously adopting a 'no position'-position.

As these occasional remarks show, Wittgenstein was not entirely immune to Pyrrhonian silliness. In his early work, at least, he also succumbed to what one might call the *myth of mere method*. This is the illusion that one can fashion philosophical methods in a presuppositionless manner, one which does not in turn draw on philosophical views, e.g. about logical necessity, linguistic meaning or the nature of philosophical problems. In the *Tractatus* the method, in particular an ideal notation for the analysis of propositions, is supposed to be put in place by propadeutic claims about the essence of representation, claims that are then disowned as nonsensical. In the *Investigations* it seems that the method is supposed to emerge automatically as a spin-off from reflections on specific philosophical problems. But the *Tractatus* procedure is self-refuting; and the philosophical problems discussed in the *Investigations* only cry out for Wittgenstein's treatment on a certain understanding of their nature, an understanding which itself is philosophically contentious.

V   Extrinsic vs. Intrinsic Interests

The nature of philosophy is itself a contested philosophical issue, and views about this issue are philosophically controversial. Although the investigation of the proper aims and methods of philosophy is nowadays known as 'metaphilosophy', it is not a distinct higher-order discipline, but an integral part of philosophy itself. By contrast to therapeutic followers like Lazerowitz (1964), who theorized about philosophy from the external vantage-point of psychoanalysis, Wittgenstein himself was aware of this point (PI §121). Once it is acknowledged that one cannot engage in metaphilosophy without doing philosophy, however, the case for Pyrhonnianism collapses. One cannot swim without venturing into the water. And one cannot address philosophical problems, the nature of philosophy included, without doing philosophy, and hence without philosophical arguments and commitments of one's own. What one can do is to ensure consistence between philosophical methods, metaphilosophical and substantive views, and to argue for the latter in as plausible and unassuming a way as possible.

The rational line for both rationalist and irrationalist *interpreters* is to acknowledge that Wittgenstein's work combines rationalist and irrationalist elements. The rational line for *philosophers* is to explore the arguments, insights and instructive errors it has to offer. This exhortation presupposes, of course, that philosophy is an enterprise based on argument. But since one cannot argue against this presupposition without self-refutation, it is one to which we should commit.

But there is another pressing issue, namely whether one's interest in Wittgenstein and his work should be philosophical to begin with. There are plenty of extrinsic alternatives to such an intrinsic perspective, even within a (loosely speaking) academic setting (see also Biletzki 2003, Ch. 11).

For one thing, as mentioned above there has been an intense *biographical* interest in Wittgenstein as a *person*. The extent to which biographical information about authors in general or Wittgenstein in particular can help in understanding the work is subject to debate (see Monk 2001 and sct. 2 above). In any event, however, we can separate the two as topics of investigation: if it is indeed the person we seek to understand, as opposed to the views she expresses or the arguments and methods she uses, then we are engaged in biography rather than philosophy.

Related to the biographical interest is the *psychopathological* interest in Wittgenstein's *frame of mind* (e.g. Sass 2001; Hintikka and Hintikka 2002). From amnesia to Aspergers, from dyslexia to schizophrenia, there is hardly a mental disorder that he has not been diagnosed with. Lack of acquaintance with the patient is no obstacle, it would appear, which just goes to show that some disciplines are progressing with an ease that philosophy can only envy.

Then there is a *sociological*-cum-*political* angle on Wittgenstein. Thus one may ponder the dynamics of his interactions with his academic environment by way of armchair sociology (Collins 1998). From a similar perspective, but intellectually a cut above, Bloor proposes to divide Wittgensteinians into 'right' and 'left', on the model of 'right' and 'left' Hegelians (1992). Bloor's left/right terminology serves mainly to distinguish those Wittgensteinians that are and those that are not sympathetic to a purportedly scientific and causal sociology of knowledge and a communitarian conception of rule-following. But the political overtones are irresistible, and have been taken up by others (e.g. Stern 2005, 176–7). There is also the overtly political question of whether Wittgenstein was a conservative in anything but the cultural sense, something asserted by Nyiri (1981) and (convincingly, to my mind) denied by Schulte (1983).

Talking about culture, there is Wittgenstein as a *cultural* and *historical* phenomenon, an issue brought to the fore by Janik and Toulmin (1973; see also Nedo and Ranchetti 1983). This approach overlaps with biographical and exegetical/philosophical studies that lay emphasis on the context of Wittgenstein's life and writings (see Klagge 2001). It differs mainly in being less concerned with Wittgenstein the individual than with his cultural and political context.

Finally there is Wittgenstein as an *aesthetic* and specifically *literary* figure. By this I mean his role not as a muse for the arts, but as an object of stylistic analysis and literary theory. There are numerous discussions of Wittgenstein's style, especially in the *Investigations*, ranging from Cavell (1962) through Binkley (1973) to Pichler (2004).

Of course it is perfectly legitimate to investigate Wittgenstein in any of these capacities. What is problematic is to maintain that these extrinsic perspectives yield the true key to his philosophical thought. Thus proponents of what I called genre interpretations are not just impressed by Wittgenstein's singular style. They also berate more orthodox interpreters for assuming that one can separate Wittgenstein's contribution to (or crusade against) philosophy from his way of writing and mode of composition (e.g. Stern 2005, 184).

This is the most plausible case of an extrinsic perspective feeding into a philosophical interpretation. For Wittgenstein had self-professed aesthetic ambitions and regarded 'correct' style as integral to good philosophizing (FL 10.–11.19; CV 39, 87). The moot question, however, is this: What aspects of Wittgenstein's writing have, or are supposed to have, what kind of philosophical relevance? One of the few sustained answers to this question is given by Pichler. The less discursive and more aphoristic style of the *Investigations* is supposed to mark a move away from the 'dogmatic' and rationalist stance of the transition period to a more 'polyphonic' and irrationalist one. But the middle Wittgenstein had already condemned dogmatism and sketched an 'undogmatic procedure' for the resolution of conceptual confusions through elenctic argument (Glock 1991, 80–3). Furthermore, in Wittgenstein's oeuvre there is no statement to the effect that the stylistic changes of the mid-1930s had this kind of grand-strategic purpose. Yet surely this is precisely what one would expect from someone so obsessed with drawing metaphilosophical lessons from his own philosophical reflections. It is more likely, therefore, that these changes are a philosophically unwelcome result of Wittgenstein's aforementioned editing process. As he himself realized, he was in constant danger of being 'enamoured to his own style' (see MS 134, 145; MS 183, 28, 101, 222).

Of course there are features of *intellectual* style which are integral to his philosophical methods, e.g. his use of language-games, of analogical reasoning, of *reductio ad absurdum* arguments, of placing concrete examples in a novel context, and his quest for the redeeming word which either summarizes a philosophical temptation or provides an antidote. But these can be transposed into a different *literary* style, as the collaboration between Waismann and Wittgenstein clearly shows. On this issue I am in strong agreement with Gordon Baker: 'the single most effective antidote to the obscurantist dogma that Wittgenstein set his face against any systematic presentation of his philosophical insights. His own lengthy participation in the project of [*Logik, Sprache, Philosophie*] is a concrete refutation of this contention' (1979, 280). Even Waismann's supremely engaging and pellucid prose is no aesthetic match for Wittgenstein's. But stylistic interpreters owe us a clear and well-argued account of what *philosophical* substance (concerning problems, arguments or insights) is lost by rephrasing Wittgenstein's thought in a more conventional manner.

Barring such an account, this kind of paraphrase is not just legitimate but imperative. Wittgenstein studies and even Wittgensteinian philosophy have gradually lost contact with mainstream analytic philosophy, to the detriment of both sides. There is a genuine danger of navel-gazing if Wittgenstein scholars and Wittgensteinian philosophers lose the ability to write in a normal academic style, or to do philosophy except through the medium of interpreting Wittgenstein. The real discovery is the one that makes us capable of stopping doing Wittgenstein exegesis whenever we need to!

Notes

1   On this topic see Stern (2004, 1) and Schulte (2005, 131–6). Schulte also provides a brief but illuminating history of Wittgenstein scholarship (113–31). On the nature of the oeuvre and the history of Wittgenstein editing see also von Wright (1982); Stern (1996) and Kenny (2005).

2   Biletzki (2003) provides a book-length account of Wittgenstein interpretation. But her approach is different. She all but ignores writings in languages other than English, and detects a chronological sequence of general perspectives – from a metaphysical one at the start to an ethical one at the end. By contrast, my piece divides into a brief and matter-of-fact sketch of the history of Wittgenstein interpretation and a discussion of four strategic controversies. There is no neat correspondence between Biletzki's general approaches and my controversies. In fact, the continuity vs. discontinuity and the immanent vs. source oriented debates do not feature in her story. Finally, I am less reluctant than Biletzki to take sides in favour of a particular line of interpretation.

3   The most important early reviews and discussions of Wittgenstein's later work are reprinted in Pitcher (1968).

4   For this reason we should accept the overwhelming external evidence to the effect that the *Tractatus* counted properties and relations among its objects (Glock 1996, 103–5) and that it countenanced the idea of things that are beyond the bounds of what can be said (see sct. 4).

5   An extreme version of this approach is adopted by Wilhelm Baum, the editor of the *Geheime Tagebücher*: 'The plan of the literary executors to turn

Wittgenstein into an atheist and positivist is definitely doomed to fail. Instead, the Christian form of life and religion constitutes the matrix by reference to which the philosopher's work must be interpreted' (1991, 175). A striking claim indeed, since it accuses Elizabeth Anscombe of giving succour not just to positivists but also to atheists!

6   Thus Stern, following Pears, suggests that the later work combines Pyrrhonian and non-Pyrrhonian elements. But he confines the latter to his being 'a patient anti-philosopher who sees the need to work through the attractions of systematic philosophy'; 'the text really does contain philosophical argument, but the author regards the argument as a ladder that we should throw away after we have drawn the Pyrrhonian moral'. This is the no-position position discussed below: it purports to remain uncommitted on all questions, including the question whether one can remain uncommitted on all questions. It also sits uneasily with Stern's own recognition that Wittgenstein came to reject the ladder image (see 2004, 37, 170, 46–7).

7   Claims to the contrary notwithstanding, it is neither the stress on the therapeutic character of the *Investigations* nor the non-metaphysical picture of the *Tractatus* that distinguishes the New Wittgensteinians, but exclusively the issue of nonsense. Thus Baker came to adopt a highly therapeutic account of the later work. Yet his groundbreaking study of how Wittgenstein's early philosophy of logic depends on a vision of the essence of the proposition (1988) is incompatible with New Wittgensteinianism, which at best concedes that the *Tractatus* inadvertently strayed into metaphysics. Like Hacker, Malcolm, Pears and Kenny, Baker propounded a metaphysical or ontological reading of the *Tractatus*, according to which the structure of thought and language has to mirror the essence of a mind-independent reality. By contrast, according to 'linguistic' interpreters like Anscombe, McGuinness (2002, Part II) and Ishiguro (2001) the *Tractatus* treats the so-called essence of reality as a mere projection of the structure of language. On occasion, these linguistic interpreters have been claimed as precursors of New Wittgensteinianism. But this is problematic, since they portray the book as committed to the idea that the essence of linguistic representation cannot be said but can be shown.

8   Even officially neutral commentators (e.g. Stern 2004, 41) regularly distort the orthodox interpretation by lumbering it with the view that the propositions of the *Tractatus* themselves show what cannot be said. This view was mooted by Black (1964, 378–86) but explicitly renounced, e.g. by Hacker (1986, 25–6), the favourite orthodoxonian target of the New Wittgensteinians. On the question of what shows what according to the early Wittgenstein see also Glock (1996, 330–6, 107–8).

9   On the basis of semantic and metaphilosophical doctrines which I have argued to be untenable and at odds with Wittgenstein's own later insights (Glock 2004).

10 I am grateful to the editors for alerting me to this second case.
11 Ironically, the equation of argument with demonstration seems to play a role in some irrationalist interpretations. Kenny (2004) acutely pinpoints obstacles for rationalist interpretations; yet he also infers from the fact that Wittgenstein's procedure is not demonstrative that it cannot involve argument, without even considering the possibility of elenctic reasoning.

Chapter 2

Wittgenstein's Method: Ridding People of Philosophical Prejudices

Katherine Morris

The later Wittgenstein made extensive use of such terminology as 'superstition' (e.g. PI p. 18n, §§49, 110; CV,[1] 5, 72, 83), 'dogma' (e.g. CV, 28), 'prejudice' (e.g. PI §340, cf. §108, LC, 49), 'myth' (LC, 51), and 'idol' (LC, III §36), and saw at least part of his philosophical task as ridding people (oneself or one's interlocutor) of such things. In grouping this diverse range of terms together, I am suggesting that their referents have something in common – or at least bear a family resemblance to one another. Without begging any questions (since part of the point of this paper is to call attention to the *different* ways in which Wittgenstein interpreters understand these), all I can say here is that each of these terms might strike a slightly discordant note in a philosophical work *given* a certain ('analytic') conception of philosophy. Though I will be, somewhat arbitrarily, centring on the word 'prejudice' in the present essay, and will be using the term 'philosophical prejudice' for that of which Wittgenstein is aiming to rid people (without, again to avoid begging questions, trying to explain yet what I understand by this),[2] I mean to invoke this whole range of terminology by my use of it.

The method of the later Wittgenstein's works has been read in a variety of ways. At least three of these ways were exemplified in Gordon Baker's work over the thirty-plus years of his professional involvement with Wittgenstein.[3] All three readings acknowledge Wittgenstein's use of the sort of terminology just reviewed and all three recognise that his philosophical method involved ridding people of what I have termed 'philosophical prejudices'. Since they view his method differently, however, it follows that each of these three readings must understand the methodological role and force of these terms differently. The principal focus of the present study is to investigate these different understandings within these different conceptions of Wittgenstein's method.

The 'Early Baker', the author of 'Criteria: A New Foundation for Semantics'[4] and 'Defeasibility and Meaning',[5] presented the later Wittgenstein as the creator of a novel, sophisticated and defensible theory of meaning, entirely different from his earlier, 'picture' theory of meaning. On this view, Wittgenstein was engaged in the same *type* of enterprise as 'analytic' meaning-theorists such as Quine, Davidson and Dummett. Philosophers in this tradition may well use words like 'prejudice' or 'dogma' (e.g. 'two dogmas of empiricism'); but in their usage it has, as one might say, purely rhetorical force: it is essentially a derogatory way of referring to positions which they believe to be fairly widespread and demonstrably mistaken; this is how such terms are understood by those who read Wittgenstein in this first way. Insofar as there is any effort to undermine such 'dogmas' and 'prejudices', it is indistinguishable from the effort to demonstrate that the position in question is erroneous. Since the methods for 'demonstrating' philosophical error are no doubt familiar, I will say nothing further about this conception of the role of philosophical prejudices in philosophical methodology.

The 'Middle Baker', the co-author, with Peter Hacker, of (most notably) the two volumes of the monumental commentary on the *Philosophical Investigations* (1980 and 1985; hereafter B&H), roundly rejected the idea of seeing the later Wittgenstein as in the business of developing a 'theory of meaning' or a 'foundation for semantics'. The principal task of true philosophy, rather, was to replace theorising with platitudinous descriptions of 'grammar'. On this conception of his method, 'myths', 'dogmas' and 'prejudices' are understood as interfering with the correct perception of grammar, leading their holders to violate grammar, i.e. to talk nonsense; a secondary task, aimed at reducing the amount of nonsense talked, is to rid people of these prejudices. This is not yet to say how philoso-phical prejudices are understood on this conception of Wittgenstein's method, nor what techniques are used for ridding people of them. The dominant voice in B&H presented these techniques in out-and-out *warfare* language (e.g. 'sapping the defences of orthodoxy', 'lines of retreat' which are 'cut off' by Wittgenstein, etc.).[6] What I want to see as essential to this second conception is not *this* – indeed it could be argued that this treats Wittgenstein's descriptions of grammar as debatable *theses* (cf. PI §128) – but the idea that there are two more or less independent tasks for the philosopher: one, the 'negative' one of ridding people of their philosophical prejudices which interfere with the perception of grammar; the other, the 'positive' one of describing grammar correctly.

The 'Later Baker' moved in yet a different direction, beginning some-where around 1986, and established with the publication of '*Philosophical Investigations* §122: Neglected Aspects' in 1991 (Baker 2004, Ch. 1). Here he began to read Wittgenstein in the light of the analogy, suggested by Wittgenstein himself and developed more fully by Waismann, between philosophy and psychoanalysis. The aim of philosophy on this conception was to provide therapy for intellectual torment whose ultimate source was unconscious pictures or analogies which functioned as dogmas or preju-dices in the economy of the individual's thinking. On this conception, there were no longer two tasks, only one: to free his interlocutors from their philosophical prejudices. But this task was not a purely 'negative' one: breaking the 'grip' of a picture *required* offering an alternative picture, a new way of looking at things. (Hence Baker regularly compared Wittgenstein's therapy, not just to psychoanalysis but to homoeopathy; see 2004 index.) This new 'picture' is emphatically not a 'correct' picture; it is a 'good' picture to the extent that it achieves the desired effect of breaking the grip of the old one.

For the sake of economy of expression, I will in what follows use 'Wittgenstein$_{1,\ 2\ \text{or}\ 3}$' to refer to the later Wittgenstein on these three read-ings respectively. Where I quote from Wittgenstein or where a claim is neutral between the three readings, I use the expression 'Wittgenstein' *sans souscrit.*

Wittgenstein$_1$ is uncontroversially an 'analytic' philosopher, a star in the analytic firmament. But what about Wittgenstein$_2$ and Wittgenstein$_3$? Without wishing to subscribe to a rigid 'analytic/Continental' distinction, I want to suggest that both Wittgenstein$_2$ and Wittgenstein$_3$ might be seen as *more* like Continental than analytic philosophers in terms of meth-odology, in particular in terms of their vision(s) of the role(s) of getting rid of philosophical prejudices within that methodology.[7] I want to make this suggestion concrete by comparing Wittgenstein's philosophical method to that of acknowledged members of the Continental canon: sc. comparing Wittgenstein$_2$ to Merleau-Ponty, and Wittgenstein$_3$ to Nietzsche.[8]

For reasons already outlined, I will say almost nothing further about Wittgenstein$_1$. I want to suggest that Wittgenstein$_2$ and Wittgenstein$_3$ share (or could be seen as sharing)[9] a conception of the 'essential' features of a philosophical prejudice, which will be sketched in §I; this conception is also to be found in Merleau-Ponty and Nietzsche. (See Baker 2004,

246–7 for the relevant conception of 'essence' here.)[10] §II expands on the differences already gestured at between Wittgenstein$_2$ and Wittgenstein$_3$, differences which also separate Merleau-Ponty and Nietzsche as I read them. §III looks at the sorts of techniques that Wittgenstein$_2$ and Wittgenstein$_3$ employ to try to rid people of philosophical prejudices, and reflects on the reasons why 'analytic' philosophers find Wittgenstein – on all three readings – difficult to understand.

I   The 'Essence' of a Philosophical Prejudice

We have seen already that Wittgenstein (on whatever reading) makes extensive use of the sort of terminology that includes the term 'prejudice', and that he (again on whatever reading) sees ridding people of philosophical prejudices as a central philosophical task. But whereas for Wittgenstein$_1$ as for other analytic philosophers, prejudices were simply widespread and widely ramifying philosophical *errors* which (so analytic philosophers fondly imagine) could be *refuted* by the usual analytic bag of tricks (counterexamples, demonstrations of logical fallacies, etc.), this, I want to claim, is *not* the conception to be found in Wittgenstein$_2$ and Wittgenstein$_3$. Nor is it simply a 'prior judgement' or 'assumption', something of which the holder may be explicitly aware and which he is prepared to give up should the evidence or arguments warrant it. For Wittgenstein on these readings, the central feature of a philosophical prejudice is what I will call a 'perverse' attitude toward evidence and argument, which in turn links the notion of a philosophical prejudice to 'the will' rather than to 'the intellect',[11] and the notion of ridding someone of a philosophical prejudice with the idea of 'liberation'. This makes a philosophical prejudice in *certain* respects akin to an 'everyday' prejudice such as racism or anti-Semitism, where the idea of 'refutation' seems out of place, and where the prejudiced person is not apt to give up his prejudice as a direct rational response to 'evidence' and 'argument'.[12] The related terms 'superstition', 'dogma', 'idol' and so on share something of this 'perversity'.

'*Perversity.*' In regard to philosophical prejudices or dogmas, Wittgenstein brings this perversity out thus: 'dogma is expressed in the form of an assertion, and is unshakable, but at the same time any practical opinion *can* be made to harmonize with it; admittedly more easily in some cases than in others' (CV, 28). So, for example, 'Imagine someone's saying: "*All* tools serve to modify something. Thus the hammer modifies the position of the nail, the saw the shape of the board, and so on." – And what is modified by the rule, the gluepot, the nails? – "Our knowledge of a thing's length, the temperature of the glue, and the solidity of the box"' (PI §14). In these last cases, the 'harmonisation' of our 'practical opinions' about what rules, gluepots and nails do with the dogma that all tools serve to modify something is less 'easy' than in the other cases; at the same time, the harmonisation *can be done*: the dogmatist does *answer* the question 'what is modified by the rule, the gluepot, the nails?' Thus, though Wittgenstein's question may look as though it is offering *counter-examples* in traditional analytic style, the dogmatist does *not* respond in the way the analytic philosopher might expect his interlocutor to respond – by modifying or giving up his 'position'. 'This is how dogma becomes irrefutable and beyond the reach of attack' (CV, 28).

Merleau-Ponty too shows a sensitive awareness of this perversity: in a particularly methodologically interesting passage, he writes:

> The relationships 'figure' and 'background', 'thing' and 'non-thing', and the horizon of the past appear . . . to be structures of consciousness irreducible to the qualities which appear in them. Empiricism will always retain the expedient of treating this *a priori* as if it were the product of some mental chemistry. The empiricist will concede that every object is presented against a background which is not an object, the present lying between two horizons of absence, past and future. But, he will go on, these significations are derivative . . . [He] must reconstruct theoretically these structures with the aid of the impressions whose actual relationships they express. (1962, 22–3)

Even without exploring the actual phenomena to which Merleau-Ponty here refers (figure-ground, the horizon of the past and so on), the movement of thought which he here ascribes to the empiricist is characteristic of someone gripped by a prejudice: he 'retains the expedient' of explaining the apparently 'contrary' phenomena *away* – 'reconstructing' them as 'derivative' of items whose existence he recognises (e.g. impressions and their 'chemical combinations'). As Merleau-Ponty acutely observes, 'On this footing empiricism cannot be refuted. Since it rejects the evidence of reflection . . . there is no phenomenon which can be adduced as a crucial proof against it' (1962, 23).[13]

As Baker stresses (see 2004: index under 'modal qualifications'), philosophical prejudices are *characteristically* expressed with modal language ('must', 'cannot', etc.) or via such language as 'all' or 'every', 'really', 'nothing but' or 'only', and so on.[14] Frequently (though by no means always) Wittgenstein and the Continental authors italicise these locutions in order to call attention to this prejudice-expressing function. Thus, for example, what Wittgenstein described as the 'craving for generality' (BB, 17) is expressed in such statements as '"There *must* be something common, or they would not be called "games"' (PI §66); what might be called a prejudice in favour of external relations is exemplified by 'the temptation to think that there "*must* be" what is called a mental process of thinking, hoping, wishing, believing, etc., independent of the process of expressing a thought, a hope, a wish, etc.' (BB, 41). Here he himself supplied the italics (and even quotation marks in the second case); though I have provided the italics in the following cases, '"*Every* word in language signifies something"' (PI §13) and '"This [sex] is *really* at the bottom of everything"' (LC, III §31) also express prejudices in their contexts. Again, what Nietzsche terms the 'faith in antithetical values' is expressed in the thought that 'the things of the highest value [e.g. 'truth' and 'goodness'] **must** have another origin *of their own* – they **cannot** be derivable from this transitory, seductive, deceptive, mean little world'; also in 'How *could* something originate in its antithesis?' (1973, I.2, bold added). Merleau-Ponty too uses such language to express the mental outlook of the empiricist, for whom all perceptual experience consists of atomic sensations and their combinations: '[s]eeing a figure can be *only* simultaneously experiencing all the atomic sensations which go to form it . . . A shape is *nothing but* a sum of limited views' (1962, 14, italics added).

Words like 'must', 'cannot', 'nothing but', as highlighted here, should alert us to the *possibility* of the operation of a philosophical prejudice; but whether a prejudice is in fact operative will depend on how the person who uses these terms reasons (i.e. whether perversely or not).

'*Difficulties having to do with the will.*' This notion of perversity might be connected with a distinction Wittgenstein drew between 'difficulties having to do with the intellect' and 'difficulties having to do with the will'. For Wittgenstein₁, prejudices count as the former type of difficulty; philosophical errors are intellectual problems. For Wittgenstein₂ and Wittgenstein₃, they count as the latter; perversity is primarily a problem to do with the will.[15] We can illuminate this by taking note of further ranges of characteristically Wittgensteinian terminology[16] – terminology which 'analytic' philosophers are highly unlikely to use, and which those who read Wittgenstein as an analytic philosopher, i.e. as Wittgenstein₁, must ignore or treat as hyperbolic.

(1) 'Craving' (e.g. BB, 17, LC, IV §12), 'urge' (e.g. PI §109), 'temptation' (e.g. BB, 18), 'revulsion' (e.g. BB, 15, 57, PG, 382), etc. The

suggestion here is that we have a powerful *desire* to look at things in a particular way (or in some cases, *not* to do so): we *want* there to be something in common, we *want* language to be something unique, we *want* all words to name objects, etc. (cf. CV, 17); what a person wants to say may 'depend on general, deeply rooted, tendencies of his thinking' (BB, 30).[17]

(2) 'Captivity' (e.g. PI §115), 'bondage' (e.g. TS, 220 §99, quoted in Baker 2004, 30), 'tyranny' (e.g. CV, 28), etc. Though these terms too connect with the will, they may seem to do so in a sense almost the opposite of the first set of terms: one is typically 'held captive' *against* one's will.[18]

(3) Yet other terms seem, in one way or another, to straddle the line between these two sets of terms. For example, terms such as 'compulsion' (e.g. BB, 47) suggest a powerful desire (like the terms under (1)) against which one struggles, typically unsuccessfully (like the terms under (2)). Terms like 'charm' (e.g. LC, III §20), 'fascination' (BB, 27) and 'bewitchment' (e.g. PI §109) suggest a powerful attraction (like the terms under (1)) which is nonetheless imposed on one by an outside force (like the terms under (2)).[19] The latter language is also highly characteristic of Nietzsche, who speaks of '*inspirational* spirits (or demons or kobolds)' (1973, I.6), 'spells' (1973, I.20), and so on.

Although these three sets of concepts have *prima facie* very different relationships to 'the will', it is not clear that we need to decide between them. They are all *analogies*, each of which captures something of the effect of a philosophical prejudice on the economy of the individual's thinking. The first suggests that the aim of 'philosophical therapy' is to persuade one's interlocutor to stop *wanting* what he wants; the second suggests *liberation* as its aim; the third, something more like *breaking a spell*. But these aims are connected: the 'urges' and 'cravings' are there only because one is 'in bondage to' or 'spellbound by' a picture which thereby functions as a dogma. I will, somewhat arbitrarily, settle on the word 'liberation', and suggest that all of these point toward the idea that 'freedom of thought is the goal of philosophical therapy' (Baker 2004, 191).[20]

Yet one might argue that a prerequisite for freeing someone from a philosophical prejudice is his somehow *feeling* it *as* a restriction on their freedom. Ryle famously asked, 'Why should the fly take the way out of

the flybottle when it is pointed out to him?' (quoted in Baker 2004, 221
26n., cf. PI §309); an answer is provided by a fourth set of terms 'having
to do with the will':

(4) 'Disquiet' (e.g. PI §111–12), 'discomfort' (BB, 26), etc. This refers
     to the characteristic philosophical unease that drives philosophers to
     ask such questions as 'What is time?' in the conviction that answering
     this question – sc. by giving a definition – will remove the unease.
     Wittgenstein suggests that this unease is not alleviated by the defini-
     tion; we immediately see the problems with it and so we try again
     with a new definition – and yet we are still unsatisfied. Wittgenstein
     compares this to 'certain states of indigestion [where] we feel a kind
     of hunger which cannot be removed by eating' (BB, 27).[21] Why do
     we keep eating – why do we continue our so-far fruitless search for
     the 'correct definition'? Because we have a '*craving* for a definition'
     (BB, 27, italics added), or we are '*tyrannised*' by the idea that every
     word can be defined (in terms of necessary and sufficient conditions),
     or the idea that every word can be thus defined exerts a '*fascination*'.
     Thus this set of concepts is *prior* to the others ((1)–(3) above); our
     disquiet is what motivates us as philosophers to ask our questions,
     our philosophical prejudices (which tyrannise us or fascinate us and
     thus make us want to see things in a certain way) make this disquiet
     incurable. One can see how the frustration of being unable to answer
     the question to one's own satisfaction could encourage one to take
     the way out of the flybottle when it is offered.

Of course, some philosophers ('or whatever you like to call them',
Z §456) no longer feel this 'mental disquiet': these are the ones who
suffer from 'loss of problems': 'everything seems quite simple to them,
no deep problems seem to exist any more' (Z §456) – like Nietzsche's
'Ultimate Man': ' "What is love? What is creation? What is longing? What
is a star?" thus asks the Ultimate Man and blinks' (1961 I, Zarathustra's
Prologue). If one wants to free such a philosopher from his prejudices,
all one can do, perhaps, is to try to *goad* (cajole, persuade . . .) him into
disquiet.

Wittgenstein₂ and Wittgenstein₃ can agree upon the idea that
philosophical therapy is liberating; but they will disagree about both
the point of this liberation (see §II) and the methods for achieving it
(see §III).

II One Philosophical Task or Two?

As I suggested in the preamble, Wittgenstein₂ sees himself as having two philosophical tasks: the negative one of getting rid of philosophical prejudices which interfere with the correct description of grammar, and the positive one of describing grammar. Merleau-Ponty's conception of philosophy is parallel: he is faced both with the negative task of ridding his interlocutors of prejudices which interfere with the correct description of perceptual experience, and the positive one of describing that experience. Thus for these two philosophers, what is *wrong* with a philosophical prejudice, from a philosophical point of view, *is* that it distorts descriptions of grammar (or perceptual experience) and thus leads its holder to talk nonsense (or misdescribe experience); philosophical prejudices are *instrumentally* bad. Thus, though Wittgenstein₂ and Merleau-Ponty do aim at 'liberating' their interlocutors from prejudice, this liberation subserves a further purpose, viz. the correct perception of grammar (or the correct description of experience). For Wittgenstein₃, and for Nietzsche, there is only one philosophical task: freeing people of philosophical prejudices. For them, what is *wrong* with a philosophical prejudice is, precisely, *that it restricts intellectual freedom.* Liberation from prejudice thus subserves no *further* purpose.[22] Hence Wittgenstein₃, like Nietzsche as I read him, is a pure anti-dogmatist.[23] This might lead, in both cases, to charges of 'relativism' (as Baker notes: see 2004 index).

Wittgenstein₂ and Merleau-Ponty. For Merleau-Ponty as well as for Wittgenstein₂, a philosophical prejudice 'blinds' its holder to the very thing that he is attempting to describe (1962, 25: 'a kind of mental blindness', cf. 1962, 95), for Wittgenstein₂, this is 'grammar'; for Merleau-Ponty, familiar experience.[24] Thus someone in the grip of such a prejudice distorts these descriptions, leading him to say something nonsensical or false.

Arguably, for these philosophers these misdescriptions are in a certain sense *culpable*, they border on *dishonesty* (cf. Merleau-Ponty 1962, ix) or even *self-deception*, because in virtue of speaking the language (for Wittgenstein₂) or of being a human being (for Merleau-Ponty), the interlocutor actually *knows better*.

> [Empiricists] *hide from us* in the first place 'the cultural world' or 'human world' in which nevertheless almost our whole life is led . . . [F]or empiricism . . . There is nothing in the appearance of a landscape, an object or a body whereby it is predestined to look 'gay' or sad', 'lively' or 'dreary',

'elegant' or 'coarse' . . . empiricism *excludes from perception* the anger or pain which I nevertheless read in a face . . . (1962, 23–4, italics added)

They 'hide' this from us – and perhaps even from themselves: after all, the empiricist is a human being too, and the 'human world' is 'the seat and as it were the *homeland*' (1962, 24) of his thoughts – just as it is for the rest of us. Hence he knows from his own experience that the perceived world contains angry faces and dreary landscapes. His empiricist prejudice has led him into dishonesty or even self-deception.

One *might* see a parallel movement of thought in Wittgenstein, especially in his activity of 'assembling reminders' (cf. PI §127): one cannot 'remind' someone of something he does not already 'know'. Thus Russell, in the grip of the dogma that names must signify simples, ends up asserting that 'this' and 'that' are the only genuine proper names. This distorts our ordinary use of the words 'name' and 'this', and Wittgenstein reminds us, and Russell, here of that ordinary use: 'If you do not want to produce confusion you will do best not to call these words names at all . . . it is precisely characteristic of a name that it is defined by means of the demonstrative expression "That is N." . . . But do we also give the definitions: "That is called 'this'." . . . ?' (PI §38).[25]

Thus prejudices distort the perception of grammar or experience, arguably in a way that amounts to self-deception; my claim is that for Merleau-Ponty and Wittgenstein₂, this is what is *wrong* with philosophical prejudices. Their negative task of ridding their interlocutor of his prejudices is independent of their positive task of describing grammar/experience, though if they want their interlocutor to *accept* their descriptions, they need to perform their negative task.

Wittgenstein₃ and Nietzsche: I want to suggest that for Nietzsche and Wittgenstein₃, what is wrong with philosophical prejudices is precisely *that* they restrict intellectual freedom; the liberation from dogma subserves no further goal. I observed earlier that this single-task conception of philosophy could by no means be seen as wholly negative: this is not simply the dual-task conception minus the second, positive task. This goes along with a certain conception of the aetiology of a philosophical prejudice: as an unconscious picture or analogy that, in virtue of being unconscious, has come to exercise a tyranny over the person's thinking, so that the person supposes that things *must* be like that. On Wittgenstein₃'s conception, a 'must' can only be countered by a 'need not be' – *not* by an 'is' as is for Wittgenstein₂ (i.e. 'this is how we speak', or for Merleau-Ponty, 'this is how we experience the world'). Thus what is required to liberate the person from the tyranny of his dogma is an *alternative* picture, an *alternative* way of looking at things. For example, someone gripped by the idea that 'there must be something common', without which the concept would lose its unity, is offered an alternative *picture*: an *analogy* with a thread whose strength 'does not reside in the fact that some one fibre runs through its whole length, but in the overlapping of many fibres' (PI §67).

Here let me note a couple of consequences of seeing Wittgenstein as a pure anti-dogmatist. One is that the same assertion could play the role of a liberating alternative picture in one circumstance, of a prejudice in another. This is a point which the later Baker stressed in regard to Wittgenstein's slogan from the early 1930s: 'Thinking is operating with signs'. As Baker comments, 'this remark has received little explicit attention from commentators. If mentioned at all, it is brushed aside as an immature idea, one superseded in his fully developed philosophy of psychology by his analysis of every form of "inner process" in terms of behavioural criteria' (2004, 144). But, as Baker argues, 'Thinking is operating with signs' is not intended as the (misguided) 'description of the logical grammar of "think"' (2004, 167), but as a *picture* which might have therapeutic value against the prejudice which makes thought something essentially private and speech a mere accompaniment of thought; should the holder of this prejudice come to acknowledge the *possibility* of looking at thinking in these terms, i.e. as 'operating with signs', he would no longer hold the prejudice. At the same time, should this new picture come to be held dogmatically (as it was by the behaviourists), *it* would demand therapy of a parallel sort, but with an entirely different picture – perhaps even a picture of thinking as something private!

A further consequence of seeing Wittgenstein as a pure anti-dogmatist is seeing him as not being dogmatic about his *way of doing philosophy*. This is again a point which the later Baker stressed repeatedly: the word '*notre*' in the title of his article '*"Notre" Méthode de Pensée sur la "Pensée"*' is in quotation marks in order to stress that the 'vision' of philosophy which, in the later Baker's view, Wittgenstein shared with Waismann, 'is deliberately not offered as an account of the *nature* of philosophy, but rather a *conception* of philosophizing'; likewise the title of Waismann's Wittgensteinian[3] article 'How I see philosophy' (Baker 2004, 150; see also Ch. 9, whose title 'A Vision of Philosophy' makes the same point).

III Techniques for Ridding People of Philosophical Prejudices

Even those who read Wittgenstein as an analytic philosopher – who co-opt him into the analytic canon in the persona of Wittgenstein$_1$ – admit that he writes in a way that is strikingly unlike 'typical' analytic philosophy.[26] What I want to suggest is that the 'stylistic' features which strike analytic philosophers as peculiar are precisely those which those who read him as Wittgenstein$_2$ or Wittgenstein$_3$ will see as being in the service of the philosophical task of getting rid of philosophical prejudices.[27] That there are similar stylistic features in the Continental authors is an additional bit of indirect evidence.

Let us begin by reflecting on the question of how one might, as a philosopher, try to rid oneself or one's interlocutor of a prejudice, understood in the Wittgenstein$_2$ $_{and}$ $_3$ sense of a way of thinking which by its very nature leads one's interlocutor to respond 'perversely' to 'evidence' and 'argument'. It would be absurd to think that there could be a *formula* for so doing, and there are many ways of attempting to divide this task up into 'sub-tasks'; I cannot hope to review all of these, nor the whole range of techniques for attempting to achieve these sub-tasks. What I will do here is to focus on two sub-tasks. One is that of creating and sustaining disquiet; techniques for attempting this will differ somewhat between Wittgenstein$_2$ and Wittgenstein$_3$. The other is a sub-task only for Wittgenstein$_3$, viz. persuading the interlocutor to acknowledge alternative possibilities.

1. *Creating disquiet.* Drury quotes Kierkegaard: 'The very maximum of what one human being can do for another . . . is to inspire him with concern and unrest', and he relates this to Wittgenstein: 'if his writings do not produce the same unrest [as his conversations] they have been misunderstood' (quoted in Baker 2004, 174 27n.).[28] We have seen already that 'mental disquiet' is what inspires typically philosophical questions, and that the prejudiced but serious philosopher (i.e. one who does not suffer from 'loss of problems') finds that his answers satisfy him only for a moment, whereupon his disquiet returns; this disquiet is essential to motivate him to *want* 'liberation' from his prejudices. Many of Wittgenstein's philosophical techniques may look at first sight (*plus ou moins*) like traditional analytic argumentative techniques; I want to suggest that we can actually make *better* sense of them if we see them as aimed at *creating* (and maintaining) such 'concern and unrest'.

We noted earlier that both Merleau-Ponty and Wittgenstein engage in an activity that might be described as 'assembling reminders', be it of familiar experiences or of the ordinary uses of words. Although at first sight this activity might look like the analytically familiar activity of providing *counterexamples* to the prejudice (understood as 'mistaken generalisation') of, for example, supposing that all experience boils down to impressions (as with Merleau-Ponty's reminders of such everyday experiences as seeing the dreariness in a landscape or the anger in someone's face, 1962, 23–4) or that all words name simples (as with Wittgenstein's reminders of the ordinary use of the word 'name', PI §38), further reflection ought to give us pause. Merleau-Ponty and Wittgenstein both anticipate their interlocutors' *responses*: the empiricist will simply say that Merleau-Ponty's descriptions of experience are 'derivative', that what we *really* experience are impressions and their combinations; Russell will similarly say, 'Of course we don't ordinarily call "this" a name, and that is just the problem: ordinary language is "inexact" and "approximate"' (cf. PI §38).[29] These 'perverse' reactions are, of course, what we would expect from someone in the grip of a prejudice, but they are *not* the 'rational' admission of defeat which analytic philosophers might expect. Merleau-Ponty's and Wittgenstein's awareness of the likelihood of this 'perverse' response might be taken as evidence that they are *not* offering their 'reminders' as counterexamples to mistaken generalisations. But, in that case, what are they doing with them? Might they not simply be aimed at making the empiricists and Russell uneasy?

The precise mechanism of this will differ between Wittgenstein$_2$ and Wittgenstein$_3$: the former will hope simply to make Russell uneasy about violating ordinary usage; the latter has no objection whatever to Russell's violating ordinary usage: 'What is pathological is not the deviance of his philosophical utterances from everyday speech-patterns, but the unconscious motives which give rise to this behaviour' (Baker 2004, 208). What Wittgenstein$_3$ hopes is that Russell will feel some *conflict* between different things he *wants* to say (Baker 2004, 153; e.g. Russell *may* find that he *both* wants to use the word 'name' in its ordinary sense *and* wants to correct ordinary language; his problem is not the latter desire but the internal conflict *between* his desires),[30] or that he will examine his own motives and ask himself why he feels *driven* to say something so out of line with ordinary usage (cf. Baker 2004, 208).

There are rather few passages in Wittgenstein that look like traditional 'analytic' arguments; but there are a number which have been *reconstructed* so as to look like traditional analytic arguments. The so-called

'Private Language Argument' (commonly located in PI §§242–315) is the most famous. The later Baker wrote extensively about this (2004, Chs. 5–7) and I won't say anything more about it here. Instead, consider again Wittgenstein's discussion of the dogma that all tools serve to modify something.[31] We have already discussed Wittgenstein's question 'And what is modified by the rule, the gluepot, the nails?' In response to his interlocutor's answer to this question, Wittgenstein, absolutely typically, asks another: 'Would anything be gained by this assimilation of expression?' (PI §14). It might be tempting to read this question as elliptical for a traditional analytic argument (though spelling that argument out in a way that does not sound massively question-begging would be a challenge). What is clear is that no such argument is to be found in the text (any more than the 'Private Language Argument' is). The *question* appears to leave it open to the interlocutor either to *say* what he thinks is gained, or to deny that anything is gained but remain unbothered by this. (Cf. PI §403: 'But what should I gain from this new kind of account? Nothing. But neither does the solipsist *want* any practical advantage when he advances his view!') Thus it seems that Wittgenstein has not convicted this dogmatist of any fallacy or otherwise refuted him. And if this argument were playing the traditional analytic role, this would be a serious *defect*. With a sufficient number of examples like this (which would in fact be very easy to give), we might well begin to wonder whether Wittgenstein deserves his reputation as a great philosopher. But 'refutation' was never his intention – at least not if one reads him as Wittgenstein₂ or Wittgenstein₃. We can see Wittgenstein's examples and his question as subserving the strategy of creating unease.

Note that this 'argument' makes central use of *questions*. So too does the 'Private Language Argument'. Those who read Wittgenstein in the manner of Wittgenstein₁ (as well as B&H, it must be said) invariably ignore the interrogative form and take the questions as rhetorical, as disguised assertions. There are numerous other 'rhetorical devices' that must similarly be ignored or treated as mere stylistic quirks if one is to treat Wittgenstein as an analytic philosopher. Both philosophers also employ humour (PI §250: 'Why can't a dog simulate pain? Is he too honest?'),[32] irony ('In this sense of "activity" even resting would signify an activity', BT, 410, quoted in Baker 2004, 210), and – in Nietzsche's case in particular – sarcasm and hyperbole. Though the case would have to be made from instance to instance, one might consider the possibility of seeing these rhetorical tropes as in the service of this same sub-task: to create and sustain disquiet.

2. *Persuading the interlocutor to acknowledge alternative possibilities.*
This is, as we have seen, a vital sub-task for Nietzsche and Wittgenstein₃.
Nietzsche even characterises those who look at philosophy as he does as
'philosophers of the dangerous "perhaps"': against the 'faith in antithetical values', he puts forward that '[i]t might even be possible that *what*
constitutes the value of those good and honoured things resides precisely
in their being artfully . . . crocheted to these wicked, apparently antithetical things.' And he adds: 'Perhaps! – But who is willing to concern himself
with such dangerous perhapses!' (1973, I.1).³³ There are numerous passages which those who read Wittgenstein as Wittgenstein₃ will understand
as subserving this sub-task – but which, therefore, those who read him as
Wittgenstein₂ must understand differently, since alternative ways of
looking at things have no methodological role in Wittgenstein₂; indeed it
is just here that Wittgenstein₂-readers come closest to Wittgenstein₁-
readers. These include Wittgenstein's numerous analogies (e.g. between
the concept of a game and a thread with overlapping fibres, PI §67; or
between tools and words, PI §11), the passages that are taken to express
Übersichten (e.g. 'the meaning of a word is its use in the language', PI
§43; or 'Thinking is operating with signs'; see above), and his modal
qualifications such as 'Here is one possibility' (e.g. PI §244) or 'Here we
might say' (e.g. PI §49). On *Übersichten*, see Baker (2004, Ch. 1). I here
focus on the last of these devices.

Wittgenstein's modal qualifications are regularly ignored by commentators who read him in either of the first two ways.³⁴ The relevant sentence
from PI §244 – 'words are connected with the primitive, the natural,
expressions of the sensation and are used in their place' – is quoted
without the preface 'Here is one possibility', and Wittgenstein is taken as
making a claim about the grammar of sensation-words (or even as making
an empirical claim about language development). The relevant sentence
from PI §49 – 'a sign "R" or "B," etc. may be sometimes a word and
sometimes a proposition' – is likewise read not only without the phrase
'Here we might say', but ignoring or playing down the caution 'though
this easily leads to all kinds of philosophical superstition'!³⁵ But here is
another possibility: that when Wittgenstein says 'Here is one possibility'
he means 'Here is *one possibility*', and when he says 'Here we might say',
he means 'Here we *might* say, i.e. here is *one* possibility'. This is how
those who read him as Wittgenstein₃ understand these passages. They
present alternative ways of looking at things which might have a therapeutic effect on a disquiet whose source is a philosophical prejudice. Thus,
for example, someone in the grip of a picture according to which all words

name objects may ask himself 'How do words *refer* to sensations?' (i.e. how is the connection between sensation-words and the objects for which they stand set up?) and find himself – at least with Wittgenstein's assistance – dissatisfied with the kinds of answers he can come up with. Wittgenstein makes two helpful moves in this paragraph. The first is to transform our way of looking at the question by suggesting that we look at it as: 'how does a human being learn the names of sensations?'[36] As long as the interlocutor retains his dogma, the sorts of answers to this transformed question that occur to him (what the commentators call 'private ostensive definitions') will also dissatisfy him. In *this* context, Wittgenstein's 'possibility' might be liberating – *not* that that liberation occurs automatically, however. Dogmas are very difficult to rid people of! Thus Wittgenstein anticipates that the interlocutor will hear his 'possibility' in the light of his own dogma: ' "So you are saying that the word 'pain' really means crying?" '. And Wittgenstein is forced to clarify: 'On the contrary: the verbal expression of pain replaces crying and does not describe it'. As we know, the dialogue continues in similar vein.

The point I have tried to make – further examples of which could continue indefinitely – is that there are things which both the Continental philosophers and Wittgenstein do in their writings which perforce must sound strange to analytic philosophers; these things have tended to make analytic philosophers ignore the Continentals altogether, and these things must themselves be ignored or dismissed as stylistic quirks by those who try to read Wittgenstein in the Wittgenstein₁ manner. Am I trying to say that Wittgenstein₂ ₐₙd ₃ and the Continental philosophers are not doing real philosophy, that their work 'does not contain any arguments that fulfill the standards of philosophical discourse'? (Glock 1991, 73). I trust that I won't be misunderstood in this way. My point might better be put by raising the question: do 'analytic' philosophers perhaps suffer from a kind of 'meta-prejudice' about what counts as philosophy and hence about what counts as an argument?[37]

Notes

1 References to CV are to the first edition.
2 The term 'philosophical prejudice' is meant to contrast these prejudices with ordinary prejudices such as racism and sexism, though on the second and third readings of Wittgenstein, there are important analogies as well. These prejudices are by no means confined to philosophers, however. In view of

this, I did consider the term 'intellectual prejudice', but that term has the problem of seeming to identify such prejudices as 'difficulties having to do with the intellect', cf. CV, 28 and below.

3 See the editor's introduction to Baker 2004.

4 Baker 1974/1986.

5 Baker 1977.

6 I know from many personal conversations that Baker became uncomfortable with B&H's militaristic language (and its concomitant tendency to think of the interlocutor as 'the opponent'), partly because it did seem to treat descriptions of grammar as controversial theses, well before he saw his way to the third reading outlined below. Careful readers of B&H will hear this subaltern voice in places even there.

7 I trust that it is clear that I am not making any claims of *historical* influence of Wittgenstein on these Continental philosophers or *vice versa*. The Continental focus on getting rid of prejudices can be traced back to Descartes' desire to 'free us from our preconceived opinions' and, more recently, through Husserl's stress on the Cartesian notions of prejudice and intellectual responsibility in the *Cartesian Meditations*.

8 It goes without saying that these other philosophers too are read in a variety of ways. It cannot be doubted that Merleau-Ponty sees himself as in the business, *inter alia*, of getting rid of prejudices, in particular what he labels the 'prejudice of objective thought' which resonates in various guises throughout the *Phenomenology of Perception* (1962). But the issue of what he understands by the term 'prejudice' is seldom addressed and the *methodological* consequences of seeing oneself as being in the business of getting rid of prejudices is not considered. By contrast, all commentators recognise at least an anti-dogmatic side of Nietzsche; he declares the subject of *On the Genealogy of Morals* (1996) to be 'the *origin* of our moral prejudices' (1996, Preface 2), and Part One of Nietzsche's *Beyond Good and Evil* is entitled 'On the Prejudices of Philosophers'; he uses a huge variety of terms for related ideas, e.g. 'dogmas' (1973, Preface, 1968, 410), 'ideés fixes' (1996, I.2), 'faith' (1973, 2, 1964, III.5, VI.5), 'evaluations', 'inspirations' (1973, 5), 'instincts' (1996, I.1), 'drives' (1973, 6), 'idols' (1964, 1979 Foreword, 2), 'superstitions' (1973, Preface, 17, 32, 1968, 422), etc. This list of terms is strikingly similar to the list of characteristic Wittgensteinian terms cited at the outset of this essay. Some commentators however see him as constructing his own alternative dogmas (e.g. the 'doctrines' of the will to power and the eternal recurrence), and I am here siding with those who see his enterprise as *consistently* anti-dogmatic.

   Since most of the works referred to here were not written in English, there are potential problems of translation which I ignore for the purposes of this essay.

9   Again, the dominant voice in the published works of B&H does not fit with this conception of a philosophical prejudice; its military tactics will do little to dislodge philosophical prejudices thus understood and indeed are rather more likely to entrench them. But I have already indicated that these tactics are not the essential feature of Wittgenstein$_2$.

10 Astute readers may notice a preference on my part for Wittgenstein$_3$, i.e. the 'later Baker' reading of later Wittgenstein. This essay fills in a couple of lacunae in Baker's discussion of the later Wittgenstein: first, though (as the index to Baker 2004 will confirm) Baker frequently focused our attention on the terminology of 'prejudice', 'dogma' and so on in Wittgenstein, he never spelled out how exactly he understood the 'nature' of a philosophical prejudice; and secondly, though he gestured at possible comparisons between Wittgenstein, Nietzsche and Merleau-Ponty (see Baker 2004 index) – admittedly I am the one who put these ideas in his head in the first place! – he never elaborated these either.

11 He referred to 'the contrast between understanding [a] subject and what most people want to see. Because of this the very things which are most obvious may become the hardest of all to understand. What has to be overcome is a difficulty having to do with the will, rather than with the intellect' (CV, 17). This is a quotation of which Gordon Baker was particularly fond, though the scholastic terminology could be misleading.

12 Sartre writes very acutely and amusingly in this vein in describing the thinking of the anti-Semite, e.g. 1948, 11–12: 'A classmate of mine at the lycée told me that Jews "annoy" him because of the thousands of injustices . . . [such as this]: "A Jew passed his agrégation the year I failed, and you can't make me believe that that fellow . . . understood . . . Virgil better than I."' This man 'ranked twenty-seventh on the official list. There were twenty-six ahead of him, twelve who passed and fourteen who failed . . . even if he had been at the top of the list of unsuccessful candidates, even if by eliminating one of the successful candidates he would have a chance to pass, why should the Jew Weil have been eliminated rather than the Norman Mathieu or the Breton Arzell? . . . [But] it was the Jew who robbed him of his place' (1948, 12–13). Again, the anti-Semite admits, for example, that Jews are intelligent and hardworking – because that makes them more dangerous; indeed it allows him to disdain intelligence because it is Jewish: 'The true Frenchman . . . does not *need* intelligence' (1948, 25).

13 'Perversity', as these examples illustrate, is not all-or-nothing. From a certain point of view (that is, to the extent that one conceives of such claims as analogous to scientific ones) there is nothing wrong with someone who holds that all tools serve to modify something trying to fit awkward examples into his generalisation, or with someone who holds that all perceptual phenomena boil down to impressions and combinations of impressions attempting to

explain apparently contrary phenomena away. Scientists do this all the time. Though flat-earthers' reasoning these days (e.g. the argument that photographs of the earth taken from the moon are mock-ups) strikes many as perverse, there need not have been anything perverse about Ptolemy's adding epicycles to the basic geocentric theory in order to accommodate recalcitrant observations. The point at which reasoning begins to strike us as perverse will be both contestable and context-dependent.

14   These are all instances of what Wittgenstein called the 'metaphysical use' of words (PI §116; see Baker 2004, Ch. 4).

15   B&H don't quite see this; a key passage here might be the well-known PI §110, where the idea that 'Language is something unique' is said to be 'a superstition (*not* a mistake!)' B&H gloss this contrast between 'superstition' and 'mistake' – with no textual justification – as follows: 'If these obscure metaphysical claims were mistaken, their negation would be true, but affirmation of their negation would not slay the chimera' (Baker and Hacker 1980, 522). Granted that Wittgenstein does not want to claim that 'Language is *not* something unique'! But it is clear from the context that what makes the idea that 'language is something unique' a superstition rather than a mistake is the 'impressiveness' of the idea: it is something that people *want* to believe, of which they are inclined to say 'It *must* be so'.

16   Baker tended to run these terms together (e.g. 2004, 182); yet as we will see they connect with 'the will' in rather different ways.

17   To Hilbert's worry that Wittgenstein was going to try to 'turn us out of the paradise which Cantor has created', Wittgenstein replied, 'I would do something quite different: I would try to show you that it is not a paradise – so that you'll leave of your own accord' (LFM, 103).

18   Although a dogma 'is not a wall setting limits to what can be believed, but more like a brake which, however, practically serves the same purpose; it's almost as though someone were to attach a weight to your foot to restrict your freedom of movement' (CV, 28).

19   Cf. 'The solution of philosophical problems can be compared with a gift in a fairy tale: in the magic castle it appears enchanted and if you look at it outside in daylight it is nothing but an ordinary bit of iron' (CV, 11).

20   Nietzsche's image of the 'three metamorphoses' in 1961, to which he alludes in 1973 Part Six ('We Scholars', esp. 211), likewise suggests 'liberation' as the goal of philosophy: the 'weight-bearing spirit', 'like a camel hurrying laden into the desert', burdens itself with such values as self-debasement and loving those who despise us; as the lion, the spirit can say 'a sacred No even to duty' and thereby 'create freedom for itself', viz. a freedom from such burdens; finally the spirit is metamorphosed into the child, which has the freedom to 'create new values' (1961 Part One: 'Of the Three Metamorphoses').

21   According to Nietzsche, with most philosophers 'it is distress that philosophizes . . . Every philosophy that ranks peace above war, every ethic with a

negative definition of happiness, every metaphysics and physics that knows some finale . . . permits the question of whether it was not sickness that inspired the philosopher . . . I am still waiting for a philosophical *physician*' (Preface to 1974, 2).

22 Cf. Nietzsche's distinction between 'philosophy as the art of discovering truth' and 'philosophy as an art of living' (1968, 449).

23 Some commentators use the term 'Pyrrhonism' for Wittgenstein as thus read. One consequence of reading both Wittgenstein and Nietzsche as pure anti-dogmatists is that it should come as no surprise to find them from time to time tackling *opposite* dogmas. For example, Wittgenstein speaks of the 'over-whelming attraction' of certain kinds of explanations: those of the kind 'This is really only this' (LC, 22), especially when the second 'this' is something 'ugly' (cf. LC, 25), e.g. Freudian explanations of dreams. Yet one of Nietzsche's more prominent targets is the opposite: the prejudice in favour of *attractive* explanations, especially attractive explanations of attractive things: this is part of what he calls 'the faith in antithetical values', against which he urges (for example) that Christian morality has its origin in ugly motives (*ressentiment*). That Nietzsche and Wittgenstein target very different prejudices is, we might say, to be *expected* in view of historical and cultural changes; e.g. Nietzsche was writing at a time when his contemporaries were in the grip of humanism and utilitarianism and had not yet absorbed Darwin, much less Freud, in their mother's milk; 'attractive' explanations came 'natu-rally' to them. When Wittgenstein and Merleau-Ponty were writing, 'ugly' explanations had taken over. When Wittgenstein cites 'our preoccupation with the method of science' (BB, 18) as a source of our 'craving for general-ity', this too might well be seen in cultural terms.

24 Note that it is *presupposed* that the individual undergoing 'philosophical therapy' is indeed attempting to describe grammar or familiar experience. The later Baker came to doubt this; e.g. Russell was not actually trying to describe the grammar of the word 'name'.

25 B&H read this *question* as implying that 'it makes no sense to explain the use of "this" by ostensive definition of the form "This is this"' (Baker and Hacker 1980, 226). We return to this interpretive strategy in §III.

26 Both Wittgenstein and Nietzsche write 'aphoristically'; why? Was Wittgenstein drowning in his own material or unable to express his arguments more straight-forwardly? We might take note of Nietzsche's comment on reading aphorisms: 'to practice reading as an *art* in this way requires one thing above all, and it is something which today more than ever has been thoroughly unlearnt . . . it is something for which one must be practically bovine and certainly *not* a "modern man": that is to say, *rumination*' (1996, Preface 8).

27 Another point that could be made here, though I don't want to press it in the present context, is that there are certain prejudices which Wittgenstein and the Continental philosophers aim to get rid of which many analytic

philosophers hold. For example, one version of what Merleau-Ponty labelled 'the prejudice of objective thought' is what he called a 'scientific point of view' (1962, ix); this includes in particular a prejudice in favour of external relations, especially causation and association, a belief that (like science) the business of philosophy is explanation and theory-construction, and a tendency towards decontextualisation, generalisation and simplification. That Wittgenstein, however he is read, objects to these movements of thought is indisputable; I suspect that it is equally indisputable that they are widespread in much analytic philosophy. A consequence is that analytic philosophers may struggle with passages where Wittgenstein is attempting to bring out internal relations, e.g. when he says that the pain 'is not a something, but not a nothing either!' (PI §304), in the service of combatting the prejudice which would externalise the relation between pain and pain-behaviour. And those who wish to read him as an analytic philosopher (i.e. as Wittgenstein₁), whether they agree with him or not, often experience some embarrassment when asked to explain Wittgenstein's injunction against advancing 'any kind of theory'. The tendency is to ignore it.

28   Cf. 'Ryle's often quoted remark that Wittgenstein did not have "a soothing bedside manner"' (Baker 2004, 221 21n.).

29   'But why does it occur to one to want to make precisely this word ['this'] into a name, when it evidently is *not* a name? – That is just the reason. For one is tempted to make an objection against what is ordinarily called a name. It can be put like this: *a name ought really to signify a simple*' (PI §39). The later Baker was particularly struck by this passage, since it seems to suggest that someone in the grip of such a 'temptation' is not trying to *describe* our ordinary use, he is trying to *correct* it, to make it conform to what it ought to be, *pace* those who read Wittgenstein in the second way.

30   This is *not* to be confused with a line sometimes taken by Wittgenstein₁ readers (e.g. Glock 1991): the point is not to convict Russell of a contradiction but to produce discomfort by highlighting conflicting *desires*.

31   B&H's exegesis of PI §14 consists of a single word: 'Straightforward' (!) (Baker and Hacker 1980, 104). What I like about this passage is that it serves as a perfect miniature exemplar of Wittgenstein₃'s philosophical method; the fact that the dogma in question is not one that is particularly likely to be held so firmly makes it all the better as a miniature.

32   Nietzsche 1973, II.25 speaks of the 'stupidity of moral indignation, which is in the philosopher an unfailing sign that he had lost his philosophical sense of humour'.

33   It requires *courage* to consider new possibilities: 'how does one pay for thoughts? The answer, I think, is with courage' (CV, 52); cf. 'he who attempts it [independence] . . . thereby proves that he is probably not only strong but also daring to the point of recklessness' (Nietzsche 1973, II.29). 'Live dangerously!'

34 See my 1994.

35 Baker and Hacker (1980, 255): 'The reply to the difficulty [raised for atomism in the previous paragraph] is that a sign such as "R" may sometimes be a word, sometimes a sentence . . . The difference, to be sure, does not lie in any mental act concurrent with its utterance (that way lie "philosophical superstitions"), but in the context of the utterance.'

36 What Wittgenstein writes is: 'This is the same question as . . .' If one reads this suggestion at face value – as making the claim that the second question really is *the same as* the first – it will surely strike one as a highly controversial *thesis*. On the reading being suggested here, we are meant to understand 'This is the same question as . . .' as 'Try looking at this question as if it were asking . . .'.

37 Earlier versions of this paper were presented over a number of years as part of my lecture series at Oxford on Sartre and Merleau-Ponty and at a meeting of Mind and Society at Cambridge in 2004, organised by Rupert Read. I would like to thank the participants on these occasions for their constructive comments. Gordon Baker, Tim Horder and Graham McFee made extensive comments on drafts of this paper, for which I am very grateful.

Chapter 3

Gordon Baker's Late Interpretation of Wittgenstein

P. M. S. Hacker

Gordon Baker and I had been colleagues at St John's for almost ten years when we resolved, in 1976, to undertake the task of writing a commentary on Wittgenstein's *Philosophical Investigations*. We had been talking about Wittgenstein since 1969, and when we cooperated in writing a long critical notice on the *Philosophical Grammar* in 1975 (much of which we were later to repudiate[1]), we found that working together was mutually instructive, intellectually stimulating and great fun. We thought that we still had much to say about Wittgenstein's philosophy, and it seemed to us that misinterpretations of passages in the *Investigations* were so extensive that it would be worth trying to write a detailed analytical commentary. It is difficult to recapture the excitement of those early days in being among the first to work on the microfilms and, subsequently, on the photocopies of Wittgenstein's *Nachlass*. We spent many hundreds of hours poring over the typescripts and the often only semi-legible manuscripts, fascinated and privileged to be able to try to follow the development of the thoughts of a great philosophical genius. We talked endlessly about what we had found in Wittgenstein's manuscripts and typescripts, and debated how it should be understood. The first fruit of our labours was *Wittgenstein – Understanding and Meaning* (1980). Its guiding idea was to draw attention to the manner in which Wittgenstein linked the concepts of meaning, understanding and explanation, and so to bypass the connections between meaning, truth and truth-conditions that so fascinated philosophers of the 1970s, and to abandon the red-herring of assertion-conditions and anti-realism.

After a hiatus of four years, during which time we wrote a controversial book entitled *Frege – Logical Excavations* and a polemical book on contemporary philosophy of language – *Language, Sense and Nonsense*, we returned to complete our work on the Commentary. We found that although we had initially thought that we could do the job in two volumes, the argument of *Investigations* §§185–242 was so complex and controversial that it required a volume in its own right. So we wrote *Wittgenstein – Rules, Grammar and Necessity* (1985). This second volume did, I think, contribute to the clarification of Wittgenstein's discussion of following a rule. It also attempted to shed fresh light on his philosophy of logic and mathematics in a 70-page essay on grammar and necessity.

During these years we gave graduate seminars together on Friday afternoons in St John's. These were popular among the graduate students of the day, and it was here that we first aired our various heresies relative to the prevalent orthodoxies, with respect to both the interpretation of Wittgenstein and (later) Frege and to current philosophy of language. Exciting and sometimes impassioned arguments were flung across the table, although good humour and merriment generally prevailed. It was here that our first clashes with Michael Dummett took place, when he attended our early seminars on Frege's logic. These, alas, later developed into an increasingly acrimonious exchange of papers in the journals.

After completing the second volume of the Commentary, we turned to compose a volume of essays that would incorporate some of the papers we had written together, as well as new material on Wittgenstein and Frege. It was while working on this joint project that I was awarded a British Academy senior research fellowship to work on the third volume of the Commentary. We had hoped to finish the volume of essays before the October 1985 deadline when I had to take up the fellowship, but Gordon had not yet completed his contribution, and I had to start alone on what was to become *Wittgenstein – Meaning and Mind*. I had been working on this for a year, showing Gordon everything I had written, to be sure, and getting the benefit of his criticisms, when disagreement broke out between us over two essays I had written on thinking.[2] The disagreement spread rapidly to its source in a much deeper emergent disagreement over Wittgenstein's conception of philosophy and philosophical method. Gordon's views had changed from the shared conception that we had advanced in *Wittgenstein – Understanding and Meaning*, and it proved impossible to reconcile our now radically diverging positions. Unlike local disagreements, this one was impossible to bracket, since it affected everything that had been and that needed to be done. This signaled the parting of our ways – sadly, since we had written five books and numerous articles together, our joint graduate seminars had been immensely enjoyable, and I had learnt a great deal from our cooperative work. Gordon continued to work on the volume of essays, which I now abandoned. The result of this was his highly illuminating book *Wittgenstein, Frege and the Vienna Circle*, which broke much new ground (and in which the growing philosophical and methodological disagreements between us are barely visible, if at all). In the meantime, I pushed on with Volume 3.

However, after *Wittgenstein, Frege and the Vienna Circle*, his disagreement with me and with our previous collaborative writings became more prominent and public in his writings. If one examines his essays on Wittgenstein from 1991 onwards, one finds increasing opposition to the interpretations we had given to Wittgenstein's philosophy in the first two volumes of our Commentary and to the interpretations I offered in Volumes 3 and 4 and in the epilogue, *Wittgenstein's Place in Twentieth-Century Analytic Philosophy*. In a series of papers written over ten years, collected in his posthumously published *Wittgenstein's Method – Neglected Aspects*, he advanced a quite different view of Wittgenstein's later philosophy.[3] He made dramatic claims for his new interpretation. The reception of Wittgenstein among Anglophone philosophers, he declared, 'constitutes an obstacle which continues to interfere with our profiting from the richness of the legacy of the *Investigations*' (p. 118). If we could surrender the preconception that Wittgenstein was practising conceptual analysis[4], he wrote, 'we might find that his work had more to teach us than we ever dreamt of' (p. 85). His interpretations, according to his own view, call for 'radical re-evaluation of the methods of concept-clarification exhibited in the whole corpus of Wittgenstein's writings' (p. 92f.). For Wittgenstein's method, contrary to the views of '*soi-disant* Wittgensteinians' (p. 276), has more affinities with Nietzsche's and Merleau-Ponty's methods[5] (pp. 222n. 43, 277) than with analytic philosophers such as Ryle (pp. 116, 181f., 217).

I find myself in disagreement with Gordon's late interpretations of Wittgenstein in *Wittgenstein's Method*. He was a reflective philosopher, bustling with ideas, and a keen student of Wittgenstein's thought. So his late understanding of Wittgenstein deserves the same serious consideration and critical examination that he himself gave to philosophers he respected but disagreed with. I shall try to explain why his psychoanalytic, therapeutic interpretation of Wittgenstein's later philosophy seems to me to be deeply mistaken.

Baker's New Conception

Gordon Baker's interpretation of Wittgenstein's methods is akin to Bouwsma's, Farrell's and Lazerowitz's, and has affinities with the methods adopted by John Wisdom. It characterizes Wittgenstein's philosophy as a form of philosophical psychoanalysis. There is, according to Baker, not merely an *analogy* between Wittgenstein's method and Freud's, but rather, as he claims Waismann showed, the conception of philosophical method is *modelled* on that of psychoanalysis. It presupposes 'reconceptualizing the boundary between logic and psychology' (p. 219). On Wittgenstein's / Waismann's view, 'dealing with compulsions, obsessions, prejudices, torments, . . . is the *proper business* of philosophy' (ibid.). Indeed, a therapeutic philosopher (such as Wittgenstein) 'has no business with anybody who is not suffering intellectual disquiet, torment, despair, distress, etc.' (p. 173, n. 12), for 'suffering is the presupposition of "our method" ', which is 'inapplicable to anybody unaffected by intellectual torment' (p. 184). Wittgenstein's method, according to Baker, is characterized by the following distinctive features:

1   It is primarily therapeutic, *on the Freudian model* (pp. 68, 178, 218). 'Wittgenstein's enterprise has closer affinities with sessions of psychotherapy' than with Rylean analytic philosophy (p. 145).
2   It is essentially *person-relative* (pp. 68, 217) and *patient-specific* (p. 163). So it is not concerned with combating general schools or styles of thought, such as dualism or behaviourism in philosophy of mind, or Platonism or Intuitionism in philosophy of mathematics (p. 68), but only with the intellectual neuroses of specific individuals. The *Philosophical Investigations* might better be viewed as a set of case histories of a GP (pp. 68, 132). Wittgenstein always sought 'to address specific problems of definite individuals' (p. 68), and to 'treat' these individuals. He never 'advocated any general positive position' (p. 68) nor undertook to give 'any general outline of the logical geography' of any part of our grammar (ibid.). His enterprise was concerned only with the treatment of specific individuals suffering from a peculiar form of intellectual torment (pp. 182f.).
3   The responsibility for philosophical confusion, like the responsibility for psychoanalytic disorder, is shifted to the patient. The ultimate goal of Wittgenstein's method is to show how to bring to consciousness our own *individual* intellectual prejudices, drives, compulsions. The

method is essentially *dialogue*, a face-to-face 'talk-cure' (p. 164). So it aims at self-knowledge and self-understanding, and its goal is the enhancement of individuals' freedom of thought (p. 200), or of human welfare (p. 218).

4   Philosophical discussion 'is less a matter of constructing rigorous arguments from secure premises than of making propaganda for alternative points of view' (p. 219). There is no attempt to assemble a dossier of grammatical facts, and no attempt to frame adversarial, coercive arguments (p. 217).

5   Since the source of philosophical torment is above all 'pictures', and since one (allegedly) cannot combat a picture with an argument, proper philosophical method consists in offering alternative pictures to those who are afflicted. Hence 'In each case, [Wittgenstein] puts before us a *picture* in order to bring about a change in our manner of seeing something, and instead of making an assertion, he does nothing more than say "Look at this" (cf. PI §144)' (p. 137).

What is the evidence for this interpretation? First, Baker claims that 'There was a definite phase of Wittgenstein's thinking in which close comparison with Freud's methods informed his own conception of philosophical investigation. This phase extended over several years, at least from the composition of *The Big Typescript* to the writing of PPI [TS 220 (the Early Draft)]' (p. 155). *This* evidence, therefore is in Wittgenstein's own writings.

Second, he avers, Waismann, in 'How I See Philosophy' 'offered a fully developed conception of philosophical therapy expressly modeled on the features of Freudian psychotherapy' (p. 146), which represents the way Wittgenstein thought about philosophy and philosophical method in the early 1930s, and arguably later too (pp. 179, 201n. 3). *This* evidence, therefore, lies in Waismann's essay and Wittgenstein's dictations to Waismann in the early thirties (p. 155). Strikingly, Baker alleges that 'the whole of "How I See Philosophy" can be seen as an elaboration of Wittgenstein's remark "Our method is similar in certain respects to psychoanalysis" ' (p. 181). We shall examine these claims below.

It seems to me that Baker's late conception of Wittgenstein's methods was unduly influenced by the work he did on the Waismann papers. I think that he misrepresents Waismann's position and its relation to Wittgenstein's. And I think that he misrepresents Wittgenstein's methodology both in the early 1930s and later. I shall try to substantiate this in the next three sections.

Waismann and Wittgenstein

Baker spent many years editing Waismann's notes of Wittgenstein's dicta-tions.[6] He also worked with Brian McGuinness on *Logik, Sprache, Philoso-phie* – the German edition of Waismann's book *The Principles of Linguistic Philosophy*, which was based on the Wittgenstein dictations – and he evi-dently spent much time reflecting on Waismann's 1956 essay 'How I See Philosophy'. All this coloured Baker's late essays on Wittgenstein. This is evident in three features.

(i) He attributed greater weight to the Waismann dictations than they merit. It seems to have been part of his exegetical method to take the dictations to be authoritative expressions of Wittgenstein's later views unless expressly repudiated.

This is methodologically unsound. First, Wittgenstein never refined or approved of the dictations. Given the extent to which he worked over his own notes and typescripts, it is perilous to assume that the 'voices of Wittgenstein' that can be heard in the dictations are voices that he would uniformly be willing to acknowledge as expressing his definitive view. Secondly, the dictations were given principally in the years 1931 to 1934/5, i.e. roughly contemporaneously with *The Big Typescript* and its revisions. Although many remarks from *The Big Typescript* were to be incorporated in the *Investigations*, it must be remembered that he was not satisfied with most of them, and revised the material ceaselessly before making his final selections from it. It is more than merely unlikely that he would have been satisfied with unrevised dictations made at the same time. I am, of course, not suggesting that the dictations are worthless as source material – only that they should be used with caution, and that greater weight be given to Wittgenstein's own typescripts and especially to his notes and typescripts of the later thirties and forties.[7]

(ii) Not only are the dictations not authoritative, but Waismann's *Logik, Sprache, Philosophie* is not either. It is noteworthy that what apparently precipitated Wittgenstein's decision to publish his later ideas in 1938 was the knowledge that Waismann was lecturing in Cambridge on the basis of the draft of the former text.[8] Hence the 1938 Preface: 'Until a short time ago I had really given up the idea of publishing these remarks in my lifetime. But the idea has been revived mainly by the fact that I have been obliged to learn that the results of my work, which I had communicated orally, in lectures and discussions, more or less mangled or watered down, were in circulation' (TS 225). This, to be sure, does not mean that the book is not an important derivative source; what it means is that it must be used cautiously and may not be treated as authoritative unless it confirms Wittgenstein's views as expressed by himself in later years. If it conflicts with his later views, it is they that must be respected. If it pronounces on a matter of importance on which he is later silent, it should be treated with great circumspection. (It is, after all, more than merely improbable that *the* key to Wittgenstein's later methodology is not even mentioned in the *Philosophical Investigations.*)

(iii) Baker assumes that the methodological views Waismann expressed in 'How I See Philosophy' were Wittgenstein's own. 'The vision of philosophy that Waismann elaborated in 1956', he wrote, 'seems to have been Wittgenstein's own at least in the early 1930s. . . . it is a **description** of a very distinctive method which appears to have dominated Wittgenstein's work at this period' (p. 179), and added in a footnote 'Arguably it continued to dominate Wittgenstein's later work' (p. 201n. 3). This is mistaken. By 1956, Waismann had come to detest Wittgenstein and everything he thought he stood for. He referred to him in conversation with Heinrich Neider as 'the greatest disappointment of his life', accused him of an anti-scientific attitude, and even of 'complete obscurantism'.[9] He wrote of him, in one of his aphorisms, 'Wittgenstein – the leading thinker of our day: namely, the one leading to falsehood'.[10] 'How I See Philosophy', although obviously hugely influenced by Wittgenstein, was written to *distance* Waismann from Wittgenstein, not to reiterate his views. This is demonstrable by a few examples.

(a) No great discoverer, Waismann wrote (HISP, 16), 'has acted in accordance with the motto "Everything that can be said can be said clearly" . . . For my part, I've always suspected that clarity is the last refuge of those who have nothing to say.' Yet Wittgenstein was not only the author of this 'motto', but also wrote 'For me, by contrast [with the scientific, progressive spirit of Western civilization] clarity, perspicuity, are ends in themselves' (MS 109, 207), and 'the clarity we are aiming at is indeed *complete* clarity' (PI §133).

(b) Philosophy, Waismann averred, is 'not only criticism of language', for thus construed, its aim is too narrow. This remark is probably directed against *Tractatus* 4.0031: 'All philosophy is a "critique of language"'. Maybe the later Wittgenstein would not have repeated his youthful remark, but not for the reason Waismann gave: namely, that what is essential to philosophy is, above all, *vision* (HISP, 32) – a theme that does not occur in Wittgenstein's reflections on philosophy.

(c) In a patent anti-Wittgensteinian sarcasm, Waismann remarked: 'To ask "What is your aim in philosophy?" and to reply "To show the fly the way out of the flybottle" is . . . well, honour where it is due, I suppress what I was going to say' (HISP, 32).

(d) Philosophers, Waismann wrote, have to 'undermine current categories' . . . 'question the canons of satisfactoriness themselves'; 'philosophy is the re-testing of standards'; 'In every philosopher lives something of the reformer' (HISP, 33). This contrasts sharply with Wittgenstein, who held that 'Philosophy may in no way interfere with the actual use of language', that 'It leaves everything [in grammar] as it is' (PI §124), that its task is to clarify existing categories, not replace them with different ones.

(e) 'To say that metaphysics is nonsense *is* nonsense', Waismann wrote, 'Metaphysicians, like artists, are the antennae of their time.' This too is intentionally asserted in the face of Wittgenstein's persistent averral that metaphysics is nonsense – a confusion of conceptual with empirical questions, and a projection of grammar (actual or notional) on to reality.

It is equally disconcerting that Baker reads into Waismann's essay things that are not to be found there at all, and, then proceeds to ascribe them to Wittgenstein. Baker claims that 'In How I See Philosophy' Waismann 'offered a fully developed conception of philosophical therapy expressly modeled on certain features of Freudian psychotherapy. He was explicit about what he understood by the maladies addressed by psychotherapy (compulsions, obsessions, neuroses) and about what methods are appropriate for their treatment. (His text suggests that he had in view primarily Freud's early writings' (p. 146)). It is, however, noteworthy that neither the word 'psychoanalysis' nor any of its cognates even occurs in Waismann's essay, nor is Freud mentioned.[11] Waismann does not in fact offer psychoanalysis as a model for philosophical method at all.[12] True, he writes of 'deep disquietude' (HISP, 3), 'alarm' or even 'terror, accompanied by slight giddiness' at Augustine's puzzle of how time can possibly be measured (HISP, 3f.), of 'mental discomfort' (HISP, 6), 'states of confusion' generated by Zeno's paradox (HISP, 7), 'obsessional doubt' about other minds and 'anxiety doubt' about freedom of the will (HISP, 8), and speaks of Frege's 'obsession' with the question 'What is a number?' (HISP, 19). But he *never* connects this hyperbole with psychoanalysis or even suggests that psychoanalytic method is a revolutionary model for philosophy.

Having insisted that there are no *deductive proofs* or *inductive confirmation* in philosophy, Waismann was eager to stress that this does not mean that there are no rational *arguments* in philosophy. So what is the philosopher up to? Waismann does offer us a model – and it is a *legal*, not a psychoanalytic one; and it is not one of combating pictures with pictures. The philosopher, he wrote, *builds up a case*:[13]

> First he makes you see all the weaknesses, disadvantages, shortcomings of a position; he brings to light inconsistencies in it or points out how unnatural some of the ideas underlying the whole theory are by pushing them to their farthest consequences; and this he does with the strongest weapons in his arsenal, reduction to absurdity and infinite regress. On the other hand, he offers you a new way of looking at things not exposed to those objections. In other words, he submits to you, like a barrister, all the facts of his case and you are in the position of a judge. You look at them carefully, weigh the pros and cons and arrive at a verdict. (HISP, 30)

The legal analogy, to be sure, is Waismann's, not Wittgenstein's.[14] The point is that this is the *sole* explicit model for the methods of philosophy in 'How I See Philosophy', and it is very far removed from the psychoanalytic model that Baker read into Waismann's paper.

Wittgenstein on the Psychoanalytic Analogy

Did Wittgenstein *really* think that psychoanalysis provided a model for his method of philosophizing? Did this idea really 'dominate' his work in the early 1930s (p. 179), and arguably even his later work (p. 201n. 3)? Certainly in the early 1930s he thought that there was an *analogy* between his methods and Freud's.[15] Nevertheless, it is noteworthy that in the *Nachlass* there are only *five* distinct remarks on the matter (though most are repeated when copied into large MS volumes, and in TSS).

(i) One is, through mistaken grammar, inclined to ask: how does one think the proposition *p*, how does one expect such-and-such to happen (how does one do it). Such mistaken questions contain *in nuce* the whole difficulty. It is a main task of philosophy to warn against false comparisons, false similes that underlie our modes of expression without our being conscious of them. 'I believe', Wittgenstein continues, 'that our method is similar here to that of psychoanalysis that also makes the unconscious conscious and renders it thereby harmless, and I think that the similarity is not merely external' (MS 109, 174).

(ii) MS 110, 230 contains an early draft of BT, 410. I give the polished version:

> One of the most important tasks is to express all false trains of thought so characteristically that the reader says, "Yes, that's exactly the way I meant it." To trace the physiognomy of every error.
>
> Indeed we can only convict someone else of a mistake if he acknowledges that this really is the expression of his feeling. // . . . if he (really) acknowledges this expression as the correct expression of his feeling.//
>
> For only if he acknowledges it as such is it the correct expression. (Psychoanalysis.)
>
> What the other person acknowledges is the analogy I am proposing to him as the source of his thought.

In *The Big Typescript*, this occurs under the chapter heading 'Philosophy shows the misleading analogies in the use of language'. This passage was incorporated into MS 142, §121 in 1936/7, and typed into TS 220, §106. It does not, however, occur in the Intermediate Draft or in the *Investigations*. It is noteworthy, however, that a similar thought *is* expressed in the *Investigations* §254, stripped of any psychoanalytic association: we do sometimes have to give a psychologically accurate account of the temptation to use a particular kind of expression. What we 'are tempted to say' is not philosophy, but its raw material . . . something for philosophical treatment.

(iii) In MS 113, 117r (MS 158, 68r), Wittgenstein observes that a mathematician will be horrified by his mathematical comments, since he has been trained to avoid indulging in such thoughts and doubts. To use an analogy from psychoanalysis (this paragraph is reminiscent of Freud, Wittgenstein notes), he has acquired a revulsion from them as infantile. Whereas Wittgenstein demands clarification of all the repressed doubts and difficulties that a child learning arithmetic is trained to pass over. This recurs in *The Big Typescript* (cf. PG 381f.).

(iv) There is a curious aside in MS 145, 58: '"Meaning has a *direction*, which no mere process has." (One could almost say: "Meaning *moves*, where any process stands still." (Psychoanalysis of grammatical misinterpretations.)'

(v) In his notes for his lectures in 1938, Wittgenstein jotted down (MS 158, 34v):

> What we do is much more akin to Psychoanalysis than you might be aware of

> Schopenhauer: "If you find yourself stumped trying to convince someone // of something // and not getting anywhere, tell yourself that it's the *will* & not the intellect you're up against."

The only other relevant passage that I have been able to find is in the *Diktat für Schlick* in which there occurs a deleted paragraph in the context of the brief discussion of Heidegger on how nothingness noths. This is derived from MS 109, 174 and adds nothing to it.[16]

That is the sum total of Wittgenstein's remarks on the affinity of his methods to psychoanalysis. The topic is not even mentioned in the *Investigations* (although the ideas of 'diseases' of thought (§593), 'treatment' (§§254–5) and 'therapies' (PI §133) are).[17]

So, what are we to make of these few remarks? Do we have here the hidden secret of Wittgenstein's method? I think not. There are important *analogies* between *some* features of Wittgenstein's methodology and psychoanalytic methods.[18] These struck Wittgenstein in the early 1930s, and he repeated them (only very occasionally) until 1938. The analogies are limited. On the basis of Wittgenstein's remarks alone, there can be no warrant in claiming that what we have is a 'very distinctive method which appears to have dominated Wittgenstein's work' in the early 1930s – not an analogy, but a 'revolutionary programme' (p. 179). Moreover, it is not merely that Wittgenstein did not repeat the psychoanalytic analogy in the *Investigations*, we know that he was furious when it was attributed to him.

In 1946 Ayer gave a talk on the BBC on contemporary philosophy. He made a facetious remark about the *Tractatus* conception of the role of the philosopher ('a park keeper whose business it is to see that no one commits any intellectual nuisance: the nuisance in question being that of lapsing into metaphysics'). He added that the effect of Wittgenstein's later teaching on his more ardent disciples 'has been that they tend to treat philosophy as a department of psychoanalysis', mentioning in this connection John Wisdom, whose work Ayer described as 'of fascinating subtlety', while expressing doubts whether curing intellectual cramps was all that the philosopher was good for. Wittgenstein, Ayer reported, was 'extremely vexed', not because of the rude comment about the *Tractatus*, but 'because of my suggestion that John Wisdom's view of philosophy could be taken as a pointer to his own. In particular, he did not admit any kinship between the practice of psychoanalysis and his own methods of dealing with philosophical confusions.'[19] Doubtless the claim that there is *no* kinship is exaggerated. But it is noteworthy that Wittgenstein had apparently come to think that the analogy is more harmful than useful,[20] and therefore suppressed it in his writings and teachings, since it can evidently lead to such excesses as Wisdom's. It seems to me that Baker's interpretation of Wittgenstein's methods would have been similarly rejected.

What remains in the *Investigations* is the therapeutic method, which is mentioned twice: first in stressing that there are *many* philosophical methods, just as there are different therapies (PI §133), and later in the suggestion that 'The philosopher treats a question; like a disease' (PI §255). In addition, Wittgenstein uses the metaphor of a philosophical 'disease' that is rooted in a one-sided diet of examples (PI §593). There is nothing further to be found in the *Nachlass* on therapy, but the medical analogy between philosophical problems and philosophical confusion, on the one hand, and diseases and illnesses, on the other, is common. But it is important to note that the seemingly insoluble philosophical problems are conceived to be 'diseases' of the intellect that have their seat *in the form of representation* (MS 115, 110) – not in the weaknesses of individuals. 'Our problems', Wittgenstein wrote in the mid-thirties, '. . . are linguistic errors // are disquietudes that arise from the essence, the depths, of our language // linguistic expressions//.' (MS 157a, 52v). Far from these 'diseases of the understanding' being exclusively person- (or patient-) specific, as Baker claims (pp. 68, 163, 217f.), they are, Wittgenstein suggested in 1946, either rooted in the very nature of language itself or characteristic of our civilization:

> Have we to do with mistakes and difficulties that are as old as language? Are they, so to speak, diseases that are bound up with the use of a language, or are they of a more special nature, characteristic of our civilization?
>
> Or also: Is the pre-occupation with the medium of language that runs through all our philosophy an ancient trend of all philosophizing // of all philosophy //, an ancient struggle? Or is it new, like our science? Or also thus: does philosophy always waver between metaphysics and critique of language? (MS 132, 7)

Wittgenstein's Methodology Reconsidered

I shall now examine the methodology that Baker imputes to Wittgenstein.

i. *Primarily therapeutic.* No one, I think, would dispute that Wittgenstein's later philosophy has a therapeutic goal – analogically speaking. Philosophy, he held, is the resolution of philosophical problems and dissolving of philosophical puzzlement. Philosophical problems are conceptual. They involve misunderstandings and misconstruals of the conceptual articulations of our language (or, in a later idiom, of our conceptual scheme). Hence they are solved (PI §133) or dissolved (BT, 421) by the clarification of the relevant grammatical structures and by the elimination of the *various* misconceived ideas that stand in the way of attaining a clear view of how a particular network of interrelated concepts hangs together. Philosophy is then therapeutic in so far as it restores the bewildered to an optimal intellectual state of good sense – akin to good health (here lies the analogy with therapy).

Wittgenstein's 'therapy', however, involves *many* methods, not one (PI §133). Salient among them is assembling reminders of how the relevant words are generally used (PI §127), getting people to remember that they really use words in such-and-such a way (BT, 419). We must draw attention to familiar grammatical rules (for 'certain grammatical rules become interesting only when philosophers want to transgress them' (BT, 425)), and arrange them in such a manner that an overview of the conceptual structure will be achieved and the philosophical problem at hand dissolved. The aim of philosophy is to stop people from transgressing the bounds of sense: 'to erect a wall at the point where language stops anyway' (BT, 425). So, 'We want to replace wild conjectures and explanations by quiet weighing of linguistic facts' (Z §447). In order to disentangle the knots we tie in our understanding (of the concept of the infinite, for example), we need a 'comparative surveyable representation of all the applications, illustrations, conceptions of the calculus [this being the example under consideration]. The complete survey of everything that may produce unclarity' (Z §273). It would be mistaken to suppose that this does not involve the *positive* task of delineating the logical geography of the puzzling concepts (of which more below). Of course, this is not *l'art pour l'art* (conceptual cartography for its own sake) – the conceptual map is produced to help us know our way about and to prevent us from getting lost.

ii. *Person-relative and patient-specific.* It is quite wrong to suppose that Wittgenstein's targets are *always* specific muddles of specific people – and I know of no place in which he declares any such self-limiting intent. The *Investigations* is *not* comparable to a GP's casebook (pp. 68, 132). Wittgenstein nowhere suggests any such thing and he aspired to achieve something far more general than this would imply. In the Preface he characterizes the *Investigations* as journeys 'over a wide field of thought' that resulted in 'sketches of landscapes' which conjunctively give one 'a picture of the landscape'. The subjects with which he is concerned, he wrote, are 'the concepts of meaning, of understanding, of a proposition, of logic, the foundations of mathematics, states of consciousness, and other things' – not 'the confusions of my friends and acquaintances in Vienna and Cambridge'. It is mistaken to suppose (p. 68) that Wittgenstein never addressed grand schools of philosophical thought such as logicism (in RFM) or intuitionism (primarily in his lectures), or grand doctrines, such as Platonism (in RFM and LFM) or idealism (via his various anatomizations of the deep errors of solipsism, e.g. in BB), or *pervasive* misconceived ways of thinking (e.g. of the mind as a private domain to which the subject has privileged access by introspection, the contents of which are privately owned (PI and RPP)).

Wittgenstein did not open the *Investigations* with a quotation from St Augustine because he was concerned with Augustine's tormented confusions – Augustine was not in the least intellectually tortured by his description of how he thought he learned to speak. Nor was Wittgenstein concerned with giving the saint a psychotherapeutic session. Rather, as he told Malcolm, he selected the passage from Augustine not because he could not find the conception there expressed as well stated by other philosophers, but because the conception *must* be important if so great a mind held it.[21] For most of mankind, he wrote, the conception articulated by Augustine is the most natural way to think about the nature of language (MS 141, 1). And this natural way of thinking is the source of widespread philosophical confusions and errors that run through much of Western philosophy. It is mistaken to suppose that the private language arguments are addressed exclusively or specifically to modern empiricists, especially Russell's *Analysis of Mind*, and perhaps Schlick and Carnap or Cambridge contemporaries (pp. 117, 138). On the contrary, in discussing the idea of a private language, Wittgenstein wrote, he was talking about the problems of idealism and solipsism (MS 165, 102). The nonsense against which he was struggling, he said, was 'the semi-solipsism that says that I know my sensations intimately since *I* have them, and then I generalize my own case' (MS 165, 150). Baker claims that to interpret the private language arguments as a *reductio* of Cartesian dualism appears to be a 'grotesque genre-misidentification', for Wittgenstein is not lodging objections to Great Philosophers and trying to score points off them, as Anthony Kenny and I are said to have claimed (pp. 138f.). I agree that *Wittgenstein* was not confronting Descartes and Locke, neither of whom he ever read. But *his arguments*, if correct, definitively undermine their philosophies – as Kenny argued with respect to Descartes, and I (and others) have argued, with respect to Locke.[22] In his lectures, Wittgenstein cited Hardy's supposition that 'a reality corresponds to mathematical propositions', and added 'The fact that he said it does not matter; what is important is that it is a thing which lots of people would like to say' (LFM, 239).

Wittgenstein thought of himself in 1931 as the destroyer of the great tradition of Western philosophy (DB, 39). He could hardly have simultaneously thought that his new method was concerned only with providing individual (tailor-made) therapies for his circle of friends and acquaintances.

iii. *A face-to-face 'talk-cure'.* Wittgenstein did indeed declare that he must find the *exact* form of expression that misleads the philosophically confused, and that this must be so done that his reader will exclaim 'Yes, that is exactly the way I meant it' (BT, 410; cf. PI §254). If an error turns on the adoption of a misconceived analogy, then one must find out exactly what it is – and the criterion of success is acknowledgement (ibid.). He also claimed that he should be the mirror in which his reader can see the errors of his ways of thinking (MS 112, 225). But it would be wrong to suppose that he was involved in 'face-to-face talk-cures' (save perhaps in his lectures and conversations). He criticized Russell's theory of desire with a crushing *reductio ad absurdum*, but did not wait on Russell's consent. He criticized Frege's conception of an *Annahme*, not offering an imaginary face-to-face 'talk-cure', but an array of counter-arguments. He relatively rarely addressed the conceptual muddles of specific people other than those of his youthful self – which he treated as exemplary. In general, he delineated forms of conceptual confusion and misconceived conceptual analogies that seemed to him to be powerfully tempting, and commonly (but not uniformly) also more or less perennial. Causal theories of belief and desire are typically adopted by empiricists and scientists, and Russell was merely an example of an error that Wittgenstein aimed to extirpate. The temptation to think of every sentence as containing in its depth-grammar a sentence-radical and mood operator is deep (and characterized much philosophy of language *after* Wittgenstein's death) – Frege merely provided an example of a general error that Wittgenstein strove to eradicate.

What is true is that Wittgenstein had a liking for the interrogative methods of Socratic dialogue (on a modest *Bemerkungen* scale) in his writings. This is indeed important (and perhaps indicates a source of Baker's misinterpretations). For Wittgenstein had an unparalleled concern with the roots of philosophical error and misconception, and he found this Socratic form the most fruitful way to characterize the genesis of a conceptual confusion and the most illuminating way to present the dissolution of such types of puzzlement. But such dialogical methods are perfectly compatible with generality in purpose and implication.

There is no passage that I know of that restricts Wittgenstein's philosophical methods to people, or to the philosophical problems of people, who are suffering 'intellectual torment'. He examined the flaws of Platonism in mathematics, but there is no suggestion that only mathematical Platonists who are in torment can learn from his clarifications. He criticized intuitionism in mathematics, but added no qualifications that his criticisms are of use only to tormented intuitionists. His ultimate goal was to clarify and disentangle conceptual confusions. He never asserted or, I fancy, would have asserted that his goal is the enhancement of human freedom of thought.

iv. *The responsibility for philosophical confusion, like the responsibility for psychoanalytic disorder, is shifted to the patient.* Baker claims that according to Wittgenstein (and Waismann) we are not the 'victims' of the grammatical features of our languages ('As if we couldn't help having problems about existence') – but only of our own prejudices and dogmas (pp. 198f.). But even in the early 1930s (when he introduced the psychoanalytic analogy), Wittgenstein attributed philosophical confusions to grammatical features of our languages. 'Why are grammatical problems so tough and ineradicable?', he queried. 'Because they are connected with the oldest thought habits, i.e. with the oldest pictures *that are engraved into our language itself*', he replied (BT, 423, emphasis added). He elaborated further:

> One keeps hearing the remark that philosophy really makes no progress, that the same philosophical problems that had occurred to the Greeks are still occupying us. But those who say that don't understand the reason it is // must be // so. The reason is that our language has remained the same and seduces us into asking the same questions over and over. As long as there is a verb 'to be' which seems to function like 'to eat' and 'to drink', as long as there are adjectives like 'identical', 'true', 'false', 'possible', as long as one talks about a flow of time and an expanse of space, etc., etc., humans will continue to bump up against the same mysterious difficulties . . .' (BT, 424)

So problems about existence *are* well-nigh unavoidable. Furthermore, Wittgenstein held that

Language contains the same traps for everyone; the immense network of well-kept // passable // false paths. And thus we see one person after another walking the same paths and we know already where he will make a turn, where he will keep going on straight ahead without noticing the turn, etc. etc. Therefore wherever false paths branch off I should put up signs which help one get by the dangerous places. (BT, 423)

So we are, to a large degree, 'victims' of the misleading forms of our language. 'Philosophy is a struggle against the bewitchment of our understanding by means of language' (PI §109).

v. *No 'dossier' of grammatical facts.* To be sure, Wittgenstein did not compile dossiers of anything. But the claim that he did not think it his business to delineate the grammar of expressions flies in the face of his writings. In a letter to Schlick of 20.11.1931, he wrote that the main difference between the conception advanced in the *Tractatus* and his new one is that he now realizes that the analysis of propositions does not turn on discovering hidden things, 'but on *tabulating*, on the surveyable representation of, grammar, i.e. the grammatical uses of words'. Our grammar, he said, is lacking in surveyability (PI §122; BT, 417). Baker suggests that by 'grammar' here (and in many other places), Wittgenstein means not the rules for the uses of words, but rather the grammarians' modes of representing those rules (p. 59). But this, as far as I know, has no textual warrant.[23] Wittgenstein's original example of the difficulty of attaining an overview of the use of a word was *the logical connectives* – the grammar of which he had erroneously represented in the *Tractatus* as exhausted by the truth-tables, overlooking the fact that a non-molecular proposition such as 'A is red' entails 'A is not green (blue, brown, etc.)' (MS 108, 31). Hence the work of the philosopher consists in assembling reminders of how words *are* used (BT, 415, 419; PI §127) – we recollect that we really used words in this way. The task of philosophy is to describe the use of words *for a particular purpose*, to tabulate the rules for the use of words, and arrange them in a perspicuous representation that will dissolve a particular problem or range of problems.

Baker thinks that establishing that a certain word is normally used in such-and-such a way risks 'falling into dogmatism' (p. 116). But there is no ground for such fear in Wittgenstein's grammatical observations. There is nothing dogmatic, nor any risk of dogmatism, about reminding ourselves that we do not say, 'When I said such-and-such I *quickly* meant that . . .'; that we do not ask '*How long* did it take you to mean that?';

that we do not say 'I decided to mean . . .', 'I tried hard to mean . . .', or
'I succeeded in meaning . . .'. Reminding ourselves of such grammatical
facts (viz. that there is no such thing as meaning something quickly or
slowly, and no such thing as deciding to mean something or trying to
mean something, etc.) enables us to resist the temptations generated by
the surface grammar of 'to mean', which resembles the surface grammar
of activity verbs and process verbs. For the sentence 'When I said ". . .",
I meant . . .' appears to make reference to a pair of acts: saying and
meaning (PI §664). But the depth-grammar of 'to mean', its multiple
connections and articulations, show that *to mean something* by a word is
not to perform an action or engage in an activity of any kind. 'To mean'
should not be compared to activity verbs such as 'to speak', but to such
verbs as 'to intend'. Hence Wittgenstein's remark (in a different context):
'In order to be able to attain an overview of these concepts, you must
compare them in ways other than their surface-grammar suggests. You
must see different parts as homologous; what looks like a jawbone should
be compared with a foot' (MS 134, 126).[24]

There is no dogmatism or any risk of dogmatism in citing mundane
grammatical facts that any user of the language will recognize. After all,
the worst that can happen is that someone may reply that *he* uses the word
differently. So be it – then Wittgenstein will hear *his* explanation of how
he uses the word, and pick up the argument from there. Baker queries
how Wittgenstein could sustain the dogmatic thesis according to which
any kind of ostensive definition requires a sample. The answer, of course,
is that he could not (since an ostensive definition of a point of the compass
(PI §28) does not), and that he never made any such claim. But he could
and did assert that if an ostensive definition does incorporate a sample,
the sample functions as part of the means of representation, not as an
object represented (and that is no 'thesis', but a description of the use of
samples). Baker asks how Wittgenstein knew that neither a sensation nor
a mental image can play the role of a sample. The answer is given in the
private language arguments: such a putative sample could not satisfy the
requirement on explanations of meaning that function as standards of
correct use that there be a difference between thinking one is using a word
correctly and using it correctly. That is not a dogmatic thesis, but the
conclusion of an argument.

What *did* Wittgenstein mean by 'dogmatism'? Certainly not the tabulating of rules for the uses of words where this is required to dissolve a
conceptual confusion. His observations on 'object' and 'elementary proposition' in the *Tractatus* were dogmatic, he wrote in the above-mentioned

letter to Schlick. 'If one wants to understand the word "object," for example, one looks to see how it is actually used.' If one thus tabulates the grammatical use of words, then 'therewith everything dogmatic that I said in the *Tractatus* about "object" and "elementary propositions" collapses.' Elsewhere he remarked that dogmatism in philosophy consists in stating grammatical rules that are not acknowledged by everyone as the rules of their language, for that again engenders the impression that there are *discoveries* to be made in philosophy (MS 110, 222), as if we might *discover* the rules that we are following in our use of words. So, contrary to Baker, it *is* part of the method to tabulate agreed rules, and far from it being *dogmatic* to describe the use of a word, it is the opposite of, and the main means of *combating*, dogmatism.

vi. *The main source of error is 'pictures', and one cannot combat a picture with an argument.* Baker holds that according to Wittgenstein the primary source of philosophical confusion ('torments') are pictures. He claims that 'pictures' cannot be combated by argument, but only with other pictures (pp. 268f.). Hence, he avers, Wittgensteinian therapy is a form of homoeopathy (p. 188).

Certainly Wittgenstein held that we are misled by 'pictures', but it should be noted that he uses the word 'Bild' in many different meanings. Sometimes 'a picture' signifies a conception (and a conception can certainly be true or false, correct or incorrect, supported or undermined by evidence and argument); sometimes it signifies a model (and a model may surely be right or wrong, adequate or inadequate); sometimes it signifies an emblematic representation, akin to Bentham's linguistic archetypes (and while these may not be true or false, correct or incorrect, they may be correctly applied or incorrectly applied). However, Wittgenstein ascribed philosophical error and confusion to many sources other than pictures. He held that we are misled by the forms of our language, by our tendency to neglect the uses of expressions, by our disposition to seek for generality where it is unavailable, by our desire to explain conceptual forms rather than merely describing them, by our tendency to construct theories in philosophy, by our disposition to emulate the methods of science, and so forth.

It is perfectly true that Wittgenstein sometimes juxtaposed one picture with another, tried to induce us to look at things differently (MS 118, 73v and 77v), and thus to change our 'way of looking at things' (PI §144). But, first, this is but one among many different methods of philosophy (PI §133) – and not the main one. Secondly, we must attend carefully, in each case, to what he meant by 'a picture'. Thirdly, it is noteworthy that in *Investigations* §144, which Baker repeatedly cites, Wittgenstein appends to his remark on juxtaposing pictures the parenthesis '(Indian mathematicians: "Look at this.")' – alluding to the fact that Indian mathematicians use pictures, namely geometrical drawings, *as proofs* (MS 161, 6) – not as 'propaganda' for different ways of looking at things (p. 219).

Wittgenstein did not hold that a picture can be combated *only* with another picture: in so far as Augustine's puzzlement about how we can measure time was rooted in a 'picture', it was a *false*, i.e. *mistaken*, picture of measuring time, and can be shown to be false by clarifying what is *called* 'measuring time' and how it differs from measuring length.[25] The author of the *Tractatus* had 'a false and idealized picture of the use of language' (PG, 211), which is shown to be so not by substituting an alternative 'picture', but by scrutinizing the use of the words 'name', 'proposition', etc. and coming to realize that they are not applied on the grounds of common characteristics (cf. PI §66), that a name *need not* signify something simple, that a proposition *need not* be a logical picture, that an elementary proposition (containing no logical constant) *can* have logical consequences, e.g. 'A is red' entails 'A is not blue, not green, etc.'. When held captive by a picture (a preconception) and trying to fathom the essence of the proposition or the name, as the author of the *Tractatus* was (PI §§115f.), what is needed is not another picture, but to ask whether the word 'proposition' or 'name', for example, is 'ever actually used in this way in the language-game which is its original home', and so to bring words back from their metaphysical to their everyday use (PI §116).[26] When we have a correct picture (as when we think that lengthening a piece of string that circles the globe by a yard is increasing its length by a tiny fraction) and misapply the picture (as when we think that the string will extend beyond the surface of the globe by the tiniest of distances), our misapplication is not discarded in the light of a new picture, but in the light of an explanation of where we went wrong (the taut string will be about six inches from the surface of the earth, and, of course, six inches, although by no means the tiniest of distances from the surface of the globe, is but a tiny fraction *of the radius of the earth*).

Baker suggests that the Augustinian picture is not combated with argument, but only with another picture, namely the picture of meaning as use (p. 269). But Wittgenstein did have arguments to support the (grammatical) proposition that the meaning of a name is not the object (if any) that it stands for, and he argued against the view that every assertion contains an assumption, as indeed he argued against the view that ostensive definition fixes the foundations of language by connecting indefinables to simples in reality that are their meanings. If he thought that his assertion that 'For a *large* class of cases – though not for all . . . the meaning of a word is its use in the language' offered us no more than an alternative *picture* to the Augustinian one, then it is puzzling that he should have said in his lectures:

> I have suggested substituting for "meaning of a word," "use of a word," because *use of a word* comprises a large part of what is meant by "the meaning of a word." The use of a word is what is defined by the rules, just as the use of the king of chess is defined by the rules. . . .
>
> I also suggest examining the correlate expression "explanation of meaning." . . . it is less difficult to describe what we call "explanation of meaning" than to explain "meaning." The meaning of a word is explained by describing its use. (AWL 48)[27]

It is equally surprising that in the Blue Book he should have said that 'The meaning of a phrase for us is characterized by the use we make of it. . . . We ask "*What* do you mean?", i.e., "How do you use this expression?"' (BB 65)[28] and later adds 'We are inclined to forget that it is the particular use of a word only which gives the word its meaning. Let us think of our old example for the use of words. Someone is sent to the grocer with a slip of paper with the words "five apples" written on it. The use of the word in *practice* is its meaning' (BB 69). This is not a picture, but part of Wittgenstein's description of the grammar of the phrase 'the meaning of a word'.

Baker claims that the Augustinian picture of language is treated by Wittgenstein as beyond the reach of any arguments based on the grammar of the concepts of name, sentence, proposition, etc. – it is, in a sense, unassailable (p. 275). It cannot be combated by giving a correct description of these concepts but only by another picture. But this was not Wittgenstein's view at all. Baker confuses Augustine's picture of the essence of language, which is implicit in the quotation from the *Confessions*, namely, that words name objects and sentences are combinations of words, with the *idea*, which has its roots in that picture, that 'Every word has a meaning. This meaning is correlated with the word. It is the object for which the word stands' (PI §1). This is *a conception* of language – 'an approach' according to which, 'naming is the essence of language' (MS 111, 15) and 'the meaning of a word is seen as the foundation of language' (MS 152, 38–40), and in which the form of explanation of words by ostension is thought to be fundamental (BT, 25), inasmuch as it links language with reality. This is 'a philosophical concept of meaning' or 'the philosophical idea of the meaning of words' (MS 152, 87). The concept of meaning it incorporates 'stems from a primitive philosophical conception of language' or 'a primitive philosophy of language' (BT 24v, 25). *These ideas* incorporate misdescriptions of the grammar of our concepts of language, name, meaning, etc. They are incorrect (as Wittgenstein laboured to show) – not *factual* errors, but conceptual ones. Far from being unassailable and irrefutable, these claims are combated *by argument*, i.e. by giving countervailing reasons, throughout Wittgenstein's lengthy and detailed discussions of these matters. For it is, for various reasons, *mistaken* to suppose that naming is the foundation of language; that all words are names; that ostensive definition is essential to language, and that it links language to reality; that the meaning of a word is the object it stands for, and that all words stand for objects. To hold such things is to exhibit misunderstanding and conceptual (not factual) confusion – including categorial confusion.

Wittgenstein and Ryle 1: Categorial Confusions

Baker insists that Wittgenstein's conception and method of philosophy is radically unlike that of Ryle (the point is made in 11 of the 13 essays in *Wittgenstein's Method*), and he castigates other interpreters of Wittgenstein, especially Anthony Kenny, for misguidedly thinking that there is any significant similarity between the two. In particular, Baker asserts that Wittgenstein, unlike Ryle, was not concerned with category mistakes and categorial confusions,[29] and that he was not interested in the 'logical geography' of concepts.[30] It is unfortunate that in the last years of his life Baker did not make use of the Bergen electronic version of Wittgenstein's *Nachlass* that was then available. Had he checked the sources with the benefit of the search-engine, I do not think that he would have made such claims. I shall deal first with Wittgenstein and Ryle on categorial confusions.

According to Baker, 'Wittgenstein refrained from pinpointing "category-mistakes" and from classifying words into logical types' (p. 91n. 51). Wittgenstein believed that the difficulty of seeing and describing the use of words 'arises from the presence of pictures of grammar which we have constructed in order to orient ourselves. If we could get rid of these obstacles, we could easily describe the use of words. The issue is no longer that of category *mistakes*' (p. 115). His method 'is not to impose some category discipline (Ryle), e.g. to pinpoint a *mistake* in seeing thinking as an **activity**' (p. 197). Indeed, he adopted a quite different method, for example, 'that calling thinking a mental process or mental activity involves drawing misleading analogies between the use of "think" and that of certain other expressions – analogies he attempted to displace in favour of other analogies' (p. 91n. 51).

I believe that Baker misrepresents Ryle and misunderstands Wittgenstein. There are many differences between Ryle and Wittgenstein[31], but the idea that the former held that many philosophical problems and confusions stem from category mistakes and categorial confusions and that the latter eschewed any such diagnosis is not one of them.

Wittgenstein frequently drew, and insisted upon, categorial distinctions, and attributed many philosophical muddles to categorial confusions. That one wants to say that the present is fleeting (constantly disappearing, cannot be grasped) is a confusion resting on the attempt 'to apply to immediate experience a category that can be applied only to the physical world' (MS 108, 27). The difference 'between two distinct categories', he asserted, is not a difference of degree (MS 108, 87). One cannot put equations and inequations on the same level as if they were just different animal species – rather the two arithmetic methods are 'categorially distinct' (MS 108, 132). The word 'tree' and the phrase 'my image (*Vorstellung*) of a tree' belong to two different grammatical categories (MS 110, 241). An infinite possibility (e.g. infinite divisibility) belongs to a 'completely different grammatical category' from a finite possibility (e.g the possibility of trisecting something) (MS 111, 121; cf. MS 106, 178 and MS 113, 88r for further observations on category differences between the finite and the infinite). A mathematical proposition with a proof 'belongs to a different category' from one without a proof (MS 113, 73v.).

It might be said that all these remarks date from the early 1930s, and he may later have changed his mind about category differences and categorial confusions. But that would be mistaken – Wittgenstein invokes these ideas just as frequently after 1945. One cannot simply say that grasping a proposition thus or thus is not an experience, he insisted, one must 'show the categorial difference' between understanding and an experience (MS 130, 278; cf. MS 130, 289). MS 133 is largely concerned with psychological concepts. On p. 55v Wittgenstein contemplates introducing a *new* nomenclature for psychological categories. Thus one could call understanding a word an 'ability'; but intending is no ability, and *meaning* a word thus and so is an intention (MS 133, 55v). Similarly, consciousness of lying 'belongs to the category of consciousness of intention' (MS 133,

88r). One often notices a difference which is indeed categorial, but one is unable to say what it consists in – then one often says that one knows the difference by introspection (MS 133, 93). The 'categorial difference' between the state of being in pain and of believing is important (MS 134, 39). An attitude belongs to 'a different category' from a psychological process (MS 135, 130). The meaning of 'to interpret' (*deuten*) is connected with that of 'to speak', but 'the two are categorially different' (MS 137, 41a). Of course, a sense-impression is not a drawing, it is not even something 'of the same category' that I carry around within me but cannot show to another (MS 137, 121b). The uncertainties about another's feelings, intentions, beliefs, mental images, etc. all belong to 'different categories', and need to be explained in quite different ways (MS 138, 29b). While discussing the concept of vision, Wittgenstein notes the distinction between seeing a thing and seeing the difference (or the similarity) between two things: what is important is 'the categorial difference between the two "objects" of vision' (MS 144, 38). 'Knowledge' and 'certainty', he asserted, 'belong to different categories' (MS 175, 37r).

The later Wittgenstein did not think that categorial distinctions are sharp and precise, as he had in the *Tractatus*. He was very aware that the *most* general terms, such as 'experience', 'event', 'process', 'state', 'something', 'fact', 'description', 'report', which in the *Tractatus* he had conceived to be sharply defined categorial terms, have an extremely blurred meaning (RPP I, §648). Contrary to what *he* had earlier thought, grammatical categories are not akin to variables with a sharply defined range of values, and failure of intersubstitutability *salva significatione* in some context is not an adequate test of categorial difference. He was not aiming at some definitive classification of psychological concepts, he wrote, but rather at showing the extent to which the existing classification of psychological concepts can be justified (*zeigen inwieweit die bestehende [Einteilung] sich rechtfertigen lässt*), and also showing that any such classification involves indeterminacies. The classification should serve only to emphasize crude differences between categories (MS 136, 131b). In this respect, he did not differ from the later Ryle, who wrote in *Dilemmas* (1954)

This idiom [of categories] can be helpful as a familiar mnemonic with some beneficial associations. It can also be an impediment, if credited with the virtues of a skeleton-key. I think it is worthwhile to take some pains with this word 'category', but not for the usual reason, namely that there exists an exact professional way of using it, in which, like a skeleton-key, it will turn all our locks for us; but rather for the unusual reason that there is an inexact, amateurish way of using it in which, like a coal-hammer, it will make a satisfactory knocking noise on doors which we want opened to us. It gives answers to none of our questions but it can be made to arouse people to the answers in a properly brusque way.[32]

No doubt Ryle had earlier made too much of the notion of a category and of a category-mistake. But it is noteworthy that even in respect of *Concept of Mind* (1949), Austin already remarked in his review of the book that *in practice*, Ryle did 'not confine himself to any single technique or method of argument, nor is the book one whit the worse for that'.[33]

Did Wittgenstein deny that we commit category mistakes? Did he 'refrain from pinpointing category mistakes'? On the contrary. When distinguishing between the grammar of 'to mean' and that of 'to think', he wrote (MS 165, 51–3):

> and there could be nothing more mistaken [*nichts Verfehlteres könnte es geben*] than to call "meaning" a mental activity. . . . once it has become clear that the different verbs, including the "psychological" ones such as meaning, thinking, fearing, being startled, expecting, etc. have categorially different // completely incomparable // uses (toolbox) then the investigation of a particular case will no longer present us with frightful difficulties.

Still later, at the end of 1947, he wrote (MS 135, vi):

> What should I call it when one takes belief, expectation, as the preparation of the organism, of the nervous system, for an event in the external world; or when one thinks that intending is an experience, because an image of what is intended may accompany the decision, and so forth?
>   It is a confusion of categories [*Vermengung der Kategorien*]. A failure to distinguish concept-types [*Ein Nicht-Unterscheiden der Begriffsarten*] and an inclination to substitute a particular concept-type for all others. A conceptual misunderstanding [*Ein begriffliches Missverständnis*].

Wittgenstein and Ryle 2: Logical Geography

We are masters of the techniques of the use of words in our native tongue, and yet we have the greatest difficulty in attaining an overview of these uses. We know how to use words, but cannot adequately describe that use. How can this be? Baker alleges that Ryle's explanation was that we all have a practical skill (know-how), but do not know the *theory that underlies this practice* (pp. 115, 135f.), and he refers to *Concept of Mind*, pp. 7–8 to substantiate this claim. One would be surprised to find Ryle asserting that there is a *theory* underlying the normal speaker's use of words. After all, this is a doctrine that post-dates Ryle. It sprang into popularity in the 1970s with Dummett's quest for a *theory of meaning for a natural language* which would constitute a theoretical representation of a practical ability.[34] If we turn to *Concept of Mind*, pp. 7–8, we find that Ryle made no such claim. What he wrote was 'The philosophical arguments which constitute this book are intended not to increase what we know about other minds, but to rectify the logical geography of the knowledge which we already possess'. We have all learnt how to apply a wide variety of mental concepts, Ryle continued:

> It is, however, one thing to know how to apply such concepts, quite another to know how to correlate them with one another and with concepts of other sorts. Many people can talk sense with concepts but cannot talk sense about them; they know by practice how to operate with concepts, anyhow inside familiar fields, but they cannot state the logical regulations governing their use. They are like people who know their way about their own parish, but cannot construct or read a map of it.

There is no mention here of ignorance of a *theory* – only of inability to sketch the logical geography of concepts. Moreover, the explanation that Ryle offered (which, to be sure, is not the *only* explanation he suggested of philosophical confusion) is also an explanation that Wittgenstein offered (although he too offered many further explanations). In MS 130, 220, he wrote: 'Naturally we all know the language-games in which psychological descriptions are used – nothing could be more familiar to us. But propositions obtrude themselves [*drängen sich immer Sätze ein*] into our descriptions the use of which we cannot survey [*deren Verwendung wir nicht übersehen*], even though we have mastered them // even though we have mastered them in the practice of the language [*obwohl wir sie in der Praxis der Sprache beherrschen*].'

Thus far there seems no disagreement whatsoever between Wittgenstein and Ryle. Is the deep difference, then, that Ryle provided his readers with the logical geography of the concepts that are under discussion, and that Wittgenstein did not do so? Is it that Wittgenstein altogether eschewed logical geography? This is what Baker suggests. In describing the principles of his own exegetical methods, he wrote: 'I suggest scrupulous attention to Wittgenstein's overall therapeutic conception of his philosophical investigations: far from advocating any general positive position . . . and far from undertaking to give any general outline of the logical geography of our language (or even of the narrower domain of "mentalistic" or "psychological" concepts), he always sought to address specific philosophical problems of definite individuals . . .' (p. 67). Baker castigates commentators (especially Kenny and me) for thinking that Wittgenstein is engaged in 'logical geography *à la* Ryle' (p. 26). 'Commentators on Wittgenstein', he wrote, 'seem to be pulled by powerful gravitational forces towards assimilating all of his remarks to factual observations about the logical geography of natural languages' (p. 70n. 4). But 'Wittgenstein's enterprise has closer affinities with sessions of psychotherapy than with didactic presentations of the logical geography of ordinary language' (p. 145). On this view, Baker contends (pp. 198f.), 'We are not hapless victims of circumstance; e.g. of syntactic features of English, or even of the grammatical categories of Indo-European languages. (As if we couldn't help have problems about existence.) . . . nor is there a "natural" explanation of our predicament; e.g. the discrepancy between practical know-how and the ability to describe (or explain) what we have mastery of (on the model of the divergence between knowing how to get around a city and being able to draw a useful map (Ryle).'

Baker misrepresents Ryle's conception of 'logical geography'; Wittgenstein *was* engaged in logical geography no less than Ryle; if he was not the originator of Ryle's metaphor, he was Ryle's precursor in inventing and invoking it; philosophical confusion, according to Wittgenstein, as we have noted above is rooted, *inter alia*, in the grammar of our languages (including the Indo-European group); and the clarification of grammar in which Wittgenstein commonly engages is typically perfectly general in intent.

First of all, what Ryle meant by 'logical geography' was not a set of factual observations about a natural language. He was concerned with the logical geography of mental *concepts*, no matter whether they are expressed in English, French or German. He was concerned with delineating the *uses* of certain expressions, and the 'logical regulations' governing the uses – and if 'denken', 'penser' and 'think' have the same use then the different languages share the same concept. Pointing out that to think is not the same as to talk to oneself, that one need not think *in* anything (neither in words, nor in pictures), that thinking is polymorphous, is not to make factual observations about English, but to make non-factual observations about thinking. Such observations are, in Wittgenstein's jargon, 'grammatical propositions'. Stating that sensations have a bodily location and that thoughts do not, that emotions have objects that may be altogether distinct from their causes, that intentions are not causes of action, delineates a fragment of the logical geography of the several concepts – but does not describe factual contingencies of any kind.

In 1933/4, long before Ryle wrote *Concept of Mind* (1949) and made famous the phrase 'logical geography', Wittgenstein told his pupils 'One difficulty with philosophy is that we lack a synoptic view. We encounter the kind of difficulty we should have with the geography of a country for which we had no map, or else a map of isolated bits. The country we are talking about is language and the geography its grammar. We can walk about the country quite well, but when forced to make a map, we go wrong' (AWL, 43). In his 1939 lectures he used a similar metaphor:

> I am trying to conduct you on tours in a certain country. I will try to show you that the philosophical difficulties which arise in mathematics as elsewhere arise because we find ourselves in a strange town and do not know our way. So we must learn the topography by going from one place in the town to another, and from there to another, and so on. And one must do this so often that one knows one's way, either immediately or pretty soon after looking around a bit, wherever one may be set down.
>
> This is an extremely good simile. In order to be a good guide, one should show people the main streets first. . . . The difficulty in philosophy is to find one's way about. (LFM, 44)

'My aim', he wrote for his pupils, 'is to teach you the geography of a labyrinth, so that you know your way about it perfectly' (MS 162b, 6v). One does not know one's way around the 'foundations' of mathematics. But this is not because one does not know what is to be done, but because the geography of the large connections is unfamiliar to us [*weil die Geographie der großen Zusammenhänge uns unbekannt ist*] (MS 126, 79). The philosopher (in philosophy of mathematics) does not have to erect new buildings, or construct new bridges, but 'to describe the geography *as it now is*' (MS 127, 199). The philosopher, Wittgenstein averred, *wants to master the geography of concepts*: to see every locality in its proximate and its distant surroundings (MS 137, 63a, my emphasis).

Baker's Wittgenstein

It may be that one reason that encouraged Gordon Baker in his psychoanalytic, therapeutic interpretation of Wittgenstein was disappointment at the extensive (largely misconceived) criticism, consequent widespread rejection, and plain disregard, of Wittgenstein's philosophy, especially by mainstream American philosophers writing in the Quinean tradition. If one reads Wittgenstein as Baker did in his last writings, the figure that emerges is indeed secure from criticism. Those who do not heed him can be alleged merely to exhibit the depth of their dogmatism, or their lack of torment and consequent superficiality (just as those who resist Freudian theories *really* confirm them). Since Baker's Wittgenstein never asserts anything, there is nothing for him or his followers to defend as being correct, and nothing for his opponents to attack as being incorrect. His philosophical position is completely immune to counter argument (p. 276; cf. p. 169). But this immunity is obtained only by means of a one-sided selection of remarks from Wittgenstein's writings that disregards everything that fails to fit the psychotherapeutic straitjacket.

Those who see Wittgenstein as one of the great geniuses of philosophy will be sad to see a figure of such originality and importance reduced to these dimensions. If Baker's interpretation were right, one of its consequences – whether intended by Baker or not – would be that Wittgenstein is a figure of very minor importance. For he is, Baker insists, relevant only for those who are suffering intellectual torment, and who need conceptual psychotherapy to ameliorate their condition. Baker's Wittgenstein is an 'intellectual GP' much influenced by Freud, with a book of case histories of individual treatments of his tormented friends and acquaintances (pp. 68, 132, 173n. 12, 184). He insists on nothing. Everything is up for negotiation (pp. 192, 194, 269, 277); nothing is forced upon one by compelling argument; nothing is refuted and no one is shown to be wrong. Maximal tolerance (e.g. for Heidegger (pp. 207–10)) is manifested in the face of absurdities (for, Baker avers, it would be 'a moral defect' to mock Heidegger's confusions concerning Nothingness and its activities, as Carnap did (pp. 219, 222n. 5.)). Alternative pictures are offered one, but one is free to accept or reject them at will. One can look at things this way, or that way – as one pleases.

This Wittgenstein is, I fancy, at best a rather remote relative of the Austrian Wittgenstein who taught in Cambridge, England, and who died in 1951. That Wittgenstein resolved many of the deep problems that have dogged our subject for centuries, sometimes indeed for more than two millennia, problems about the nature of linguistic representation, about the relationship between thought and language, about solipsism and idealism, self-knowledge and knowledge of other minds, and about the nature of necessary truth and of mathematical propositions. He ploughed up the soil of European philosophy of logic and language. He gave us a novel and immensely fruitful array of insights into philosophy of psychology. He attempted to overturn centuries of reflection on the nature of mathematics and mathematical truth. He undermined foundationalist epistemology. And he bequeathed us a vision of philosophy as a contribution not to human knowledge, but to human understanding – understanding of the forms of our thought and of the conceptual confusions into which we are liable to fall.[35]

Notes

1   Published in *Mind* (Baker and Hacker 1976), it was written under the influence of the idea that Wittgenstein's conception of meaning was a form of anti-realist, assertion-conditions semantics. This we later came to think was completely mistaken. We rewrote our essay comprehensively when Stuart Shanker asked us whether he could reprint it in his four-volume anthology of papers *Ludwig Wittgenstein: critical assessments* (Shanker ed. 1986).

2   'Thinking: methodological muddles and categorial confusions' and 'Thinking: the soul of language' in *Wittgenstein: Meaning and Mind* (Hacker 1990).

3   Baker 2004. All unflagged page references in the text are to this volume.

4   He added the clause 'as this phrase is now understood', but left it opaque how he thought it to be then understood or what other licit ways there were of understanding it. On p. 179 he added that in many respects, the therapeutic method 'is radically different from established procedures of conceptual analysis in analytic philosophy'. On p. 217 he made it clear that he took Wittgenstein's method to be 'very far removed from the paradigms of "conceptual analysis" to be found in Carnap and Ryle'. That Wittgenstein's later methods were very far removed from Carnap's is uncontroversial. That they are *very* far removed from Ryle's forms of conceptual analysis is more debatable – see below, pp. 109ff.

5   Although the only affinity mentioned is that they were all concerned to combat prejudices and superstitions.

6   This dedicated labour resulted in the posthumous publication of *The Voices of Wittgenstein* (VW; 2003).

7   Similar caution must be exercised with respect to students' notes of Wittgenstein's lectures. Drury reports his saying to a student who was taking comprehensive notes during his lectures 'If you write these spontaneous remarks down, some day someone will publish them as my considered opinions. I don't want that done. For I am talking freely now as my ideas come, but all this will need a lot more thought and better expression.' (Drury 1981/DC, 155).

8   B. F. McGuinness, 'Manuscripts and Works in the 1930s', repr. in McGuinness 2002, pp. 281–3.

9   See Wolfgang Grassl, 'Friedrich Waismann on the Foundations of Mathematics' in his edition of Waismann's *Lectures on the Philosophy of Mathematics* (Waismann 1982), p. 10.

10 'Wittgenstein – der führende Denker unserer Zeit (nämlich der ins Falsche führende).'

11 Equally, it is noteworthy that in the voluminous dictations of *Voices of Wittgenstein* there is only one mention of the psychoanalytic analogy (p. 69), namely in the *Diktat für Schlick*, in which it was a *deleted* paragraph, evidently derived from MS 109, 174.

12 In Baker's essays 'Thinking about thinking' (1997) and 'A vision of philosophy' (1999), reprinted in *Wittgenstein's Method*, this fact is not mentioned. He does mention it in his posthumously published essay 'Friedrich Waismann: How I See Philosophy' (Baker 2003a). On the opening page there, Baker notes for the first time that Waismann mentions neither Freud nor psychoanalysis, but, Baker avers, Waismann delineates a 'distinctive form of intellectual therapy', which 'from independent evidence (PLP, 179) we know he thought to have some striking resemblances with psychoanalysis'. Baker then repeats much the same points that are in the previous two articles. If we turn to *The Principles of Linguistic Philosophy*, we find that Waismann remarks only that 'Our method is in certain respects similar to that of psychoanalysis' in bringing unconscious analogies to consciousness (p. 179), and adds (rightly) 'this comparison could be carried further'. But what he does *not* say, *pace* Baker, is that Freudian psychoanalytic therapy provides not an *analogy* but a *model* for philosophical method.

13 Baker castigated '*soi-disant* analytic philosophers' for having 'a definite ideal of philosophical argument, as case building', which they misguidedly impute to Wittgenstein (p. 269). If so, then Waismann shared the same 'definite ideal'.

14 But cf. the legal interpretative analogy in BT, 424f., discussed by H.-J. Glock (1991, 79). See also BT, 415.

15 For illuminating discussions of Wittgenstein's attitude towards Freud's thought, see Brian McGuinness, 'Wittgenstein and Freud', repr. in his *Approaches to Wittgenstein* (Routledge, London, 2002), pp. 224–35, and Jacques Bouveresse, *Wittgenstein Reads Freud* (Princeton University Press, Princeton, New Jersey, 1995).

16 I exclude the remark on the 'dynamic theory of the proposition' (analogous to Freud's 'dynamic' theory of dreams) in TS 220, §93 (cf. TS 226, §113 and TS 239, §109), since it refers to the *Tractatus'* account of the proposition, not to a methodological analogy in Wittgenstein's later philosophy.

17 But one might quite legitimately see an analogy between rendering latent nonsense patent (PI §464) and psychoanalysis, although Wittgenstein does

not use the terms 'latent' and 'patent', and does not draw the analogy in this remark.

18 They are spelt out in P. M. S. Hacker, *Wittgenstein – Meaning and Mind* (1990), Exegesis §255.

19 A. J. Ayer, *Part of My Life* (1977, 304–6). Malcolm reports Wittgenstein as twice saying, in connection with this episode, that his way of doing philosophy and psychoanalysis 'are different techniques'; see Norman Malcolm, 1984, 48.

20 As indeed, by 1946, he had come to think that Freud's 'fantastic pseudo-explanations' had done more harm than good (MS 133, 11v).

21 Malcolm 1984, 59f.

22 Kenny, 'Cartesian Privacy' 1973a, pp. 113–28, Hacker, 1972, 224–31, Anthony Flew, *Hume's Philosophy of Belief* (1961), Ch. 2. To be sure, one could pick on many other 'Great Philosophers', not to score points off them, but to show how they fell victim to an array of powerful intellectual illusions the source of which lies in the misunderstandings and misconstruals of our language that Wittgenstein pinpointed in the private language arguments.

23 Baker held that the colour-octahedron is meant to be a second-order representation of the grammar of colour-words, i.e. not an *expression* of the rules for the use of colour words at all. Accordingly, the colour octahedron does not itself belong to grammar (pp. 24f.). But Wittgenstein wrote that 'The colour octahedron is grammar, since it says that you can speak of a reddish-blue but not of a reddish-green, etc.' (PR 75), that it is a perspicuous representation of the grammar of colour words precisely because it 'wears the rules of grammar on its face' (PR 278). It is 'really a part of grammar . . . It tells us what we can do: we can speak of greenish-blue but not of greenish-red, etc.' (LWL 8). When I pointed this out to Baker in 1991, he shrugged his shoulders and said that perhaps there was no coherent position in Wittgenstein at this point. But the position is perfectly coherent.

24 In his paper 'Wittgenstein's "Depth Grammar"' (p. 91n. 48; Ch. 3 in Baker 2004), Baker cites this passage (misidentified as occurring in Vol. XII, 132) as supporting his interpretation of the depth-grammar of words as having to do with the integration of *sentences* into human activities, the *uses of sentences*, the context-dependence of the senses of *sentences*, the invocation of imaginary language games as objects of comparison, etc. He mistranslates the passage, confusing 'Kiefer' (jawbone) with 'Käfer' (beetle) and speculates what 'far-fetched comparisons' [as between a beetle and a foot] Wittgenstein might have had in mind. Wittgenstein didn't have any far-fetched comparisons in mind – his metaphor remains within the domain of comparative skeletal morphology. (The choice of *Kiefer* (maxillary) is perhaps a deliberate allusion to Goethe's discovery of the *Zwischenkieferknochen* (intermaxillary), which is singularly apt, given the affinity between Wittgenstein's morphological methods in conceptual analysis and Goethe's morphological methods in

botany and zoology (see 'Chor und Gesetz: Zur "morphologischen Methode" bei Goethe und Wittgenstein' in Schulte 1990, 11–42).) The comparisons Wittgenstein had in mind were indeed such things as comparing 'to mean' not with 'to say' or 'to speak', but with 'to intend'. Baker's construal of Wittgenstein's conception of the depth-grammar of *words* specifies things that are not *grammar* at all, and that concern not words but *sentences* and their uses. But Wittgenstein (in §664) is concerned with the deceptive surface-grammar of the *word* 'to mean' (meinen): namely, that it looks like a verb of action; and the sentence 'When I said ". . .", I meant . . .' looks as if it refers to two actions that I performed. The next thirty remarks show that the grammar of 'to mean' is more akin to that of 'to intend' than to activity or process verbs.

25   Baker intimates that a 'picture' can be false only in the sense that it is held unconsciously and misleads (p. 158). His editor summarizes his view thus (p. 10): 'Wittgenstein is not in the business of demonstrating that this or that *picture* or *analogy* is *mistaken* . . . it makes no *sense* to call a picture or analogy "false" in the sense of "*mistaken*" ', and adds (p. 17, fn. 30) that 'Wittgenstein was often tempted to use such phrases as "false analogy" or "misleading picture", but he also regularly indicates misgivings about these expressions by putting wavy lines under "false" or "misleading" in these phrases (e.g. MS 110, 300, BT, 409)'. In fact Wittgenstein uses the phrase 'false analogy' ('falsche/(falschen) Analogie') 45 times in the *Nachlass*, 44 times without misgivings as far as I was able to detect. The *only* time in which he manifested qualms is in the example Dr. Morris cites in MS 110, 300. In BT 409 he manifests qualms about 'incorrect analogy' ('dass diese Analogie nicht *stimmt*'). 'Misleading analogy' occurs seven times, without qualms. 'Misleading picture' is used rarely, but without any misgivings.

26   In his article 'Wittgenstein on Metaphysical/Everyday Use' (pp. 100f.; Ch. 4 in Baker 2004), Baker claims that a 'metaphysical use' of words is any use in which one tries to state the essence of a thing, and that 'ordinary use' has nothing to do with normal or ordinary usage, but simply means 'non-metaphysical'. His evidence for this is that in the ancestor of PI §116 in BT 411f., Wittgenstein wrote 'What we do is to bring words back from their metaphysical use to their *correct* // normal // use in language', thus indicating unease about the word 'correct'. Baker takes this to show that Wittgenstein started from the word 'metaphysical' and 'then tried to find some down-to-earth expression that means "non-metaphysical". The term "everyday" in §116 seems to represent yet another attempt to solve this same problem.' His radical interpretation of Wittgenstein's plea to return to ordinary use rests on this conjectural basis. But his conjecture is unwarranted.

First, Wittgenstein's qualms concern the fact that one cannot say that ordinary use is *correct* use; rather, ordinary use sets the standard of correctness, and is itself neither correct nor incorrect. A use of a word is correct (if no stipulation, or metaphorical or technical use is intended), if it is *in accordance with* ordinary use. That is why Wittgenstein opted first for 'normal' and then for 'ordinary', rather than 'correct'.

Secondly, none of these terms *means* 'non-metaphysical' – any more than in the contrast between *scientific* and *religious*, 'religious' *means* 'non-scientific'; and there is no reason whatsoever to suppose that Wittgenstein was looking for a word that meant 'non-metaphysical', or for thinking, as Baker did, that of the pair 'metaphysical use' and 'ordinary use', the former 'wears the trousers'.

Thirdly, BT 429f. notes:

> In the theories and battles of philosophy we find words whose meanings are well-known to us from everyday life used in an ultra-physical sense.
>
> When philosophers use a word and search for its meaning, one must always ask: is this word ever really used this way in the language which created it // for which it is created//?
>
> Usually one will find that it is not so, and that the word is used against // contrary to // its normal grammar. ("Knowing", "Being", "Thing".)

Here it is evident that ordinary use wears the trousers, and that the ultra-physical (metaphysical) use is aberrant.

It is curious that Baker holds that *any* use of words that tries to state the essence of a thing is, according to Wittgenstein, 'metaphysical', since Wittgenstein held that '*essence* is determined by grammar' (PI §371). It is grammar that tells us what kind of object anything is (PI §373). Indeed, Wittgenstein insisted, 'we too in these investigations are trying to understand the essence of language, its function, its structure' (PI §92) – only not by analysis that reveals something hidden beneath the surface of language (ibid.). 'What is the essence of dogmatism?', Wittgenstein queried; to which he replied 'Isn't it the assertion of a necessary proposition about all possible rules' (MS 111, 87); and surely did not think of himself here as engaged in the metaphysics of dogmatism. There is nothing metaphysical about stating the essences of things that have essences. What is objectionably metaphysical is to think that essences are language independent, and that the rules of our grammars are necessary rules that could not be otherwise, as he had thought of the rules of logical syntax when delineating the metaphysics of symbolism in the *Tractatus* (that only simple names can represent simple things, only relations can represent relations and only facts can represent facts).

27   In the preceding paragraph of Ambrose's lecture notes, Wittgenstein remarks that he will not proceed by enumerating different meanings for the words 'understanding' and 'meaning', but instead 'draw ten or twelve pictures that

are similar in some ways to the actual use of these words'. It is, however, far from clear that the above paragraph was meant to delineate one such 'picture', especially given the frequency with which Wittgenstein elsewhere associated meaning and use, without any mention that this was but one 'picture' among others. He repeated the same point in his talk to the Moral Science Club meeting on 23.2.1939, remarking 'In a vast number of cases it is possible to replace "the meaning of a word" by "the use of a word" without making any claim that this is a 'picture' – it is, he observed, a slogan, and a very useful one at that. There are many dozens of remarks in which "Bedeutung" is linked with "Gebrauch", but none, as far as I know, that state that the 'slogan' is but a picture.

28   Baker suggests that the occasional qualification 'for us' (as here in the quotation from BB) or 'in our sense' (PG, 60) is the mark of an optional 'picture' rather than of a dogmatic assertion about the use of the word 'meaning'. I agree that it is not a dogmatic assertion about the use of the word 'meaning' – it is an undogmatic assertion about that use. Wittgenstein sometimes qualified his remarks on meaning in the early thirties in this way in order to contrast this use of meaning (*Bedeutung*) with Frege's use (and his own use in the *Tractatus*) – which was, in fact, a misuse, or with the empiricist use of 'meaning' to signify a characteristic sensation accompanying the use of a word (PG, 60) – which was a muddle.

29   See pp. 23, 70n. 8, 74, 76, 91n. 5, 94, 95, 105n. 13, 109–12, 115, 121, 131, 176n. 45, 177n. 52, 181, 197, 199.

30   See pp. 26, 52, 70n. 4, 74, 145, 165, 171, 260, 276.

31   For a brief and highly compressed discussion of the differences, see Hacker 1996a, pp. 168–70. The subject merits article length treatment.

32   Ryle, *Dilemmas* (1954, 9). Baker claims that Ryle went so far as to suggest that *all* philosophical problems arise from category mistakes (p. 176n. 45), but does not give any reference for this claim. What is true is that in 1938 Ryle wrote that all philosophical propositions are category-propositions (Ryle, 'Categories', repr. in *Collected Papers*, vol. 2 (Hutchinson, London, 1971), p. 184).

33   Austin, 1970, pp. 48f.

34   M. A. E. Dummett, 'Can Analytic Philosophy Be Systematic and Ought It to Be?' (1978, see p. 451), and 'What Is a Theory of Meaning? (II)' (1976, see p. 69).

35   I am grateful to Professor H.-J. Glock, Professor O. Hanfling, Professor H. Oberdiek, Professor D. Patterson, Professor H. Philipse, Dr Joachim Schulte and to the editors of this volume for their comments on earlier drafts of this paper.

Chapter 4

The Interpretation of the *Philosophical Investigations*: Style, Therapy, *Nachlass*

Alois Pichler

I Introduction

Interpretation of Wittgenstein's *Philosophical Investigations* (PI)[1] is divided by a number of debates. The following two seem to be of a more fundamental nature: the text-immanent vs. contextual debate and the theory vs. therapy debate. The first concerns the question: Shall the PI be read text-immanently or contextually? To read the PI text-immanently means to read it without reference to text-external data. To read the PI contextually means to read it with reference to text-external data; this includes, for example, reading it in the context of Wittgenstein's life, his *Nachlass*, his other writings, the works of other authors, or with a special focus on a context of reception.[2] After an increasing number of Wittgenstein's texts came to light, the contextual standpoint seems to have become the more prominent one and is held by a great number of Wittgenstein and PI interpreters. The contextual approach was, however, most forcefully challenged by Eike von Savigny, who consciously adopted the method of strict *text-immanent interpretation* in his PI commentary (1988ff.).

The theory vs. therapy debate concerns the PI's relation to theory and theses in philosophy (on my use of these concepts see further down); more specifically: Shall the PI be read as advancing philosophical theses and theories, or shall it rather be read as dissolving philosophy as a theory- and theses-oriented discipline by means of a number of 'therapies' for philosophical problems? Whereas one group of scholars, though on different levels and to varying degrees, sees the PI as a work advancing both philosophical theses and theories, another sees it as a work which aims to dissolve philosophical problems through a number of not necessarily systematically related therapies. While this latter conception is often seen to oppose philosophy as such, it in fact establishes a new function and field of work for philosophy, since, according to the therapy view, philosophical problems will continually arise due to our tendency to misunderstand the workings of our language (see PI §109). When defending a theses or a theory understanding of the PI, one typically holds that the PI, in order to *solve* philosophical problems, itself proposes philosophical theses and arguments. In contrast to this, defenders of a therapeutic understanding of the PI typically hold that the PI *dissolves* philosophical problems by bringing to light their illusory nature (i.e. by showing the absence of any substantial claim and thus theory), rather than by developing and putting forward new theses and arguments to answer these problems (see for example Diamond 1995, 13ff.; Crary 2000a). A particularly interesting case in this context is Gordon Baker, who in his early Wittgenstein scholarship took the theory stand (e.g. Baker 1979), but later changed to the therapy view (Baker 2004). One of the strongest expressions of this change is found in his "*Philosophical Investigations* §122: Neglected Aspects" (first published 1991), where he states that in the PI

> [n]o fact (even one about 'our grammar') is stated, no thesis advanced. There is nothing to attack, hence nothing to defend against criticism. Wittgenstein advocated nothing more (and nothing less!) than different possible ways of looking at things which he offered in particular argumentative contexts for certain specific purposes. (Baker 2004, 44f.)

Despite the fact that representatives of the theory approach often invoke Wittgenstein's view of philosophy as *therapy*, they nevertheless read the PI as itself elaborating important theses and arguments to counter a number of wrong or unsatisfactory solutions to problems in systematic philosophy. Where they claim that the PI proposes philosophical therapies, they are just as willing to regard them as connected within a system, or as functioning as elements for building a theory; even their most minimalist interpretation would understand the PI as developing and defending theses, e.g. about grammar and linguistic rules. This places Wittgenstein's thought alongside that of other systematic philosophers in such a way that it then becomes natural to think that, like theirs, his work wants to be consulted for cognitive data to help solve current problems within contemporary analytic philosophy of mind, language, or other disciplines. While some interpreters seem to suggest that such use of the PI may not always be true to Wittgenstein's intention, most still seem to think that this is the only way we can make good use of the book in academic philosophy. In fact, it is sometimes conceded that there may be a striking contrast between the way Wittgenstein wanted the PI and himself to be understood, and the way in which one wants to understand and utilize the work itself. Eike von Savigny is one of the strong view-holders also in this debate. He not only clearly states his belief that the PI should be read as a book which presents arguments, theses, and a theory, but he also defends the view that the book is meant and designed by the author to do so, though it is disturbed by certain stylistic features and does not always proceed in a systematic, linear, and thus, theory-apt way (von Savigny 1997). Consequently, the strongest version of the theory reading, as von Savigny develops it, claims not only that the PI is best read as defending theses and theories, but, moreover, that it is intended for this purpose.[3] But while the PI is characterized by a peculiar form and contains passages and structures that make a theory reading seem doubtful (something which Cavell stressed early on; see Cavell 1962/1976, Ch. 2), a reading in the theses and theory spirit may still want to explain them away by claiming that Wittgenstein did not always, and surely not in every passage, achieve his objective of writing a linear and systematic work, all the while maintaining that this surely was his intention and that he worked hard on it.

From this background, we can single out four basic approaches to the PI which we can call text-immanent, contextual, theory, and therapy or therapeutic approaches. In practice, these approaches combine into four principal readings: (i) a text-immanent theory reading; (ii) a contextual theory reading; (iii) a text-immanent therapeutic reading; (iv) a contextual therapeutic reading. If we associate each reading with a representative and organize approaches and proponents, we get the following distribution:

Approach	Theory	Therapy
Text-immanent	(i) E. von Savigny	(iii) S. Cavell
Contextual	(ii) Early G. Baker	(iv) Late G. Baker

My paper seeks to explore the logical framework for an argument in favour of the therapy interpretation of the PI, thus for readings (iii) and (iv). It seems to me, that, although this view is widely held, the argument for it is not yet firmly in place. Where it is argued for, textual (text-immanent) and extra-textual (contextual) issues are often intermingled, and where it is held that the style of the PI is important in this context, essential features of the style are often underexploited, if noticed at all. In my paper, it is asked whether, and in what sense, the Wittgenstein *Nachlass* can and should provide help for such an argument. In section II, attention is drawn to certain aspects of the PI, termed *skandala*, which represent apparent incoherencies and contradictions in the text. I think that Gordon Baker's psychoanalytic-therapeutic understanding of the PI provides crucial clues to understanding these *skandala*, thereby allowing us to view them as functional, rather than as "only" stylistic idiosyncrasies and/or shortcomings of the author. At the same time, it is argued that Baker tends to commit fallacies when he invokes contextual evidence for his standpoint. My paper thus, on the one hand, identifies Baker's psychoanalytic interpretation of the PI as a valuable methodological tool for the argument in question, while on the other tries to secure and improve the contextual evidence which should and justly can be utilized with it. Consequently, a type of contextual methodology is proposed and developed, which, while utilizing evidence from the *Nachlass*, attempts to be more correct and adequate than standard, including Baker's, ways of using the *Nachlass* for PI-interpretation. To summarize, the paper brings a number of issues together which have partly characterized and partly gone unnoticed in PI scholarship, including recent debates between text-immanent and contextual approaches, on the one hand, and therapy versus theory approaches on the other. Moreover, I think that if an argument for a therapeutic view of the PI shall succeed, these issues ought to be brought together in the way sketched here.

At this point, the use of certain terms relevant to this paper needs to be clarified. *Thesis* is understood as any philosophical assertion which claims truth and generality. *Theory* or *system* is a coherent set of such theses, while an *argument* develops conclusions which support such systems. *Linearity* is a key-feature of such arguments, and means that the argument (or more generally the discourse) proceeds step by step and in a cumulative way towards the conclusion or intended result. *Therapy* is understood as being problem- and person-specific: the therapy is a therapy for a specific problem and in a specific context; it would thus be wrong to treat it as a general remedy for all cases which seem alike. Also, it is person-centred, since it is, first and foremost, a therapy for the person who suffers from this problem. To others it may seem difficult either to see the problem or how it is dissolved, or even both. This does not, however, exclude the possibility of a more general applicability of the therapy and its elements. While I am aware that these are contested views, I think they are nevertheless central to therapeutic PI interpreters (see for example Baker 2004, 173).[4]

II   The Issue of Textual Difficulties and Style

A close text-immanent reading of the PI cannot ignore the dominant presence of incoherence as well as inconsistencies in the text, e.g. frequent ambiguities in phrasing, and more generally, a prevalent lack of precise meaning. We meet obstacles, tensions, frictions and disturbances, and more generally, *difficulties*. They are difficulties both of a structural nature and difficulties at specific points in the text. A word which I would like to associate with these difficulties is *skandalon* (Greek for "stumbling block"), because they make the reader stumble, pause, and ask certain questions. Such a question can be, for example, 'How does remark A fit together with remark B?'; or similarly we might be astonished by the fact that a certain remark is awkwardly ambiguous; or even that we cannot help but think that a specific statement which the PI seems to make is utterly wrong. These difficulties create textual and intellectual *tensions*, and we experience these tensions as intellectual discomforts when reading and trying to understand the text.

PI §1 and how it is further developed in the text already provide striking examples of such difficulties.[5] One directly concerns questions regarding what *mistake* Augustine made in his description of the acquisition of language as well as what assumptions lie behind it. This issue is continuously re-assessed in the text, the last time (explicitly) in §32. §1 states that Augustine's description of learning language does not pay sufficient attention to the fact that different word classes exist, since it suggests that there is only *one* word-class, namely the class of names. While from a first reading one may find this paraphrase and interpretation of Augustine's description satisfactory, the text itself adds many more views on the issue and expands into a many-fold assessment. It can reasonably be taken to develop a number of perspectives under which Augustine's description is assessed, and to present a number of paraphrases of Augustine's "mistake" which actually conflict with each other.

Part of the text in §1 and §6 attributes to Augustine the belief that "All words are names." Besides pointing out that this belief is mistaken – since it rests on a faulty generalization – it states that Augustine does not even describe language correctly concerning names. In contrast to this, however, §§3–4 concede that Augustine does correctly describe language with regard to names. A further message is yielded by the phrase

> If you describe the learning of language in this way you are, I believe, think-ing primarily of nouns like 'table', 'chair', 'loaf', and of people's names, and only secondarily of the names of certain actions and properties; and of the remaining kinds of word as something that will take care of itself. (§1)

Here we understand that Augustine's description may reveal a mistake of attitude rather than a mistake of reasoning; it is neither a wrong position nor faulty generalization which lies at the heart of Augustine's description. Rather, the problem lies with an attitude of neglect or of drawing our attention to *one* aspect only, or an attitude of "name-imperialism" (though he *knows* that there is more to language than only names). While these interpretations of Augustine's "mistake" can all be traced back to the text, they are not consistent with each other. From the analogy in §4, we indeed learn that Augustine's description is, though not correct for the entire field of language, still correct for the field of names. The description of a script in which the letters are "used to stand for sounds, and also as signs of emphasis and punctuation" (§4) is correct insofar as it describes the script's function as representing sounds, and incorrect, i.e. incomplete, only inasmuch as this script functions in other ways, namely to signify emphasis and punctuation. Such an incomplete description of the script as a whole can thus be said to be correct for a certain dimension of the script, and it is this to which Augustine's description is compared. But in contrast to such an assessment of Augustine's mistake, parts of §1 and §6 reject that Augustine's description is correct even for the field of names. §6 criticizes the conception of ostensive definition if it is assumed that ostensive definition functions in pure terms of a name-object relation.

The text presents difficulties also on another level. The fact that Augus-tine's description even enters the level of philosophical interpretation, not to mention the way in which it does so, are *skandala* as such. To begin with, the text refers us to a familiar and nevertheless challenging situation: the situation of describing and reflecting on learning language. It introduces us to a misrepresented – though perhaps only slightly so – description of this situation, namely Augustine's description. Then, it gives us a translation of the description, produced by Wittgenstein himself,[6] which in fact *misrepresents* the original Latin on important points, for example, by strongly attending to names, a focus which was much less present in the original Latin.[7] Furthermore, it links the description to a philosophical interpretation, which additionally overemphasizes certain aspects in the translation.[8] We may above all wonder about the fact that Augustine's report is made the centre of a *philosophical* issue, i.e. is both attributed as much philosophical potential as is done in §1 and met with such harsh intellectual critique. However, further down in the text we meet, rather unexpectedly, a voice which is very different and rather conciliatory, and which gives room for the fact that the author of the description at stake, Augustine, may have thought his description to be primarily about *y*, and not about *xyz*. Thus, the critique expressed would apply first of all only in the latter case, namely if he had intended to describe *xyz*. Indeed, in §2 a "language" is introduced – later referred to as "language (2)" – for which Augustine's description actually is said to be valid, i.e. a language which is supposed to function in terms of the name-object scheme presupposed by Augustine's description, the "builders' language."[9] But while in §2 we are asked to conceive of "language (2)" as a *complete primitive language*, in §6 there is no longer talk about a complete ("vollständige") primitive language only, but this language is conceived as the *whole*, entire ("ganze") linguistic activity of a community. A *complete primitive language* will be complete with regard to the functions it is thought to perform in certain contexts; we could, for example, speak of the completeness of certain terminology. However, to regard "language (2)" as the *whole* language of a linguistic community, as §6 proposes, seems to be far-fetched.[10]

One could continue to add to this list of difficulties or *skandala* when reading further into the PI text. The important question, though, is how we respond to them. If we are confronted with places containing ambiguity, unclearness, contradiction, or incoherence, should we try to make sense of these tensions, or should we rather see them as accidental stylistic idiosyncrasies or attribute them to a weakness of Wittgenstein as a writer? The latter would be the standard procedure, but I think that as long as it is not shown to be irrelevant and inadequate, it is fair and adequate to begin with the first approach. The late Baker has with his psychoanalytic-therapeutic view of Wittgenstein's work (2004), shown a way to make sense of and understand the function of the *skandala*. But let us start by looking more into the standard view, which is well-developed by Stephen Hilmy and refers in particular to Wittgenstein's supposed "incapability" to produce a linear and systematic text (e.g. see Hilmy 1987, 15–17). Hilmy thinks that Wittgenstein himself wished to advance theses, and that he wanted to achieve a systematic and linear presentation of these theses, but that he did not succeed. Consequently, we should supplement what

Wittgenstein himself was unable (but wanted) to achieve by providing the text of the PI with an explication of its inherent, though stylistically contaminated, argumentative structure, thus rendering the thesis content visible and systematic. This endeavour is paradigmatically carried out by Eike von Savigny in his PI-commentary. An alternative to the standard approach, however, is to regard the difficulties not as accidental mistakes and deficiencies, which Wittgenstein himself would have wanted to avoid, but to try to go along with the text as it stands, without attempting to unify its contents into a linear argument or improve on the passages where we find a *skandalon*. This is an approach which was exemplified early on, at least in nuance, by Stanley Cavell (1962/1976 Ch. 2). It is therefore held in this paper that, at least in principle, therapy readings like Cavell's are much more able to integrate the *skandala* functionally into their reading than are theory readings like Hilmy and von Savigny's. While it is problematic for a theory reading to handle the *skandala* without either ignoring them, playing them down, or re-constructing the text so that the difficulties disappear and the scheme of an overall coherent interpretation is satisfied, therapy readings can focus on them as their strongest text-immanent evidence. Even more, one is able to link them internally to Wittgenstein's conception of what philosophical problems are and what is required to deal with them well.

According to therapy readings, the PI conceives of philosophical problems as something which are "Luftgebäude" of "nonsense" (§§118, 464), rather than as genuine problems which have substance. They are made up of incoherent and inconsistent tangles of views, beliefs, temptations, thoughts, requirements, actions, etc. What one needs to do in order to deal with this tangle, its incoherencies and inconsistencies, is to make the philosopher see and help untangle them. For this, the philosopher may first need to be exposed to the same processes which produced the tangle in the first place. With this conception of philosophical problems and their required treatment in mind, one can explain the function of inconsistency and incoherency in the PI in a way which seems hard for theory readings to match. Therapy readers may for example say that in the beginning of the PI Wittgenstein attempts to expose the philosopher to the roots of the philosophical problems of word-object relation and meaning (see Goldfarb 1983, 266). In order to show these roots, the text neither needs to be consistent, nor shall be. In fact, since the sources and roots of the problem are themselves incoherent and inconsistent with each other, it should be no surprise that their depiction is too. This, however, is not the place to show how this approach is to be applied in detail, i.e. how the *skandala* function bit for bit both to lay out and help dissolve the philosophical problem. Nonetheless, I think that a therapeutic reading of the PI should pay attention to and utilize these *skandala*, and that the late Baker's psychoanalytic approach presents an adequate frame for doing so.

In this context, Wittgenstein's phrase "übersichtliche Darstellung" (perspicuous re/presentation; §122), which is widely referred to and discussed in PI scholarship, receives a new and illuminating meaning. It would no longer be correct to understand it as an ordering of language and linguistic usages into a system of grammatical propositions (cf. Baker and Hacker 1983, 308; Glock 1996, 278ff.). Rather, in the spirit of the late Baker's approach, one should take it to mean an overview and synopsis of the parts which *produce* the tangle underlying the philosophical problem ("übersehbar machen"): Wittgenstein views the philosopher as experiencing "an internal tension or conflict. What needs clarification are the motives which occasion such a conflict" (Baker 2004, 208). The PI states:

> It is the business of philosophy, not to resolve a contradiction by means of a mathematical or logico-mathematical discovery, but to make it possible for us to get a clear view of the state of mathematics that troubles us: the state of affairs *before* the contradiction is resolved. (And this does not mean that one is sidestepping a difficulty.) (§125)

"Übersichtliche Darstellung" thus shows the roots of the problem, rather than a system of rules the obeying of which shall provide the solution. It is thus an explication of the *pre*-conditions and premises which are internal to the problem, rather than a description of legitimate usage which enters the arena *post factum* as an external corrector.

Although Baker's therapy reading seems apt for large parts of the PI, it may be too hasty to see all of the PI as an exemplification of psychoanalytic method in philosophy (cf. §133), a qualification Baker would surely agree to. Sometimes, an attractive picture immediately helps us to refocus and to see in new and relieving ways the things which previously were knotted together in problematic ways. Such a picture is included in §18, which encourages us to look at language as "an ancient city [. . .] surrounded by a multitude of new boroughs." Suddenly, we learn that borders need not be exact in the way we had thought, that language is both grown and planned, that there are connections between its parts, that language changes, etc. Or we are helped and inspired by an enlightening comparison: it is helpful to compare utterances with pictures, both in terms of portraits and genre-pictures (§522), or to ask what the understanding of an utterance has in common with the understanding of a musical theme (§527). This is not the place to describe and discuss in detail the entire range of PI therapies. Yet, a crucial element is surely the utilization of "language games." They help us to recognize and face the philosophical problem at hand and to ask: How do we place this particular philosophical question, phrasing, description, statement, problem? Where does it come from and where is it at home? The PI will try to find the place for it: the model to which it belongs, the "language game" which suits it. We can ask, where is the claim "Only I can know whether I am really in pain" (§246) at home? It is in the conception and model of a "private language." What the PI continuously does, is to make us see and reflect upon specific contexts where views and concepts responsible for philosophical problems seem to function; however, these contexts are most likely very different from those where *we* function, and it is indeed hard for us to see how they can function even in fictitious contexts.

Theory readers will find it difficult to read the PI or parts of the PI in the ways described in this section. Even if one agrees regarding the difficult nature of the text and to the view that it contains *skandala*-type incoherencies and contradiction, one may still not think that these *skandala* are functional in the way described here. One may want to see them as personal shortcomings, rather than as elements of methodological function. Holding a therapy view of the PI, I think, ought to mean agreeing that the "shortcoming"-approach may unjustifiably neglect a substantial dimension of the text and, consequently, may preclude us from understanding an all-important aspect of the PI, one which we would not discover by denying these difficulties any functionality in the first place. A therapy reading along the lines of the late Baker's understanding of the PI is, in contrast, able to create a space where the *skandala* can receive an authentic place and function by reflecting and carrying the tensions and misunderstandings which produce our philosophical problems. Philosophical therapy, then, does not follow linear and systematic methods; it follows the paths by which a problem was occasioned in the first place. But, in addition to the *skandala*, is there other evidence that a systematic and linear presentation is not essential to the PI and its tasks, and that it rather aspires to a different form?

III   The PI Preface

Although we can find important evidence in a very specific PI text (the so-called philosophy chapter to which we will return further down), it is in particular the preface we shall focus on here. The preface tells us that the natural order of the author's thoughts was non-linear and non-systematic, and that the book resulting from them follows this natural order. It tells us also that the nature of the subjects investigated actually demands a non-linear and "criss-crossing" method of investigation and presentation. Consequently, inasmuch as theory and argument are tied to a linear and systematic presentation, therapy readers of the PI can say that according to the preface, the author consciously chose a form for the book which is not the form of system, theory, and argument. Yet, as we have seen earlier, many interpreters have challenged this view and think that the non-systematic and non-linear form of the PI is connected neither with its subjects of investigation, nor its method, but rather with a personal shortcoming. They may claim that Wittgenstein was not sincere and made a virtue out of necessity when he said that the subjects investigated demand a form different than linearity and systematization. The preface remark which theory readers consider the most important evidence for their stand is the following: "I should have liked to produce a good book. This has not come about, but the time is past in which I could improve it." I will refer to this remark as the "discontent-remark." A key issue is then how we are to understand this remark. Does the preface state that the features of non-linear and non-systematic form, as well as inconsistencies and incoherencies in the text, are what make the author discontented with the book? There is, however, another passage in the preface which is central to the context of this discussion and which we shall call the "album-remark": "Thus this book is really only an album." Can we plausibly connect the discontent-remark and the album-remark in a way which does not support the personal shortcoming interpretation? Is it possible that the preface expresses discontentment not with the album form, but with something else? Though this deviates from standard interpretations, there is indeed a way to read the two remarks which does not leave Wittgenstein discontented with the book because it is (partly or wholly) an album: Wittgenstein wants the book to be an album and he is quite happy with much he has achieved in this direction. However, the book is in some parts (still) too little an album, and therefore Wittgenstein is dissatisfied with the book. In short: Wittgenstein could have been discontented with the book because it is not yet enough album.

If the *skandala* and the preface are regarded to lend support to the therapy reading, theory readers may still challenge this by questioning the authority of the underlying text. This leads to our second debate, the text-immanent vs. contextual debate. The question with which theory readers may challenge the evidence just gained is: Does the preface really belong to the PI? And is the PI edition reliable? What if that which you call *skandala* results from editing rather than Wittgensteinian authorship? And the general methodological question which makes its entrance here is: How do we relate our research to the Wittgenstein *Nachlass* from which the PI is edited, and more generally, which role can and shall *Nachlass* research have for the interpretation of the PI? How shall we utilize these materials to interpret the PI? Von Savigny has been very critical about using the *Nachlass* for PI interpretation. But he would surely accept utilization of *Nachlass* evidence such as the following. Let us first repeat the question which leads us into *Nachlass* research: What if the preface was not part of the PI and we thus mistakenly considered it relevant for understanding the PI? What if the PI editors added the preface and other parts to the text?[11] And more generally: How reliable is the PI edition on which our text-immanent study and reading are based? The space provided here does not permit a detailed and text-critical engagement with the materials. Yet, we can be confident that the PI text, as it was published in 1953 and reissued in later editions, is on the whole both reliable and faithful. Joachim Schulte noted only a handful of mistakes in the text when he prepared the genetic-critical edition of the PI (PI 2001b), and only "two or three of them were more or less important."[12] But what interests us most at this moment is the question whether the PI preface belongs to the PI or not. In short, the answer is yes, and it is based on the following consultation of the *Nachlass*: on page 1 of the two preserved carbon copies of TS227[13] we find the title, the motto, and the beginning of the preface. The preface ends on page 4, the same page on which §1 of the PI main text begins. Thus, there can be no doubt that the preface belongs to the PI. So if it is true that the PI text, including the PI *paratexts* with the preface, supports a therapeutic reading, then such a reading cannot be validly countered by the claim that it is based on a PI edition or PI text which is not authentic and authorial.[14]

IV   Baker's Contextualism

But what then is the broader role of *Nachlass* research for the interpretation of the PI? Clearly, as von Savigny stresses, use of the *Nachlass*, and contextual evidence more generally, is not as unproblematic and straight-forward as in the above case where the published text was compared to its original. Baker has also been paradigmatic in this arena, though not without fault, as I will try to show in this section. This concerns both the early and the late Baker whose justifications often seem both problematic and contextually fallacious, regardless of whether he is arguing for or against the therapy view. In contrast to his late views, the "early" Baker stated that Wittgenstein's collaboration with Waismann on a systematic presentation of his philosophy showed that Wittgenstein, including his PI, was positive about systematic philosophizing and theory, and that therefore, "it cannot be mistaken in principle to try to fit Wittgenstein's remarks together into a philosophical system" (Baker 1979, 245). This reasoning seems to rest on faulty thinking which is interesting for our context. First, the justification for "fitting" an author's work "into a philosophical system" is clearly not dependent on whether this undertak-ing is in agreement with the author's intention ("intentional fallacy"). We have a range of prominent examples which show how it is possible and accepted to fit an author's work into a system and theory even though the author himself did not intend such a utilization of his work, or even spoke out against it. In the context of Wittgenstein scholarship, Kripke is one such person who consciously took this path, and clearly addressed the issue (Kripke 1982, 3ff.). Many commentators may want to say that Kripke's Wittgenstein is not a figure with which Wittgenstein himself would agree. But this is not a point of importance in this context, for it is not a premise for Kripke's undertaking that it is based upon an inter-pretation and utilization of Wittgenstein's PI in its own spirit. Thus, the intentional fallacy falsely construes an inference from the context of origin to the context of utilization and justification; reference to an author's intention is neither necessary nor sufficient in order to interpret ade-quately. However, such reference would naturally be crucial for picking the same interpretation as the author would pick. Thus, in this fallacy "adequate interpretation" and "author's interpretation" were confused. Second, the fact that Wittgenstein may have been positive about system-atic philosophizing at a certain point does not entail that this is also valid for the Wittgenstein of the PI. It is surprising how often, in doing biog-raphy and history of philosophy, too little space is given to possible inco-herencies, tensions, and changes in a thinker's intellectual life. In some cases it might for an author even be desirable or advantageous to produce different works with different and perhaps even contradictory messages. Moreover, what is continuously neglected, is a difference which we are all acquainted with from our own writing, namely the differences between our notebooks and drafts, on the one hand, and works prepared and polished for publication, on the other. It is a contextual fallacy to infer from the fact that Wittgenstein thought and conveyed, or simply, wrote, X at point $t1$ that he also thought and wanted to convey X at point $t2$, or, from the fact that writing $Y1$ conveys the message $M1$, that the message of writing $Y2$ is or shall be made coherent with $M1$. We can call this the "coherentist fallacy." A special branch of this fallacy is the "genetic fallacy" which entails interpreting PI remarks in the light of earlier versions of these remarks according to the following reasoning: "PI section n means x because PI section n's earlier version n' means x or x'." This fallacy is explicitly addressed and attacked by Eike von Savigny, who justly dismisses this kind of reasoning as methodologically unviable: the meaning of a text is not determined by the meaning of an earlier or other version of this text, neither in necessary nor sufficient terms. A third type of contextualist fallacy can be termed the "*already there* fallacy." In short, it consists in inferring from the fact that a remark or a group of remarks is "already there," be it in the same or a different form or context, at an earlier date, that this determines in a substantial sense the function or meaning of this remark or group of remarks at a later stage; or that the meaning and function of the later remark or group of remarks is already present at the earlier point.

Contextual fallacies or mistakes deceive defenders of both the theory and the therapy approaches, in particular, when they argue their respective and opposed approaches to the PI with reference to earlier or later statements made by Wittgenstein. Such mistakes are partly due to the fact that Wittgenstein scholars in general often adopt an uncritical attitude to the issue of the special place the PI occupies, or at least, might occupy, in the context of Wittgenstein's work. Views valid for certain parts of Wittgenstein's work after 1929 are extended to the whole "later Wittgenstein," including the PI, or views valid for the PI only, are extended to the whole "later work."[15] In opposition to the early Baker, the late Baker argues for a *therapeutic* reading of the PI; but where he does so on a contextual basis, he tends to make the same contextual mistakes the early Baker made, arguing for his view by reference to contextual evidence with questionable legitimacy.[16] So, where does this leave us with regard to our principal issue of theory vs. therapy reading and the issue of how contextual evidence is to be utilized for handling this issue? I think that there is indeed a way of legitimately extracting evidence from the *Nachlass*, one which differs from both "passage-hunting" and under-reflected use of material on the one hand, and safe text-critical collation on the other hand. The kind of evidence which I am thinking of here can be called genetic evidence, but it is genetic in a very specific sense, one distinguished from a general reference to earlier versions of a remark.

V Applying the Right Kind of Context

We have thus far focused on the question whether text-immanent evidence supports a therapeutic reading of the PI. We have concluded this is plausible. In the following, this issue will be pursued further into the realm of contextual data. In the previous section we had to remind ourselves that contextual confirmation can include different things and can be used in faulty ways: often, scholars invoke passages which are not found in the PI itself to support the view that Wittgenstein and the PI have a therapeutic programme. Or similarly, commentators interpret remarks from the PI in light of the meaning and function of their pre-PI versions by applying the following reasoning: "The ambiguity of section *x* is clarified if we interpret *x* in the light of section *y*, which is a precursor of *x*. Therefore, we should understand *x* along the lines of *y*." This kind of methodology is habitually used in Wittgenstein scholarship; however, it can, as I have tried to argue, be fallacious. In contrast to such utilization of contextual evidence, the support which we shall refer to here is of a different kind. It is related to the specific textual and stylistic developments that occurred at the very moment(s) when the PI was composed, rather than to precursors, ancestors, and relatives of PI remarks. Instead of, for example, interpreting the meaning of certain remarks in the context of earlier remarks or meanings, we shall focus on the text genesis and see, in the making of the PI, what new elements were introduced and what old elements left out. Consequently, the kind of contextual evidence which I think is indeed applicable is intimately connected with the shaping of the PI and its remarks themselves.

As a valid argument which utilizes such relevant contextual support, I want to suggest the following.[17] In late 1936, Wittgenstein dismissed the form of the *Brown Book* as suitable for his envisaged book, and thus adopted a different form for the PI. This is documented by the text-genetic development from the second part of MS115 (German translation and revision of the *Brown Book*, published as EPB in 1970) to MS142 (the PI's "*Urfassung*") and a number of preface drafts to the PI which are preserved in the *Nachlass*. This development can be interpreted in the sense that Wittgenstein consciously abandoned linearity and systematization in favour of the album form,[18] and insofar as this new form, shaped by opposition to linearity and systematization, also opposes theory and supports therapy, it corroborates the view that a therapeutic reading of the PI is proper. Furthermore, it can be claimed that the genesis of individual remarks and parts of the PI, including the adding of simile and pictorial elements, is best explained as a conscious redaction of a text meant to promote therapy rather than theory. That fits well with the experience of PI remarks being much "clearer" in their earlier versions. Consequently, according to this reasoning a study of the genesis of the PI remains crucially incomplete if it does not include a comprehensive assessment of the PI's relation to the *Brown Book*.[19] It is often said that §§1–188, which have remained a stable part of the PI since 1937, do not differ much from the *Brown Book*. But a close examination of the changes which took place when Wittgenstein left the *Brown Book* behind and started his PI, shows that the differences between the two are much deeper and more substantial than is usually described. Wittgenstein rejected the *Brown Book* with disapproving words,[20] and immediately afterwards began what we today refer to as the PI. What was it that made him abandon the *Brown Book* in the first place? G. E. Moore and Rush Rhees record that Wittgenstein was unhappy with the method which he employed in this piece (BBB 1984, 12ff.). In his first preface to the PI from 1938, Wittgenstein refers to the new text as a "fragment": "I begin this publication with the fragment of my last attempt to arrange my philosophical thoughts in a series. This fragment has perhaps the advantage that it relatively easily conveys an idea of my method. This fragment I want to let follow a mass of remarks in more or less loose arrangement" (TS225: ii, my translation).[21] With the "last attempt" ("mein letzter Versuch"), I think he means the *Brown Book* together with the "Fragment" MS142, or TS220 respectively, into which MS142 was dictated. TS220 is a fragment because it still contains parts and dimensions of the "last attempt." However, in addition to new texts being added which never could have been included in the *Brown Book*, like the philosophy-chapter as well as many sections with simile and pictorial rather than argumentative language (like §18), these parts of the "last attempt" have been changed and adapted to fit the new form. In short, the linear and systematic structure of the *Brown Book* was broken for the PI, and what before had been one linear string of text, was then fragmented. With the "mass of remarks" ("Masse von Bemerkungen"), Wittgenstein meant, I think, TS221, which was to follow the "fragment," but which, as it is said, was not in as equally adequate an arrangement as the "fragment." Consequently, it is foremost PI §§1–188

(TS220) which should be studied closely in order to identify the PI's character and method. This part also contains the so-called philosophy-chapter (PI §§89–133) which therapy readers consider important evidence.

It is often said that the philosophy-chapter of the *Big Typescript* (TS213) from 1933 formed the basis of the philosophy-chapter of the PI (e.g. see Hilmy 1987, 35); but this statement is in need of modification (see also Stern 2005, 180ff.). Most of the PI's philosophy-chapter was in fact drafted anew, and only certain and comparatively few parts were included from the *Big Typescript*'s philosophy-chapter. Studies of correspondence between the TS213 philosophy-chapter and the PI "*Urfassung*" (1937) and "*Frühfassung*" (1938) philosophy-chapters show that relatively little text from the first has been used in the second. In fact, the changes from the *Big Typescript* to the "*Urfassung*" were much more substantial than any subsequent changes. Here we meet rupture and a new beginning, rather than continuity. For his new book, Wittgenstein worked on "meta-philosophy" for quite some time in the period November 1936 to February 1937, including the issue of ideals and demands in philosophy. Only for some parts was significant use made of the earlier *Big Typescript* philosophy-chapter, in addition to new remarks being produced.[22] Thus, evidence from the text genesis of the philosophy-chapter clearly shows that this text was directly created for the PI and is therefore to be seen as performing a crucial function in that work. Wittgenstein obviously felt at this very point of composing the PI that the issue of philosophy and demands in philosophy were crucial, but that he had up until then not satisfactorily dealt with them, thus necessitating new work. From this analysis, therapy readers may conclude that the work carried out on the philosophy-chapter during late autumn 1936 and early spring 1937 would seem unreasonable if the PI really was intended to advance theses.

VI   Conclusions and Further Issues

In this paper, I have tried to show that both text-immanent evidence and contextual evidence, in the sense of genetic-contextual evidence intro-duced in the previous section, lend support to the therapy view of the PI. If it is the case that our text-immanent reading ends up with a theory reading, then we may need to ask ourselves whether this is due to our conception of and demands on philosophy – a subject which is directly tackled in the PI philosophy-chapter – and thus depends on *text-external* factors of reception, rather than on the PI text as such. If one lets go of certain demands on philosophy, including the demand that it has to advance theses and theories, one has good reasons to claim that, already on a text-immanent basis, a therapy reading is more proper than a theory reading.

Another, though connected, topic of this paper was to address the text-immanent vs. contextual debate and to find the proper place for the results of contextual readings, in particular *Nachlass* research, for PI interpretation. As a result of *Nachlass* research studying the specific developments in text and form that occurred when the PI was composed, we may have to free ourselves from some of the most prominent pictures which Wittgenstein scholarship treasures. The PI is neither a point nor span on a line of development from 1929 (1913) to 1951, yielded without serious rupture from the previous, and developed further into the "latest" Wittgenstein. The PI is above this line and not on the line, and the textual and conceptual development into the (therapeutic) PI should be seen in *editorial* rather than in *chronological* terms. This makes it possible to understand that texts later than the PI can (again) have a theory focus while the PI does not. I think, then, it is right to say that there are *two* Wittgensteins; however it is not the early and the later Wittgenstein, but rather the Wittgenstein of the manuscripts (*Nachlass*) on the one hand, and the Wittgenstein of the works prepared for publication, the *Tractatus* and the PI, Part I, on the other hand. It is primarily to these two principal works we have to refer for Wittgenstein's philosophical "will."[23] This is not to say that *Nachlass* research becomes less important. In fact, it implies the opposite. The *Nachlass* is a background and "object of comparison" (§122). Without it we cannot understand the PI as it understood itself and its philosophical mission. My point, that we have to approach the *Nachlass* and PI methodologically differently, is therefore not to discourage *Nachlass* research, but to encourage it in order to get a better grip on both the two principal works as well as the 20,000 challenging pages which Wittgenstein additionally left us, and to recognize the rights demanded by their distinct natures and functions. With such methodological concerns in mind, we are enabled to see that the so-called later Wittgenstein in fact can contain both theory and therapy. We will, therefore, be careful not to override the PI's messages with, for example, messages taken from TS213. A therapy reading of the PI cannot then be endangered by other texts authored by Wittgenstein which defend doctrines, whether earlier or later than the PI. Which of the texts is more valuable for philosophy is, however, a different question which is not answered here.

Yet, this is not at all to say that a therapy reading of the PI cannot be challenged on a different level. Jaakko Hintikka thinks that Wittgenstein's (therapeutic) conception of philosophy and his belief that there cannot be proper problems and theses in philosophy, are linked to his view that language cannot represent itself, and that any attempt to do so leads to inconsistency ("inexpressibility-view," Hintikka 1996, 280). If this view fails, Wittgenstein's specific conception of philosophy and philosophical therapy would also fail. It also needs saying that many readings which are critical towards theory readings are not, therefore, necessarily therapy readings. David G. Stern's "How many Wittgensteins?" (Stern 2005) describes the PI as displaying a struggle between philosophical therapy and systematic and theory-oriented philosophy, rather than as working toward liberation from the latter. On this view, the PI is neither therapy nor theory, but rather displays how philosophy oscillates between the two and how the two are interrelated in Wittgenstein's own work and philosophy. This is a reading of the PI which Stern himself traces back to Stanley Cavell and Robert Fogelin's work on Wittgenstein.

This paper does not claim to do justice to the wide range and variety of therapeutic readings. It rather concentrates on themes of principal relevance within the debate between therapy and theory readers. One principal point was to argue for the view that the style of the PI and its *skandala* may essentially belong together with its therapeutic aims, and that therapeutic readings should, therefore, find it attractive to show and explicate their role in detail. However, there are still many crucially relevant themes which have not been addressed adequately in this paper. This includes the issue of the PI's "multivoicedness." In contrast to a "polyphonic" conception of the PI (Pichler 2004, 18ff.), is it not assumed in my paper that some PI sections, e.g. from the philosophy-chapter, are more authoritative than others, and indeed express views of the author, rather than a possible stand in a philosophical debate which the author himself does not need to defend, but is still part of the therapy which the reader has to undergo? Therapy readers would claim that much of what is attributed to the PI in terms of theses and theory content, e.g. the "use theory of meaning," represents stands in a philosophical debate which the book gives voice to, rather than its authorial outcome. What then about the remarks on philosophy? Are they more authentic and authorial? One may answer that the question regarding what is authentic and authoritative is not important during the process of reading since, for the process to be therapeutic, everything is to be taken at face value. Consequently, since responding to theses and inconsistencies simply as theses and inconsistencies may be an essential element of the therapy, it would be wrong on the basis of the view that the PI does not end up with theses, to read a thesis not as a thesis and to treat an inconsistency not as an inconsistency. But if we return to the PI text after having undergone successful therapy, and find our experience of therapy described therein, we may then take these remarks as authoritative. [24]

Notes

1   I am concerned with *Philosophical Investigations*, "Part I", only (PI 2001a).

2   Hanjo Glock speaks of and defends the "genetic or source-oriented" approach and contrasts it with von Savigny's "immanent approach" (Glock 1990, 153). What I mean by "contextual" approach includes, but is broader than, Glock's "genetic or source-oriented" approach.

3   This is developed in detail in von Savigny's commentary (1988ff.).

4   The choice of the "theory" vs. "therapy" terminology may raise questions on a more principal level. However, it is prominent in the texts of many scholars central to the debate, including the two main heroes of this paper. Eike von Savigny, in the introduction to his commentary on the PI (1988), states that it is proper to speak of Wittgenstein's *theory*, while the late Baker explicitly defends *therapeutic* readings of Wittgenstein (Baker 2004). Other labels used for "theory" readings of the PI are "constructive", "analytic", "systematic", "dogmatic", "cognitive", or "position" readings.

5   This has been observed earlier: see Cavell 1996; Pichler 1997, 107ff.; Raatzsch 2003, and, recently, H. Johannessen ("While reading Wittgenstein, *Philosophische Untersuchungen* §§1–19", in preparation).

6   That this passage from the *Confessions* was translated by Wittgenstein is shown by von Savigny; see von Savigny 1994, 36.

7   Clearly, this translational misrepresentation is not covered by principal difficulties of inter-lingual translation. Rather, the messages of the source text are focused and moved to the territory of name-object relations. This is confirmed by von Savigny 1994, 34f.

8   So too von Savigny 1994, 35.

9   In §2, "language (2)" is already *learned* and *in use*. However, Augustine's description, as it was presented at the beginning of §1, was concerned with how he learned language rather than with the issue of the structure of language and its use, and, consequently, to call the "builders' language" a

language "for which the description given by Augustine is right" includes some shortcuts and thus adds to the difficulties.

10 Around "language (2)" a discussion has arisen regarding whether it can qualify as a language at all; cf. for example Rhees 1970 and Malcolm 1989.

11 Indeed, these questions were posed in PI scholarship; e.g. see Raatzsch 1996, 254, 257.

12 Personal communication, November 2005. There is, though, an issue concerning the PI edition's rendering of the graphics (see Biggs 1995), and the placing of the slips found in the typescript ("Randbemerkungen"). Schulte (PI 2001b) puts them in text boxes in the main text, while the previous editions had printed them at the foot of the page.

13 References to Wittgenstein *Nachlass* manuscripts and typescripts follow von Wright's classification (von Wright 1982, 35–62, latest revision von Wright 1993a). Quotations follow the *Bergen Electronic Edition* (BEE 2000).

14 A different issue, though, is whether it was indeed TS227 which was to be published, and not another typescript, maybe derived from TS227. As yet, we do not have the evidence to suppose that this is the case. An argument to this extent would involve complex philological studies of the kind developed in Rothhaupt 1999.

15 A recent example is Weiss' study on the *Big Typescript*. Notwithstanding the merit of Weiss having shown that the *Big Typescript* contains a coherent theory or at least aptly responds to a theory reading, it does not follow from this that "the later Wittgenstein is a constructive, analytical theorist" (Weiss 2004, iii). What follows is what Weiss has shown, namely that this is valid for the *Big Typescript*, but not more.

16 Surely, many other scholars seem to commit the same mistakes. Although Hanjo Glock himself is very much aware of the problematic nature and critical of what he calls "passage-hunting" (Glock 1990, 152; see also Glock's essay in this volume), he can nevertheless be criticized for inaptly invoking contextual evidence, for example when he refers to a remark from the *Big Typescript* in order to give support to his "cognitive" understanding of the PI's view on philosophy: "His own philosophizing he describes as the 'rejection of wrong arguments' [. . .]" (Glock 1991, 73f.). It is a fact that this remark from the *Big Typescript*, "Philosophieren ist: falsche Argumente zurückweisen" (TS213, 409), did not make it into the PI, and it may be significant, that it did *not* make it.

17 The following is drawn from Pichler 2004.

18 It needs mentioning that the word "album" itself was not introduced before 1945 (Pichler 1997, 34f.).

19 With *Brown Book*, here the entire complex of MS141 (1933–34), TS310 ("Brown Book", 1934–35) and the second part of MS115 ("Versuch einer Umarbeitung", 1936) is meant.

20 "Dieser ganze 'Versuch einer Umarbeitung' von Seite 118 bis hierher ist
    nichts wert." (MS115, 292: "This entire 'attempt of rewriting' from page
    118 up to here is not worth anything"; my translation.)
21 TS225 is from August 1938, even though earlier versions of this text dating
    back to 1937 exist (see Pichler 1997, 24).
22 We meet the first drafts to the philosophy chapter in MS152 (81–96), which
    were begun in late autumn 1936. They are continued in MS157a (45r–71r,
    9.2.1937 and later) and MS157b (1r–18v, 27.2.1937 and later), where
    remarks from the *Big Typescript* were brought in (see list in MS157b: 13v).
23 See also Stern 1996, 445. For a general discussion of the problematic nature
    of the notion "work by Wittgenstein", see Kenny 2004 and Schulte 2005a.
24 This article is an extended version of Pichler 2005. Earlier versions of this
    paper have been presented at seminars and conferences in Bertinoro (2003),
    Innsbruck (2004), Lisboa (2004), and Kirchberg (2005). I would like to
    thank the organizers and participants of these events for discussions and
    comments. For valuable comments on drafts I would like to thank K. Cahill,
    J. Conant, H. Johannessen, K. S. Johannessen, O. Kuusela, J. Rothhaupt, S.
    Säätelä, J. Thompson, T. Wallgren, and P. K. Westergaard. My deepest
    thanks go to G. Bengtsson, C. Huitfeldt, R. Jewell, H. Nyvold, and D. Smith,
    who helped me shape the paper in a series of discussion circles at the Witt-
    genstein Archives in Bergen in Autumn 2005. I am particularly indebted to
    Deirdre Smith for tidying up my English.

Chapter 5

Ways of Reading Wittgenstein: Observations on Certain Uses of the Word 'Metaphysics'

Joachim Schulte

I

In one of his last published papers Gordon Baker draws our attention to one paragraph of a remark of Wittgenstein's *Philosophical Investigations*. This paragraph (§116b) consists of a single, often-quoted sentence: '*Wir führen die Wörter von ihrer metaphysischen, wieder auf ihre alltägliche Verwendung zurück.* – What *we* do is to bring words back from their metaphysical to their everyday use.' In the course of his discussion Baker points out the importance of paying attention to the genesis of individual remarks in Wittgenstein's texts as well as peculiarities and changes of the wording of these remarks. In what follows I shall first look at some of the passages examined by Baker and his comments. As a second step, I shall then proceed to investigate the question whether it may prove helpful to supplement Baker's approach by additional considerations. My chief interest lies in exhibiting by way of examining examples certain features of Wittgenstein's style and technique of writing that can be found useful in attempting to understand and explain the meaning of his remarks.

In his discussion of §116b Baker wishes to convince us that certain standard interpretations of what Wittgenstein was up to in his later philosophy are mistaken. The sort of interpretation he has in mind would want to place Wittgenstein in the neighbourhood of what used to be, and sometimes still is, called 'ordinary language philosophy', generally associated with eminent Oxford figures like Gilbert Ryle and J. L. Austin. This is not the place to go into the question whether or not Baker's reading of these authors will ultimately prove entirely correct. The characteristic of their philosophy emphasized by him is their tendency to rely on 'standard speech-patterns of the English-speaking peoples' (Baker 2004, 93). Readers of Wittgenstein's later writings who regard him in a similar light will then be inclined to understand Wittgenstein's talking of our bringing words back to their everyday use as amounting to the claim that 'describing everyday use is a matter of establishing facts about a public normative practice', where 'it is presumed to be relatively uncontentious (objective?) what these facts are'. Accordingly, the expression 'everyday use' is treated 'as synonymous with "ordinary speech (language)" ' (Baker 2004, 93, 94).

Baker continues to say that by reading the *Investigations* that way one will fail to do justice to the role played by the contrastive term in Wittgenstein's remark, i.e. the notion of a 'metaphysical' use of words. By regarding the expression 'everyday use' as the one which 'wears the trousers' such readers will in Baker's opinion be misled into thinking that metaphysical uses of words are among those that do *not* conform to ordinary speech, and can hence without further ado be condemned as nonstandard, deviant, or violating the rules of common usage.

In Baker's eyes this sort of interpretation gets off on the wrong foot by ignoring a possibility favoured by Baker himself, viz. the possibility of taking 'metaphysical use' as the expression which wears the trousers. If one allows for this possibility one will, according to Baker, see that the term 'metaphysical' can be given a content in harmony with a number of occurrences of this word in Wittgenstein's writings, eventually leading to a reading of 'everyday use' which explains the meaning of this expression in terms of what is '*non*-metaphysical'. This would have the consequence that the term 'everyday' need not be read as meaning 'conforming with standard speech-practice' (Baker 2004, 100).

Baker's surprising result depends on a number of factors. One is his list of passages illustrating Wittgenstein's use of the term 'metaphysical'. Another one is the use he makes of Austin's well-known ploy of identifying one term of a pair of contrastive expressions as the one whose use 'wears the trousers'[1] and declaring the other one the dependent use. As regards the question what strategies of reading Wittgenstein can be seen to lead to fruitful insights it will be of general importance to find out whether this notion of an expression's wearing the trousers fits §116b and other passages in Wittgenstein's writings. But before we can usefully get down to exploring this point we shall have to look at some of the details of Baker's discussion to see if his researches and comments shed light on textual difficulties.

It is a particularly commendable feature of Baker's treatment of §116b that, true to his and Peter Hacker's previous work on their *Analytic Commentary on the Philosophical Investigations*, he takes the trouble to examine some of the fine points of Wittgenstein's German text. Thus, he mentions the fact that Wittgenstein underlines the word 'we', which is likely to be a means of stressing a difference between Wittgenstein's own specific way of doing philosophy and the ways favoured by other authors.[2] Then Baker elucidates various aspects of 'bringing something back' – Wittgenstein's word is 'zurückführen'. Baker illustrates possible uses of that expression by describing various situations in which a person or an animal is by one means or another directed back to the right or desired place or path. For instance, a rambler who has lost his way can be led to the right path, and then we may give him additional instructions how to reach his destination. In view of the 'ordinary language' reading opposed by Baker it is a matter of particular concern to him to find out 'to what extent Wittgenstein's conception of bringing words back to their everyday use respects the freedom or independence of his interlocutors. Is it a case of beating somebody with the stick of grammar? Or of gently leading him somewhere with his own consent?' (Baker 2004, 93).

Clearly, this way of posing the problem is partly due to Baker's overall interest in discrediting a competing approach to Wittgenstein. But, of course, the immediate context of §116b contains an element pointing in the direction indicated by Baker's reflections. The question concluding the first paragraph of §116, i.e. the formulation immediately preceding the sentence we are interested in, contains the suggestive word 'Heimat': 'is the word ever actually used in this way in the language which is its original home?'[3] To be sure, there is an associative link between the original home mentioned in §116a and the idea of being brought back to the fold accentuated in Baker's explanation of the import of 'zurückführen' in §116b. However, this associative link by no means exhausts the full meaning of Wittgenstein's German phrase. On the contrary, it tends to obscure the literal, and perhaps part of the intended, meaning of Wittgenstein's words.

One must not overlook that the relevant expression used by Wittgenstein is a complex one: 'zurückführen auf'. This phrase is typically used to express that something has been traced back to its origin or that one has succeeded in finding its basic cause, as in 'I have traced the word's development back to its roots in Latin' or 'The peculiar taste of this wine can be traced back to its having been tampered with by the vintner'. A related but distinguishable meaning of the phrase can best be rendered by the English word 'reduce'. Thus 'Wir haben die Arithmetik auf die Logik zurückgeführt' would be the German equivalent of 'We have succeeded in reducing arithmetic to logic'. If you want to express 'bringing back' in the sense suggested by Anscombe's translation or Baker's explanation, you would in many standard cases have to use a different preposition in German, e.g. 'in' or 'zu'. Wittgenstein's formulation as it stands contains various oddities which it would take a long time to make clear.[4] Suffice it to say that Wittgenstein's choice of words is idiomatically, if not grammatically, eccentric and clearly involves an expression ('zurückführen auf') which is generally associated with historical, causal or reductive explanation, and hence difficult to reconcile with Wittgenstein's view that philosophy is totally different from all kinds of *Wissenschaft*.

Part of the point I want to make by mentioning these facts of German idiom and grammar is that there is no straightforward way of penetrating or cutting through the maze constructed by Wittgenstein's seemingly simple words. I think that ultimately something to the effect of what is expressed by Anscombe's translation really is the basic content of Wittgenstein's remark, but all the same we are surely meant to bear the idea of a causal or a reductive explanation in mind. This may serve to give a special flavour to the 'metaphysical' use alluded to or simply amount to poking fun at some of Wittgenstein's pet bugbears – either reading makes sense but neither is directly borne out by Wittgenstein's actual words.

As his next step, Baker tries to achieve clarity about the contrastive pair of expressions 'metaphysical'/'everyday'. As he has reasons to mistrust the self-explanatory power of the latter expression and, at least in his own view, even stronger reasons to mistrust what he regards as a particularly widespread explanation of the expression, he turns to the former and looks at a number of passages where Wittgenstein uses the word 'metaphysics' or its cognates. The result of this investigation is summed up by saying that in Wittgenstein's texts 'the term "metaphysical" has a definite and quite traditional meaning: it belongs to a semantic field that includes "necessary," "essence" and "nature" ' (Baker 2004, 100).

In a way (leaving the word 'definite' aside), this result is unexceptionable; at the same time, however, it is neither exciting nor unexpected. Why would Wittgenstein, who for many reasons – but in particular for being able to play games with words of the kind pointed out with regard to 'zurückführen' – relies on there being at least vaguely circumscribed and accepted standard meanings of words, want to use this umbrella term in an unusual way?[5] On the other hand, there is something a little disappointing about the list supplied by Baker (2004, 96–97): the vast majority of his references are to the *Blue Book*, which of course was not written in German but dictated in English. This fact makes it a precarious source, especially if there is a largish number of passages taken from it for which there is no parallel in any of Wittgenstein's German writings.[6]

However, on the strength of his list of passages involving uses of the word 'metaphysical' and his result that Wittgenstein's own use tends to conform to tradition, Baker takes a further step by helping himself to a premise which is not obviously derivable from anything that was demonstrated, or alluded to, before. He says: 'Granted that the phrases "metaphysical use" and "everyday use" are mutually exclusive, the term "everyday" must be glossed as "non-metaphysical"' (Baker 2004, 100). But has Wittgenstein, or has Baker on Wittgenstein's behalf, said anything that would warrant granting that? Or, even more to the point, would Wittgenstein want to use these terms in a fashion that would make them mutually exclusive?

One reason to wonder about Baker's claim is the general consideration that Wittgenstein appears to have had an aversion to neat distinctions.[7] One gets the impression that once in a while he feels attracted to drawing a pat distinction, but in most cases of that kind he bothers to take it back, to relativize it or to shroud it behind a veil of further distinctions that are hard to bring into line with the original one. If this observation is correct (and I think it is), then it seems unlikely that Wittgenstein really had a very sharp distinction between two mutually exclusive terms in mind when he contrasted metaphysical and everyday uses.

The question involved in this is of general relevance, both as regards our reading of Wittgenstein's philosophical attitude and as regards the possibility of gaining insight into characteristics of his style and tone. To get closer to an answer I shall first follow Baker in doing what he calls 'textual archaeology', that is, I shall look at some earlier versions of our sentence. This will lead to a discussion of the role of context and what it may mean to take the context of a remark into consideration. Afterwards, I shall return to the question of the intended contrast to a 'metaphysical' use and try to find out whether an examination of additional passages, which were not taken into account by Baker, will help us to find an answer.

II

The first ancestor of our remark discussed by Baker is to be found in TS 213, generally called the 'Big Typescript' (BT) – a name given to it by Wittgenstein's literary executors. This is by no means the earliest version we know: that was written down on 4 February, 1931, on p. 34 of MS 110[8] and then transferred through a series of typescripts to p. 412 of the BT. The wording remained unchanged. However, while in the original manuscript source our sentence (§116b) appears as a separate remark, in the BT it is the first paragraph of a remark comprising three paragraphs:

> What we do is to bring words back from their metaphysical to their correct use in language.
> (The man who said that one cannot step into the same river twice said something wrong; one *can* step into the same river twice.)
> And this is what the solution of all philosophical difficulties looks like. Their answers, if they are correct, must be homespun and ordinary.[9] But one must look at them in the proper spirit, and then it doesn't matter. (PO, 167, 169)

In the third paragraph, three expressions were marked by a typed broken line, indicating dissatisfaction or doubt. Further changes or marks of doubt were added at an unknown later date in handwritten form. Some of them concern the marked expressions of the third paragraph. An arrow-like sign plus the words '["Schlichter Unsinn"]' indicate that a fourth paragraph was to be added to this remark, viz., the well-known sentences making up PI §119 about plain nonsense and bumps that our understanding gets by running up against the limits of language, which were to be found on p. 425 of the BT. In the earlier manuscript, the three paragraphs forming the above-quoted remark of the BT follow each other in the same order in which they occur here. In the manuscript, the four remarks preceding our sentence as well as the two remarks following the series preserved on p. 412 and quoted above were eventually transferred to another part of the BT (§48); some of them survived and became PI §435. The theme of the entire manuscript sequence is the question whether the speed of thinking and speaking results in hiding the truth from us. Our sentence has a clear reference back to the remark preceding it, where Wittgenstein contrasts our ordinary use of a word like 'escape' or 'flee' to the meaning intended by phrases like 'everything flows',[10] quoted on the same page and probably the direct motive for mentioning the alleged impossibility of stepping into the same river twice. At any rate, the manuscript remarks do have a theme; it is connected with the notion that the unstoppable passage of events, thoughts and utterances may hide the truth about things from us. No doubt this is a metaphysical notion, and our sentence summarizes the point of looking at normal (non-metaphysical) uses of our words: it helps us to see that 'nothing is hidden' (cf. PI §435).

The context of our sequence BT, 412 is quite different. The title of this three-page section of the BT is 'Where does the feeling that our grammar is fundamental come from?', and the connection with what precedes our sequence is not immediately obvious. On the other hand, the two remarks following it are clearly connected with the content of that sequence. They run as follows:

> Where do the old problems get their significance from?
>   The law of identity, for example, seemed to have fundamental significance. But now the proposition that this 'law' is nonsense has taken over this significance.[11]

Whatever way you look at this last remark, it clearly has an as it were Neurathian flavour: metaphysics and all attempts to express something metaphysical are nonsense; the feeling that a certain phrase expresses something important is no substitute for putting words together in such a way that they make sense. This would chime quite well with the remark about plain nonsense and bumps (PI §119) which Wittgenstein wanted to insert between our sequence and the two remarks following it. And if you read this back into the sentence about bringing words back from their metaphysical use, then the contrast would simply be that between important-sounding nonsense on the one hand and talking sense on the other. But if this was Wittgenstein's attitude towards metaphysics, it appears unlikely that he discriminated so finely between various aspects of metaphysics as Baker reads into the passages he relies on. However, if the term 'metaphysical use' is to wear the trousers, this notion will have to be a well-circumscribed one with a clear content; otherwise, it will not have the right kind of physiognomy to wear trousers.

There is another important feature of the text of our sentence as presented in the BT to which Baker draws our attention. While the words 'hausbacken' and 'gewöhnlich'[12] in the third paragraph of our sequence bear typed marks of doubt or dissatisfaction, the word 'richtige' in the first paragraph has a handwritten wiggly line under it and the word 'normale' written above it. So Wittgenstein had become dissatisfied with the word 'correct' and now proposed 'normal' as a possible alternative. According to Baker, this 'suggests that [Wittgenstein] starts from the word "metaphysical" and then tries to find some down-to-earth expression that means roughly "non-metaphysical" ' (Baker 2004, 100). Now, this seems to be a tendentious reading of what went on when Wittgenstein revised this part of the BT, especially in so far as it intimates that Wittgenstein had a clear and at the same time sophisticated and well-circumscribed notion of metaphysics while what he intended by 'correct' was less clear to him.

To my mind, what happened when Wittgenstein revised this passage is fairly clear and agrees with his procedure in thousands of other passages of this kind. Obviously, he was dissatisfied with the word 'richtig', and one reason for his dissatisfaction may have been the fact that this is a particularly bland word while Wittgenstein preferred more expressive, distinctive and specific words that can affect, and be affected by, the context in which they occur. Of course, 'normal' is hardly a better choice in this respect. This is the word Wittgenstein first used at the next stage of his revision of the text (in MS 142, the Urfassung of PI; see PIKr), where the next alternative submitted is the somewhat unlikely word 'practical', which suggests that he really was at a loss. Both 'normal' and 'practical' were crossed out, and 'everyday' was inserted. This may well have happened when he decided to move the paragraph that became PI §116a from the opposite page (117) to the place we are familiar with, that is, before PI §116b (116). As we have noticed earlier, 'alltäglich' fits 'Heimat' in a suggestive way; so thinking about a better place for that paragraph containing the word 'Heimat' may have suggested 'alltäglich' to replace the problematic pair of alternatives 'normal/practical'. Naturally, all of this presupposes that he was looking for a better word to contrast with 'metaphysical', but none of it requires that he had a particularly clear or well-circumscribed idea of the meaning of 'metaphysical'.

There is another aspect of the contextualization of our sentence emphasized by Baker that we have not mentioned yet. Baker draws our attention both to the remarks preceding §116b in the BT version and its continuation in the early versions of PI. The former seem of little relevance to me; the latter, however, is clearly important and of independent interest, also because it is an elaboration of our paragraph's original manuscript context. In the manuscript as well as in the early PI versions Wittgenstein goes on to talk about the alleged impossibility of stepping into the same river twice. I suppose that many readers share my feeling that this observation of Wittgenstein's is not particularly clever; moreover, it is uncharacteristically insensitive to the potential points of Heraclitus' dictum or of quoting it. Now, in the early PI versions of the list of (presumably 'metaphysical') blunders and our ('everyday', 'ordinary' or 'trivial') responses to them, the responses are supplemented by additional observations. The following is the version cited by Baker:

> (The person who said that one cannot step twice into the same river said something false; one *can* step twice into the same river. – And an object sometimes ceases to exist if I cease to see it, and sometimes not. – And we *do know* sometimes what colour another sees, and sometimes not.) (Baker 2004, 101, 102; TS 220 §111 (p. 89))

Baker stresses the function of the many modal terms occurring here, but I cannot believe that this is Wittgenstein's point: it would amount to the 'insensitive' sort of reply criticized above in simply contradicting the metaphysical pronouncements, even if the contradictions sound less doctrinaire than the pronouncements. I think that the point of adding new items to the list of anti-metaphysical replies was to drive home the jocular character of the enterprise; after all, telling a metaphysician that sometimes he will be right and sometimes wrong is a deliberate misunderstanding of what he strives to express and the urgency he wishes to bestow on this expression.

Wittgenstein admits as much when he crosses out the original words 'But one must look at [our replies] in the proper spirit, and then it [their ordinariness and triviality] does not matter' and replaces them by the words 'For these replies as it were poke fun at the [philosophical, metaphysical]¹³ question' (MS 142, §128 [130], TS 220, §111 [113]). In the next version (TS 239) he adds a qualification by saying that explanations rendering philosophical (metaphysical) questions intelligible behave differently, that is, they do not ridicule philosophical (metaphysical) questions. At this point Wittgenstein must have noticed that the whole continuation of our §116b was hopeless – it was neither funny nor particularly enlightening. So he crossed it out, and all that remained of what was then §126 of the *Investigations* was our sentence §116b, which only at the next stage of textual revision (in the so-called 'intermediate' version) was joined to §116a. The emphasis on 'We', by the way, was added in the last typescript, and that in only one of the two extant copies of TS 227; hence it may be of dubious authenticity.

A description of Wittgenstein's use of personal pronouns would surely deserve a chapter of its own. It is remarkable how easily he moves from the impersonal 'one' or the personal 'you' to 'I' or 'we' or 'he' etc. without arousing any suspicion on the part of his readers. But as soon as one pays attention to these changes one may well become puzzled, and sometimes irritated, as one finds it increasingly difficult to identify the person or group of people ostensibly referred to by Wittgenstein's pronouns. To mention just one striking example: in PI §120 he oscillates between 'I', 'we', 'you' and 'one' (in her translation Anscombe uses the impersonal 'you'). At the same time, the dialogical structure of the exchange reproduced in the first five paragraphs is quite clear.

What is much less clear are many other occurrences of the first person plural pronoun 'we'. In several of the remarks PI §§89ff. 'we' seems to refer to the author of the *Tractatus*, but at other times (e.g. §90b: 'Our investigation is therefore a grammatical one') it evidently refers to Wittgenstein's later self. What is decidedly odd is that Wittgenstein manages to use this form without sounding in the least pompous ('royal plural') or stilted (as in certain scholarly texts – 'As we remarked in footnote 7 on p. 659 of our work on . . .'). Still, certain juxtapositions can seem surprising. Think of the sequence §115: 'A *picture* held us captive . . .', §116a: 'When philosophers use a word . . .', §116b: 'What we do . . .' followed by a curiously impersonal formulation (§117): 'Man sagt mir' – 'Someone tells me'. Here the first 'we' clearly refers to the author of the *Tractatus*[14] and, perhaps, to other philosophers like him (or to later selves), while the second 'we' (in §116) seems to draw a line between 'philosophers' on the one hand and 'us' on the other, which gives the impression that 'we' are *not* philosophers. Of course, this would be a strange thing to say in a context where Wittgenstein tells us, among other things, how to do philosophy. There is something *obviously* odd about this contrast; so it may be advisable to take the apparent statement introduced by 'we' with a pinch of salt. Perhaps 'we' are not so different from those 'philosophers', after all.

III

Our discussion has shown that as regards this sort of question it is generally important and useful to take the context of the relevant phrase or remark into account. There may, however, be different ways of specifying a context; and different kinds of context may give rise to different questions and different answers to these questions. In many cases the differences between various kinds of context will be obvious and easy to see, but occasionally it will be useful to pay attention to these divergences or to insist on the value of looking at a particular kind of context.

The first kind of context are the words in the immediate vicinity of the phrase or remark under discussion. Here it is important to remember the distinction between *remarks* (in the technical sense of this word) and *paragraphs* within a remark. In Wittgenstein's manuscripts a remark is generally separated from other ones by a blank line before and after. A new paragraph within a remark is indicated by an indentation (without a blank line). In his typescripts Wittgenstein tends to follow the same convention, but in addition he often numbers his remarks (but not paragraphs within a remark) in the way readers know from the example of the *Investigations*.

If one tries to trace the history of individual remarks (not necessarily in the technical sense of that term), one will often notice that what used to be a separate remark (in the technical sense) has later become a paragraph within a larger remark, or vice versa. Sometimes paragraphs or entire remarks are joined to form a new, more comprehensive, paragraph; in such cases Wittgenstein often places a dash (in some cases a particularly long dash) where the line between different paragraphs used to be. It is clear that it is important for readers to pay attention to these different lines of separation (dash, new paragraph, new remark) as they represent Wittgenstein's own ways of signalling what to count as the immediate context of a given phrase or thought.

These, however, were not Wittgenstein's only means of indicating and separating the immediate context of his remarks. He often used marginal signs to designate whether he was satisfied or dissatisfied with or in doubt about what he had written or that he felt uneasy about its location. Normally, such marginal signs refer to remarks, but where they are used to comment on paragraphs this may be taken to show that Wittgenstein has changed his mind about the closeness of the link between those paragraphs. Another sign used by Wittgenstein to indicate context or, rather, separation from what seems to be context are vertical strokes placed before and after a remark or paragraph to signal that the text between these strokes is not continuous with what goes on on the rest of the page.[15] At the same time the occurrence of these strokes may occasionally be taken to reveal that the parts of text outside – before and after – the strokes are closely connected and may hence be seen as forming an immediate context.

Whilst identification of this kind of context tends to be unproblematic and uncontroversial, the second type of context I wish to distinguish is much more difficult to pinpoint. What I mean may perhaps be called the visible context of composition: it comprises, first, the page or pages of the manuscript book visible to Wittgenstein while he was actually working on certain remarks and, second, pages from other manuscripts or typescripts he is certain or likely to have had open on his desk when writing a given passage. An example of the first kind was mentioned earlier in this paper where I talked about Wittgenstein's decision to move the text of PI §116a from the right hand page of his manuscript book to the left hand page before what became §116b. I also suggested that this decision may have influenced his choice of the word 'everyday'. At any rate, it can evidently be quite instructive to look at what Wittgenstein is likely to have seen while working on his remarks, and to do so may sometimes help to explain surprising choices of words or illustrations.

Of course, examples of the second kind will often be a matter of speculation unless we are dealing with one of those not very infrequent cases where Wittgenstein himself made explicit reference to other manuscripts or typescripts. A fairly clear and often impressive case is the use Wittgenstein made of his pocket notebooks 157a and 157b when composing the Urfassung of the *Investigations*. An example I have discussed elsewhere is Wittgenstein's use of the expression 'pneumatic conception' in PI §109, which was surely influenced by his perusal of one of those notebooks. An equally interesting example is his use of the expression 'Vorurteil' ('prejudice', 'preconceived ideas') in the sentence before the one mentioning the 'pneumatic conception'. As a matter of fact, this may well be a mixed case: on the one hand, when he was writing down what became PI §109 (and the remark before that) he probably had both notebooks (157a and b) in front of him. There he could see the word 'Vorurteil' underlined on a page he had just used in writing down what became §108a. Most of this paragraph containing the underlined word 'Vorurteil' can be found on the same page as §109, so it is likely that the Vorurteil mentioned in §109 is the same as the one talked about in §108. This spatial proximity, which at the same time may be a proximity of thought, is obscured, not only by the fact that in the English edition of the *Investigations* §108 happens to be on the page before §109 (and hence out of readers' sight), but also by the circumstance that the editors took the perhaps erroneous decision to print the content of a loose sheet of paper as §108b-d, thus separating by twelve lines of text and an unhappily placed footnote (quoting Faraday) what used to be, and were probably intended to be, two contiguous paragraphs (even though separate remarks).[16]

A third kind of context, whose identification is particularly relevant when studying Wittgenstein's manuscripts (as opposed to his typescripts), is the 'diurnal context', i.e. the context of remarks written on the same day as the one(s) under discussion. Since Wittgenstein frequently, but by no means always, noted down the date of composition, identification of this sort of context is quite easy in a great number of cases. It can be of interest for various reasons, most of them connected with the fact that what Wittgenstein wrote in one sitting tends to be part of one train of thought or one chain of associations. Thus you will often find him using one colour-word ('red' or 'yellow' etc.) on one day and another colour-word on another day. (Noticing this may be important when confronted with the question whether a change of example is likely to be relevant or irrelevant to the philosophical point in question.)

Or take an example mentioned above, PI §120. The six paragraphs forming this remark were written down on a single day (29 June, 1931) in the same order in which they are given in PI and only twice interspersed with short remarks that were not used in later versions. As observed above, the dialogical structure of the first five paragraphs (§120a-e) shows that they are closely connected and how they are connected. On the other hand, paragraph f (culminating in a comparison between words and money – money and cow vs. money and use) is not obviously connected with the paragraphs preceding it. This is especially so in the German original, where Wittgenstein changes pronouns and introduces the impersonal form 'man' that was not used before. But the fact that in the first manuscript these paragraphs were written in the same order and in one sitting makes it particularly urgent to look for a uniting thread running through the whole sequence of paragraphs – an urgency that might be absent or felt in a different way if we were unaware of this fact.

A fourth kind of context is the context of the 'chapter'. Of course, except for the BT, none of Wittgenstein's manuscripts and typescripts has actually been divided into chapters by the author himself. But as commentators have shown, this kind of division is possible and useful in the case of the *Tractatus* and the *Investigations* and, to a much smaller extent, also in the case of a few further writings. If you read PI §89ff. basically as a discussion of themes connected with the *Tractatus*, you will understand a number of remarks quite differently from someone who regards the apparent references to the early work as purely external and more or less irrelevant to the argumentative core of this sequence of remarks.

This is one kind of importance of the chapter context. In the case of the BT, on the other hand, which really was divided into titled chapters and sections by Wittgenstein himself, the matter is quite different. Here readers will often wonder why on earth Wittgenstein put the remarks he assembled into one and the same chapter and why he did so under the title he gave it. Let us take the example of our remark §116b. Baker takes the chapter context in the BT very seriously and prints the relevant passage as follows:

> Where does this observation get its importance from: the one that points out to us that a table **can** be used in more than one way, that one **can** think up a table that instructs one as to the use of a table, that one **can** also conceive of an arrow as pointing from the tip to the tail, that I **can** use a model as a model in different ways?
>   What we do is to bring words back from their metaphysical to their // correct//normal// use in (the) language. (Baker 2004, 101)[17]

Baker then goes on to say:

> Is the second paragraph not meant to be a straightforward description of the tactics illustrated in the first? The series of statements highlighting 'can' are evidently to be understood as antitheses to statements framed with 'cannot'. It is the presence of these modal qualifications that make those (implicit) theses *metaphysical* uses of words. The denial of these 'cannot's is precisely what makes the antitheses everyday or *normal* uses of the very same words. (Baker 2004, 101)

Now, this is certainly quite ingenious and additionally supported by leaving out the separating blank line between those two remarks as well as the preceding remark[18] (which provides a more natural context for the first one) and highlighting all those **can**'s. But if you tend to be struck by the *lack* of organization of many chapters and sections of the BT, the proximity of those remarks may fail to impress you. You will then wonder why Wittgenstein placed these remarks next to each other, and one possible answer would be related to but not the same as Baker's: seeing the possibility of reading a table or interpreting a sign in a different fashion from the usual one is in a way similar to noticing that you understand the phrase 'same river' in more than one way and that in one of those senses you *can* actually step into the same river twice. That would connect the first remark quoted by Baker, not with the content of §116b, but with the second paragraph of the BT sequence ['(The man who said . . .)', quoted above, p. 150]. This is surely not the only way of finding a connecting link between these remarks. But my basic point here was that different ways of understanding the chapter context will considerably affect one's reading of individual remarks.

The fifth (and last) type of context I want to distinguish is the overall, or project, context. This refers to the general question 'What was Wittgenstein up to in this manuscript or typescript?' or, more generally still, 'What was he up to at the time of writing this?' Perhaps one would at first want to distinguish between philosophical and stylistic aspects of this question but ultimately, I think, there is no clear way of keeping these aspects separate: asking what he wanted to say shades into asking why he said what he did say the way he said it. And helpful answers to these questions will not respect supposed boundaries between those aspects either. In the light of enquiring after the overall context of what Wittgenstein wrote in the BT, for instance, we may wonder if a determinate and well-circumscribed notion of metaphysics could be seen to play a useful role in terms of the project of that typescript. Naturally, there is no straightforward project description to be found in any of his writings.[19] On the other hand, the general question 'What was his project in writing this?' and the question 'Can concept X be seen to play a useful role in terms of that project?' can sometimes be asked in tandem, and it may be practicable to ask them in such a way that a rough answer can be given to both. One possibility of approaching this pair of questions is by way of exploring Wittgenstein's use of crucial terms, especially those that may be found relevant in the course of looking into questions of the second type, i.e. questions involving the role potentially played by apparently crucial concepts.

Of course, this is not the place to try to be even approximately exhaustive about this sort of question. But I think that a few examples will serve to show what kind of consideration may be helpful and, in particular, how looking into the details of Wittgenstein's use of words may assist us in our attempts at getting a grip on what his project was in working on certain texts.

IV

In Wittgenstein's extant writings one will find four or five dozen really different remarks involving the word 'metaphysics' or its cognates (there is a fair number of repetitions of many of these remarks).[20] The greatest concentration of such remarks can be found in the *Blue Book* (9 remarks). There may be various reasons for that. Perhaps the occasion – dictating a kind of summary of his views to students – demanded a more graphic setting up of contrasts than he required in his manuscript writings. Several of the points he tends to make in connection with metaphysics are in other contexts made in speaking of 'philosophy' (cf. note 13). After all, sometimes he did talk about philosophy in a way which suggests that he wanted to wash his hands of the business.

There are two obvious and supplementary ways of dealing with Baker's claim that in PI §116b (and other remarks of a similar kind) the word 'metaphysics' wears the trousers. The first one consists in considering features frequently or emphatically connected with that term and partial or near synonyms if there are any. The second consists in looking for notions explicitly or implicitly contrasted with that term and near antonyms if any can be found. Baker, in his article (96–100), mentions four more or less general features associated by Wittgenstein with his notion of metaphysics. The first feature is the use of expressions of necessity and impossibility (e.g. 'must' and 'cannot'). The second is the use of words without antitheses. The third feature is the making of non-scientific statements exhibiting the form of scientific explanations. The fourth feature is the occurrence of statements about word-use making reference to the alleged nature or essence of things.

I think that Baker is basically right about these things, although I am not sure about the importance of the first feature, nor about the significance of speaking of the 'form' of scientific explanations. But it seems that there are various further features that tend to be associated with metaphysics. To enumerate just a few: inconceivability of the opposite (MS 114, 124, TS 213 [BT], 97v), nontemporality (MS 116, 117), similarity with striving for metalogical or metapsychological accounts (MS 148, 32r, TS 213 [BT], 1).

Of course, Wittgenstein also uses the term 'metaphysics' as an equivalent, or near-equivalent, of a certain kind of 'nonsense' or 'illusion'. The *Tractatus* provides what is surely the best-known instance of this use (6.53), but there are further examples in his later writings that go in the same direction (cf. MS 114, 133, MS 179, 35v, MS 142, §126 [128]).[21] These expressions of a straightforward and at the same time fairly undiscriminating anti-metaphysical attitude accord well with the following battle-cry noted down in June 1931: 'We chase metaphysics out from all its hiding-places' (MS 110, 194). In particular, they harmonize with the fact that Wittgenstein tends to use as antonyms of the term 'metaphysics' two or three expressions that are clearly seen in a positive light. In more than one passage of his writings does Wittgenstein contrast metaphysics with common sense ('gesunder Menschenverstand': MS 120, 68, MS 151, 44), and he leaves no doubt about it that common sense is a good thing while metaphysics exists owing to a dangerous tendency of the philosophical mind:[22] he complains about the difficulty of sticking with common sense, that is, 'to say nothing about the use of a word but what is obvious while at the same time casting light on every corner' (MS 120, 68v). Another contrast invoked several times is that with grammar (or 'Sprachkritik', MS 132, 8, quoted below); and it goes without saying that grammar is in Wittgenstein's good books. I do not want to claim that Wittgenstein had one clear view of grammar, but there can be no doubt that for a few years in the 1930s the idea of grammar was at least a partially defining mark of his overall project. Both passages from MS 120 alluded to just now make the contrast with grammar explicit. Some further passages (and among them are a few of those mentioned by Baker) draw on typically 'grammatical' features, e.g. the lack of contrast or 'antitheses' characterizing certain metaphysical uses of words.

These considerations should suffice to show that PI §116b as well as most passages relevant to it can be understood without assuming that it is the term 'metaphysics' which wears the trousers.[23] There are, however, a few passages in Wittgenstein's writings invoking uses of the term 'metaphysics' etc. that are not covered by any of the contrasts we have considered so far. While I do not believe that these uses exemplify an independent meaning of 'metaphysics', allowing for certain nuances of the tone and colouring displayed by these uses may inspire us to additional reflections upon passages like PI §116b in this new light. And it may well be that this sort of reflection will lead us to see that Baker, in drawing our attention to the significance of 'metaphysical', was right in a way not anticipated by himself: perhaps there really are essential shades of the meaning of 'metaphysical' that are not exhausted by what the contrasts with common sense, grammar, everyday use etc. seem to suggest.

The first passage I want to mention is the following one, which was written down in November 1948:

Strangely enough, [Wilhelm] Busch's drawings may often be termed 'metaphysical'. Thus, there is a way of drawing which is metaphysical.[24] – One might say, 'This is seen against the background of the eternal'. This, however, is something those strokes can mean only in a whole language. And it is a language without a grammar; one could not specify its rules. (MS 137, 88b (4.11.1948)/CV, 143)[25]

Obviously, this is an interesting remark, also as regards what it says or implies about language, grammar and rules. Here, however, I shall focus on Wittgenstein's use of the term 'metaphysical'. To make sense of this remark you will have to have seen drawings by Wilhelm Busch. In German-speaking lands these drawings from the second half of the nineteenth century used to be immensely popular, and to some extent they still are part of the intellectual world most German-speaking people grow up in. Many of these cartoons belong to longish series of pictures-cum-verses telling the stories of eccentric or nasty characters, stock figures or animals. Many of the situations described are tragicomic, some are cruel, none is straightforwardly happy. Often Busch's pictures and his poetry have been associated with Schopenhauer's pessimism, and a good portion of the latter's disillusioned wisdom can certainly be found in Busch's drawings.

Now, what can be meant by a 'metaphysical' way of drawing? The only hint we are given seems to lie in Wittgenstein's pointing out that one might say, 'This is seen against the background of the eternal'. Given the lack or extreme sketchiness of background in Busch's drawings this hint cannot be intended to underline a feature of the pictures themselves, nor is it likely to be meant to bring out the timelessness of the scenes depicted. I can think of no other solution than this: that by referring to what is eternal, Wittgenstein wants to say that these drawings, by being executed a certain way, manage to evoke in us something that is not clearly present in these pictures regarded by themselves. Perhaps one might even say that, by way of negation, they intimate that despite a certain desolateness of the stories told there is still hope – surely not for a better world but maybe for just punishment, maybe for redemption. This is no doubt a speculative reading of Wittgenstein's words, but it may none the less succeed in conveying one facet of the meaning of 'metaphysical' that Wittgenstein had in mind.

The second and perhaps even more intriguing passage I want to mention was written in August 1946 and runs as follows:

Love for cruelty involves something approaching an artist's love for the eerie, the as it were paradoxical, form of the deed. What is horrible, for instance, is lent a tinge of the ridiculous. And thereby it is so to speak lent a metaphysical kind of horribleness, something eerie.

A murder committed with irony will in its victim set something in motion which is quite different from what is aroused by a murder committed in wrath or desperation. (MS 130, 273)[26]

Perhaps the most striking feature of this remark is the fantastic mixture of seemingly disparate elements: love and cruelty (the phrase 'Liebe zur Grausamkeit' must be the fruit of a very deliberate choice of words), art and eeriness, the horrible and the ridiculous, murder, wrath and desperation. Moreover, in this passage Wittgenstein himself uses the two words which may be central to every promising attempt at characterizing what it is about, viz. the words 'paradox' and 'irony'. Only that these words appear in odd combinations: it is the *form of the deed* which is called paradoxical, and it is claimed of a *murder* that it might be committed with irony. In the midst of this bewildering hotchpotch the notion of metaphysics is used to clarify the idea of eeriness, where metaphysical horror seems to result from adding a dose of ridiculousness to ordinary horror. The basic idea appears to be that pondering on a mixture of certain extreme and apparently divergent feelings may lead to the possibility of entertaining a new and intensified quality of feeling: real eeriness. The essential intensification involved in this is due to the paradoxical combination of otherwise incongruous features. To exaggerate just a little: the horrible and the ridiculous may under certain conditions add up to something metaphysical.

Admittedly, this is a bit vague, but in its very vagueness it seems to provide a quite natural bridge to the last passage I want to quote. This is actually a fairly well-known quotation, belonging to a sequence of remarks inspired by Wittgenstein's reading of Frazer's *Golden Bough*. In this context Wittgenstein writes: 'I now believe that it would be right to begin my book with remarks about metaphysics as a kind of magic.'[27] He emphasizes that while he should not ridicule magic he must not plead its case either. What he wants to retain of magic (and, by implication, of metaphysics) is its 'depth' – an idea which is given a characteristic twist in the *Investigations* (§111), where he talks of the depth of grammatical jokes and says that this is the same as philosophical depth. In earlier and much longer versions of this remark he mentions specific 'grammatical' jokes told by Lichtenberg or Lewis Carroll (see MS 142, §§111 (113) ff.). He is fascinated by the idea that the neutralization of magic (metaphysics) has itself the character of magic (metaphysics). What he seems to have in mind is what Frazer calls 'homoeopathic' magic, a set of techniques for driving out, neutralizing or eliminating like by like (cf. 'The magic in *Alice in Wonderland*: of drying out by reading the driest thing there is' (PO, 129)). In the context of this sequence of remarks Wittgenstein elaborates on the similarities between magical practices and metaphysical, or at any rate philosophical, procedures. A particularly enlightening example is the resemblance of magical practices of the voodoo kind or burning in effigy to philosophical ideas of representation – and the *Tractatus* principle of *Stellvertretung* is by no means the only case in point that could be mentioned here.

It is clear that all those magical practices of identification, personification or invocation have strict parallels in philosophical theories of all kinds. What becomes obvious and may at the same time be perplexing is, as Wittgenstein stresses, the fact that magical practices, procedures and rituals correspond to deep-seated inclinations of the human mind. And here, one may feel, there could be a deep reason for Baker's claim that it is the term 'metaphysics' which wears the trousers: the metaphysical tendency, as opposed to common sense or the grammatical attitude or a philosophical notion of our everyday use, appears to be deeply rooted in human nature, in our instincts and inclinations. But perhaps one ought not to be too sanguine about that: after all, Wittgenstein himself wonders whether doing philosophy does not 'continuously oscillate between metaphysics and a critique of language' (MS 132, 8). If this is right, it would count in favour of thinking that, besides our metaphysical instinct, we also have a critical instinct, an instinct driving us to bring words back from their metaphysical to their everyday use.

Notes

1   Austin 1962, 70–71 (section VII). Austin's example is the word 'real': 'But with "real" [. . .] it is the *negative* use that wears the trousers. That is, a definite sense attaches to the assertion that something is real, a real such-and-such, only in the light of a specific way in which it might be, or might have been, *not* real.'

2   Cf., however, what is said on p. 153 about the history of this emphasis.

3   Baker avoids actually quoting Anscombe's extremely free but presumably defensible translation '. . . in the language-game which is its original home'. In the following I consult existing translations, but whenever it suits my purpose I modify or ignore them without explicitly drawing the reader's attention to this fact.

4   Thus, in standard German, one reading of the sentence would run: '*Wir* führen die metaphysische Verwendung der Wörter wieder auf ihre alltägliche zurück' (where 'wieder' sounds strange while Wittgenstein's own use of 'von' is grammatically odd if the 'trace back'/'reduce' sense of 'zurückführen' is in question).

5　As a matter of fact he does so use it, but not in this type of context. See below, section IV.

6　To mention a well-known example of non-parallelism: In the *Blue Book* (BB) Wittgenstein draws a distinction between 'object' and 'subject' uses of the word 'I'. But, as far as I know, there is no parallel to this distinction to be found in Wittgenstein's other writings. (MS 147, 26r has the words '"Ich" als Subjekt & als Objekt', but this jotting is evidently closely connected with the dictation of the BB, and thus does not constitute an independent parallel.) I myself find that distinction hard to reconcile with Wittgenstein's more clearly articulated view, and one reason why I am in doubt about it is its very patness.

7　Of course, Wittgenstein does occasionally draw neat distinctions, but much more frequently does he seem to be concerned to avoid or qualify them. Cf. what I said about the BB distinction between 'subject' and 'object' uses of 'I' in note 6. Another kind of example of Wittgenstein's anxiety to avoid a certain sort of neatness of formulation is his decision not to use 'Worüber man nicht reden kann, darüber muß man schweigen' with its too obvious parallelism (*worüber – darüber*) as the last sentence of the *Tractatus* (cf. Brian McGuinness, "Some Pre-*Tractatus* Manuscripts", in his 2002, 268).

8　There may well have been earlier versions, e.g. in a lost pocket notebook, but none has survived.

9　Variant (handwritten): 'Our answers, if they are correct, must be ordinary and trivial.'

10　Cf. PR, 84–85, where Wittgenstein observes that 'everything flows' cannot be *said* for the reason that uttering these words would be an attempt at describing a feature of the essence of the world.

11　The German original reads as follows: 'Woher nehmen die alten philosophischen Probleme ihre Bedeutung? / Der Satz der Identität z. B. schien eine fundamentale Bedeutung zu haben. Aber der Satz, dass dieser "Satz" ein Unsinn ist, hat diese Bedeutung übernommen.'

12　Which of course belong to the same spectrum of meanings as 'richtige' in the first paragraph.

13　There is in Wittgenstein's writings a certain use of the word 'philosophy' ('philosophical', etc.) which is not clearly distinguishable from a use he makes of the word 'metaphysics' (etc.). One can find a number of passages where these two words could be used interchangeably. In MS 110, 220 he crosses out the words 'Zusammenhang der Metaphysik mit der Magie' ('connection of metaphysics with magic') and replaces them by 'nach der alten Auffassung – etwa der der großen westlichen Philosophen –' ('according to the old view – e.g. that held by the great Western philosophers –'). In MS 115, 190 (EPB, 169, cf. BB, 117) he uses the phrase 'metaphysischer Unterschied' and then goes on to speak of the senselessness of 'many general philosophical principles'. And in the BB (p. 48) he wonders whether our belief in another person's being in pain is 'a philosophical, a metaphysical belief'.

14   As Peter Hacker points out, originally the *Urfassung* of this passage had 'Das *Bild* hielt mich gefangen.' It is interesting to speculate about Wittgenstein's possible motives for this change of formulation. Cf. Baker and Hacker 2005, Part II, 251 (with reference to §115).

15   A number of these remarks can be found in *Culture and Value*. An example will be discussed below (see the remark from MS 137 mentioning the drawings of Wilhelm Busch).

16   For more information, see PIKr, 142–3, and Schulte 2006, which owes a lot to an unpublished piece by Brian McGuinness on what Wittgenstein owed to Sraffa.

17   I have modified the translation slightly to bring it in line with the remark preceding the quoted ones.

18   This remark, which later came to form the first two sentences of PI §118, begins with the very same words as the remark quoted by Baker: 'Where does this investigation get its importance from, since it seems only to destroy everything interesting, that is, all that is great and important? (As it were all the buildings, leaving behind only bits of stone and rubble.)'

19   Of course, his prefaces are quite revealing, but one would not want to call them 'straightforward' descriptions of what he wanted to do.

20   The most frequently repeated remark was written on 23 August, 1930; it figures in much truncated form in BT §43 (p. 183), and ends up in Geach's arrangement of fragments (*Zettel*), where it appears as an uninspiring statement to the effect that 'Like everything metaphysical the harmony between thought and reality is to be found in the grammar of the language' (§55). The first version was actually quite interesting in speaking, not only of a harmony, but of a *pre-established* harmony between thought and reality and claiming that this metaphysical harmony was due, not to grammar, but to the *limit of language* (MS 109, 31).

21   'This kind of illusion is expressed by the metaphysical use of our words.' This is followed by words well-known from PI §104: 'For one predicates of the thing what lies in the way of representing it. We take what strikes us as a possible comparison for a perception of an highly general state of affairs.' It was only in the final version of PI that the first sentence was crossed out and the rest of the remark transferred to its present position. The word 'denn' (in 'Denn man prädiziert von der Sache . . .') was dropped when Wittgenstein revised the first typescript of the early version of PI.

22   Oskari Kuusela begins his paper 'From Metaphysics and Philosophical Theses to Grammar: Wittgenstein's Turn' (Kuusela 2005) with the following quotation which highlights what Wittgenstein regarded as a menacing aspect of metaphysics: 'In philosophizing the greatest danger threatening the mind arises from that metaphysical tendency which takes hold of the mind and

completely displaces the grammatical tendency' (MS 120, 136v).

23   If one takes 'grammar' as the paradigmatic term, Wittgenstein's choice of the word '*richtig*' ('correct') in the MS 110 and BT precursors of PI §116b seems apt enough. As these issues are complicated anyway and as additional complications are brought in by quoting passages written at different times of Wittgenstein's life, this may be a good place to indicate my own position on three interconnected points: (1) I agree that assimilating Wittgenstein's thought to an ordinary-language position as characterized by Baker tends to be misleading. However, as I have said above, I am not sure if Baker's characterization does justice to the thought of philosophers like Austin or Ryle – but that is a problem which need not bother us here. (2) There is no way of giving a succinct account of what Wittgenstein said or implied about grammar in his manuscripts written between the early 1930s and his last notebooks. At many places of the earlier writings it is important to distinguish between 'grammar' in the sense of an envisaged philosophical enterprise of analyzing and tabulating the meanings of linguistic expressions and their interrelations on the one hand and 'grammar' in the sense of a structured network of rules shaping language and its 'logic' on the other. (For the notion of grammar, cf. various passages in VW, e.g. the section of the justification of grammar, 232ff.) Especially in Wittgenstein's writings from the early 1930s, grammar in the second sense is frequently alluded to and the idea informs a large part of Wittgenstein's thought during that period. It is not difficult to see, however, that this notion of grammar can reveal itself as a highly metaphysical one by Wittgenstein's usual standards. Many later criticisms of metaphysical views can be seen to apply to his own earlier views on grammar. I have discussed this difficult point in various papers, e.g. in the above-mentioned piece on the 'pneumatic conception' (see above, n. 16) and in Schulte 2006a. (3) There is a point I have deliberately refrained from mentioning in the body of this paper, as it would require a very involved discussion of various questions. This is connected with the fact that Wittgenstein's word for 'use' in §116b is not '*Gebrauch*' but '*Verwendung*'. It stands to reason that terminologically different translations of these words (e.g. 'employment' vs. 'use') might have been helpful. There are connotations of '*Verwendung*' which are not expressed by standard uses of '*Gebrauch*', but the matter is so uncertain that I should not want to rest my case on differences in shades of meaning normally attributed to these words. It is, however, extremely important to remember that an everyday employment of a certain word need not be one of its standard uses (as specified in a dictionary entry, for example). There may be everyday employments (e.g. in religious rituals, jokes, teaching situations, songs or poems, etc.) that would strike us as at least as strange or non-standard as certain metaphysical employments. I think this is a significant point but it is not addressed in Baker's article, nor in my own observations.

24 Perhaps this should in effect read: 'Does this mean that there is a metaphysical way of drawing?'

25 The German original reads as follows: 'Es ist merkwürdig, daß man die Zeichnungen von Busch oft "metaphysisch" nennen kann. So gibt es also eine Zeichenweise, die metaphysisch ist. – "Gesehen, mit dem Ewigen als Hintergrund" könnte man sagen. Aber doch *bedeuten* diese Striche das nur in einer ganzen Sprache. Und es ist eine Sprache ohne Grammatik, man könnte ihre Regeln nicht angeben.'

26 The German original reads as follows: 'Die Liebe zur Grausamkeit schließt auch eine beinahe künstlerische Liebe zur unheimlichen, gleichsam paradoxen, Form der Tat ein. Was grauenhaft ist, erhält z. B. einen Anstrich des Lächerlichen. Und erhält dadurch sozusagen noch ein metaphysisches Grauen, das Unheimliche. | Ein Mord, der mit Ironie begangen wird, setzt im Opfer noch ganz anderes in Bewegung als einer, der im Zorn oder in der Verzweiflung geschieht.' Rush Rhees has an interesting report of a conversation with Wittgenstein in the course of which the latter tried to imagine what it might be like to commit a series of murders in a state of extreme despair. See Rhees ed. 1984, 176.

27 'Remarks on Frazer's *Golden Bough*', in PO, 116. The German original was written down on 19 June, 1931. The passage reads: 'Ich glaube jetzt, daß es richtig wäre, mein Buch mit Bemerkungen über die Metaphysik als eine Art von Magie zu beginnen' (MS 110, 177).

Chapter 6

Metaphysical/Everyday Use: A Note on a Late Paper by Gordon Baker

Hilary Putnam

In "Wittgenstein on Metaphysical/Everyday Use" (reprinted as Chapter 4 in Baker 2004),[1] after giving a "representative sample" (96) of uses of "metaphysical" by Wittgenstein, Gordon Baker tells us (97) that "There is no single pattern visible in all these cases, but several patterns seem immediately evident[.]" He lists four:

1   "*Expressions of necessity and impossibility*, statements that feature 'must' and 'cannot'." (97–98)
2   "The use of words *without antitheses* If every word in the language *must* be a name then there is no such thing as a word's *not* being a *name*, or if every (real) *pain* is mine, then there is no such thing as a pain being *yours*." (98. Baker's emphasis in all these examples)
3   "*Non-scientific* statements having the *form* of *scientific* explanations (theories): formulations of essences often take the form of simple formulae giving definitive answers to questions of the form 'What is . . .?'" (98)
4   "Statements about word-use giving *explanations grounded in the natures* of things: For example, it looks to us as if we were saying something about the **nature** of red in saying that the words 'Red exists' do not yield a sense." (99. Bold font in original – this font seems to be used by Baker for extra emphasis.)

After giving the above list (which I have shortened only by omitted further examples and explanations of each of the four), Baker concludes that:

The outcome of this investigation seems clear. Within the corpus of Wittgenstein's texts, the term 'metaphysical' has a definite and quite traditional
meaning; it belongs to a semantic field that includes 'necessary', 'essence',
and 'nature'. More precisely, the four features just listed seem to characterize various instances of what Wittgenstein picks out as 'metaphysical statements' or 'metaphysical uses of words'. (The textual evidence does not
support any distinction in meaning between these two phrases.) In this way,
he focuses attention on a tolerably well-defined family of propositions
having various definite and interrelated characteristics. The most conspicu-
ous is their containing expressions of modality. But whether or not they
contain 'must' or 'cannot', they are to be understood as stating necessities
and impossibilities. (100)

Here Baker fleshes out his claim that, in the antithesis "metaphysical/
everyday use," it is the term "metaphysical" that does the real work by
giving us what amounts to *an essentialist account of metaphysics* – or at
least he attributes such an account to Wittgenstein.

To see how Baker's interpretation of Wittgenstein's later philosophy
works, we must, however, also see how Baker thinks Wittgenstein would
typically go about treating confusions which are "metaphysical" in the
sense Baker attributes to him. Baker seems to list only two approaches in
"Wittgenstein on Metaphysical/Everyday Use." The first is to show that
the supposed "necessity" arises in the mind of the philosopher because
he has been so struck by a picture, one which indeed "fits" *some* cases,
that he has acquired a compulsion to force it onto *all* cases. (An example
Baker gives from Wittgenstein MS 113, 115: "I *can always only* conjecture
the/a/ cause" (97).) At this point the philosopher who is in the grip of
this picture will begin to use the "expressions of modality" of which Baker
speaks (e.g. "can always only"). The second is to show that the philosopher has confused a conceptual with a scientific investigation. (Wittgenstein says, in a passage cited by Baker, that "The essential thing about
metaphysics: that the difference between factual and conceptual investigations is not clear to it. A metaphysical question is always **in appearance**
a factual one, although the problem is a conceptual one." (RPPi §949;
Baker's emphasis; cf. BB, 35). In this connection, Baker also quotes,
"Philosophers [. . .] are irresistibly tempted to ask and answer questions
in the way that science does. This tendency is the real source of metaphysics" (BB, 18; Baker's emphasis). The therapy recommended by Baker
is to "investigate how we use *words*" (99). I am not sure whether Baker's
advice to avoid asking certain questions is part of this advice or a sort of
preventive therapy:

Being advised by [Wittgenstein] to avoid asking the question, '*What is* a proposition?' (PI §92), we should presumably take him to avoid asking such questions as '*What is* the meaning of a word?', or '*What is* following a rule?', and equally to avoid giving answers that formulate the *essences* of these things. (103)

Baker's example of what happens when one fails to follow this advice is interesting, and important for our examination of his interpretation. He writes (103):

> Is it reasonable for us to interpret [Wittgenstein] as asserting, 'The meaning of a word **really is** its use in the language' (PI §43), or 'Following a rule **must** be a social practice (*custom*)' (PI §199)? The philosopher who makes such claims (allegedly on Wittgenstein's authority!) is apparently using words while trying to grasp the *essence* of the things. Thereby he himself makes a *metaphysical* use of words; and his example serves as a paradigm of 'The dogmatism that we so easily fall into in doing philosophy'. (PI §131)

A remark about this charge that Baker here makes so briefly against the many Wittgenstein interpreters who have attributed a "use theory of meaning" and a "communal practice theory of rule following" to Wittgenstein. Now, I have no brief for either of these theories, or for attributing either one of them to Wittgenstein.[2] But the argument Baker offered against making statements of the form "A *is* such and such" in philosophy was that such statements typically present themselves as statements about the *nature* of things, as scientific (or rather super-scientific statements), thus flouting the distinction between conceptual truths and empirical truths. (Even this is rather quick – is Wittgenstein, then, supposed to assume a "conceptual/empirical" dichotomy?) But the "Wittgensteinians" who attributed the above theories to Wittgenstein thought they were giving conceptual analyses or clarifications, ones that they claimed to find in Wittgenstein's text. The advice Baker gives to "avoid asking such questions as '*What is* the meaning of a word?', or '*What is* following a rule?' " seems to prohibit in advance a search for an insightful conceptual clarification of these notions. Arguably, the search for such clarifications is typically a search for a reductive account. People who find a "use theory of meaning" and a "communal practice account of rule-following" in Wittgenstein do typically see themselves as *reducing* meaning to use and rule-following to communal practice; but they also see themselves as talking about the *grammar* of "to follow a rule" and the *grammar* of meaning-locutions; they do not see themselves as "trying to grasp the *essence* of the things" in a way that ignores "the difference between factual and conceptual investigations." Before "treating" the confusion of these Wittgensteinian philosophers, it would be necessary to show them that they *aren't* just making conceptual discoveries. It seems that Baker thinks we can do this by just "reminding individuals of their own everyday (non-philosophical) uses of words" (103). But the purpose of "Wittgenstein on Metaphysical/Everyday Use" is to argue that "everyday (non-philosophical) uses of words" just means "*non-metaphysical* uses of words" where " 'metaphysical' seems [. . .] to bear a traditional meaning" (100), and "everyday uses" has no *independent* meaning. ("Metaphysical" does all the work.) To convict the "Wittgensteinian" philosophers he criticizes for not using words in their "everyday use," he would, then, have to argue that the "use theory of meaning" they attribute to Wittgenstein is metaphysical *where "metaphysical" bears a traditional meaning*. What is likely, I think, is that when Baker wrote "reminding them of their own everyday (non-philosophical) uses of words" he simply *ignored* the claim that *metaphysical* (in a "traditional" sense) "wears the trousers."

A question that must of course be raised about Baker's interpretation is the following: is it textually correct as an account of the sense in which Wittgenstein used the word "metaphysical" *when he said that what he does is "to bring words back from their metaphysical to their everyday use"*? In other words, was Wittgenstein's "target" really restricted to philosophical theories that erroneously seek to state "necessities and impossibilities"?

Before addressing this textual question, however, let us stop to see whether the most famous metaphysical debates in the analytic philosophy of the last half century really can be illuminated by construing them as misguided examples of essentialism, examples of the four types of error Baker listed, and treated by the two strategies Baker attributes to Wittgenstein, or whether this does not turn out to be a strategy for, at best, forcing all philosophical confusions into a Procrustean bed. If it does, then it will follow that either Wittgensteinian philosophy simply fails to provide a fruitful way to approach those debates (which I do not think is the case), or else Baker's account, even if it sheds light on certain passages in Wittgenstein, badly underestimates both the variety of philosophical confusions as Wittgenstein saw them, and the variety of strategies a philosopher who has learned from Wittgenstein might have to clear up specific kinds of confusions.

On anyone's list of such debates, the following would certainly have to figure:

1 The controversy over "realism" and "antirealism" in Michael Dummett's sense as accounts of the semantics of "true."
2 The controversy over functionalism in the philosophy of mind.
3 The debate over the "innateness hypothesis" in linguistics.
4 The debate about "realism," "nominalism" and "quasi-realism" in philosophy of mathematics.

Now each of these is about an issue that is "metaphysical" in a traditional sense. But *the arguments are not traditional metaphysical arguments.* Firstly, Dummett's argument for antirealism is supposed to be in Wittgenstein's spirit; he sees himself as clearing up the confusions of the realist side, not doing "ontology." And Dummett's critics, including myself, see themselves as defending our everyday conception of truth, but *not* in a sense of everyday which is defined *simply* by contrasting it with metaphysics in a "traditional" sense. Secondly, "functionalism" claimed to be an *empirical* hypothesis – the possibility that the metaphysician may pretend to be a natural scientist goes missing in Baker's account. Thirdly, the "innateness hypothesis," as its name suggests, likewise claimed to be an *empirical* hypothesis. Fourthly, the arguments in defense of "realism," "nominalism" and "quasirealism" in philosophy of mathematics are a mixture of conceptual arguments and analyses of the role of applied mathematics.

Of course, it might be that Baker's notion of "the traditional meaning" of the word "metaphysical" could be *stretched* to cover all of these debates. But to me it seems clear that Wittgenstein would have had (and Wittgensteinians should have) *plenty* to say about all of these debates, and that the question as to whether this or that side or argument in any one of these debates is metaphysical "in a traditional sense" is totally unhelpful.

I don't think that taking "everyday" as the word that "wears the trousers" would be any help either – but that is a matter for another occasion.

Notes

1 All subsequent references are to this paper/chapter unless otherwise stated. The paper appeared first in *The Philosophical Quarterly* 52/208 in 2002.
2 I criticized the idea that Wittgenstein thinks we can always identify differences in use with differences in meaning in *Renewing Philosophy* (1992) and the idea that he defends a communal practice account of rules in "Was Wittgenstein *Really* an Anti-Realist About Mathematics?" (2001).

Chapter 7

Wittgenstein and Transcendental Idealism

A. W. Moore

Introduction[1]

What follows, though I refer to it from time to time as an essay, is really a pair of independent essays, each with its own separate provenance. Part I, which addresses the question whether the early Wittgenstein was a transcendental idealist, is a much abridged version of an essay that is due to appear in another volume.[2] Part II, which addresses the question whether the later Wittgenstein was a transcendental idealist – or rather, which takes an early stance on that question as a preliminary to mooting a somewhat more oblique relation between the later Wittgenstein and transcendental idealism – is adapted from a section of my book *Points of View*.[3] The two parts are very different in style, approach, and intent, and I have made no effort, except at a purely cosmetic level, to integrate them. On the contrary, I have tried to ensure that each can be read independently of the other. But I hope and believe, for what I take to be obvious reasons, that there is some interest in their juxtaposition.

As will transpire, my own verdict is (with qualifications) that the early Wittgenstein was a transcendental idealist and the later Wittgenstein was not. Interpreters can be found who represent every combination of views on these two issues, including the combination which is diametrically opposed to mine, and including scepticism about whether either issue is a genuine one. What would Gordon Baker's verdict have been? Since I nowhere engage with Baker in what follows, I am glad of this opportunity to say that I share his view, so wonderfully paraded in his later work, that philosophy can be (and in Wittgenstein's hands was) an open-ended, exploratory, non-dogmatic, highly contextual affair in which individuals are freed from the constraining effects of certain unhelpful pictures associated with their concepts.[4] I hope that his verdict would not have been that my obsessive concern to locate Wittgenstein in relation to this abstruse piece of Kantian metaphysics clamours for just such treatment; that it is itself the constraining effect of an unhelpful picture of the relations between language, thought, and reality. I *hope* that his verdict would not have been that. I suspect otherwise.

I   Was the Early Wittgenstein a Transcendental Idealist?

1. Imagine a dispute between two readers of the *Tractatus*[5] that would be readily settled once both parties had acknowledged that Wittgenstein holds the propositions of logic to be true. An example would be a dispute about whether he advocates a principle of bipolarity for all propositions, whereby only what could be false could be true. There is a clear sense in which any such dispute ought not to survive an appeal to the 4.46 s. These numbered remarks indicate clearly that Wittgenstein does indeed hold the propositions of logic to be true. It would be captious to object that, by the very lights of the *Tractatus*, these remarks are themselves nonsensical, and that, in his most authentic mode, Wittgenstein would not have assented to 'The propositions of logic are true,' but would rather have urged that we had not yet given any meaning to certain signs in this pseudo-proposition (cf. 6.53). There *could* be an interesting exegetical dispute about *that* too. Two readers could disagree about why, or even whether, Wittgenstein would indeed have regarded this as a nonsensical pseudo-proposition. But relative to the dispute about bipolarity, even to raise this issue would be cavilling. Relative to *that* dispute, the idea that the propositions of logic are true is simply there in the text. And its being simply there in the text is a matter of our prescinding from the book's self-renunciation at the end and pretending that what we have before us in the 4.46 s are what we appear to have: straightforward affirmations. The early Wittgenstein, in a clear and unproblematic sense, held that the propositions of logic are true.[6]

Would it be fair to say that, in just the same sense, the early Wittgenstein was a transcendental idealist; that, subject to all the obvious caveats about the *Tractatus*'s self-renunciation, transcendental idealism is 'simply there in the text'? There are all sorts of reasons why it would not. First, there is the entirely non-trivial issue of what transcendental idealism *is*. Second, even given an account of what transcendental idealism is, there will still be an issue about whether it is 'there in the text'. For there is no reasonable account of what transcendental idealism is on which it can be said to receive unambiguous expression there, of however vicarious or disingenuous a kind. And third, most significantly, even given some compelling reason for thinking that transcendental idealism *is* there in the text, there will still be, or there should still be, an issue about whether it is 'simply' there in the text, in other words – in Peter Sullivan's words – about 'what it's doing there'.[7]

Why do I describe this third issue as the most significant? Partly, though not exclusively, for a reason that is admittedly intra-mural. As Sullivan indicates in the context from which I have just quoted, he and I would be in substantial agreement about the first two issues; and this part of my essay is largely a continuation of a dialogue between us about the third.[8]

Let me say, then, far more briefly than is really warranted, what I take to be the gist of our agreement about the first two issues. There are, in the *Tractatus*, notably in the 5.6 s, remarks in which the limits of language and the limits of the world appear not merely as *limits*, not merely as essential features, but as *limitations*, as features that at some level exclude certain possibilities. Because these features appear to exclude certain possibilities, they also appear to admit the question why they are as they are. The answer implied in those same remarks involves the subject, who both understands language and has thoughts about the world, and who somehow sets the limits – *is* a limit – of each. And this is a version of transcendental idealism.[9]

Granted this broad characterization of our shared reaction to the first two issues, the third, to repeat, is what such transcendental idealism is doing in the text. It is easy to overlook this third issue. It is easy to treat the *Tractatus* as a relatively uniform sequence of apparent affirmations, 'framed' by some remarks near the very beginning and near the very end which are themselves genuine affirmations concerning the status of what they 'frame'.[10] On this crude way of regarding the *Tractatus*, whether a view can be attributed to Wittgenstein, in the relatively relaxed sense that is of concern to us here, is a matter of whether there is, among the apparent affirmations that constitute the bulk of the book, an apparent affirmation of the view in question, or at least a set of apparent affirmations that apparently commit Wittgenstein to it.

I said that it is easy to treat the *Tractatus* in this way. Perhaps I should have made a more cautious autobiographical claim: I myself have slipped into treating the *Tractatus* in this way. I have in the past attributed transcendental idealism to the early Wittgenstein[11] as though this were no more contentious than attributing to him the belief that the propositions of logic are true, or the belief that objects are simple (2.02). But, as Sullivan has helped me to appreciate, to proceed as though these attributions are of a piece is to do scant justice to the subtleties of this extraordinary text, a text in which ideas are variously developed and suppressed, and temptations are variously indulged and dispelled, all within a context that allows for the eventual recognition that some of the words being put to critical use in these tasks are being put to use without meaning.

Sullivan has in various places developed a reading of the *Tractatus* whereby these apparent affirmations of transcendental idealism are altogether more dissembling than the apparent affirmations of various other doctrines that Wittgenstein wants us to throw away once we have used them to climb up beyond them (cf. 6.54). Sullivan draws a contrast with Wittgenstein's treatment of logical categories.[12] For Wittgenstein, the logical category to which anything belongs is determined by the formal variable within whose range it lies. But this means that the very use of the word 'anything' in this formulation of the doctrine – 'the logical category to which *anything* belongs' – cannot have its intended generality. It is impossible to generalize about things of different logical categories (as indeed this very admonishment purports to do). Wittgenstein brings us to an understanding of these matters which involves our 'coming to share with him an appreciation that the best that can be done in the way of trying to express this understanding will be to produce formulations which the understanding itself enables [us] to recognize as nonsense.'[13] Sullivan contrasts this with the case of transcendental idealism. The two cases may look analogous. We may think that, for Wittgenstein, language has certain limitations which, for that very reason, it cannot be *said* to have; hence that, here too, Wittgenstein brings us to an understanding of the matters which involves our 'coming to share with him an appreciation that the best that can be done in the way of trying to express this understanding will be to produce formulations which the understanding itself enables [us] to recognize as nonsense.' But on Sullivan's view, this is seriously to understate Wittgenstein's eventual repudiation of transcendental idealism. On Sullivan's view, although Wittgenstein both feels and indulges a sympathy for transcendental idealism, his ultimate aim is to dispel it completely, that is in such a way that it no longer serves even as a 'self-consciously nonsensical and knowingly futile attempt to express the understanding [we have] of its sources.'[14] Kant, from whom of course transcendental idealism derives, remains very much in the picture for Sullivan, but only as the enemy. Once transcendental idealism has collapsed into its opposite, which it does so spectacularly in 5.64, Wittgenstein can be seen as proceeding to a case-by-case repudiation of a Kantian conception of the a priori.[15] Transcendental idealism, by the end of this exercise, can in no way be said to be 'simply' there in the text.

I am suspicious of this contrast with Wittgenstein's treatment of logical categories. It seems to me that, in the case of the doctrine of logical categories just as in the case of transcendental idealism, 'seeing the world aright' (6.54) involves acquiescing in the lack of whatever alternatives would make limitations out of limits, for instance an alternative in which a formal variable can correspond to more than one logical category; and that, again in the former case just as in the latter case, this is a prize that we can be helped to win by watching claims whose implications are being followed out strictly, for instance the claim that things belong to different logical categories, collapse into their opposites, in this instance the claim that things do not belong to different logical categories (cf. 5.64).[16] So when Sullivan offers me the analogy with the doctrine of logical categories as one that he himself rejects, I am not inclined to be proud: I am inclined to welcome his cast-off.

The contrast with Wittgenstein's treatment of logical categories is one of two that Sullivan draws. The second is with Wittgenstein's later work, where there is, Sullivan avers, a commitment of some kind, at some very deep level, to transcendental idealism.[17] I do not want to say anything about that now.[18] Sullivan's second contrast does however provide me with an opportunity to correct a false impression that I may have given about how I see the relation of transcendental idealism to the early work. I suggested that, in the *Tractatus*, Wittgenstein brings us to transcendental idealism by indulging an urge that we have to transcend our limitations; and I further suggested that the limitations in question are those that ground and shape our concepts.[19] I may thus have given the impression that I see Wittgenstein as grappling with the complex of biological and cultural contingencies which, for reasons and in ways that Sullivan indicates, are undoubtedly crucial to any proper understanding of how transcendental idealism beckons in the later work. If I had seen Wittgenstein in this way, then I would of course have owed an explanation for why, in the *Tractatus*, despite an allusion to the complexity of the human organism (4.002), Wittgenstein does not seem to be the least bit interested in reckoning with any of the actual manifestations of that complexity. But I do not see Wittgenstein in this way. I had in mind something more Kantian.

There is a kind of scope distinction here. My idea was not that, given whatever such limitations we are subject to, we aspire not to be subject to them. It was rather that we aspire not to be subject to any such limitations at all. It is ultimately the very finitude of our thinking that we have an urge to transcend: the very fact that our thinking is answerable to something.[20] This is not to suggest that there is any alternative to our thinking's being thus finite. Our urge may be utterly ill-conceived. What *is* true is that for our thinking to be thus finite is for there to be an alternative to whatever *qualifies* it as thinking which is thus finite – to whatever equips it to answer to that to which it is answerable, namely reality, or the world. (By way of analogy: even if there is no alternative to a stick's having some finite length, for a stick to have some finite length is for there to be an alternative its having whatever finite length it has.) So, for example, our thinking involves our using signs in some particular way (3.1 ff.), where what this means is our using them in some way rather than some other that would have equipped us to think just as well (3.326–3.327).

One example of our using signs is, in Tractarian terms, our naming objects. Let us reflect for a while on the naming of objects. This will provide us with an indication of how these ideas connect with transcendental idealism. Our thinking does not depend on our actually naming objects (5.526; cf. also 4.002). But it does depend on our being, so to speak, at one remove from naming objects, in as much as each of our thoughts can be analyzed into simple thoughts in which objects are named. Our thinking is *about* objects (3.2 ff.). This is how it touches reality. If our thinking did not touch reality in this way, then it would not be able to answer to reality (2.15–2.1515 and 5.542). For our thinking to be about objects in this way, we need to know the objects it is about (6.2322). But our knowing an object does not itself consist in our thinking anything: we cannot *say* what we know when we know an object.[21] That our thinking depends on our having such inexpressible knowledge is therefore another fundamental mark of its finitude. But it is just such fundamental marks as this that we have an urge to transcend. Thus one particularly significant way in which our urge is liable to manifest itself is through the attempt to say what we know when we know objects; to say *what* objects are, not just *how* they are; to put objects themselves into words (cf. 3.221). This connects with transcendental idealism in two ways.

The first connection is a direct one. This attempt is itself liable to issue in some version of transcendental idealism. For it is an attempt to say what grounds the very essence of reality, conceived as something to which not even logic is prior (5.552). It is an attempt to say, not how things are, nor yet how things must be, but what it is, in some deep metaphysical sense, for things to be how they are. It is an attempt to say, not how *things* are, but how their limits are. And this is liable to involve casting those limits as limitations. It is liable to involve embracing some version of transcendental idealism.[22]

The second connection with transcendental idealism is less direct, but more significant as far as the project of the *Tractatus* is concerned. Our understanding of why the attempt to express our inexpressible knowledge of objects is ill-conceived is itself inexpressible. Like our knowledge of objects, it does not itself consist in our thinking anything: it is part of our understanding of what thinking is. And the attempt to express *it* is liable to issue in some version of transcendental idealism. We are liable to say that reality consists of how objects are, not of what they are, not of the objects themselves – or, in somewhat more familiar terms, that the world is the totality of facts, not of things (1.1) – intending this as a corrective, as a way of signalling that only our knowledge of *facts* is a form of thinking, answerable to reality, and apt to be expressed. But if we do say this, then we shall be violating an admonishment that Wittgenstein himself gives in the *Tractatus*:

> We cannot say in logic, 'The world has this in it, and this, but not that.' – For that would appear to presuppose that we were excluding certain possibilities, and this cannot be the case, since it would require that logic should go beyond the limits of the world; for only in that way could it view those limits from the other side as well. (5.61)

Wittgenstein's admonishment, which of course he himself violates, is an admonishment precisely against treating limits as limitations.[23] In saying that the world is the totality of facts, not of things, we do exclude certain possibilities; and we exclude them, moreover, on the grounds that they are not consonant with the nature of our thinking. In sum, we embrace a version of transcendental idealism.

This second connection with transcendental idealism is worth pondering for a little longer. While the first connection illustrates one source of our temptation to construe limits as limitations, namely the urge to transcend our own limitations, the second reveals another: the very urge to counter that first urge. At some level we recognize the incoherence of construing limits as limitations, and, in recognizing this incoherence, we have an urge to forbid any reference to the possibilities that limits exclude, in such a way that we ourselves make reference to the possibilities that limits exclude, and hence in such a way that we ourselves construe limits as limitations. There is a general pattern here. Having seen through the appearance of sense in some piece of nonsense, we have an urge to repress the appearance by redeploying the nonsense, using some such formula as 'It does not make sense to say that . . .' And if, furthermore, we attempt to say *why* it does not make sense to say this thing that we have just said, then we are liable to indulge in yet more nonsense of the same general sort, trying to characterize both sides of a border between that which we can characterize and that which we cannot. This is how we get to transcendental idealism: a kind of nonsense born of the urge to combat nonsense of that very kind; a disease for which it itself purports to be the cure.[24] And that is what I think we find in the *Tractatus*.[25]

Still, Sullivan has convinced me that, even if I am right about this, it does not settle any dispute between us. For there is still the question of what such transcendental idealism is *doing* in the *Tractatus*.

My own view is that Wittgenstein has put it there *in propria persona* – or at least, as much *in propria persona* as is compatible with an exhortation to recognize it as itself nonsense that we must ultimately transcend (6.54). It is there as a result of an unsuccessful attempt to express certain inexpressible insights into the limits of language and into the incoherence of attempts to violate those limits, insights which, on the one hand, are supposed to be fostered by seeing that such nonsense is the result of an attempt to express them and, on the other hand, are supposed to foster seeing that such nonsense is nonsense. (Again I appeal to the analogy with the doctrine of logical categories.)

Sullivan thinks that this is to accredit Wittgenstein with more sympathy for transcendental idealism than he has. On Sullivan's view, there is a much greater critical distance between Wittgenstein and the transcendental idealism in his book. It is there as if in scare quotes. Wittgenstein does feel its allure, and he quite deliberately exploits that allure, but only so that it will eventually no longer have any hold on us. His aim is to repudiate the doctrine entirely. He wants us to acquiesce in viewing the limits of language as precisely that: limits, not limitations.[26] We are to recognize that there is no way for things to be which is not how they can be represented as being. Language is the totality of propositions; the world is the totality of facts; and the limits of these totalities coincide, that is to say any possible proposition expresses some possible fact and any possible fact is expressed by some possible proposition. But they coincide not because the limits of either are limitations somehow set by the other, nor yet because the limits of both are limitations somehow set by the subject, but precisely because they are the *limits* of two formal totalities that are to be conceived in terms of each other.[27]

In sum, then – and this is a cartoon sketch – where I take Wittgenstein to be a transcendental idealist, Sullivan takes him not to be. But of course, that *is* a cartoon sketch, and one of the reasons why settling our dispute presents such a challenge, or so it seems to me, is that it is enormously difficult to say what *exactly* is at issue between us. I have still not really pinpointed it. In §2 I shall approach this dispute from a somewhat different angle, in the hope that this will go at least some way towards helping me to identify it. I shall also try to give an indication of why I am still inclined to take the same side. This will involve a brief digression on Kant. It will also involve an attempt to take due account of what seems to me to be in many respects the most striking and most significant fact about the appearance of transcendental idealism in the *Tractatus*, a fact that has been completely absent from the discussion so far.

2. Kant too is exercised by the limits of thought and the limits of reality. That is, he is exercised by the limits of thought which, in his terms, has *content*, thought which is about objects of sensible intuition (A51/B75); and he is exercised by the limits of *empirical* reality, the reality to which such thought is answerable (A26/B42 ff.).[28] He takes the limits of each of these to be limitations. He contrasts thought which has content with thought which lacks content; and he contrasts empirical reality with the reality of things in themselves (Bxxv–xxvii).[29]

The fact that Kant effects these two contrasts, and takes the limits of thought and the limits of reality to be limitations, signals that he is an unregenerate transcendental idealist. And one of the ways in which he arrives at his transcendental idealism is by seeking an explanation for why these limits coincide in the way they do. This is something that he insists demands explanation. Furthermore he sees only three possible explanations: one is that the limits of reality are determined by the limits of thought; a second is that the limits of thought are determined by the limits of reality; and a third is that the limits of each have some common determinant. But it is only the first of these (that the limits of reality are determined by the limits of thought) which he thinks can account for our a priori knowledge of their coincidence. In neither of the other two cases, where the limits of thought would be determined by something else, could we have any way of foreseeing (to use a Wittgensteinian word (4.5

and 5.556)) that the limits of reality would always conform to them. Hence Kant's transcendental idealism.[30]

But, as Wittgenstein helps us to appreciate, if these limits really were *limits*, and not limitations, then there would be no question of any such determination and no need for any such explanation. The limits would be as they are because, in the most austere sense of the word 'could', they *could* not be otherwise. And their coincidence would still be knowable a priori. Kant arrives at his transcendental idealism by taking as a datum the existence of a priori knowledge that is not merely of limits, but of limitations; not analytic, but synthetic (Introduction, §§IV and V). Wittgenstein, in direct opposition to this, insists that 'there is no a priori order of things' (5.634).[31] That is, there is no a priori knowledge of limitations. And this is how, for Wittgenstein, transcendental idealism is to be resisted. On this Sullivan and I are in agreement. And yet . . .

Why does Kant see limitations where Wittgenstein sees only limits? Well, for Kant, thought which has content is thought which is capable of becoming knowledge; thought which lacks content is thought which is not capable of becoming knowledge.[32] *Kant needs the contrast.* As he famously says in the Preface to the second edition of *Critique of Pure Reason*, 'I had to deny *knowledge* in order to make room for *faith*' (Bxxx, his emphasis). Faith, for Kant, 'is reason's moral way of thinking . . . [It] is trust in the attainability of an aim whose promotion is a duty but the possibility of whose realization we cannot have any insight into.'[33] It is directed at our freedom, at our capacity to exercise our wills either by obeying the moral law or by disobeying it, at our immortality, at the existence of God, and, quite generally, at whatever is ultimately of value, all of which Kant sees as lying beyond the reach of discursive knowledge. Freedom; the good or bad exercise of the will; the moral law; immortality; God; value: these cannot but ring extremely loud bells for any student of the *Tractatus*. They also provide me with a good cue to reveal what I had in mind when I referred earlier to what seems to me to be in many respects the most striking and most significant fact about the appearance of transcendental idealism in the *Tractatus*. I had in mind the fact that it appears, not only in the 5.6 s, on which we have so far been concentrating, but just as blatantly, if not more so, in the 6.4 s.[34]

It seems to me that, when we take the Kantian strain of the 6.4 s duly into account, we can see an isomorphism, albeit a rough one, between, on the one hand, Kant's contrast between thoughts which have content and thoughts which lack content and, on the other hand, Wittgenstein's contrast between propositions which have sense and certain nonsensical pseudo-propositions.[35]

	Left-hand side	Right-hand side
Kant	Thoughts with content	Thoughts without content
Wittgenstein	Propositions with sense	Certain nonsensical pseudo-propositions

And, granted this isomorphism, we can say that, for both Kant and Wittgenstein, transcendental idealism lies on the right-hand side; furthermore, that it serves in helping us to *see* that it lies on the right-hand side. But obviously, if that were all it served to do, then we need have nothing more to do with it. To use an analogy that I have used before, it would then be like a plinth whose sole purpose was to support a sign reading 'Mind the plinth'.[36] One reason why it is of greater use than that is that it also serves, for both Kant and Wittgenstein, in helping us to see what else is on the right-hand side. But its greatest service, I submit, again for both Kant and Wittgenstein, is in helping us to do justice to what is on the right-hand side, or, more strictly, in helping us to do justice to the forces at work when we produce what is on the right-hand side.

Neither Kant nor Wittgenstein thinks that our rational engagement with things – that part of our engagement with things which is made possible by the fact that we are rational, thinking beings – is exhausted by whatever finds expression in items on the left-hand side. It does obviously include whatever finds expression in items on the left-hand side, which for both Kant and Wittgenstein has as its paradigm discursive knowledge, the kind of knowledge that is embodied in natural science.[37] But, for Kant, it also includes each of the following:

❖   faith;
❖   hope;
❖   the practical use of pure reason;
❖   aesthetic judgement;

and, overlapping some of these, what he sometimes calls

❖   practical knowledge.[38]

(Kant takes it to be a fundamental mark of our finitude that our rational engagement with things fractures in this way.)[39] That we *recognize* ourselves as engaging with things in these various ways itself involves our engaging with things in a way that is not just a matter of discursive knowledge. And in articulating what we recognize, we are led to transcendental idealism. For we contrast what finds expression in items on the left-hand side with our other modes of rational engagement with things, and we come to regard empirical reality – that to which all items on the left-hand side must answer – as correspondingly restricted. What it is restricted to, Kant insists, are objects of sensible intuition.[40] But, *in* so insisting, he sees himself as allowing for due acknowledgement of our other modes of engagement with things, which find expression, or at least partial expression, in thoughts that are not about objects of sensible intuition, but about value, about freedom, about God, and the like; items on the right-hand side.[41]

I think we can see the same structure in Wittgenstein. Admittedly, there are profound differences in how the structure is instantiated. Thoughts without content, for Kant, are none the less thoughts. They involve the genuine exercise of concepts (B146). And they are true or false (A820–831/B848–859). By contrast, nonsense, for Wittgenstein, is just nonsense. It comprises words to which no meanings have been assigned (5.4733 and 6.53). Thus, while Kant can countenance that which finds bona fide (if partial) expression in items on the right-hand side, Wittgenstein can at most countenance that which finds *apparent* or *attempted* expression in items on the right-hand side – what we might call, echoing the fact that items on the right-hand side are for Wittgenstein pseudo-propositions, pseudo-expression. Wittgenstein can *at most* countenance that. The point, however, is that he does. Like Kant, he recognizes modes of rational engagement with things other than that which finds expression in items on the left-hand side. That is, he recognizes modes of rational engagement with things other than thought. I discussed one example in §1:[42]

❖   knowledge of objects,

which is also in effect understanding of names. There are other kinds of understanding too, including

❖   understanding of propositions (4.022, 4.024, and 4.1212),

and, quite differently, the state that we are supposed to get into as a result of reading the *Tractatus*:

❖   understanding of Wittgenstein (6.54).[43]

Then there are:

❖   the practice of philosophy (4.11–4.115);
❖   logical inference (5.13–5.133 and 6.12–6.1201);
❖   the practice of mathematics (6.2–6.211 and 6.233–6.234);

and, most significantly of all, all that comes under the head of

❖   evaluation,

including feeling the world as a whole, exercising the will, and being happy or unhappy (6.43 and 6.45).[44] *None* of these consists in having thoughts. *All* of them find pseudo-expression in items on the right-hand side.[45]

Sullivan casts Kant in the rôle of enemy throughout the 6 s. I cannot see this. I think that in the 6.4 s we see something profoundly Kantian. To be sure, Wittgenstein does want to dismantle a Kantian conception of the a priori, and he spends much of the early part of the 6 s doing just that. But this is because he wants us to appreciate that what we produce when we endorse transcendental idealism, of which the Kantian conception of the a priori is an integral part, is utter nonsense. What *leads* us to endorse it, on the other hand, continues to command Wittgenstein's deepest respect, and this is what we see most clearly in the 6.4 s. '*The book's point*,' he famously wrote in a letter to Ficker, '*is an ethical one.*'[46] And part of that point is to uphold a fundamental separation of fact and value. It is in trying to come to terms with this separation that we construe the world as the totality of facts, that is to say as the totality of what can be thought and said, *to the exclusion of* value (6.41), that is to say to the exclusion of what can be affected by acts of will (6.43). There are, for Wittgenstein, genuine insights that lead us to cast the limits of the world as limitations in this way; genuine insights that lead us to endorse this version of transcendental idealism. They are inexpressible insights into what it is to think, into what it is to exercise the will, and into what separates these.

In conclusion, then, while I am still not entirely confident that I have got the dispute between Sullivan and myself into proper focus, I hope at least to have given some indication of why I want to answer my title question in the way I do, a way that marks a relatively clean division between us. And just to be clear about what my answer is: *was* the early Wittgenstein a transcendental idealist? *Not* in any straightforward sense – he thought that transcendental idealism was a tissue of nonsense – but, in the sense in which he held the propositions of logic to be true, or objects to be simple, yes he was.

II   Was the Later Wittgenstein a Transcendental Idealist?

The later Wittgenstein, I claim, was not a transcendental idealist.

This is a bald, bold, cryptic claim which, among other things, cries out for a definition of 'transcendental idealism', and I shall supply one in due course.[47] But it also stands in need of an immediate qualification. In claiming that the later Wittgenstein was not a transcendental idealist, I am not suggesting that he confronted transcendental idealism and came to regard it as false, still less that he adopted some other 'ism' in its stead. That would have been completely antithetical to Wittgenstein's conception of philosophy. On Wittgenstein's conception, philosophy is a kind of therapy. Its purpose is to cure us whenever, through the misuse of our own language, we become troubled by unanswerable pseudo-questions posing as deep problems. It is not the point of philosophy to advance 'isms'. If, in the course of doing philosophy, one affirms anything, then it will be by way of showing the use of certain words. What one affirms will as likely as not be a platitude, or an item of common empirical knowledge, not something to be debated.[48] So, depending on how exactly transcendental idealism is defined, it is either of no concern to philosophy or, more probably, a bit of nonsense to be flushed out of the system by means of some suitable philosophical purgative.

Very well, then, how do I define transcendental idealism? By transcendental idealism I mean one of two species of idealism, the other being empirical idealism. Idealism, as I understand it, is the view that the limits of that to which our representations[49] answer, by which I mean the essential features of that to which our representations answer, are set, in part, by some feature of the representations themselves. *Empirical* idealism includes the rider that the setting of these limits lies within them; it is itself an aspect of that to which our representations answer. *Transcendental* idealism includes the rider that the setting of these limits lies beyond them; it is not itself an aspect of that to which our representations answer, and the limits are, relative to it, limitations.[50]

Now I said above that, on Wittgenstein's conception of philosophy, transcendental idealism is either of no concern to philosophy or a bit of nonsense to be flushed out of the system.[51] And I do not want to retract that. The later Wittgenstein, to repeat, *was not a transcendental idealist.* Nevertheless, the main burden of Part II of this essay is to show that his relevance to transcendental idealism – or again, its relevance to him – lies not in his giving us license to ignore it, nor in his supplying the methods for finally disposing of it, but, on the contrary, in his providing an inducement, in spite of himself, to embrace it. Transcendental idealism, for all that its outright endorsement would be so utterly un-Wittgensteinian, has an important place in Wittgenstein's work; or better, it has an important place in Wittgensteinian exegesis.[52]

For Wittgenstein, philosophy involves self-conscious attention to the use of language. This means commanding a clear view of how words are used, reflecting on what does and does not make sense, feeling one's way around inside one's outlook, or one's various outlooks. (Here and elsewhere in Part II I use the term 'outlook' to denote a way of seeing the world. To have a particular outlook is to treat some things as relevant to others, to be disposed to make various connections between things, to be struck by certain similarities and differences, to find some things natural foci of attention, and suchlike.) Self-conscious attention to the use of language also means recognizing certain propositions as necessary. A simple example is the proposition that aunts are female. Such propositions do not embody substantial claims about the world. They register the interrelations of concepts. For Wittgenstein, saying, 'Aunts are female,' is enunciating a rule rather than making an assertion. Saying, 'Aunts *have* to be female,' is alluding to this fact. We will not count somebody as an aunt unless we also count that person as female.

Notice how necessity is thereby grounded in contingency. Wittgenstein is keen to dispel the view that, in exploring meaning in the way described, we are exploring some unchanging super-physical landscape, as though the concept of an aunt and the concept of femaleness were things we just stumbled across, the one an inseparable part of the other. It is on our own contingent practices that we are focusing. Moreover, part of Wittgenstein's genius is his special gift for drawing attention to how deep the contingencies lie. It is of course contingent that we use particular words (particular sounds and particular inscriptions) in the way in which we do. (We might have used the word 'aunt' to denote uncles.) But when we reflect self-consciously on our actual classifications, we are inclined to see these as subject to certain constraints. Imagine people who in some circumstances use a word to denote green things, and who in other circumstances use that same word to denote blue things. We are inclined to say that they cannot have one concept in mind: they do not count as carrying on in the same way. Wittgenstein, applying some of his own philosophical methods to this very inclination of ours, urges us to think again about what is involved in 'carrying on in the same way'. It is not that he has in mind some favoured view of this that he wants to argue for. Rather, by means of a careful interlacing of hints, suggestions, and descriptions of different imaginable cases, he gets us to explore in greater depth the view we already have. We come to see what a huge amount we take for granted whenever we count someone, or refuse to count someone, as carrying on in the same way. Had various facts of nature, including facts of human nature, been different from how they are, then all sorts of behaviour might have constituted carrying on in the same way. (Thus imagine the green/blue case supplemented as follows. Suppose there are periodic atmospheric conditions that temporarily turn green things blue, and blue things green.) The contingencies of language use include all such facts. In particular, and centrally, they include our shared sensibilities, our shared senses of the natural and the salient: our shared outlooks. Without these, communication would break down. As Stanley Cavell marvellously and famously puts it:

> That on the whole we . . . [make, and understand, the same projections of words into further contexts] is a matter of our sharing routes of interest and feeling, modes of response, senses of humour and of significance and of fulfilment, of what is outrageous, of what is similar to what else, what a rebuke, what forgiveness, of when an utterance is an assertion, when an appeal, when an explanation – all the whirl of organism Wittgenstein calls 'forms of life'.[53]

Wittgenstein describes 'forms of life' as 'the given'. They are what has to be accepted.[54] Part of what he means is that it is in our biological nature to have certain outlooks. This comes out in the fact that, ultimately, we just do respond to our environment in certain ways, ways that help to sustain communication among us. But the phrase 'form of life' indicates more. We have also been inculcated into certain social practices. As a result, we value certain things, we take certain things for granted, we defer to certain authorities, we accept certain canons of rationality, and we adopt certain modes of interpretation. All these things help to mould our natural outlooks into the full sophisticated outlooks in accord with which we produce our linguistic representations.[55]

Now Wittgenstein is adamant that the exploration of language that characterizes philosophy cannot be a scientific exploration. There are many things he means by this. For instance, he means that philosophy must be shorn of any pretensions to theory and systematicity. He means that philosophy must be descriptive rather than explanatory.[56] But something else that he means, or at least something that is very closely related to this and that he certainly thinks, is that philosophy can never be completely *detached*. We might have thought that the kind of description of our own linguistic practices required in philosophy would be something whose content could in principle be grasped by one who did not already understand the language. Nothing less, we might have thought, could have any purchase on one who *mis*understood the language. But for Wittgenstein, such detachment is neither necessary nor possible. Bernard Williams puts well the kind of thing that Wittgenstein envisages instead:

> [On a Wittgensteinian conception] we can . . . make [our language] clearer to ourselves, by reflecting on it, as it were self-consciously exercising it; not indeed by considering alternatives . . . but by moving around reflectively inside our view of things and sensing when one begins to be near the edge by the increasing incomprehensibility of things regarded from whatever way-out point of view one has moved into. What one becomes conscious of, in so reflecting, is something like: *how we go on*. And *how we go on* is a matter of how we think, and speak, and intentionally and socially conduct ourselves.[57]

How then are we supposed to engage with those who misunderstand the language (very probably ourselves in another guise)? Well, through what we say in the course of these reflections, we give them the same kind of exposure to the language as we give infants. We do not so much tell them what the language is like as show them what it is like. By exposing them to the language we prompt them (encourage them, invite them) to reach a proper understanding of the language not from without, that is to say not by interpreting it in terms of some other language that they antecedently understand, but from within. However, this is not just a matter of our using the language while they watch. We do also describe the language: we make conceptual connections explicit, we distinguish between different forms of speech, we expose pieces of nonsense, and suchlike. The significant thing is that even when we do all this, we do it in terms that are ultimately unintelligible except to those who understand. We have no choice. Our descriptions cannot be acknowledged except from the point of view of such understanding. The exploration of language that Wittgenstein is envisaging is thus a reflective, reflexive, self-conscious process: it is a moving to and fro in which we maintain a certain conceptual point of view, partly by producing representations that cannot be produced except from that point of view, with the constant aim of keeping the point of view itself in focus.

But what *is* this point of view? I have characterized it as the point of view implicit in an understanding of our language; but what *is* that? This question is connected to two others. How exactly is 'language' being understood here? And who, in this discussion, are 'we'? These two questions come together as follows. What, in this discussion, is 'our language'?

Not English. It is not any empirically identified language of that kind. The example about aunts being female might have looked like an example concerning English. But if it were, there would be no reason to think that the relevant linguistic practices cannot be described except to those who already understand the language. There is no impediment to describing the use of the words 'aunt' and 'female' in, say, French. No, the example has nothing specifically to do with English. The relevant linguistic practices are such as our refusing to count somebody as an aunt unless we also count that person as female. And 'we', here, include monolingual speakers of French, who participate in this practice through their use of the expressions 'tante' and 'le sexe féminin'.

'Our language', then, is something more like our range of conceptual resources. Certainly this makes it clearer why anyone should think it impossible to describe our language without using it. It also absolves Wittgenstein of a kind of empirical idealism, a rather crazy and uninteresting kind of empirical idealism at that. As I observed before, it is contingent that the English word 'aunt' is used in the way in which it is. Had Wittgenstein meant to ground necessity in such contingencies as this – had he meant that the necessity of aunts' being female was due to English speakers using 'aunt' and 'female' in a certain way – then he would in effect have been saying that the limits of reality are set, in part, by certain historical accidents involving the actual mechanics of linguistic representation.

One thing that belies such idealism is that it would still have been necessary that aunts were female, and *a fortiori* aunts would still have been female, even if the words 'aunt' and 'uncle' had had their meanings interchanged. True, it would not then have been correct to utter the sentence, 'Aunts are female,' but that is another matter. In fact, aunts would still have been female whatever we had got up to. That is part of what is meant by saying that aunts *have* to be female.

There are forces in Wittgenstein, however, that make it very difficult to keep a grip on this. Wittgenstein does not ground necessity in simple contingencies of word use. But he does ground it in contingencies. 'Our language' might have been different. Does this not mean that we might have admitted the possibility of male aunts? And if so, does it not follow that there might have been male aunts? Or that twice two might have been five rather than four? To be sure, Wittgenstein will insist that twice two is four of necessity. That twice two is four, he will say, is a rule.[58] And yet – it is a rule only because of our contingent linguistic practices (and not just in the sense that we might have used different sounds or inscriptions to express it). Are there not Wittgensteinian reasons for saying that, had those practices been different, twice two would not have been four, a conclusion which, when it is not giving us a thoroughly unnerving sense of vertigo, seems to be just false, another affirmation of a crazy empirical idealism?

Well, Wittgenstein need not in fact say any such thing. These quandaries are real enough for him. But they are real in a way that is compatible with his having a clear solution to them. (I shall have more to say in due course about what I mean by this.) Wittgenstein can respond as follows. It is not that, had our practices been different, twice two would not have been four. Rather, had our practices been different, we would not have had such a rule. We would not have thought in those terms. It remains the case that twice two is four of necessity. Nothing is to count as a proper calculation if it stands in violation of that. Again, 'our language' might have been different, not in the sense that we might have admitted the possibility of male aunts – which is not something we could have done, for our concept of an aunt and our concept of maleness would not have been those concepts if they had not excluded each other – but rather in the sense that we might not have *had* those concepts. Similarly, the contingency of our linguistic practices is the simple contingency of their existing at all. And as we have seen, it is a deep contingency. We are lucky, for instance, that we do not come to blows over whether elementary sums have been performed correctly.[59] But in so far as this means that there is a contingent grounding for what is necessary, it neither threatens the necessity nor indicates the setting of any limits of reality by some feature of our representations.

As regards the question of who 'we' are, there is no reason why this question should not admit of a perfectly definite answer once various matters have been resolved – though there is also no pressing need to resolve them, since nothing in what has just been said hinges on their resolution. The matters in question include: whether being one of 'us' means sharing various outlooks, or merely being able to share them; if the latter, in what sense of 'able'; and either way, which outlooks. However these matters are resolved, 'we' are not just English speakers. On some ways of resolving them, 'we' are a certain group of human beings. On others, 'we' are all human beings. On others again, 'we' include any beings, actual or potential, with whom humans can communicate, or any beings whom humans can recognize as producing linguistic representations.

Wittgenstein can be exonerated, then. The problem is that it is extremely difficult to stop there. It is extremely difficult not to envisage the 'we' expanding as it were to infinity. Once we have considered the various possibilities above, we find it hard ultimately not to think of 'ourselves' as all *possible* producers of linguistic representations. One of two things can then happen. First, the contingency can disappear altogether. 'Our language' comes to admit of no alternative. Any evidence that something is a use of language at all is *eo ipso* evidence that it is a use of 'our language'.[60] The references to 'us' and to 'our language' are then in effect redundant, and philosophy must once again be seen as the exploration of some unchanging super-physical landscape. The second thing that can happen is that the contingency is retained. 'Our language' does admit of alternatives. But given the nature of its expansion they are not 'real', representable alternatives. 'We', and 'our language', are to be understood transcendently – not as an aspect of that to which our representations answer, but as a limit of that to which our representations answer. Neither possibility would be acceptable to Wittgenstein.

Somehow, if his view is to be safeguarded, the urge to see the 'we' expanding in this way must be resisted. But again, there are forces in Wittgenstein himself that make that urge almost irresistible. Indulging in the kind of self-conscious reflection that Wittgenstein advocates, we cannot help asking, 'But what, ultimately, does somebody's being an aunt *consist in*? What does something's being green consist in?' We cannot help asking these questions because we cannot help wondering about the essential nature of that to which our representations answer, that whose character gives our language its point and helps to make it possible. We know that aunts have to be female, and we know that females have to have a certain biological constitution. Such are our rules. But what does it *take*, ultimately, for things to be configured in such a way that somebody is an aunt? Or in such a way that something is green? On a Wittgensteinian view, there is nothing we can summon in response to such questions that is clearly demarcated from the language itself. Someone who wants to know what something's being green consists in cannot just focus attention on a green thing and think, '*That* is what it consists in.' It is not clear what they are referring to by 'that'. Anyone who wants to know what something's being green consists in must observe us communicating with one another and exercising various discriminatory capacities that we possess. Not only that. Such a person must understand our acts of communication and see the point of our classifications. Such a person must become, or already be, one of us. What something's being green consists in is, at least in part, how we carry on. And the only way to prevent this from being a crazy empirical idealism (an idealism entailing such empirical falsehoods as that, had human beings not had the colour system they have, grass could not have been green) is to let the 'we' expand to infinity; or in other words, assuming that the concept of being green cannot be regarded as part of some super-physical landscape, to let the idealism turn transcendental.

So – how can Wittgenstein resist such transcendental idealism?

By disallowing the questions that led to it. We must not ask, 'What does something's being green consist in?' Or at least, we must not ask it with a certain metaphysical intent. (It may be a perfectly good scientific question, with a perfectly good scientific answer concerning wavelengths and the rest.) Somehow we have to see these questions themselves as pseudo-questions, symptoms of an illness awaiting Wittgensteinian therapy.

The fact remains that it was assimilation of Wittgenstein's work that led us to pose the questions. It was assimilation of Wittgenstein's work that tempted us to affirm the transcendental idealism. Moreover – a point but for which this entire exegetical approach to Wittgenstein would be altogether harder to justify – there is evidence that Wittgenstein himself feels the force of the temptation. The question about how far our mathematics depends on us, for instance, is one that he himself grapples with, very uncomfortably. Consider this quotation:

> 'But mathematical truth is independent of whether human beings believe it or not!' – Certainly, the propositions 'Human beings believe that twice two is four' and 'Twice two is four' do not mean the same. The latter is a mathematical proposition; the other, if it makes sense at all, may perhaps mean: human beings have *arrived* at the mathematical proposition. The two

propositions have entirely different *uses*. – But what would *this* mean: 'Even though everybody believed that twice two was five it would still be four'? – For what would it be like for everybody to believe that? – Well, I could imagine, for instance, that people had a different calculus, or a technique which we should not call 'calculating'. But would it be *wrong*?

And consider this:

We have a colour system as we have a number system. – Do the systems reside in *our* nature or in the nature of things? How are we to put it? – *Not* in the nature of numbers or colours. – Then is there something arbitrary about this system? Yes and no. It is akin both to what is arbitrary and to what is non-arbitrary.[61]

And consider Williams's just reply:

The diffidence about how to put it comes . . . [from the problem:] how to put a supposed philosophical truth which, if it is uttered, must be taken to mean an empirical falsehood, or worse . . . [Wittgenstein's theory of meaning] points in the direction of a transcendental idealism . . . [We are] driven to state it in forms which are required to be understood, if at all, in the wrong way.[62]

There is a real aporia here. My own view is that a proper response to this aporia has to draw on Wittgenstein's earlier work.[63] But that is an undertaking for another occasion.[64]

Notes

1   I am extremely grateful to the editors of this volume, especially Edward Kanterian, for their help and encouragement during the preparation of this essay.
2   [A. W.] Moore (forthcoming). I am grateful to the editors of that volume for permission to publish this version.
3   [A. W.] Moore (1997), Ch. 6, §3. I am grateful to Oxford University Press for permission to re-use material from that book.
4   See Baker (2004).
5   All unaccompanied references to Wittgenstein in Part I are to this (Pears and McGuinness translation).
6   This is an example only, not my main topic in Part I. Even so, I cannot resist remarking on the surprising number of interpreters who deny that the early

Wittgenstein held the propositions of logic to be true. See e.g. McGuinness (1985), p. 312; and Floyd (2000), p. 241.

7   Sullivan (2003), footnote 41.

8   This dialogue was initiated by the pair of essays that constitute the broader context from which the quotation from Sullivan is taken: [A. W.] Moore (2003) and Sullivan (2003).

9   A somewhat fuller definition of transcendental idealism, and of its contrast with empirical idealism (which need not concern us now), is proffered in Part II below.

10   This is an allusion to the kind of reading of the *Tractatus* that has come to be associated with Cora Diamond and James Conant. Cf. Conant (1991), p. 159; Conant (2000), p. 198; and Diamond (2000), pp. 149–151. But I am not suggesting that either Diamond or Conant treats the *Tractatus* in this overly crude way.

11   E.g. see [A. W.] Moore (1997), pp. 149 and 206.

12   Sullivan (2003), pp. 217 ff.

13   Ibid., p. 218.

14   Ibid., p. 216.

15   See Sullivan (1996), pp. 197–198; and note in particular the wonderful footnote 9 (p. 213) in which he makes clear how the organization of the 6 s reflects topics that are of central concern to Kant. See Sullivan (1996) more generally, and Sullivan (2002), esp. §3.3, for his detailed defence of such a reading.

16   Cf. the transition from the first sentence of 4.126 to the first sentence of 4.1274. Note that we must regard the 'opposite' of any such claim, which in the case of transcendental idealism is some kind of realism, as being no less a nonsensical pseudo-proposition than the claim itself.

17   Sullivan (2003), pp. 221–222.

18   The relation of transcendental idealism to the later work is, of course, the principal topic of Part II below.

19   [A. W.] Moore (2003), pp. 189–190.

20   Cf. Kant (1998), B145. Henceforth in Part I all unaccompanied references to Kant are to this book.

21   The distinction between the two German words that are both rendered as 'know', namely '*kennen*' and '*wissen*', is obviously pertinent here. Cf. also PI §78.

22   Cf. in this connection various currents in 2.02–2.0272 and 5.55–5.5571.

23   In saying that Wittgenstein himself violates this admonishment, I am referring back to 1.1. An obvious reply on Wittgenstein's behalf is that he uses the word 'world' differently in 1.1 from how he uses it in 5.61: whereas in the former case he uses it to refer to the realm of the actual, in the latter case he uses it to refer to the realm of the possible. I incline to the view that he uses it to refer to the realm of the actual throughout the *Tractatus*; and that

what enables him to refer to the realm of the possible in 5.61 is his use of other words and phrases, notably 'limits' and 'in logic'. But even if I am wrong about that – even if Wittgenstein's use of 'world' is ambiguous in the way proposed – what he says in 1.1, with its clearly implied application to any other possible world, is still surely offensive to the spirit of what he says in 5.61.

24   Cf. Karl Kraus's famous remark about psychoanalysis, which Bernard Williams applies to Wittgenstein's later philosophy: see Williams (2006), p. 208. For further discussion of this idea, see [A. W.] Moore (1997), p. 248.

25   Cf. [A. W.] Moore (2003), pp. 189–190; and cf. Sullivan's helpful gloss on this in Sullivan (2003), p. 219.

26   Sullivan (2003), pp. 219 ff.

27   See Sullivan (1996), principally §IV, and Sullivan (2002), pp. 59–60. Relevant remarks in the *Tractatus* include 1, 4.001, 4.5, and 5.4711.

28   Henceforth, whenever the two terms 'thought' and 'reality' are used without qualification, in connection with Kant, they are to be understood elliptically, as standing for thought which has content and for empirical reality respectively.

29   John McDowell, in the opening section of McDowell (1996), denies that Kant effects the first of these two contrasts. I think that McDowell has not properly taken into account passages such as A253–254/B309.

30   A92–93/B124–126 and B166–168. Note that only in the second of these two passages does Kant touch on the third possible explanation, specifically in theistic terms.

31   Cf. also 2.225, 3.04–3.05, 6.31, and 6.3211.

32   See Bxxvi, footnote; B146; B166, footnote; A492–493/B521–522; and A771–772/B799–800.

33   Kant (2000), 5:471–472, translation adapted by me.

34   See also material shortly before and shortly after the 6.4 s: 6.373–6.374 and 6.52–6.522.

35   As far as the left-hand side is concerned, cf. 3.13. Note: I caution that this isomorphism is rough for all sorts of reasons. One is that analytic thoughts appear on both sides of Kant's contrast (A52–55/B76–79 and A258–259/B314–315), whereas analytic propositions appear on neither side of Wittgenstein's (4.461–4.4611 and 6.1–6.11). Another is that the right-hand side of Kant's contrast involves the exercise of concepts, whereas the right-hand side of Wittgenstein's contrast involves pure and utter nonsense (see further below, with references). A final caveat: what Wittgenstein means by 'thoughts' are simply propositions with sense (4).

36   [A. W.] Moore (2003), p. 184.

37   Cf., in the case of Kant, A792/B820; and, in the case of Wittgenstein, 4.11 and 6.53.

38 For references to practical knowledge (translated as 'practical cognition') see Kant (1996), 5:103, and Kant (2000), 5:195.
39 See, for example, B135, B138–139, and B145. Cf. Descartes (1985), Pt I, §23.
40 See again B147–148.
41 See, for example, Kant (1996), 5:141.
42 There is a sense in which §2 is a generalization of §1.
43 For discussion, see [A. W.] Moore (2003), §§V–VIII.
44 The fundamental distinction between fact and value that is implicit here is also the primary theme of LE ("Lecture on Ethics"). NB (the pre-*Tractatus* notebooks) likewise contains highly pertinent reflections: e.g. see pp. 76–89. For helpful commentary on all of this material, see: Stenius (1960), esp. Ch. XI; Janik and Toulmin (1973), esp. Ch. 6; Hacker (1986), esp. Ch. IV; Diamond (2000); and Wiggins (2004).
45 This is perhaps most tendentious in the case of mathematical practice. I am thinking of the fact that mathematical practice consists in manipulating items on the right-hand side in a way that can look for all the world like expressing thoughts (6.2 and 6.2341).
46 EL, 143, his emphasis.
47 Have I not already defined transcendental idealism in Part I above? I have identified one particular version. What I shall supply here is a somewhat broader definition which will also effect a contrast with empirical idealism, a contrast that is going to be of some service later. In any case, as I said in the Introduction, each of these two parts is intended to be self-contained.
48 E.g. PI §§122–133.
49 By a *representation* throughout Part II I shall mean anything with a content that makes it true or false – such as a thought, an assertion, a judgement, or a theory.
50 I am not much concerned about whether this usage coincides with anybody else's, though my ultimate inspiration is obviously Kant, from whom the terminology derives: see Kant (1998), A490–491/B518–519. A more immediate inspiration is Williams (1981), p. 148. For a discussion relevant to what 'setting the limits' means in this context, see Sacks (1989), §1.2.2.
51 In fact I take it to be the latter. In PI §§90 ff., where Wittgenstein is engaging with his own former self, I take him to be trying to counteract some of what once made transcendental idealism so enticing to him. True, he himself makes claims in the course of this discussion which can themselves sound very transcendentally idealistic, e.g. §§103 and 114. But I take him to be merely emphasizing the contingency of 'how we go on', and, with it, the contingency of what concepts we possess. To hear these claims as *already* transcendentally idealistic – to hear them as already making limitations out of limits – is to commit the very error that he is trying to guard against: see e.g. §108. Indeed this is an error that he tries to guard against not only here

but again and again throughout his later work: thus PI §§241–242, and OC §98.

52 The exact relation between Wittgenstein's later work and transcendental idealism has been the focus of much recent discussion. The idea that there is a form of transcendental idealism in his later work is associated primarily with Williams: see Williams (1981). The idea is sympathetically pursued in Lear (1984), Lear (1986), Garver (1994), and Forster (2004). It is explored in Anscombe (1981) and Sacks (1997). And it is attacked in Bolton (1982), Malcolm (1982), and, less directly, McDowell (1993).

53 Cavell (1969a), p. 52.

54 PI, p. 226.

55 Cf. John McDowell on 'second nature' in McDowell (1996), pp. 84 ff. For various points in the discussion so far, see for example PI §§217, 241, 372, and 569–570, and PI II, §xii; RFM I, §4; and OC §204.

56 See for example PI §109.

57 Williams (1981), p. 153, his emphasis, tenses adapted.

58 Cf. his claim that '3 + 3 = 6' is a rule as to the way in which we are going to talk, quoted by G. E. Moore in [G. E.] Moore (1959), p. 279.

59 Cf. PI §240.

60 Cf. PI §207, and Davidson (1984).

61 Respectively: PI, pp. 226–227, his emphasis; and Z §§357–358, his emphasis.

62 Williams (1981), p. 163.

63 In particular it has to draw on the distinction between saying and showing which Wittgenstein had earlier thought gave him special license to 'endorse' nonsense – including, if the argument of Part I above is correct, transcendental idealism.

64 See [A. W.] Moore (1997a), Chs 7–9.

Chapter 8

Simples and the Idea of Analysis in the *Tractatus*

Marie McGinn

1. On one well-established interpretation, the *Tractatus* presents a realist theory of meaning, which conceives the representing relation as consisting of a direct link between bits of language (words) and bits of the world (objects). On this view, language's ability to represent possible states of affairs is grounded in the links that are forged between individual expressions and objects that exist prior to and independently of language. Interpreters who have found a realist theory of meaning in the *Tractatus* include G. E. M. Anscombe (1959), Max Black (1964), A. J. P. Kenny (1973), P. M. S. Hacker (1986 and 1996a), Norman Malcolm (1986) and D. F. Pears (1987).

For example, according to Pears, Wittgenstein's early view is that the possibility of factual discourse depends upon the existence of simple objects, each with its intrinsic set of possibilities for combining with other objects in states of affairs. These simple objects correspond to the simple names in a fully analyzed proposition. A name is 'first . . . attached to an object in something like the way envisaged by Russell', but it continues to represent the object 'only as long as the possibilities presented by the proposition in which it occurs are real possibilities for that object' (Pears, 1987, 103–4). A name's possibilities for combining with other names to form propositions must mirror the intrinsic possibilities of the object for combining with other objects in states of affairs. Thus, the logical structure of language is imposed on it from outside 'by the ultimate structure of reality' (Pears, 1987, 27). It is in virtue of this isomorphism between the logical structure of language and the independently constituted structure of reality that the connection between language and the world is made.

The idea that Wittgenstein endorses a form of realist metaphysics in the *Tractatus* has always had its detractors. Rush Rhees (1960, 1963,

1966 and 1969a), Peter Winch (1981 and 1987a), Hide Ishiguro (1969), and Brian McGuinness (1981) have all argued against the view that Wittgenstein set out, in the *Tractatus*, to provide a metaphysical basis for the logical structure of our language.[1] On their "anti-metaphysical" reading of the work, Wittgenstein is engaged in a logical investigation that is internal to language. His aim is to lay bare how the expressions of our language function and there is no attempt to reason from the system of representation to something outside it. For example, Ishiguro argues that the concept of an object is properly understood as an intensional one, which emerges in the context of understanding the role that is played by the logical constituents of propositions, and it cannot be understood independently of this. Brian McGuinness also denies 'that there is something by which our grammar is determined', and argues that Wittgenstein 'did not try to infer features of the world' from our language (McGuinness, 2002, 62). It is this line of interpretation – with much indebtedness to the work of these interpreters – that I want to defend here. It is undoubtedly Wittgenstein's remarks on simples that present the greatest challenge to this style of interpretation. The question I want to explore is: Is there a plausible reading of Wittgenstein's remarks on simples that does not commit him to making claims about the ontological structure of an independently constituted reality?

2. Wittgenstein first introduces the notion of simples in the *Notebooks* in April 1915:

> It always seems as if there were something that one *can regard as a thing*, and *on the other hand* real simple things. (*NB*, 43, 25.4.15)

Up to this point he has spoken of 'objects hav[ing] been arbitrarily correlated with [a proposition's] elements' (*NB*, 12, 15.10.14), of 'the arbitrary correlation of sign and thing signified' (*NB*, 25, 3.11.14), of names as 'representatives of things' (*NB*, 26, 4.11.14), of names as 'go[ing] proxy for objects' (*NB*, 37, 25.12.14, 29.12.14), and of 'the component parts' of a proposition representing 'those of the situation' it presents (*NB*, 27, 5.11.14). But it is only at this stage that he raises the question whether we 'can manage without simple objects in LOGIC' (*NB*, 46, 9.5.15). The question of simples then remains a central topic of discussion until July 1915. There then occurs a gap in the *Notebooks*, from July 1915 until April 1916. The entries from April 1916 until the end of the *Notebooks* in January 1917 quickly become dominated, first, by thoughts about solipsism, and then by thoughts about ethics. In the Preface to the 1996 edition of the *Prototractatus*, McGuinness suggests that the gap in the *Notebooks* from July 1915 until April 1916 corresponds to the time in which Wittgenstein first tried to write down his thoughts in the form of a treatise (now lost). McGuinness holds that what Wittgenstein wrote was an early version of the first 70 pages of the *Prototractatus*;[2] McGuinness calls this the proto-*Prototractatus*.

Some of the remarks on simples and complexes that Wittgenstein makes during the period from April 1915 to July 1915 survive into the *Tractatus*. However, there are striking and significant differences between the remarks on simples that occur in the *Notebooks* and the corresponding sections on simples in the *Tractatus* and the *Prototractatus*. In the *Notebooks*, Wittgenstein makes a number of remarks that strongly invite the sort of realist reading that I want to argue against. For example, he makes a number of remarks that suggest he is tempted to think of naming in terms of a direct relation between a name and an independently existing object that is made outside the context of a proposition:

> *By* my correlating the components of the picture with objects, it comes to represent a situation and to be right or wrong. (*NB*, 33–4, 26.11.14)

> It would be vain to try to express the pseudo-sentence "Are there simple things?" in symbolic notation.
>   And yet it is clear that I have before me a concept of a thing, of simple correlation, when I talk about this matter.
>   But how am I imaging the simple? Here all I can say is always " '*x*' has reference". (*NB*, 45, 6.5.15)

He also speaks of simple signs as signs 'which have an immediate reference' (*NB*, 46, 9.5.15), or which have a reference immediately.

It is in the context of the idea of naming as a direct relation between a name and a thing, set up by an act of correlation, that Wittgenstein raises the question whether we can name a complex spatial object. In a number of remarks, Wittgenstein seem to be prepared to consider the possibility that a logically simple sign – a name – might stand for a complex thing whose existence is a contingent matter:

> For it seems – at least so far as I can see at present – that the matter is not settled by getting rid of names by means of definitions: complex spatial objects, for example, seem to me in some sense to be essential things – I as it were see them as things. – And the designation of them by means of names seems to be more than a trick of language. Spatial complex objects – for example – really, so it seems, do appear as things.

But what does all this signify?

At any rate that we quite intuitively designate these objects by means of names. – (*NB*, 47, 13.5.15)

When I say " '*x*' has reference" do I have the feeling: "It is impossible that '*x*' should stand for, say, this knife or this letter"? Not at all. On the contrary. (*NB*, 49, 19.5.15)

The feeling of the simple relation which always comes before our mind as the main ground for the assumption of "simple objects" – haven't we got this very feeling when we think of the relation between name and complex object? (*NB*, 49–50, 23.5.15)

It is quite clear that I can in fact correlate a name with this watch just as it lies here ticking in front of me, and that this name will have reference outside any proposition in the very sense I have always given that word, and I feel that that name in a proposition will correspond to all the requirements of the 'names of simple objects'. (*NB*, 60, 15.6.15)

It seems that as long as we think of naming – in the way Russell does – as a direct correlation between a sign and the thing that it signifies, there is nothing to motivate the idea that a name must signify a simple. The act of correlating a name and an object, by means of which the name comes to signify the object, may, it seems, be performed in relation to the familiar, complex spatial objects of everyday life. Thus, the motivation for holding that a name must stand for intrinsically simple elements must come from elsewhere. Wittgenstein ultimately finds the source for the requirement that names stand for simple objects in the demand for definiteness of sense and the possibility for complete analysis. He writes:

[W]hat we mean by "complex objects do not exist" is: It must be clear in the proposition how the object is composed, so far as it is possible for us to speak of its complexity at all. – The sense of the proposition must appear in the proposition as divided into its *simple* components. . . .

When the sense of the proposition is completely expressed in the proposition itself, the proposition is always divided into simple components – no further division is possible and an apparent one is superfluous – and these are objects in the original sense. (*NB*, 63, 17.6.15)

He continues the next day:

The demand for simple things *is* the demand for definiteness of sense. (*NB*, 63, 18.6.15)

Thus, at the end of analysis, we must arrive at propositions whose component expressions are logically simple names. The demand that these logically simple constituents of a fully analysed proposition stand for simple objects arises from the requirement 'for definiteness of sense'. It seems that if sense is to be 'definite', then there cannot be a perspective from which the objects that the logical constituents of a fully analysed proposition stand for can be seen as complex. Any complexity that is recognised as complexity shows that further analysis is possible, until we arrive at a point 'where no further division is possible and an apparent one is superfluous'. At this point we have arrived at what is – from the perspective of those who understand the proposition – no longer complex. Insofar as Wittgenstein recognizes that the watch on the table is complex, that complexity must be something that can be revealed through the analysis of propositions about it. Only when we arrive at what we recognize as intrinsically simple elements will analysis come to an end and the sense of the proposition be made completely definite and perspicuous.

The connection between the demand for simples and the demand for definiteness of sense does not, of course, rule out a realist interpretation. And there are remarks in the *Notebooks* in which Wittgenstein exhibits a temptation to think of the analysis of propositions in terms of uncovering a complexity that is there, independently, in the world:

> . . . a completely analysed proposition contains just as many names as there are things contained in its reference. (*NB*, 11, 11.10.14)

> When the proposition is just as complex as its reference, then it is *completely* analysed. (*NB*, 46, 9.5.15)

> It does not go against our feeling that *we* cannot analyse PROPOSITIONS so far as to mention elements by name; no, we feel that the WORLD must consist of elements. (*NB*, 62, 17.6.15)

> The world has a fixed structure. (*NB*, 62, 17.6.15)

These remarks suggest that Wittgenstein is tempted to think of the structure of the world, in the way that Pears describes, as something intrinsic, as something that is there independently of language and which language must reflect. He also seems to suggest that we have intimations of this intrinsic structure and that we can recognize that the world must ultimately break down into simples:

> Even though we have no acquaintance with simple objects we *do* know complex objects by acquaintance, we know by acquaintance that they are complex. – And that in the end they must consist of simple things?

We single out a part of our visual field, for example, and we see that it is always complex, that any part of it is still complex but is already simpler, and so on. (*NB*, 50, 24.5.15)

3. There is, then, clear evidence of realist tendencies in Wittgenstein's thought in the *Notebooks*. A number of the themes that have, in one way or another, been important for the realist interpretation of the *Tractatus* are clearly represented there: the idea of a direct correlation between a name and an object, the idea that a name has reference outside any proposition, and the idea that analysis uncovers a complexity that is there in an independently constituted reality. However, it is striking that the remarks quoted above – and others like them – are not only not included in either the *Tractatus* or the *Prototractatus*, but that the latter include remarks that appear to be in direct opposition to the ideas identified above. Thus, although the *Tractatus* and the *Prototractatus* contain the apparently metaphysical remark:

> In logic nothing is accidental: if a thing can occur in a state of affairs, the possibility of the state of affairs must be written into the thing itself. (*PT* 2.012; *TLP* 2.012)

The *Prototractatus* comments on this as follows:

> What this comes to is that if it were the case that names had meaning both when combined *in* propositions and outside them, it would, so to speak, be impossible to guarantee that in both cases they really had the same meaning, in the same sense of the word.
>   It seems to be impossible for words to appear in two different roles: by themselves, and in propositions. (*PT* 2.0122; cf. *TLP* 2.0122)

Thus, the idea that we correlate a name with an object, or that a name has reference outside any proposition, is apparently abandoned. A name is identifiable as a name only insofar as it is a logical constituent of a proposition: 'only in the nexus of a proposition does a name have meaning' (*PT* 3.202; *TLP* 3.3). He no longer talks of 'This' being identical with the concept of an object (*NB*, p.61, 16.6.15); there is no longer any '*This*' outside of 'This is how things stand' (*PT* 4.4303; *TLP* 4.5). The question whether a name can stand for a complex, or whether a complex can figure, logically, as an object also disappears. The issue now seems to have been settled:

> A complex can be given only by its description, which will be right or wrong. (*PT* 3.20105; *TLP* 3.24)

A complex can only be represented by means of a proposition that is either true or false; a complex, in Wittgenstein's early thought, is equivalent to the fact that its constituents are connected in the way that is represented by the proposition that describes it. Thus, what can be named *cannot* be complex: what is complex is given '*only* (my emphasis) by its description, which will be right or wrong' (true or false).

In the *Prototractatus* and the *Tractatus*, Wittgenstein also abandons the idea of the 'reference' of a proposition, and with it the idea that the aim of analysis is to arrive at a proposition that 'is just as complex as its reference' (*NB*, 46, 9.5.15). Instead, he picks up on a strand that is also represented in the *Notebooks*, although it is in prima facie tension with the view of analysis just expressed, in which Wittgenstein describes the aim of analysis in terms of making the *sense* of a proposition perspicuous. He writes:

> The sense of the proposition must appear in the proposition as divided into its simple components –. And these parts are then actually indivisible, for further divided they just would not be THESE. In other words, the proposition can then no longer be *replaced* by one that has more components, but any that has more components also does not have *this* sense. (*NB*, 63, 17.6.15)

The next day he continues:

> If the complexity of an object is definitive of the sense of the proposition, then it must be portrayed in the proposition to the extent that it does determine the sense. And to the extent that its composition is *not* definitive of *this* sense, to that extent the objects of this proposition are *simple*. THEY *cannot* be further divided. –
>
> The demand for simple things *is* the demand for definiteness of sense. (*NB*, 63, 18.6.15)

There is no longer the suggestion that analysis aims at uncovering a complexity that is there, independently, in the world. Whatever complexity there is in a proposition is definitive of its sense and thus internal to the proposition itself. The aim of analysis is merely to make the complexity that is definitive of the sense of a proposition explicit. The emphasis is on uncovering the logical structure that is there in our language – i.e. in the sense of the propositions that are expressed by means of the sentences of our language – and any suggestion that we are concerned with a claim about the ultimate structure of an independent reality evaporates. Thus, the aim of analysis is described in the *Tractatus* as follows:

> In a proposition a thought can be expressed in such a way that elements of the propositional sign correspond to the objects of thought.
> I call such elements 'simple signs', and such a proposition 'completely analysed'. (*TLP* 3.2–3.201)

Interestingly, these remarks do not occur in the same form in the *Prototractatus*. A version of *TLP* 3.2 occurs in the *Prototractatus*, but in it Wittgenstein is still feeling the temptation – clearly one he corrects for in the *Tractatus* – to speak of analysis in terms of correspondence to the objects of reality:

> In a propositional sign the simple signs correspond to the objects of reality. (*PT* 3.14)

All of this, I want to suggest, gives encouragement to the idea that when Wittgenstein breaks off from the *Notebooks* to write the first draft of his treatise, he has made a serious breakthrough in his thoughts about simples. Certain strands in his thought, which he has come to recognize as mistaken, are thrown off, while others are preserved and sharpened. This thought seems to be confirmed by the brief remarks on simples that open the *Notebook* entries for April 1916. He writes:

> We can only foresee what we ourselves construct.
> But then where is the concept of a simple object still to be found?
> The concept does not so far come in here at all.
> We must be able to construct the simple functions because we must be able to give each sign a meaning.
> For the only sign which guarantees its meaning is function and argument. (*NB*, 71, 15.4.16)

These remarks are very brief and very obscure. However, they seem to express Wittgenstein's coming down clearly on the side of the view that the concept of a simple symbol must be internal to a language in which states of affairs are represented, that is, it must emerge as an *a priori* or logical requirement on representation as such. This does not on its own rule out a realist interpretation of the *Tractatus*, but it suggests that there is an important shift away from at least certain realist tendencies in his thought between July 1915 and April 1916. He gives up the inclination to think in terms of the essential structure of an independently constituted reality, or in terms of a direct link, or direct correlation, between a name and an object. He now focuses instead on the idea that the concept of a simple symbol arises as an *a priori* requirement for signs that 'guarantee' their meaning: a name is essentially a logical constituent of a fully analyzed proposition with sense. There must, therefore, be nothing hypothetical in the concept of a simple object that constitutes the meaning of a logical constituent of a fully analyzed proposition.[3] The fact that the corresponding sign is an unanalyzable logical constituent in a proposition with sense must be enough to guarantee its meaning. Thus, Wittgenstein begins to think about simples entirely in relation to the analysis of the sense of propositions and within the framework of some version of Frege's context principle: 'It is enough if the proposition taken as a whole has sense; it is this that confers on its parts also their content' (Frege 1980, §60, p. 71). It is not, as I've tried to make clear, that this way of thinking is *absent* from the *Notebooks*. However, it is as if Wittgenstein has been able to resolve the tensions that characterize the discussion of simples in the *Notebooks*, by completely rejecting the realist tendencies that are expressed in the remarks quoted above.

There are remarks in the *Notebooks* that suggest that Wittgenstein is fully aware of the tensions in his pre-*Tractatus* thought about simples:

> It keeps on looking as if the question "Are there simple things?" made sense. And surely this question must be nonsense! – (*NB*, 45, 5.5.15)

It shouldn't look as if the question concerns anything hypothetical, anything that would have to be settled by experience. The question cannot be one of whether something exists or does not exist. Yet as long as he thinks in terms of a direct link between a name and an object, made outside the context of a proposition, the question of what we are acquainted with, and whether we're acquainted with simples, seems to arise and to make sense. Wittgenstein gives expression to what I'm identifying as the alternative approach to the question of simples as follows:

> The question [whether " 'complex objects' in the end satisfy just the demands which I apparently make on simple ones"] might . . . also be presented like this: It seems that the idea of the SIMPLE is already contained in that of the complex and in the idea of analysis, and in such a way that

we come to this idea quite apart from any examples of simple objects, or of propositions which mention them, and we realize the existence of the simple object – *a priori* as a logical necessity.

So it looks as if the existence of the simple objects were related to that of the complex ones as the sense of *-p* is to the sense of *p*: the simple object is *prejudged* in the complex. (*NB*, 60, 15.6.15)

The next day he adds:

(This is NOT to be confused with the *fact* that its *component* is prejudged in the complex.) (*NB*, 60, 16.6.15)

It has, in other words, nothing to do with a question about the physical composition of complexes, but with the essential logical structure of expressions that represent them. Thus, just as the sense of *-p* essentially presupposes the sense of *p*, so the possibility of representing what is complex essentially presupposes that there are signs that stand for simples. Clearly, it is this strand in Wittgenstein's pre-*Tractatus* thought that is developed in the *Tractatus* and the *Prototractatus*. What I want to argue is that the idea that the question about simples is to be understood as a question about the essential nature of a symbolism in which states of affairs are represented means that it cannot be the case that the argument for simples involves any hypothetical claim about the ultimate constituents of an independently constituted reality. To think that the argument for simples makes a claim about the ultimate constituents of reality, conceived independently of its representation in language, is to make the same mistake as to think that the propositions of logic express maximally general truths about the world, or to think that the question whether there are subject-predicate propositions is a question whether a certain logical form exists in reality.[4] In all these cases, we are making the mistake of treating what is internal to a symbolism in which we express propositions that can be compared with reality for truth or falsity, as if it were a question of fact. However, all this still leaves us with the question whether the argument for simples in the *Tractatus can* be interpreted in a way that exonerates Wittgenstein from making any quasi-factual claim about the ultimate constituents of reality, conceived independently of its representation in language. In the space remaining I want to sketch the bare bones of such a reading.

4. At *TLP* 3.23, Wittgenstein repeats the idea we saw him express in the *Notebooks*: the demand for simple signs arises out of the requirement that sense be determinate:

> The requirement that simple signs be possible is the requirement that sense be determinate.

I believe that we should see Wittgenstein's commitment to the determinacy of sense as one of a number of preconceptions concerning language that form the overall framework within which he undertakes the logical investigation of the nature of a proposition. Thus, Wittgenstein carries out his central task of clarifying how a proposition expresses its sense within the context of a preconception that where there is sense there is logic, and where there is logic there must be perfect logical order: it is this that gives rise to the requirement that sense must be determinate. That is to say, there must be no question whether a proposition expresses a sense or of what the sense that it expresses is: a proposition must be essentially connected with the unique situation that it represents. However, as Wittgenstein sees it, the requirement that a proposition is essentially connected with the unique situation that it represents just is the requirement that the simple signs that occur in a fully analyzed proposition cannot stand for something that is logically complex: if sense is to be determinate, then the simple signs that are the logical constituents of a fully analyzed proposition must be signs that '*cannot* be anatomized by means of definitions' (*TLP* 3.261). The logically simple constituents of propositions must be indefinable symbols that cannot be further analyzed, if there is to be such a thing as determinate sense. Moreover, he holds that *any* sign that stands for a complex is a sign, not only that *can*, but *must* be anatomized by means of a definition. It follows from all this that the demand for simple indefinable symbols *is* the demand for names that stand for logically simple objects, i.e. for objects that *cannot* be described by means of a proposition.

Wittgenstein makes the same point at *TLP* 2.0211–2.0212 as follows:

> If the world had no substance, then whether a proposition had sense would depend on whether another proposition was true.
>
> In that case we could not sketch any picture of the world (true or false).

The substance of the world is constituted by the logically simple objects for which primitive names stand. Thus, we could rewrite *TLP* 2.0211 as follows: if there were not primitive expressions that stand for logically simple objects, then whether a proposition had sense would depend on whether another proposition was true. The force of the above remarks, therefore, is that the existence of primitive expressions, which stand for logically simple objects that are the simple constituents of states of affairs, is a condition of our sketching any picture of the world, true or false. The question is: How are we to understand this claim?

Suppose that a propositional sign, $F(A)$, contains a simple sign, 'A', that stands for a complex. Given that what the sign 'A' stands for is complex, it can be described in a proposition, aRb, that is either true or false. If we hold that 'A' is, nevertheless, a logically simple constituent of the propositional sign $F(A)$, then whether $F(A)$ has a sense, i.e. a truth-condition, will depend on whether the proposition, aRb, is true. But in that case $F(A)$ is not a logical picture of a state of affairs, for we cannot know, on the basis of knowledge of how its constituent expressions are combined in a propositional sign, what state of affairs is represented by $F(A)$, for we do not know whether $F(A)$ represents a possible state of affairs (i.e. has a sense) at all. Wittgenstein's fundamental idea is that a picture stands in an internal relation to the fact that it represents. The internal relation consists in rules of projection whereby we can derive from a picturing fact a representation of a state of affairs that either exists or does not exist. It is essential to the internal relation that holds between a picturing fact and the fact that it pictures that everything essential to the picture's representing what it does is determined by the system of representation to which the picture belongs, and does not depend upon anything's being the case.

Our ability to use a propositional sign to communicate a possible state of affairs depends, therefore, upon the existence of primitive signs whose meanings are not in question. In a remark from the *Prototractatus* that does not survive into the *Tractatus*, Wittgenstein writes:

> The analysis of signs must come to an end at some point, because if signs are to express anything at all, meaning must belong to them in a way that is once and for all complete. (*PT*, 3.20102)

The idea is that the meaning of a primitive sign belongs to it 'in a way that is once and for all complete' or 'ready-made' insofar as it is determined by the sign's place in a system of representation and does not depend upon the existence of any state of affairs, i.e. on anything hypothetical.[5] That is to say, determinacy of sense requires the existence of primitive signs that stand in an internal relation to the constituents of states of affairs; the existence of the constituent must be guaranteed by the existence of a primitive sign that has a use within a system of representation that stands in a projective relation to the world. It must be the case that 'if everything behaves as if a sign had meaning, then it does have meaning' (*TLP* 3.328). A sign's behaving as if it had meaning – i.e. its being used in propositions with sense – is what constitutes its having a meaning; there is no more to the meaning of a primitive sign than its being in propositions that can be compared with reality for truth or falsity. It is, therefore, impossible that the constituents of states of affairs for which names stand should be describable by means of propositions that can be compared with reality for truth or falsity; whatever is describable by means of a proposition is something that can either exist or fail to exist, namely, a state of affairs. We use signs that stand for objects that are constituents of states of affairs in propositions that describe those states of affairs, and in this sense we can be said to speak about them. But these objects can only be named; they cannot be characterized in propositions. The simple signs that are the primitive constituents of propositions – the basic indefinables – constitute the elements of representation; the meaning of these signs is fixed by their use within a system of representation that stands in a projective relation to the world, and thus we can use them to construct propositions that communicate a new sense. Wittgenstein calls the constituents of states of affairs that constitute the meaning of simple names 'objects'.[6] Thus:

> Objects can only be *named*. Signs are their representatives. I can only speak *about* them: I cannot *put them into words*. Propositions can only say *how* things are, not *what* they are. (*TLP* 3.221)

Wittgenstein approaches the question of the need for the existence of primitive, indefinable names in another way, at *TLP* 3.261. Once again, suppose that a propositional sign, *F(A)*, contains a simple sign, '*A*', that stands for a complex. Suppose that the complex that '*A*' stands for is described by the proposition, *aRb*. Given this description of the complex, we could introduce another sign, '*B*', which is the contraction of the symbol that describes the complex into a simple sign: *B*=(def)*aRb*. The proposition expressed by a propositional sign of the form *F(B)* is analyzable as follows: *F(a)&F(b)&aRb*. However, we now have two signs, '*A*' and '*B*', that both stand for the same complex, but one of them, '*A*', is allegedly primitive (i.e. unanalyzable) and the other, '*B*', is defined. Wittgenstein clearly thinks that this is completely unacceptable: 'Two signs cannot signify in the same manner if one is primitive and the other is defined by means of primitive signs' (*TLP* 3.261). Signs that signify in the same manner must be the same symbol. We must, therefore, assume that the original sign, '*A*', also signifies via the signs that could be used to define it. Thus, '[e]very sign that has a definition signifies via the signs that serve to define it; and the definitions point the way' (*TLP* 3.261).

It follows from this that if a propositional sign contains a sign, '*A*', that stands for a complex, then the meaning of '*A*' is given by means of a definition: $A=(\text{def})aRb$. The sense of the proposition expressed by the propositional sign in which '*A*' occurs is perspicuously expressed by a propositional sign in which the sign '*A*' has disappeared and is replaced by a proposition, aRb, that describes that complex completely. Thus, the logical form of a proposition expressed by the propositional sign *F(A)* is perspicuously represented as a complex proposition that has aRb as one of its conjuncts. The truth of aRb is, in that case, not a condition of the sense, but of the truth of the proposition expressed by a propositional sign of the form *F(A)*. If aRb is false, then the proposition expressed by *F(A)* is false, and not senseless. Once again, it follows from all this that a genuinely primitive sign is one that 'cannot be dissected any further by means of a definition' (*TLP* 3.26). Thus, '[n]ames *cannot* be anatomised by means of a definition' (*TLP* 3.261). Wittgenstein goes on: '(Nor can any sign that has a meaning independently and on its own)'. I believe that we should understand this to mean any sign whose meaning does not depend on the meaning of its parts, i.e. it includes all the basic indefinables that are the simple constituents of a proposition.

5. On this interpretation, Wittgenstein's conception of a simple name does not express a version of realism, in which names are held to forge a direct link between language and the world. The object for which a name stands is not something that exists over and against language, in an independent or transcendent realm, but is what we grasp when we grasp the meaning of the name, i.e. when we grasp the contribution that the name makes to determining the sense of a class of propositions. Thus, at the level of simple names, we cannot understand two names without thereby knowing whether they have the same or a different meaning:

> Can we understand two names without knowing whether they signify the same thing? – Can we understand a proposition in which two names occur without knowing whether their meaning is the same or different?
>
> Suppose I know the meaning of an English word and of a German word that means the same: then it is impossible for me to be unaware that they do mean the same; I must be capable of translating each into the other. (*TLP* 4.243)

It's now clear why Wittgenstein believes that the same holds for simple signs: to grasp the *Bedeutung* of a simple sign is equivalent to grasping the meaning of the sign (i.e. the contribution it makes to propositions with a sense), and to grasp the *Bedeutungen* of two simple signs is necessarily to grasp whether they have the same or different meaning. The simple signs are the basic representational elements – the words – that are combined in elementary propositions. The most plausible examples of the simple constituents of fully analyzed propositions are names of spatial or material points, colours, temporal points, etc., and functions of these. To understand a sign that stands for any one of these elements is necessarily to grasp the whole system of representation within which it has a place. The existence of the system does not depend upon a prior correlation between the elements and something that lies over and against language, but upon the system's standing in a projective relation to the world, i.e. upon the existence of a rule that determines, for each combination of elements in elementary propositions, what it is for the proposition to be true, and thereby, what it is for it to be false.

Thus, on a particular occasion on which an elementary proposition in which the name of a simple occurs – let's say 'Red at such-and-such a place at such-and-such a time' – is true, it describes what is the case. The simple object that constitutes the meaning of the name 'red', say, is a constituent of the state of affairs described by the proposition insofar as it is a common constituent of a class of states of affairs described by means of propositions that contain the name 'red' as an element. To say that the object for which the word 'red' stands is a constituent of an existing state of affairs is just to say that the state of affairs is correctly described by means of a proposition in which the word 'red' occurs. If the state of affairs does not exist, the simple sign does not lose its meaning. Similarly, for expressions that give spatio-temporal co-ordinates, or the distribution of material points: it is the system of representation that gives these elements of representation their meaning, not a direct correlation between name and object. Sense is determinate insofar as there are primitive signs whose meaning is determined by their place in a system of representation that stands in a projective relation to the world, which can be used to describe states of affairs independently of the truth or falsity of any particular proposition.

On this interpretation, we use the propositions of ordinary language on particular occasions to express a determinate sense that is perspicuously represented by means of a conjunction of elementary propositions. Thus, the propositions of ordinary language, as they are used on an occasion to say something, are logical pictures. It is in virtue of being a logical picture that a proposition, as it is applied on a particular occasion, expresses a sense. We can read off from the fully analyzed proposition that perspicuously expresses this sense the determinate state of affairs that the proposition represents. The essential idea of a logical picture is that there is nothing in common between the picture and the state of affairs it represents, over and above what is common to all pictures that can represent that state of affairs. Wittgenstein makes the point clearly at *TLP* 3.34–3.341:

> A proposition possesses essential and accidental features.
>
> Accidental features are those that result from the particular way in which the propositional sign is produced. Essential features are those without which the proposition could not express its sense.
>
> So what is essential in a proposition is what all propositions that can express the same sense have in common.
>
> And similarly, in general, what is essential in a symbol is what all symbols that can serve the same purpose have in common.

Thus, a symbol signifies what it does in virtue of its logical properties, i.e. in virtue of those properties that are common to any symbol that can serve the same purpose.

It is essential to a proposition's expressing a sense that it is logically articulate and that the logically simple constituents of a fully analyzed proposition constitute the basic indefinables. A fully analyzed proposition is one in which the structure of the proposition mirrors the structure of the thought that it expresses. The structure of the thought is the logical articulation that is essential to any sign's expressing *this* sense. Anything that is essential to the thought's expressing its sense will be reflected in the structure of what is projected, namely the state of affairs it represents. Thus, there must be exactly as many logically simple parts in a fully analyzed proposition as there are in the state of affairs that it represents:

> In a proposition there must be exactly as many distinguishable parts as in the situation it represents.
>
> The two must possess the same logical (mathematical) multiplicity. (*TLP* 4.04)

On this interpretation, this idea does not represent an external constraint on language, and it does not commit Wittgenstein to the idea that language must fit something that is conceived independently of it. It is rather a reflection, on the one hand, of the internal relation that exists between language and the reality that it depicts, and on the other, of what is essential to any proposition's expressing the sense that it does. The logical multiplicity of a fully analyzed proposition – that is to say, the number of logically distinguishable parts – is determined insofar as it is part of what is essential to its expressing its (essentially determinate) sense: all propositions that can be used to represent a particular state of affairs must share this logical multiplicity. If there are elementary propositions of the form 'aRb', then any symbol that represents the state of affairs that is represented by 'aRb' will have parts that correspond to 'a', 'b' and 'xRy'. The logical articulation of the state of affairs is mirrored in the essential logical articulation of any symbol that represents it.

6. It is impossible to deny that the remarks with which the *Tractatus* begins appear to present a fundamental ontology that is held to be the foundation of our ability to picture the world in propositions. On all interpretations of the work, the remarks that follow force the reader to a reassessment of these opening paragraphs and to recognize that their status must be other than it originally appears. On the interpretation of Wittgenstein's remarks on simples that I have put forward, the reassessment that is called for requires us to see that the impression that the opening remarks say something about the essential structure of a transcendent reality that our language somehow hooks onto is a false one. What we come to see is that what Wittgenstein is doing in these remarks is nothing more than tracing the logical order that is essential to any language's ability to express propositions that can be compared with reality for truth or falsity. The idea is that once the central task of clarification has been accomplished, and the internal relation between propositions and the reality they depict has been made perspicuous, then the opening remarks undergo a change of aspect. We see that what appeared to be a series of metaphysical remarks that describe the *a priori* order of reality, which it possesses independently of our means of representing it, is, at bottom, an articulation of the logic, that is, the essence, of description. The idea that we are getting outside the symbolism and saying something about its relation to a transcendent realm with an intrinsic structure is an illusion; the illusion lies in our taking what belongs to the logic of our language, in which we express propositions that can be tested for truth or falsity, for substantial doctrine. What we come to see is that what Wittgenstein is doing in these remarks is not metaphysics but logic.

Read in this light, Wittgenstein's remark that objects are common to all possible worlds amounts to nothing more than the claim that we describe worlds – actual or possible – in language and that the elements of representation are common to all our descriptions. It makes no sense to ask whether objects exist or do not exist, not because they *necessarily* exist, but because they are elements of representation. The meaning of simple signs is determined by their place in a system of representation that stands in a projective relation to the world; it is the states of affairs that are represented that exist or do not exist. The substance of the world is not, therefore, to be understood as a metaphysical stuff that exists through all change. It is constituted by the meanings of the basic indefinables that we use to characterize the world as we imagine it. It is equivalent to logical space, i.e. the space within which all states of affairs are represented. It exists independently of what is the case insofar as logical space is autonomous: the system of representation within which we describe what is the case is independent of the existence or non-existence of any particular state of affairs. It depends only on whether a certain sort of projection has been made. Insofar as a fact is what is represented by a true proposition – the existence of a state of affairs – facts exist in logical space. The logical space in which facts exist is not prior to or independent of the logical space in which propositions exist. There is one and only one logical space and it is common to language and the reality it describes.

Finally, on the interpretation I've presented, Wittgenstein's commitment to simples in the *Tractatus* does not arise out of an attempt to ground the structure of our language in the structure of an independently constituted reality. If there is a mistaken philosophical conception lying behind Wittgenstein's argument for simples, then it is his commitment to the determinacy of sense and the conception of meaning as something that is correlated with a word: simple objects are the meanings that correspond to the simple, indefinable signs that are the constituents of elementary propositions. Wittgenstein is later critical of both of these ideas, and of the idea of simples that depends upon them. However, I've tried to show that the fundamental impulse behind the argument for simples that Wittgenstein gives in the *Tractatus* lies in his commitment to the autonomy of language, i.e. to the idea that whether a proposition has sense cannot depend on whether another proposition is true. The argument for simples is part of Wittgenstein's attempt to show that we do not have to worry about language, that whether a proposition has sense depends only on whether a certain projection has been made, that the relation between a proposition and the situation it represents is internal or essential and does not depend on anything hypothetical. I want to end by suggesting that the concern to show that the meaning of the

expressions of our language is independent of anything hypothetical continues in the later philosophy, that the impulse that drives the argument
for simples is not rejected, but re-thought. What we find is that Wittgenstein does not reject the impulse that leads to the idea that '*a name ought
really to signify a simple*' (*PI* 39), but that he responds to it differently.
The later turn towards language-in-use means that he now believes that
we have only to look at the actual employment of language within our
everyday lives, to see how language takes care of itself. If we are tempted
to think that the autonomy of language calls for words that stand for
simples, then 'we must focus on the details of what goes on; must look
at them *from close to*' (*PI* 51).[7]

Notes

1   The realist interpretation has been criticized more recently by Cora Diamond
and James Conant, who have put forward a reading of the *Tractatus* known
as the 'resolute' reading (see Diamond 1988 and Introduction to 1991;
Conant, 1991 and 2002). Their interpretation shares with the anti-metaphysical reading, of Rhees *et al.*, the rejection of the idea that Wittgenstein ever
engages in the sort of theorizing about the relation between language and an
independent reality that the realist reading claims. However, while Rhees and
others allow that Wittgenstein sets out to achieve positive insights into how
language functions, Diamond and Conant want to see Wittgenstein's aims as
purely therapeutic. Other resolute readers of the *Tractatus* include T. Ricketts
(1996), W. Goldfarb (1997) and M. Kremer (2001).
2   That is to say, those sections that deal with the nature of a proposition, and
excluding those concerned with the discussion of solipsism and ethics.
3   Wittgenstein expresses the idea that philosophy is 'purely descriptive' as early
as 'Notes on Logic' (October 1913; *NB*, 93ff.). The central idea of the sort
of anti-metaphysical interpretation I want to defend is that Wittgenstein sees
his task in the *Tractatus* as one of clarifying how a proposition expresses its
sense. Wittgenstein's conviction that his task is purely one of clarification arises,
in part at least, from his conviction that 'I cannot need to worry about language' (*NB*, 43, 27.4.15): 'We must recognize *how* language takes care of
itself' (*NB*, 43, 26.4.15). Everything that is essential to how a proposition
expresses its sense must be manifest in the way language functions. His aim is
not, on this understanding, to give a theory of how language connects with
the world. Insofar as '[t]he way language signifies is mirrored in its use' (*NB*,
82, 11.9.16), the task is purely one of clarification or description: we have
only to look at the use of language to see how it signifies, that is, represents
possible states of affairs in the way that it does. The nature of a proposition

must be something that language itself makes clear. However, it is also the case that Wittgenstein's whole conception of this central task of clarification is governed by a preconceived idea of logic as the essence of language and by a commitment to the idea of determinacy of sense.

4   At the beginning of the *Notebooks*, Wittgenstein writes:

> Then can we ask ourselves: Does the subject-predicate form exist? Does the relational form exist? Do any of the forms exist at all that Russell and I were always talking about? (Russell would say: "Yes! That's self-evident." *Ha!*)

> Then: if *everything* that needs to be shewn is shewn by the existence of subject-predicate SENTENCES etc., the task of philosophy is different from what I originally supposed. But if that is not how it is, then what is lacking would have to be shewn by means of some kind of experience, and that I regard as out of the question. (*NB*, 2, 3)

These remarks suggest that Wittgenstein is beginning to move away from Russell's conception of the task of philosophy, which he regards as mistaken just because it makes what are essentially *a priori* questions appear as if they involve something that *could* only be settled by experience, and that is absurd. The idea of the interpretation I'm presenting is that Wittgenstein continues, in the *Notebooks*, to give expression to the realist tendencies that he acquired from Russell, but that he finally shakes them off in July 1915. He has now come to see his task as an investigation of what is essential to a symbolism in which states of affairs are represented. One of the consequences of the investigation that he undertakes is that we come to see that what is essential to representation belongs to the method of projecting signs, and not to what obtains in reality.

5   Cf. Winch: 'A name has meaning if it behaves in language just as though it had one; in fact its having the meaning it does just consists in its "significant use"' (Winch, 1987, 9). Both Peter Hacker (1999) and Cora Diamond (2005) object to Winch's view on the ground that it entails that all names that share a logico-syntactic form are the same symbol, and that the only difference in meaning is difference in form. However, the objection takes no account of the fact that the meaning of a name consists in its contribution to the sense (i.e. the truth-conditions) of the propositions in which it occurs and that propositions which share a logical form will be true or false in different circumstances. Only names that are substitutable everywhere *salva veritate* are the same symbol. It is the being true or false that constitutes the relation of propositions to reality and confers content on their propositional constituents.

6   Although Wittgenstein uses the terms '*bedeutet*' and '*Bedeutung*' to describe the relation between a name and an object, I want to argue that the role that

the concept of an object plays in the *Tractatus* brings it much closer to the notion of the meaning of a name than to the notion of the bearer or reference of a name: simple objects just are the meanings that correspond to the simple, indefinable signs that are the constituents of elementary propositions. I want to claim that the fundamental mistake that lies behind Wittgenstein's talk of the meaning of a name as the object for which it stands is the mistake of thinking that the meaning of a word is something correlated with it, something that we grasp when we understand a word, whereas use (which is also central to the *Tractatus*-understanding of a name) is something extended in time.

7   I develop this anti-metaphysical interpretation of the *Tractatus* more fully in *Elucidating the Tractatus: Wittgenstein's Early Philosophy of Logic and Language* (Oxford: Oxford University Press), 2006. I would like to thank members of the audience at the Sterling Workshop on the *Tractatus*, and at a day conference on the *Tractatus* at the School of Advanced Study, University of London in January 2006, for very helpful discussion of an earlier draft of this paper. I would also like to thank Edward Kanterian for his helpful critical comments.

Chapter 9

Words, Waxing and Waning: Ethics in/and/of the *Tractatus Logico-Philosophicus*

Stephen Mulhall

(1) Gordon Baker's later philosophical work on Wittgenstein's later philo-sophical writings bears a striking but ambiguous relation to work on Wittgenstein's writings, both early and late, produced by authors some-times known as the 'New Wittgensteinians', prominent among whom are James Conant and Cora Diamond.[1] On the one hand, Baker's very strong sense of the degree to which the later Wittgenstein aims to eschew theses, to adopt a therapeutical stance to philosophical problems, and to view even his own grammatical remarks as without authority in the face of an interlocutor's rejection of them, seems uncannily reminiscent of the 'New Wittgensteinian' approach to the *Philosophical Investigations*. And this convergence engenders a further similarity: for insofar as one reads Witt-genstein as attempting to eschew theses, one faces the difficulty of finding a way of bringing out this aspect of his work in one's commentaries upon it that does not itself result in attributing theses to Wittgenstein – not even the thesis that there are no philosophical theses. Baker's post-humously published collection of late essays (Baker 2004) shows him confronting these reflexive challenges with respect to Wittgenstein's later writings with just as much persistence and sophistication as the 'New Wittgensteinians' show in their work on Wittgenstein's writings throughout his career.

On the other hand, Baker's work on the *Tractatus* – whilst offering a far from orthodox reading of the details of, and the underlying rationale for, that text's pronouncements on reality, thought and language – appears to accept that those pronouncements must indeed be intended to convey necessarily ineffable insights into the essence of its subject-matter (see Baker 1988). By contrast, the 'New Wittgensteinian' approach contends that attributing any such intention to the author of the *Tractatus* runs contrary to that text's explicit conception of the nature of nonsense, and more generally fails to appreciate the degree to which the text as a whole has an essentially therapeutic purpose of the kind that both they and Baker attribute to the *Philosophical Investigations* – one designed in this case to disabuse us of the very idea that there might be ineffable insights into the essence of things.

This way of reading the *Tractatus* (commonly called 'resolute') is of course a hugely controversial one, and it faces a number of challenges if it is properly to establish itself as a viable approach to the text. But since its broad outlines seem to fit so well with the conception of Wittgenstein's later philosophical methods advanced and defended by Gordon Baker in his last papers, it seemed to me that it would be a fitting tribute to his work as a scholar, philosopher and teacher to explore in more detail one aspect of the *Tractatus* that might seem at once to invite and resist a resolute reading: its treatment of ethics.

Diamond and Conant have both written in some detail about this – about the later remarks within the text on apparently ethical topics, and about the possibility that the text as a whole might be seen as having an ethical point. More specifically, with respect to the first of these issues, Cora Diamond has argued that the text invites us to acknowledge a distinction between philosophical and ethical nonsense, according to which our realization that any attempt to make remarks about ethical value will result in simple nonsense does not (as it does in the case of philosophical uses of language) result in our learning to dispense with the impulse to make such remarks, but rather leaves that impulse untouched (see Diamond 2000). In apparent contrast, Conant has argued that we should rather pursue the thought that Wittgenstein's treatment of ethics and his treatment of logic in fact converge in a multitude of significant ways – although his essay (preoccupied as it is with undermining more familiar ways of reading these parts of the text) does not spell out those convergences and their significance in any real detail (see Conant 2005).

In this essay, I aim to show in concrete detail that, whilst the text does provide good reason to believe that its author's remarks on this topic have a peculiarly self-subverting quality, and hence can be seen to support the general claims of the resolute reading, the precise ways in which these words put their own status in question do not obviously require that we invoke (even provisionally) the distinction around which Diamond's account pivots, although they do give some support to Conant's general intuitions. And in so doing, of course, I cannot avoid confronting the question that Wittgenstein himself inevitably confronted – namely, that of finding an appropriate form for a philosophical text whose burden is that there cannot be theses in philosophy. For this cannot consistently be presented as itself a (philosophical) thesis about philosophy; and more specifically, insofar as one takes Wittgenstein to have found the appropriate textual form for the message he wants to convey to his readers, one in which a certain kind of work is left for the reader herself to perform, then what room does that leave for work that a commentary might legitimately do on that reader's behalf? In more Derridean terms: what form could a non-subversive supplement to such a text take?

(2) If we want to establish Wittgenstein's early views on ethics, it seems self-evident that we should examine that portion of the *Tractatus Logico-Philosophicus* that explicitly concerns itself with the realm of value: sections 6.4–6.522. This assumption certainly appears to be confirmed by the *Tractatus* numbering scheme, which tells us that these sections fit within a more general discussion that is initiated by Wittgenstein's climactic identification, in section 6, of the general form of the proposition – his claim that every proposition is a truth-function of elementary propositions, pictures of possible states of affairs. The first-level comments on this claim (the 6.x's) proceed to identify and account for the nature of uses of language that do not appear to fit, or should not properly be seen as fitting, this descriptive or depictive paradigm. Abstracting the skeleton of that discussion, we arrive at the following 'list of contents' for the concluding pages of the *Tractatus*:

6.1   The propositions of logic are tautologies.
6.2   Mathematics is a logical method.
      The propositions of mathematics are equations, and therefore pseudo-propositions.
6.3   Logical research means the investigation of all *regularity*, and outside logic all is accident. (A discussion of scientific laws follows.)
6.4   All propositions are of equal value.
6.5   For an answer which cannot be expressed, the question too cannot be expressed.
      The riddle does not exist.
      If a question can be put at all, then it *can* also be answered.

The structural implication seems clear. After analyzing in turn logical propositions, mathematical propositions, and formulations of scientific laws, the 6.4's (and the 6.5's) analyze propositions of value; each sub-section of the 6's is devoted to a determinate and distinguishable sector or domain of language use, each of which diverges in a particular way from the propositional paradigm articulated in section 6.

But from the outset, the notoriously compressed and allusive sequence of remarks that makes up the 6.4's and 6.5's resists our expectations. For what section 6.4 actually says is that 'All propositions are of equal value'. And this is not a general claim about value-propositions, it is a claim about the value of propositions as such – all propositions, any symbolic employ-ment of signs whatever. And what it claims is that, with respect to – from the perspective of – value, all propositions are equal. It does not claim that propositions (perhaps because they are, on Wittgenstein's account, a species of fact) are utterly unrelated to the realm of value, and hence of zero value, of no worth or significance whatever. Rather, it claims that no proposition is any more or less valuable than any other. This is, of course, a formulation that is entirely consistent with the belief that the degree of value all propositions share is zero; so we are not exactly prevented from taking it in that way. But it could hardly be regarded as the most obvious or straightforward way of articulating such a conviction. What this claim rather more naturally suggests is that each proposition (the fact that it is, and hence the possible fact that it pictures) is of some value, possessed of a non-zero degree of worth or significance that it shares with every other proposition.

If, however, seeing propositions aright, from the perspective of value, is a matter of refusing to differentiate between them rather than entirely rejecting their relevance, the following questions arise. Would distinguishing propositions of value from other kinds of (pseudo-) proposition be exactly the kind of internal differentiation that any proper evaluation of propositions must refuse? And if so, would dis-tinguishing within the *Tractatus* between those of its propositions which concern themselves with value and those which do not – would such a reading strategy itself be an exemplary instance of such improper evaluation?

(3) Perhaps we should set these questions aside for the moment; their pertinence or ineptness will doubtless emerge as we explore the elabora-tions Wittgenstein offers of the true ramifications of his opening claim. The first such elaboration – section 6.41 – runs as follows:

The sense of the world must lie outside the world. In the world, everything is as it is and happens as it does happen. *In* it there is no value – and if there were, it would be of no value.

If there is a value which is of value, it must lie outside all happening and being so. For all happening and being-so is accidental.

What makes it non-accidental cannot lie *in* the world, for otherwise this would again be accidental.

It must lie outside the world.

These sentences move us immediately from linguistic to material mode – from talk about propositions to talk about value and the world. The hinge or pivot of this transition is Wittgenstein's use of the term 'Sinn' (sense, meaning or significance), perhaps most naturally at home in linguistic contexts, in conjunction with that of 'Welt'. It is striking that this opening conjunction avoids the more familiar association of 'Sinn' with 'Leben', and hence the thought that one can as easily talk of the meaning of life as one can of the meaning of a word or sentence. (Perhaps one is meant to assume that no sense can be made of the idea of a human life that is anything other than worldly – to take seriously some version of the Heideggerian claim that human being is Being-in-the-world.) It is clearly far less natural to talk of the world, of everything that is the case, the totality of facts, as possessed of meaning or significance; but perhaps the issue here is again one reminiscent of Heidegger – the question of whether and how the way things are in the world might matter to us at all, might be worth our attention or interest or concern. Certainly, this kind of question seems rather different from such everyday ethical questions as 'If I stay at home in this terrible weather, will I be letting her down?' or 'Must I take responsibility for his unreasonable demands yet again?' One might say that it puts in question the very point or substance of such mundane ethical challenges and difficulties; it gives expression to a bewilderment about how and why ethical judgements are so much as possible, and hence marks a point at which ethical life has somehow engendered, and is now taken over by, philosophical reflection on ethics.

Nevertheless, it seems clear enough that if one can make sense of such talk, then the sense about which one is talking cannot lie within the world. For if the sense of the world really were the sense of some part of the world, how could it be the sense of the whole of which it is a part? To put the point in a manner that brings out its Kierkegaardian resonance: if the sense of the world as a whole is in question, how can one resolve the difficulty by assuming that some part of that whole has a sense, let alone by assuming that it can then confer it on the whole? In a more Wittgensteinian linguistic register: in such circumstances, our talk of 'the sense of the world' would refer not to the sense of the world but to the sense of some subset of it, the sense of a fact or set of facts; we would be saying something other than we meant to say.

Wittgenstein, however, appears intent on reaching this conclusion another way. His argument might be summarized thus: whatever exists and takes place in the world is accidental (contingent – a matter of happenstance); value is non-accidental; therefore value cannot lie within the world. This argument takes it for granted that (essentially accidental) facts and (essentially non-accidental) values are essentially unrelated to one another. It thus adopts without question the less natural reading of 6.54, according to which every member of that subset of facts we call propositions must have zero value. But the actual presentation of the argument is far less perspicuous than my summary would suggest – it is in fact littered with puzzles and opacities.

These begin to appear in the third sentence of the sequence: '*In* [the world] there is no value – and if there were, it would be of no value.' This sentence first presents the absence of value from the world as a definitive feature of both value and world; then it contemplates the contrary possibility, thereby implying that the original claim is at best contingently true; and then it cancels that implication. In so doing, however, it constructs a puzzling category – that of values that are of no value; and the following sentence of the sequence accordingly finds itself reiterating the basic claim of the section in terms of the contrary (equally puzzling) category – that of values that are of value. If there are such things, we are told, they must lie outside the world – the realm of accident. But to talk of values that are of value is to imply that being of value is something that a value might lack; and to talk of what must be the case if there are such values is to imply that there might not be or have been such values. So what began as an unqualified assumption about the utter lack of relation between absolute value and the contingent fact or accident ends by concluding that, if there are any values that happen to be of value, they must lie outside the realm of existence and happenstance.

The source of this self-subverting incoherence appears to be the first half of the third sentence of the sequence. For the assertion that '*In* [the world] there is no value' is what immediately prompts the thought of its contrary, with its chain of consequences; and it prompts us in this way because it presents itself as a claim about the world, and about value, that is true, and hence as a claim that might have been false. In other words, it implies that the absence of value from the world is a fact about the world and about value; and it is this implicit assumption that generates the resulting sequence of conditional claims about value – claims that being of value is a property that some values possess and others do not, and claims that values that are of value might or might not exist. The problem is that any attempt to articulate the assumption underlying the whole pattern of reasoning (that value is non-accidental, and so essentially beyond the realm of the factual, no element of which can accordingly be of any value whatever) – for example, by saying as emphatically as possible that value is not in the world – transforms or deforms it into something that might have been otherwise, a merely contingent feature of value and of the world. And this is because (as the *Tractatus* showed us much earlier) propositions are pictures of possible states of affairs, and hence at best capable of presenting us with contingent truths, with states of affairs that might not have been actual.

(4) This enactment in miniature of the process by which we run up against the limits of language in the domain of ethical reflection thus appears to prepare the way very smoothly for Wittgenstein's second remark elaborating on the significance of 6.4–6.42's claim that 'there can be no ethical propositions. Propositions cannot express anything higher'. But 6.421, presented as a gloss on 6.42, in fact engenders a certain discomfort with 6.41's repeated claim that value and significance must lie outside the world; for it invokes an idea from earlier in the *Tractatus* that implicitly questions the assumption that any phenomenon that does not lie inside the world must lie outside it, by reminding us that the world not only has an inside and an outside, but also a framework or scaffolding – a boundary or limit.

It is clear that ethics cannot be expressed.
Ethics is transcendental.
(Ethics and aesthetics are one.)

The idea of the transcendental first appears in 6.13: 'Logic is not a theory but a reflexion of the world. Logic is transcendental.' The propositions of logic, understood as tautologies or contradictions, are regarded by the *Tractatus* as degenerate or limiting cases of propositions, and hence as indicative of the limits of the world. A proposition of logic says nothing (its constituent elements being so combined as to cancel out any informational content), but that logical propositions are tautologies shows something about the formal properties of language (i.e. that elementary propositions have sense and names have meaning) and hence of the world (i.e. that the world is the totality of facts, and that objects are its substance). In short, insofar as logical propositions say nothing about but rather show the limits of language, so they offer no theory of but rather mirror the limits of the world.

Perhaps, then, we can avoid the incoherencies which appear to be engendered by any attempt to talk of value as outside the world by relating value (via the idea of the transcendental) not to the outside of the world but to its limits. But the central difficulty with this strategy is that Wittgenstein's account of propositions of ethics is significantly different from his account of the propositions of logic. His view in 6.42 is that there are no ethical propositions; it is not that they are a recognizable species of proposition, not even a degenerate instance of the genus. The propositions of logic say nothing, although they do show something; but this distinction can be drawn only because such propositions have logical form, and hence count as genuine propositions. But Wittgenstein's conclusion about the inexpressibility of ethics does not invoke any version of the saying/showing distinction; it turns rather on the assumption that value, being non-accidental, is not expressible in bipolar propositions. Since, according to the *Tractatus*, there can be no such thing as a proposition that is not a truth-function of essentially bipolar elementary propositions, it follows that there can be no propositions of ethics. Propositions cannot express anything higher because, if what they expressed genuinely was the higher, they would not be genuine propositions. They would not be senseless (tautologous) but rather nonsensical.

Accordingly, if what makes logic transcendental is that logical propositions, being tautologies, mirror the limits of the world, then ethics cannot be said to be transcendental in the same sense. So why use the term at all here? Is it that Wittgenstein wishes to detach the idea of ethics as not a theory but a reflexion of the limits of the world from its original home in an account of the nature and significance of tautologies? If so, how is the use of such a picture of world-mirroring in this new context to be justified or re-grounded? And should we expect to find that ethics shares other distinctive characteristics of the domain of logic without exactly participating in its underlying nature – perhaps a recurrent air of the tautological, or the essential dispensability of the relevant kind of proposition, or the absence of surprises or discoveries? Should we perhaps be seeking some ethical equivalent of the thought that our grasp of logic is not sayable (in the form of contentful propositions) but is shown in our everyday linguistic competence, in the various untroubled ways we implicitly acknowledge the logical relations between propositions in whatever we say, in the way our specific opinions, questions and judgements cohere with one another?

Without getting clearer on the answers to some of these questions, it seems unlikely that we will be able to appreciate the full significance of Wittgenstein's parenthetical association of ethics with aesthetics – his assertion, from the point of view of the transcendental, of a unity that is not an identity.

(5) Wittgenstein's second major attempt to clarify 6.42 is section 6.422:

> The first thought in setting up an ethical law of the form 'thou shalt . . .' is: And what if I do not do it? But it is clear that ethics has nothing to do with punishment and reward in the ordinary sense. This question as to the *consequences* of an action must therefore be irrelevant. At least these consequences will not be events. For there must be something right in that formulation of the question. There must be some sort of ethical reward and ethical punishment, but this must lie in the action itself.
>
> (And this is clear also, that the reward must be something acceptable and the punishment something unacceptable.)

This passage picks up the idea of limits invoked by the earlier association of ethics with logic, and tries to indicate how that idea might be seen as both at home in, and distinctively inflected by, the domain of ethical value. But its lack of success in this task is hard to overlook. To be sure, ethical laws or principles can be thought of as setting up or reflecting limits, perhaps most naturally limits on actions; but their canonical formulation inevitably undercuts what is distinctive about those limits – their necessity or absoluteness. For even a categorical imperative, in commanding us unconditionally to do (or not to do) something, nevertheless implies that not doing (or doing) that thing is at least conceivable, that disobedience makes sense, and hence raises the question 'What if I don't do what is categorically imperative?' And if we persist in thinking that there is something right about asking that question, we will find ourselves forced to construct a distinctively ethical notion of the consequences, more specifically the rewards and punishments, attendant upon acknowledging or denying those limits. Since the ordinary sense of consequences of our actions refers to events or occurrences that are literally consequent upon those actions, hence subsequent to and separable from them, the nonordinary or ethical consequences must not be so separable; they must lie in the actions themselves. The idea seems to be that mirroring the limits of the ethical in our actions is its own reward, and failing so to mirror them is its own punishment.

So far, we might think, so good. But then we encounter another of Wittgenstein's concluding parenthetical remarks, reminding us that distinctively ethical rewards and punishments must, like any other kinds of rewards and punishments, be acceptable (pleasant, congenial, welcome) and unacceptable (unpleasant, uncongenial, unwelcome) respectively. And at this point, the linguistic wheels are surely beginning to lose friction, to spin emptily. For this parenthesis might as well be saying that ethical rewards must be rewarding and ethical punishment punitive – which is as near to a tautology as makes no difference.

The interesting question is: what has brought us to the point of resorting to such a tautological formulation – quite as if it were a reminder of a substantial truth we were in danger of overlooking? There are, it seems to me, two ways of answering that question. The first is to deny that this parenthetical remark really is a tautology. For if ethical reward and punishment must lie in the action itself, and ethical action is a matter of mirroring ethical limits (or failing to), then one might say that acting ethically is a matter of finding those limits acceptable as opposed to unacceptable – of acknowledging as opposed to denying them. To act, to live, ethically is to see nothing punitive in the limits to which one is subject as a worldly being, to overcome any tendency to apprehend the limits of the world as limitations, the conditions of language and existence as constraints. To live unethically is to be unreconciled to those limits, to allow them to be reflected in one's existence as a kind of punishment, an unacceptable imposition, as if they deprived one of something, fenced one off from something that lies beyond them.

The second way of answering my question is to recall that the need to recall ourselves to such a tautological point about anything worthy of the name 'reward' and 'punishment' is ultimately a consequence of our accepting the idea that talk of reward and punishment in an ethical context has an extraordinary sense or meaning. It is only once we have accepted that assumption that we need to be reminded that those terms must retain some connection with their ordinary uses if they are to be worth employing in this context at all. And what drives us to the thought that ethical reward and punishment are *sui generis* is the prior thought that the contrary of any ethical command is conceivable – the thought that there is something (the unethical, the evil) that lies beyond the limits of the ethical, from which we are being prohibited or fenced off (by specific kinds of rewards and punishments), the thought that there is something (anything) right about formulating the question 'But what if I do not do what the law commands?' But the idea of ethical limits as absolute or unconditional is precisely supposed to entail that there is no such alternative; to think otherwise is to regard what is supposedly absolute or unconditional as contingent or accidental.

According to this second way of answering my question, then, the most appropriate way of acknowledging the unconditionality of the ethical is not to proceed to work out a conception of ethical reward and punishment that effectively enforces or polices ethical limits by incorporating such rewards and punishments into our actions themselves; it is to overcome the tendency to think that unconditional limits require any such enforcement – for to do so is already to fail properly to acknowledge their unconditionality. To invoke an idea of ethical reward or punishment, even one which is sharply distinguished from reward and punishment in the ordinary sense of those terms, reflects a failure to appreciate the nature of the ethical – even when that idea is invoked in the service of demonstrating that others have failed to appreciate the absolute nature of the ethical. For it implicitly reinforces the very misperception it castigates. Hence, if one incorporates into one's existence the desire to provide a philosophical demonstration of the non-contingency of the limits of the ethical, then to that degree one's existence fails properly to reflect or mirror the non-contingency of those limits. For then one's actions qua philosopher amount to a failure to acknowledge those limits as limits, a failure properly to reflect them in one's reflections. A life which properly acknowledges that ethical action is its own reward will not include advancing a theory to that effect; and it must not regard its abstention from such theorizing as a constraint or imposition, even a self-imposed one. Rather, it must overcome the tendency to think of this reflection of the limits of the ethical in one's reflections on ethics even as an abstention – for from what does it abstain?

(6) Wittgenstein's third gloss on 6.42 runs as follows:

> Of the will as the subject of the ethical we cannot speak.
> And the will as a phenomenon is only of interest to psychology.

In one sense, 6.423's focus on the will makes for a very natural transition from 6.422, with its stress on ethical commandments; quite apart from the impeccably Kantian ancestry of the thought that anything categorically imperative is applicable primarily to the orientation of one's will rather than to the action in which the will's orientation is made effective, Wittgenstein's suggestion that living ethically means accepting the limits of the world itself implies that the subject of ethical evaluation is not any particular thing one does but one's attitude or orientation to life in general, to the world as such. And the distinction that 6.423 then goes on to draw between the will as bearer of the ethical and the will as phenomenon seems equally natural; for just as action, being one more happening or occurrence in the world, cannot be of ethical interest, so too the will, if understood as another such happening, is equally irrelevant to ethics. Since, however, as we saw, the orientation of one's will appears nevertheless to be the sole locus of ethical interest, we find ourselves having to construct a distinctively ethical notion of the will to be the subject of that distinctive interest.

But 6.423, consonant with its origin in 6.42, in fact tells us that the will in its ethical aspect is something of which we cannot speak. From which it appears to follow that we cannot speak either of a distinction between the ethical and the phenomenal will; there is no ethical sense of the term 'will'. Hence we can no more demarcate the species of ethical propositions from the genus of propositions as such by reference to a distinctively ethical sense of the term 'will' than we can by reference to a distinctively ethical use of the terms 'reward' and 'punishment'. The end result of this long elaboration of 6.42 is thus exactly what one might have expected from the outset. It is not that there is a species of distinctively ethical proposition that tries but fails to express the ethical (the higher), but rather that there is no such distinctive species of proposition.

If this is indeed the moral of Wittgenstein's remarks about the ethical, however, then we must acknowledge its full reach. For his talk about distinctively ethical laws must fall under the same critique, and hence so must the talk of distinctively ethical limits that it is an attempt to gloss. And this might begin to clarify one positive implication of 6.421's association of logic with ethics. For if there is no intelligible distinction to be drawn between ethical as opposed to logical limits, but ethics is nevertheless to be understood as a matter of reflecting the limits of the world, then the limits thereby reflected must be none other than the limits shown by the propositions of logic. One might, then, say that ethics and logic are not just transcendental, they are one. Living an ethical life, insofar as it means reflecting in that life the world and its limits, is not separable from the task of acknowledging the nature of logic – of acknowledging that it is not a theory but a reflexion of the world, and of acknowledging what it reflects. It is thus because logic does not have a distinctive subject-matter (i.e. logical propositions do not picture anything or say anything) that ethics does not constitute a distinctive subject-matter (i.e. that there are no ethical propositions); in the task of acknowledging the limits of the world, no proposition is of any more value than any other, because any and every proposition – insofar as the whole of logic is given with it – makes equally manifest the limits of language and hence of the world.

(7) It is, therefore, striking that 6.43, Wittgenstein's third comment on 6.4, happily continues to employ the vocabulary of the ethical will:

> If good or bad willing changes the world, it can only change the limits of the world, not the facts; not the things that can be expressed in language.
>
> In brief, the world must thereby become quite another. It must so to speak wane or wax as a whole.
>
> The world of the happy is quite another than that of the unhappy.

It therefore will come as no surprise that the dialectical structure of these paragraphs, too, is deeply unstable. They begin by offering a hypothesis about the ethical will's capacity to change the world, then they tell us that any such change must affect the limits rather than the content of that world; then they further specify such limit-changes as ones which make the world quite other to itself, and finally they gloss this notion of otherness in terms of a lunar metaphor evocative of an alteration in volume. But the final step in this sequence self-evidently subverts its predecessors.

The lunar metaphor neatly incorporates the earlier idea of reflection, since the moon's waxing and waning is a function not of any objective alteration in the moon itself but in the degree to which it reflects the light of the sun. But this already undermines the preceding idea upon which it is supposed to be a gloss – that good and bad willing actually changes the world by changing its limits. It rather implies that the world itself is unchanged; what alters is its appearance to us, the aspect it presents to us – more precisely (given that the lunar cycle is a function of the relative positions of earth, sun and moon), our orientation or attitude towards it. This at least respects the thought that the limits of the world with which ethics concerns itself are nothing other than the limits logic makes manifest, since those limits are not themselves alterable. What the implicit logic of Wittgenstein's metaphor rather invites us to acknowledge is the ease with which we are inclined to regard those limits as subject in principle to alteration, and hence as contingent rather than absolute or unconditional. Once again, our attempt to articulate the absoluteness of ethical value results in our articulating something other than we took ourselves to mean.

It is further worth noting that both standard translations of the moon metaphor invert the order of the German terms for waxing and waning. The second paragraph of 6.43 in fact speaks of the world as waning and waxing, not waxing and waning. This matters because there are two other paired expressions with which this lunar pair is correlated – good and bad willing, and the worlds of the happy and the unhappy; and in both cases, goodness and happiness come first in the pairing. Hence the rhythm of the German text suggests that we should link goodness and happiness not with the waxing of the world but with its waning. And this in turn suggests that properly to acknowledge the limits of the world amounts to their vanishing or being rendered invisible as limits – that to the good or happy person, the limits of the world are not experienced as something limiting, as something she continually runs up against or confronts. It is the unhappy or bad person for whom the world is nothing but a limit, a punitive imposition on her will rather than a condition for its possibility and hence no punishment or limitation at all. This is why Wittgenstein's term for the happy person ('Glücklich') might be better rendered as 'fortunate' – for the person for whom the limits of the world have waned as a whole is one for whom there is only what happens, and for whom anything and everything that happens is equally a matter of good fortune, equally capable of being turned to good account, of being acknowledged as of just as much worth or significance from the ethical point of view as any other eventuality. For the unhappy or unfortunate person, by contrast, the person for whom the world (the totality of facts) is nothing but limit, everything that happens is experienced as an imposition, as being as much a punitive limitation on the will as any other eventuality.

This way of conceiving of the happy and the unhappy recalls the biblical reminder that 'the rain falls on the just and the unjust alike'. The happy person apprehends what happens simply as what happens, as sheer contingency – it carries no more or less ethical significance than anything else that happens, or that might have happened. This amounts to a rejection of the idea that the realm of contingency is one of ethical reward or punishment at all; it means seeing no connection whatever between acting and living well and having pleasant or congenial things happen to one, as if in recompense. It might further include the sense that whatever way things turn out in the world can equally be turned to good ethical account – as when Jesus not only rejects his disciple's assumption that a blind man's blindness must be a punishment (the only question being 'Directed at whom? – himself, or his parents?'), but claims instead that it is an opportunity for making the glory of God manifest (through healing).

The unhappy person's unhappiness consists in her refusal or inability to relinquish this idea of a connection – in her thinking of what happens to her as reflecting her (real or imagined) merits; she is therefore made unhappy or resentful when the rain falls on her (what have I done to deserve this?), and no less so even when the sun shines (because of the knowledge that it might as easily have been raining). In this way, the world as such appears as essentially an obstacle or limit to her, a stumbling block or scandal; every element in the totality it constitutes is turned to bad account.

But it then follows that happiness is attained not so much by reconceiving the idea of ethical reward or punishment but by abandoning it altogether; one must give up not only the idea that what happens as a consequence of one's deeds is a reward or punishment, but also the idea that one's deeds are their own reward and punishment (since, being occurrences in the world, they are no more intrinsically of value than any other occurrence). And in giving up that latter idea, one entirely gives up any desire to use the terms 'reward' and 'punishment' in an ethical context. Once again, then, we find ourselves having to discard a pair of what might otherwise have appeared to be distinctively ethical terms.

Returning to the metaphor of the moon's phases, it is worth noting that, given the essentially reflective element in the process of the lunar cycle, Wittgenstein's rhyming of happiness with waning further suggests that happiness is effected by the withering away of any substantial reflection of the world and its limits, by their absence from one's reflections on ethics as well as from every other aspect of that existence. And one way of developing this thought would be to put in question the appropriateness of any talk about limits in these ethical contexts – even if in so doing one avoids any talk of distinctively ethical limits. For the idea of a limit appears inevitably to suggest that there is a beyond to that limit, somewhere further to go in the same direction, and hence to suggest that limits are limitations. But the world does not prevent us from living in certain ways, any more than logic prevents us from thinking or saying certain things; every existential possibility is legitimately realizable, just as every possible proposition is legitimately constructed. Once again, then, we find ourselves saying something other than we mean to say – constructing turns of phrase that imply the very thing that we want them to criticize. The resolution of this difficulty must therefore lie in the withering away of its reflective as well as its non-reflective expression. If the happy person is one for whom the world's limits are not encountered as limitations, then anyone who finds herself running up against the limits of language (and hence, of the world) to that extent declares her inhabitation of the world of the unhappy.

(8) The next three remarks in the text (6.431–6.4312) constitute a gloss on Wittgenstein's first gloss on 6.43:

> As in death, too, the world does not change but ceases.
>
> Death is not an event of life. Death is not lived through.
>
> If by eternity is understood not endless temporal duration but timelessness, then he lives eternally who lives in the present.
>
> Our life is endless in the way that our visual field is endless.
>
> The temporal immortality of the soul, that is to say, its eternal survival after death, is not only in no way guaranteed, but this assumption in the first place will not do for us what we always tried to make it do. Is a riddle solved by the fact that I survive for ever? Is this eternal life not as enigmatic as our present one? The solution of the riddle of life in space and time lies *outside* space and time.
>
> (It is not problems of natural science which have to be solved.)

This sequence begins by making explicit the pressure that was implicitly applied to the idea of a change in the limits of the world, and to the idea of a limit itself, in 6.43. Just as the worlds of the happy and the unhappy are wholly other but unaltered in their limits, so death does not effect a change in the world but rather a cessation of it. It seems all-but-unavoidable to think of our mortality as a limit on our life; but given that limits can in principle be exceeded or passed through, their invocation inevitably engenders the idea of something beyond the limit, hence of that beyond as essentially continuous with that which it goes beyond, from which the limit bars us. Hence, we think of our mortality as providing us with only a finite quantity of life, and think of our death as depriving us of more of the same – more life; and we imagine that acquiring an unlimited quantity of life would solve the problem of sense or meaning with which our mortal existence can appear to confront us.

However, going beyond this limit in the way that the idea of a limit itself suggests in no way resolves the problem that the limit, so apprehended, creates. For if mortal, spatio-temporal or worldly, existence is apprehended as enigmatic or bewildering, as if its significance is put in doubt by its sheer conditionedness, then this riddle would not be solved by gaining unlimited amounts of what is apparently available only in limited quantities. For even of an eternal life, one can ask: what does it mean? What is its sense, or significance? Gaining more of such life merely extends the scope or range of that for which a meaning is sought.

Only a qualitative change can effect what is needed; only if we conceive our finite, mortal life otherwise than under the aspect of 'limit' can we achieve what we seek. If, for example, one can live in the present without apprehending the present as limited by (as opposed to conditioned or made possible by) the past and the future, then time vanishes under its aspect as limit without vanishing as such, and hence the temporality of life is no longer seen as a punitive imposition on the will, a withholding of something.

But of course, attaining such an orientation to our temporality does not amount to answering a specific problem that temporality poses to us; it rather amounts to no longer seeing temporality as posing a problem at all – it means accepting temporality as essentially unproblematic. This is certainly not the way in which a problem in natural science is solved; it is not a question to which the uncovering of further facts about the natural, empirical realm might conceivably contribute an answer. But then neither is it something to which the uncovering of super-natural facts might contribute an answer. And yet, that is precisely what Wittgenstein's emphatic suggestion that the solution to the riddle of mortal life must lie *outside* space and time implies. For that formulation pictures what lies beyond the empirical realm as continuous with it, as the world outside a window is continuous with the world inside it; and it is precisely this conception of space and time as limits that must be transcended or overcome.

However, we cannot avoid the charge of self-subversion here simply by avoiding any reference to what is outside space and time, and restricting ourselves to denying that what we seek can be found inside space and time. For of course, the notion of that which is inside space and time gains its content from an implicit contrast with what is outside space and time; so if we give up the latter notion, we must give up the former as well. In other words, Wittgenstein's italicizing of 'outside' is meant to make us stop and think just as much about the rather more implicit emptiness of 'inside' in the same context. If space and time really are conditions for the possibility of our existence, there is nothing beyond them by reference to which we can make any sense of the thought that we lead our lives within them. But there seems to be no way of articulating that awareness that does not betray it, by presenting what is unconditionally necessary as if it might have been otherwise. Once again, then, it appears that the only way that our reflections on ethics might adequately reflect our understanding of it is by entirely dispensing with the terms in which it could alone be articulated. Either we say something other than we mean, or we say nothing.

(9) Section 6.432 is Wittgenstein's second major gloss on 6.43, and it comes with its own gloss:

> *How* the world is, is completely indifferent for what is higher. God does not reveal himself *in* the world.
> The facts all belong only to the task and not to its performance.

The facts do not belong to the performance of the ethical task (more accurately – both to the German and to the chains of association it thereby sets up with preceding and succeeding remarks – to the solution of the problem or riddle of existence) because that task is precisely to apprehend and accept the facts as facts – to acknowledge that whatever is is, which means acknowledging that it might have been otherwise and acknowledging that whatever way the world is has no more ethical significance (say, as a reward or a punishment for one's deeds and mode of existence, or as an opportunity for doing good or evil) than any other way it might have been. The happy person apprehends the world as nothing but a totality of facts; she has overcome the apprehension of the limits of the world as limits, as a constraint or restriction. Whatever that totality of facts may be, she accepts it, and the goodness of her will consists in her capacity to accept whatever way the world is *as a whole*, without picking and choosing among that totality.

(10) Section 6.432's reference to the divine prepares the way for Wittgenstein's next two major glosses on his master-remark in 6.4, sections 6.44 and 6.45:

> Not *how* the world is, is the mystical, but *that* it is.
> The contemplation of the world sub specie aeterni is its contemplation as a limited whole.
> The feeling of the world as a limited whole is the mystical feeling.

Wittgenstein's invocation of the idea of the world as a limited whole is highly qualified or specific; the formulation is used to characterize a

feeling, and the content of an image, picture or view (far better translations of 'Anschauung' than 'contemplation'), and hence is never advanced
as an idea we must regard as valid or even comprehensible. Indeed, it
rather forces us to ask what sense can be made of the idea of a limited
whole; what, for example, would an unlimited whole be like? What 6.45
implies is that the notion of limitation enters here together with the
notion of a view of the world sub specie aeterni – what section 6.432
prepares us to think of as a God's eye view of the world; to view the world
as a limited whole is to view it from outside that world. But of course,
that perspective is not open to mortal beings, ones whose existence is
spatio-temporal; more precisely, it is not obvious that we can give any
content to the idea of such a perspective, since it trades on precisely the
contrast between inside and outside whose coherence 6.4312 led us to
question.

If so, then the attempt to articulate the orientation of the happy person
to which we were led in the previous section of this paper is doomed to
failure, since it relied precisely upon a thought of the world as a whole,
as a totality of facts. But if our attempts to articulate our ethical understanding in ethical reflection once again subvert themselves, they do so in
this instance in a manner that also explicitly threatens the broader Tractarian account of logic and metaphysics. For that account famously begins
with the claim that 'The world is everything that is the case. The world
is the totality of facts, not of things.' And our difficulties here suggest that
this, too, is a remark that could only be made from a God's eye view on
the world, a view sideways on, from which the way the world necessarily
is appears as something that might have been otherwise (it's a totality of
facts, not of things; but that implies that we can make sense of the idea
of its being a totality of things, and hence implies that it is merely accidental that it is not – quite as if the world's being a totality of facts constitutes a limitation on it, a determination of it as lacking something it
might have possessed). If, then, talk about the world as a whole must be
transcended ethically, must it not also be transcended logically? And what
might that indicate about the terminology and propositions of the
Tractatus as a whole?

In the light of these anxieties, it is interesting that 6.44 invokes an idea
of the mystical that does not depend upon the idea of the world's limits,
or of a God's eye view. Instead, it relies on a contrast between how the
world is and that the world is, thereby reminding us that talk (as in 6.432)
of how the world is appears to make sense only insofar as we can make
sense of some contrasting mode of approach to the world's existence. But

how much sense can we make of the contrasting thought *that* the world is? This makes the world's existence sound like a fact – something that might have been otherwise (the world's being the case as opposed to not being the case); but the *Tractatus* has always characterized the world as the totality of what is the case, and the existence of that totality cannot be a part or constituent element of it. So, this way of articulating the idea of the mystical turns out to be as empty as the way essayed in 6.45; but the emptiness of 6.44 more directly casts doubt on the intelligibility of the earlier Tractarian talk of the happy person as having a specific kind of orientation to the facts as facts, to how the world is. One begins to wonder: are any of the *Tractatus*' attempts to articulate its understanding of ethics anything other than empty forms of words?

(11) To this question, section 6.5, and the ensuing two major glosses upon it, appear to provide Wittgenstein's answer:

> For an answer which cannot be expressed the question too cannot be expressed.
> *The riddle* does not exist.
> If a question can be put at all, then it *can* also be answered.

> Scepticism is *not* irrefutable, but palpably senseless, if it would doubt where a question cannot be asked.

> For doubt can only exist where there is a question; a question only where there is an answer, and this only where something *can* be *said.*

> We feel that even if *all possible* scientific questions be answered, the problems of life have still not been touched at all. Of course there is then no question left, and just this is the answer.

> The solution of the problem of life is seen in the vanishing of this problem.

> (Is this not the reason why men to whom after long doubting the sense of life became clear, could not then say wherein this sense consisted?)

> There is indeed the inexpressible. This *shows* itself; it is the mystical.

Sections 6.52 and 6.521 seem to be pivotal in this sequence. For the fact that, even if all possible questions have been answered, the problem of life would remain unaltered, shows that the problem of life is not a question at all. One cannot solve this problem by being told something that counts as an answer to some specific question; it is rather a matter of no longer viewing life as a problem. As the notion of 'vanishing', with its recollection of the earlier metaphor of the waning moon, implies, the sense or significance of life becomes clear not when we acquire something to say in response to the question 'what exactly is the sense or meaning of existence?', but when we no longer apprehend existence as questionable in this way. For once we do so apprehend it, nothing could conceivably count as a satisfactory answer; for any such answer would involve the specification of a particular fact or state of affairs, when it is the whole to which any such fact belongs that we are, by hypothesis, apprehending as questionable. To achieve happiness is to overcome this apprehension of our worldly existence as questionable in this way; it is to apprehend that existence as acceptable, as essentially ethically unproblematic – to acknowledge its contingency as such, and to see the way things are and the way things happen as neither more nor less than how things are (not, for example, as modes of ethical reward or punishment). The unhappy person finds that everything that happens raises the question 'why?' (Why should I do this rather than that? Why do I exist, and why should I continue to exist, at all? Why this rather than that? Why something, anything at all, rather than nothing?). For the happy person, existence asks no such questions; more precisely, it asks only questions that can be answered – the only questions there are.

It is worth noting that, given the broader context in which it is located, it is by no means self-evident that the discussion of scepticism in 6.51 is (as so many commentators tend to assume) intended to focus primarily on epistemological doubts about the existence of the external world. On the contrary, the kinds of doubts with which Wittgenstein is here concerned are anxieties about the sense – the meaning or significance – of the world, and of our existence within it. To be sure, if such sceptical anxieties find a reflective formulation in terms of a question, then they are self-evidently nonsensical; but to apprehend the world as questionable, to find that its sense or significance is utterly enigmatic, is not thereby rendered unreal or illusory. So to apprehend the world is to live the life of an unhappy person; and if one attempts to articulate these anxieties in ethical reflection, one will inevitably find oneself utilizing formulations that betray themselves (e.g. by presenting this anxiety as a question or set of questions). But that is simply part of one's unhappiness with life, one of the ways in which one's life reflects or gives expression to one's inability to find satisfying articulations of one's anxieties, or to find a way of overcoming the drive to entangle oneself in such unsatisfying forms of reflection, to encounter limits as punitive or otherwise unacceptable. Of course, that unhappiness will be manifest in other ways, ways in which one is unable to accept the events and happenings of the world for what they are – contingencies and accidents – but rather as enigmatic obstacles or riddling problems (for example, under the aspect of punishment or reward).

By the same token, what shows itself in the life of the happy person (what Wittgenstein calls the mystical) is neither an expressible nor an inexpressible answer to the question 'What is the meaning of life?'; what shows itself is that, for this person, life poses no such question, is essentially unproblematic. It shows itself in the fact that this person accepts each and every event or occurrence as the accident it is; and in the fact that this person has no specific moral-philosophical expertise at his fingertips, to be deployed in answer to ethical difficulties – in the fact that he eschews, has no need of, ethical reflection of this kind, that he has nothing whatever to say about the ethical at this level. In this sense, the happiness of one's life is manifest in the way it is entirely taken up with dealing with genuine questions (questions of natural science, practical problems arising from one's plans and purposes in the world, specific ethical challenges and conflicts, and so on), by finding genuine answers to them – by the way in which such straightforwardly intraworldly problems entirely occlude the 'problem' of the meaning of life, in which that 'question' finds absolutely no foothold in one's life.

(12) Section 6.53, the number of which presents it as a further gloss on the thought that 'the riddle does not exist', might appear to effect a change of topic:

> The right method of philosophy would be this. To say nothing except what can be said, *i.e.* the propositions of natural science, *i.e.* something that has nothing to do with philosophy: and then always, when someone else wished to say something metaphysical, to demonstrate to him that he had given no meaning to certain signs in his propositions. This method would be unsatisfying to the other – he would not have the feeling that we were teaching him philosophy – but it would be the only strictly correct method.

This appearance is, however, misleading; for if 6.53 is an accurate description of the correct method for philosophizing in general, it must also accurately describe the correct way to go about doing moral philosophy. And what this description suggests is that there is and can be no such thing as moral philosophy, if that is understood as a branch of reflection with a distinctive subject-matter – that of ethical value, or of the ethical species of the genus proposition. For 6.53 (suitably adapted) tells us that all possible propositions are empirical propositions, no subset of which concerns ethics; and it further tells us that anyone who attempts to say something ethical will find that he has failed to give any meaning to certain signs in his propositions. Demonstrating this emptiness in any putatively ethical proposition is, in Wittgenstein's view, the only strictly correct method of philosophical ethics.

One might say that this would amount to a rigorous excision of this kind of ethical reflection in one's life – and hence an excision of the most obvious respect in which an apprehension of the world as ethically questionable might make itself manifest. But the paragraph also suggests that one's overcoming of any such apprehension of the world is equally manifest in every intelligible use of language. Saying only what can be said whatever the topic under consideration (striving to accept anything and everything that is the case as such – perhaps by striving to construct an adequate scientific theory, or an accurate account of an historical episode, or an acceptable solution to a problem in engineering, mathematics, tailoring, architecture or personal relations) is just as much an expression of one's happiness as one's avoidance of empty ethical reflection. Achieving such acceptance in any and every aspect of one's life is precisely the way in which 'the ethical problem' is solved – or rather it is the way in which the appearance of such a problem is entirely dissolved, leaving behind the only genuine problems there are.

But if this is on the right lines, it will follow that what Wittgenstein is here characterizing as the correct method for philosophy as such (not just moral philosophy) will itself be of ethical significance – will, let us say, have an ethical point. For even if one's philosophical concern is, say, logic, if one achieves in that field an adequate solution to the genuine problems in the area together with an avoidance of any talk that outruns the limits of its own intelligibility, then one will to that degree have attained the orientation of the happy person in one's existence. One will have overcome any conception of this aspect of one's worldly existence as questionable in a way that goes beyond any specific questions it poses (to which there must in principle be specific answers). In this respect, the application of the strictly correct method in philosophy will itself be an ethical achievement. Hence, philosophical labours, just as much as scientific, historical, mathematical and aesthetic ones, might in principle have an ethical point. Once again, we find ourselves returning to the master-remark, section 6.4: all propositions are of equal value. Any remark, about any kind of subject-matter – whether or not it employs such uncontroversially ethical concepts as 'promising', 'lying', stealing' and so on – might in principle have ethical import.

(13) But, of course, it seems clear that the propositions of the *Tractatus* itself cannot easily be regarded as the result of applying the strictly correct philosophical method that section 6.53 outlines. Hence the need for section 6.54, which characterizes the way Tractarian propositions are meant to have their effect on their readers:

> My propositions are elucidatory in this way: he who understands me finally recognizes them as senseless, when he has climbed out through them, on them, over them. (He must so to speak throw away the ladder, after he has climbed up on it.)
>
> He must surmount these propositions; then he sees the world aright.

If, once again, we adapt the import of these remarks to the sequence of remarks (beginning with 6.4) from which they emerge, then it would appear that the (strictly speaking) incorrect method in moral philosophy – the method that has some chance of satisfying one's interlocutor – is one in which one advances putatively ethical propositions, and then gradually allows their latent lack of sense or emptiness to become manifest, with the ultimate aim of weaning one's readers from their inclination to become entangled in such nonsensicalities, to take nonsense for sense. To see ethics aright one must give up one's inclination to construct such ethical propositions, indeed give up one's inclination to think that there is such a species of the genus 'proposition', and hence give up one's inclination to think that there is such a thing as moral philosophy.

This seems to be a fairly accurate characterization of the experience of reading the remarks in section 6.4ff. Time and again, we have found ourselves concluding that the implications of the various apparently substantive claims about the distinctive nature of ethics that Wittgenstein advances, when properly followed through, subvert their own presuppositions, to the point at which their very intelligibility is put in question. The idea of the world as a limited whole with an inside and an outside, of ethical laws and ethical limits, of ethical reward and punishment, of the ethical will, indeed the very idea of ethical value as such – the uses to which Wittgenstein puts each and every such concept eventually undercut their own point, inexorably misrepresenting as accidental what they purport to regard as necessary, and misrepresenting our mortal immersion in the world as a God's eye view upon it. Each such foray into moral philosophy thus overcomes itself, reveals itself to be another way of running up against the limits of language (and hence of the world); and when we surmount them, we see that even to utilize moral philosophy to attempt to demonstrate its own self-overcoming, because it involves utiliz-ing the very expressions whose transcendence we are urging, must also be transcended. If we are to be truly happy, we must excise from our exis-tence even the inclination to demonstrate philosophically that we must excise moral philosophy from our existence. We must, in short, simply excise it – throw it all away, even those ultimately self-subverting proposi-tions whose provisional stability was the means by which we came to see the need for such excision.

But of course, Wittgenstein means his remarks in 6.54 to apply to all the elucidatory propositions of the *Tractatus*, not just to those apparently concerning ethical value. Hence, insofar as any philosophical exercise consists in (even a strictly incorrect) attempt to come to see the world aright, to see that everything is what it is and not another thing, to say of something only what can be said and otherwise to say nothing at all, then to that extent the successful application of this philosophical method will constitute an expression of the orientation of the happy person – a capacity to accept the world and its limits, to overcome any apprehension of oneself as limited, constrained or punished thereby. In this sense, one might say that the *Tractatus* as a whole, and not just the 6.4's and 6.5's, has an ethical point.

(14) It is worth noting in conclusion that, if the *Tractatus* itself can be thought of as having an ethical point, so too might any form of writing that makes manifest the attitude or orientation of the happy person in more strictly correct ways – in its capacity to say whatever is to be said about a given topic, and resolutely to abstain from misbegotten reflections on the limits thereby observed, in what one might think of as the utter absence of any sense that the limits of language, life and world are ques-tionable, problematic as such. Faraday's *History of a Candle* might be one such text; Uhland's poem 'Graf Eberhards Weissdorn' another, and Dickens' portrayal of Mark Tapley's response to seasickness in *Martin Chuzzlewit* yet another; whereas the Brothers Grimm's tales 'Rumpel-stiltskin' and 'The Fisherman and his Wife', and Hawthorne's story 'The Birthmark', might appear as portraits of the inverse attitude to life.

But this highly partial list of examples suggests a reason for Wittgen-stein's association of ethics with aesthetics in section 6.421; for it implies that any form of writing that has ethical point does so through a certain stylistic achievement, a certain art of language. And this suggestion might in turn engender the thought that the art of the *Tractatus*, as that mani-fests itself in the passages purportedly dealing with ethics, is more complex even than the self-portrait of its strictly incorrect philosophical method in section 6.54 implies. For cutting across the rhythmic waxing and waning of the text's repeated, self-subverting attempts to articulate genuinely ethical propositions, there is another linguistic rhythm or register. It is exemplified in its overlapping, inflected chains of concepts, and of associations invoked by individual concepts (such as that leading from 'acceptable and unacceptable' to 'waxing and waning' ['Einwachsen' to 'Abnehmen'], and 'waning' to 'vanishing' ['Abnehmen' to 'Verschwinden'], or that connecting worth or value to reward and punishment and thence to recompense and compensation ['Wert' to 'Lohn'], or that linking 'performance' to 'solution' ['Lösung']); in the way in which terminology anchored in an earlier context detaches, reorients and reroots itself for new purposes (the constellation of logical terms and characteristics – transcendentality, tautology, dispensability, the absence of surprises or discoveries); in the metaphor around which these passages as a whole pivot – that of the waxing and waning moon; and in the aphoristic, epigrammatic concision of every sentence in every numbered remark.

There is, in short, a dual aspect to this writing, which indicates that it works to make its ethical point in two rather different ways. The first seeks to attract its readers by articulating, elaborating and subverting their impulse to run up against the limits of language, inviting them to grasp that their unhappiness can ultimately be overcome only by overcoming the impulse to give propositional expression to their dissatisfaction, or indeed to its overcoming. The second uncovers and deploys a non-propositional, figurative register of language, one which demonstrates a way in which words can work for us and upon us without either rebounding from or going beyond the bounds of (in a sense, without reference to) logic and the world.

The complex satisfactions that this stretch of the *Tractatus* devotes itself to providing are not, I think, appreciable or even imaginable in the absence of these cross-cutting dimensions of its impact; and in this respect they demonstrate the degree to which Wittgenstein is prepared to acknowledge the legitimacy (if not the indispensability) of certain non-propositional uses of language. It is as if his prose works to reveal that language stands in a doubled relation to ethics: assertorically, it wanes to vanishing point (showing us the ultimate emptiness of the category 'ethical propositions', and hence of the idea of ethics as a delimited region of our lives), and aesthetically, it waxes to one kind of fullness (showing us how language might, in unpredictable and undelimitable ways, nevertheless figure or picture the ethical, providing a node around which a certain attitude or orientation – a way of living – might crystallize, articulate or shape itself, and so showing ethics to be an organizing dimension or aspect of our lives as a whole). If so, then the ethical point of Wittgenstein's remarks is not graspable without grasping their doubly indirect literary achievement.

What, then, might be said of this commentary on the aesthetico-ethical point of the putatively ethical portion of a philosophical text? How might it best be located in this complex mapping of ways in which one might convey an ethical insight? Does its very existence imply a lack of confidence in the text it claims so extravagantly to admire, or a lack of understanding of the full reach of the implications of that text's urging of its readers to stop engaging in ethical reflection, in the articulation of would-be ethical propositions? Or can it present itself as simply one more (rung of the) ladder – to be used if useful, but ultimately to be thrown away?

Note

1   See, for example, the collection of essays by Read and Crary eds. (2000).

Chapter 10

The Uses of Wittgenstein's Beetle: *Philosophical Investigations* §293 and Its Interpreters

David G. Stern

293. If I say of myself that it is only from my own case that I know what the word "pain" means – must I not say the same of other people too? And how can I generalize the one case so irresponsibly?

Well, everyone tells me that *he* knows what pain is only from his own case! —— Suppose everyone had a box with something in it: we call it a "beetle." No one can look into anyone else's box, and everyone says he knows what a beetle is only by looking at *his* beetle. – Here it would be quite possible for everyone to have something different in his box. One might even imagine such a thing constantly changing. – But suppose the word "beetle" had a use in these people's language? – If so it would not be used as the name of a thing. The thing in the box has no place in the language-game at all; not even as a *something*: for the box might even be empty. – No, one can 'divide through' by the thing in the box; it cancels out, whatever it is.

That is to say: if we construe the grammar of the expression of sensation on the model of 'object and name' the object drops out of consideration as irrelevant.[1]

What is Wittgenstein attempting to show by his analogy of the beetle in the box? How successful is his use of the analogy?[2]

I   Introduction: Baker on the Private Language Argument

In a series of three papers on the "private language argument," Gordon Baker raised a number of far-reaching objections to traditional interpretations of *Philosophical Investigations* section 243ff. as a *reductio ad absurdum* of Cartesian dualism. He proposed a very different framework of interpretation, one on which Wittgenstein's primary aim in those sections of the *Investigations* was "the elimination of prejudices that stand in the way of our noticing important aspects of what is perfectly familiar."[3]

Baker's critique of traditional approaches to Wittgenstein on private language turns on his demonstration that a number of widely shared assumptions about the nature of Wittgenstein's argument are mistaken, assumptions that are clearly stated in the influential early reviews of the *Philosophical Investigations* and are still taken for granted by many leading interpreters today. Two of the leading claims he advances in the course of his wide-ranging discussion are:

(i)   Wittgenstein's aim is not to provide a *reductio* argument against a particular conception of privacy, but rather to get his reader to see that such conceptions are absurd.

(ii)   His principal targets are not the views of leading figures in the history of philosophy, but his own earlier views, and the broader framework within which debates between "Cartesians" and "anti-Cartesians" take place.

This paper aims to critically evaluate and further articulate Baker's interpretive proposals by means of a close examination of the history of the interpretation of one strand in the "private language argument." Wittgenstein's "beetle in a box" argument (*Philosophical Investigations* section 293), usually construed as one of the principal expositions of such a *reductio ad absurdum*, is the focus of this paper, with the aim of casting light on broader concerns in the history of Wittgenstein interpretation.

The story of "Wittgenstein's beetle," like the story of the builders in section 2 of the *Philosophical Investigations*, is one of a small group of imaginary scenarios which play a leading role in that book's central argument. It is also one of the most frequently retold, and most frequently cited, passages in the book. Like Plato's cave, it has taken on an afterlife, both as a standard item in the philosophy curriculum, and as a parable that has been read in a bewildering variety of ways. It has even given its name to a recent collection of such philosophical narratives, Martin Cohen's *Wittgenstein's Beetle and Other Classic Thought Experiments* (2005). In this essay, I provide a brief and selective history of the beetle story's reception.

II   Strawson's and Malcolm's Interpretations of the Beetle Story

Peter Strawson's and Norman Malcolm's reviews of the *Philosophical Investigations*, two of the most influential early readings of that book, both give §293 a central role in their interpretations of Wittgenstein on private language. Strawson's leading objection to Wittgenstein's discussion of private language is that he moves back and forth "between a stronger and a weaker thesis, of which the first is false and the second is true." Strawson sums up the "weaker thesis" in words that also serve to summarize the main lines of the standard interpretation of the private language argument in much of the subsequent literature:

> The weaker thesis says that certain conditions must be satisfied for the existence of a common language in which sensations are ascribed to those who have them; and that certain confusions about sensations arise from the failure to appreciate this, and consequently to appreciate the way in which the language of sensations functions. (Strawson 1966, 42)

The "weaker thesis," in other words, is Strawson's term for the positive view about the relationship between language and sensation that he believes can be retrieved from the discussion of private language in the *Philosophical Investigations*. However, he regards it as mistakenly interwoven with the "stronger thesis," which "says that no words name sensations (or 'private experiences'); and in particular the word 'pain' does not" (Strawson 1966, 42). Immediately after these words, Strawson adds a parenthetical citation to §293, an indication that he considers §293 to be a particularly clear illustration of this error.

While Strawson does not provide a detailed reading of §293, the discussion of the "stronger thesis" that follows makes it quite clear how such a reading would go. Strawson construes the main line of Wittgenstein's positive argument as a demonstration that a language whose terms referred to the sensations of the language user is impossible, because "the hypothetical user of the language would have no check on, no criterion of, the *correctness* of his use of it" (Strawson 1966, 42). So far, this is a version of the weaker thesis, on which the notion of a criterion is used to specify a condition that must be satisfied for the existence of a common language. However, Strawson alleges, Wittgenstein mistakenly takes the weaker thesis to be *all* that there is to be said about the meaning of sensation words. In other words, once we have specified "what *criteria* people can use for employing [a word] or for deciding whether or not it is correctly employed," there is nothing more to be said about its meaning (Strawson 1966, 42). This, in turn, "leads [Wittgenstein] to deny that sensations can be recognized and bear names." On this reading, the point of the beetle story is that the criteria for the use of the word "beetle" in the game in §293 exhaust its meaning: "beetle" cannot refer to anything private, for the criteria are entirely public, and quite independent of whatever is in a particular person's box. Applying that point to sensation talk leads Strawson to conclude that Wittgenstein's broader moral is that just as "beetle" does not name whatever is in the box, "pain" does not name a sensation. Strawson replies that it simply does not follow from any of the points that Wittgenstein does make that 'pain' is not the name of a sensation (Strawson 1966, 49). Indeed, he claims that this is an obvious fact that cannot be denied.

Norman Malcolm's review of the *Investigations* offers a very different reading of the beetle story. He puts particular weight on §293c,[4] the final paragraph of §293. This is an appealing strategy, for it appears to state the point of the preceding story. Crucially, it is a conditional: it tells us that **if** "we construe the grammar of the expression of sensation on the model of 'object and name'" **then** "the object drops out of consideration as irrelevant."[5] On Malcolm's reading, then, the aim of the story is "to prove that attending to a private object can have nothing to do with learning words for sensations" (Malcolm 1966, 79). Because we conceive of our talk of pain and other sensations as analogous to the relationship between an ordinary name and the everyday object it stands for, we think of it as a matter of naming an inner, private object, which only the person who has pain can directly experience. The core of Malcolm's reply to Strawson is that Wittgenstein rejects that model, not the fact that we can talk about our sensations.

Malcolm observes that Strawson's approach to sensation leads to the view that each sensation-word "will have both a public and a private meaning" (Malcolm 1966, 98). The public meaning is unproblematic, at least in principle, for both Malcolm and Strawson; they agree that it consists in the criteria that govern our use of the relevant sensation-words when talking about others' pain. Strawson construes Wittgenstein's denial that there is also a private meaning when one talks about one's own pain as a denial that we can talk about our sensations, and thus is driven to insist that sensations can be recognized and named. Malcolm responds that this insistence arises out of Strawson's attraction to the very model Wittgenstein rejects. On Malcolm's interpretation, my experience of a pain is not a matter of applying inner criteria that enable me to identify the pain as pain, but is simply a matter of my having the pain under the appropriate circumstances:

> The fact that there is no *further* process of identifying a particular sensation is a reason why "the object drops out of consideration as irrelevant" when "we construe the grammar of the expression of sensation on the model of 'object and name'" (293) . . . If my use of a sensation-word satisfies the normal outward criteria and if I truthfully declare that I have that sensation, then I *have* it – there is not a further problem of my applying the word right or wrong within myself. (Malcolm 1966, 100)

To sum up: Malcolm agrees with Strawson in reading Wittgenstein as denying that we can refer to "private experience." However, Malcolm construes this denial as purely a matter of rejecting a mistaken philosophical theory about the language of experience. We do have sensations, but the self-ascription of sensation is not a matter of making an identifying reference to an inner object. Strawson, convinced that we do have private experiences, would respond that we must be able to make identifying reference to them. Malcolm, convinced that the notion of private experience is ultimately illegitimate, replies that pain is not a "private experience," and I can talk about my sensations without making identifying reference to them.

Malcolm and Strawson provide a convenient introduction to the question of how to read §293, not only because they were early and influential contributors to the debate over how to understand Wittgenstein on private language, but also because they exemplify the two interpretive poles to which subsequent interpreters are drawn. Strawson reads §293 negatively, as denying what we ordinarily say about pain; Malcolm reads it positively, as a matter of correcting a philosophical misunderstanding of everyday language.

Malcolm is surely right that Strawson misreads §293 by failing to take the closing paragraph seriously. However, Strawson's reading does give voice to some of the leading views about the mind under attack in §293, and so not only provides a convenient foil for Malcolm, but is also one of the first of many readings of §293 that responds to the passage by vigorously defending those views.

While there is much one might debate about how best to read §293c, it clearly tells us that the author of those words takes the point of the previous paragraph to be a conditional one, and that the last two sentences of §293b are a statement of that conditional's consequent. The story of the beetle-boxes is generally taken in the subsequent literature as drawing an analogy between the rules of the beetle-box game, that is, the rules governing what the beetle-box-owners can say and do with the beetle-boxes, and the rules for the use of sensation words. Just as the thing in the box cancels out in the beetle story, so on a certain conception of sensation the object of sensation "drops out of consideration as irrelevant." In this way, we are supposedly given a compelling reason to reject a certain model, picture, or theory of sensation. However, this general interpretive framework leaves room for a wide variety of detailed interpretations, which disagree about many of the details: not only about the precise nature of the view under attack, but also about the rules of the beetle-box game and the point of the story.

III   Pitcher's, Cook's, and Donagan's Interpretations of the Beetle Story

During the second half of the 1960s, Pitcher's (1964), Cook's (1965), and Donagan's (1966) discussions of the beetle-box story acquired a canonical status. Both Cook's and Donagan's papers, reprinted in Pitcher's very widely read anthology of essays on the *Philosophical Investigations,* include a critical response to the provocative interpretation of §293 in the chapter on "Sensations and talk of them" in Pitcher's *The Philosophy of Wittgenstein* (1964). As a result, they map out a set of options that provided a convenient point of departure for subsequent discussion of §293.

Pitcher, like Strawson, highlights Wittgenstein's attack on the assumption that words such as 'pain' are "the names (in a non-trivial sense) of sensations which people sometimes experience" (1964, 285). This is the first of three assumptions, which Pitcher jointly calls "View V": Pitcher's construal of the theory of sensation under attack. The other two are:

[ii] when I assert truly . . . "I am in pain," I am describing the state of my consciousness (i.e., I am asserting there is included in it a sensation called . . . "pain")

[iii] when I assert of another person . . . "He is in pain," I claim that he is experiencing the same sort of sensation that I do when I . . . am in pain. (1964, 285)

Pitcher takes Wittgenstein to be denying each of these claims, and so to be arguing that "pain" is not the name of a sensation and that "I am in pain" is not a description of my consciousness. However, Pitcher's Wittgenstein is by no means a behaviourist, for he only denies that we can *talk* of sensations, not their existence. This is an odd balancing trick, and his irresolute exposition of this point walks on both sides of that very fine line.[6] The exposition, which immediately follows his quotation of §293b, reads as follows:

The analogy with pain is perfectly clear. If 'pain' is supposed to denote a somewhat (including a nothing) which each person can observe only in his own case, then the somewhat 'cancels out'; and if the sole function of the word 'pain' is to denote it, the word is at once deprived of any use. (Pitcher 1964, 298)

However, we are then provided with two important qualifications, which make it clear that the analogy is very far indeed from being perfectly clear. First, Wittgenstein is "not denying that when a person is in pain, he very often . . . feels something frightful, nor even that this something is terribly important to the person himself and to others" (Pitcher 1964, 298). Pitcher surely intends these words to indicate the truth about sensation that is left after Wittgenstein's critique of View V. For he goes on to say that all Wittgenstein is denying is "a particular thesis about language," namely that "the word 'pain' names . . . this something that the person feels, in a way which is remotely like the way that the words for publicly observable things name . . . them" (Pitcher 1964, 298). Furthermore, Pitcher counterbalances his denial of View V by maintaining that View V is only a view about what can be said in language; sensations exist, but "do not enter into pain language-games" (Pitcher 1964, 299). For:

Everyone acknowledges that sensations are private, that no one can experience another person's sensations, so that the special felt quality of each person's sensations is known to him alone and no other. (Pitcher 1964, 297)

Thus, another's private sensations "are completely unknown to us; we have no idea what he might be feeling – what the beetle in his box might be like. But this is no epistemological tragedy, no metaphysical stumbling-block to the playing of the language-game, for they are not in the least needed" (Pitcher 1964, 299).

There is a striking parallel here between Pitcher's handling of View V, and the *Tractatus'* treatment of solipsism. In both cases, the overall point is supposedly that "what it *means* is quite correct, only it cannot be *said*, but shows itself" (TLP 5.62). This is no accident. For Pitcher attributes to Wittgenstein a theory of sensation that divides into two parts, which are supposedly consistent, but form an odd couple: a behaviouristic philosophy of language, on which there can be no talk of sensation, and each person's epiphenomenal inner world, made up of sensations. This is a "semi-solipsistic" theory of sensation.[7] The semi-solipsist agrees with the solipsist that I only know what pain means from my own case. Unlike the solipsist, the semi-solipsist also maintains that this is true of each of us. The meaning of "pain" is a private object for each of us. This is a view that Wittgenstein explored in some detail in the years immediately after his return to philosophy, in his discussions of phenomenological and physicalistic languages, and provided a point of departure in the development of his discussion of private experience in the mid-1930s.[8]

However, this semi-solipsism, without Pitcher's inexpressibility proviso, is the very view that is advocated in the opening words of the first two paragraphs of §293:

> If I say of myself that it is only from my own case that I know what the word "pain" means – must I not say the same of other people too? . . .
>
> Well, everyone tells me that *he* knows what pain is only from his own case!

But these sentences are an interlocutor's statement of the very view about pain, and my knowledge of it, that the narrator of the beetle story, responds to, models, and 'cancels out' in the words that follow it.[9] In this way, Pitcher, like Strawson, provided a convenient foil for the next stage of the debate, by defending a semi-solipsistic view of sensation and attributing it to Wittgenstein. Indeed, Pitcher's reading should remind us of Malcolm's observation that the aim of the beetle story is not to convince us that we cannot communicate about what pain is like, but that if we conceive of pain as an inner object, we commit ourselves to its incommunicability.

John Cook replies to Pitcher, as Malcolm does to Strawson, that the beetle analogy is not to "our use of words, but the philosophical use of those words" (Cook 1965, 312). "Rather than showing that sensations cannot have names," the analogy shows that "we must reject the view that sensations are private" (Cook 1965, 312). Cook's problem, like Malcolm's, is to convince us that the view that sensations are not private can do justice to our ordinary ways of talking about own experience. In other words, that he has not thrown out the baby – our ordinary ways of talking about sensation – with the bathwater – the semi-solipsistic view that everyone knows what pain is only from his own case. If we read Wittgenstein as simply discarding the "false grammatical analogy" (Cook 1965, 314) that leads to the semi-solipsist's inner world of private objects, we may seem forced to accept the other half of semi-solipsism: an outer world and a language which only speaks of that world.

Donagan replies to Pitcher along Strawsonian lines, arguing that Wittgenstein comes very close to accepting View V, once one qualifies it to acknowledge that "the internal character" of experience – whether it "is the same for you as for me is irrelevant to the meaning of the word 'toothache'" (Donagan 1966, 348). Donagan contends that Wittgenstein's definition of pain in terms of both "its external circumstances" and their "private and non-dispositional accompaniment" (Donagan 1966, 348) allows him to bring together talk of the inner and outer in a single, unitary theory of sensation. This allows Donagan to resolve the tension between the two halves of Pitcher's account of sensation by removing the inexpressibility proviso. He thus readmits talk of the existence of one's own sensations into our common language, but not comparisons or descriptions of them because private experience "plays no part in determining the meanings of the words and phrases that refer to sensations" (Donagan 1966, 345).

One problem with all these responses to the beetle story is that while each of them clearly takes one side or another in the dispute set out in §293, they do little to clarify how the different views under discussion there are related. Indeed, §304, a recapitulation of that dispute, can also be read as a summary of their disagreement. Wittgenstein's interlocutor defends the position advocated by Strawson, Donagan, and Pitcher's View V; Wittgenstein's narrator replies along the lines advocated by Malcolm, Cook, and Pitcher's reply to View V.

[Interlocutor:] But you will surely admit that there is a difference between pain-behaviour accompanied by pain and pain-behaviour without any pain?

[Narrator:] Admit it? What greater difference could there be?

[Interlocutor:] And yet you again and again reach the conclusion that the sensation itself is a *nothing*.

[Narrator:] Not at all. It is not a *something*, but not a *nothing* either! The conclusion was only that a nothing would serve just as well as a something about which nothing could be said.

Furthermore, none of the authors clearly distinguishes the expository work of stating the competing views under discussion in §293 from the interpretive task of evaluating their strengths and weaknesses. Instead, each identifies a strand in the discussion of the beetle-box that he finds most promising, and then supplements it with various assumptions about Wittgenstein's philosophical commitments.

IV   Cohen's Repudiation of the Beetle Story

Martin Cohen, in his *Wittgenstein's Beetle and Other Classic Thought Experiments*, observes that

> There is a whole literature on Wittgenstein's so-called Private Language Argument, in which a few cryptic Wittgensteinisms (like the Beetle experiment) are dissected, mulled over and prodded for signs of life. . . . A substantial body of work . . . has built up, all striving to present a definitive interpretation of what Wittgenstein meant. But at the end of the day, each new version relies upon the introduction of extra assumptions and new material, because the original accounts are just too sparse and too ambiguous to lead to any conclusion. (Cohen 2005, 109)

Cohen's sceptical conclusion has its attractions, and the material we have reviewed so far could easily be deployed in a way that would lend it considerable plausibility. However, like much of the work he criticizes, Cohen pays very little attention to the primary text. In fact, he cites none of the published scholarly work on the topic. The only secondary sources he draws on are a handful of websites that include some discussion of the beetle story, rapidly quoted to convey the impression that no clear conclusions can be drawn from such a confusing and confused discussion, one in which different interpreters come to quite different conclusions. On the other hand, it is remarkable how many contemporary "interpretations" of the beetle story amount to little more than a quick summary, rapidly followed by the claim that one philosophical theory or another has been vanquished.

While Cohen does quote the beetle story in full, there is no mention of 293a and 293c, and very little discussion of how the story works.[10] Instead, he simply asserts, without any further argument, that

> Wittgenstein's Beetle is supposed to show that people assume that because they are using the same words, they are talking about the same thing, when in fact they may be discussing different matters, and what's more, doing so in quite different ways . . . And the beetle is supposed to be like words and concepts generally. It is supposed to sever the link between concepts in our heads, and things in the world, by way of words. Today, the beetle is claimed by linguists, doctors and psychologists, artists and aesthetes to radically transform the conventional view of the stability of meaning and language. (Cohen 2005, 87–88)

In other words, Cohen claims that the story works by drawing a parallel between the beetle in the box and sensations such as pain: "Everyone has such sensations. But only they can look at them, and they cannot allow others to 'open the box' " (Cohen 2005, 106). In fairness to Cohen, we have seen that there is a long tradition of reading the beetle story along these lines, going back to Strawson. Moreover, Cohen has no trouble in finding an online passage, taken from Carl Elliott's testimony to the US President's Council on Bioethics, which reads the beetle story in much this way:

> Now, what's the point, you're asking yourself. Well, the point is that the words that we use to describe our inner lives, our psychological states, words like "depression" or "anxiety" or "fulfillment," those words get their meanings not by referring and pointing to intermental states, things in our heads. They get their meaning from the rules of the game, the social context in which they're used.
> They're like the word "beetle" in Wittgenstein's game. We learn how to use the words not by looking inward and naming what we see there. We learn how to use the words by playing the game. The players don't all need to be experiencing the same thing in order for the words to make sense.
> I say I am fulfilled. You say you're fulfilled. We both understand what the other means. Yet that doesn't mean that our inner psychic states are the same. Right?
> We can all talk about our beetles, yet still have different things in our boxes.[11]

Yet we have seen that this is not the point of the beetle story in its original setting. Instead, Elliott polemically invokes Wittgenstein's authority to bolster his contention that once we appreciate the implications of the fact that the language we use to describe mental disorders is one we learn from others, we will be able to see "why mental disorders are so flexible in their application, and so apt to expand and contract, depending on the language-game in which they are applied."[12] Elliott, it should be noted, does not draw the globally sceptical conclusions about the stability of meaning that Cohen attributes to him; he only applies the argument to terms for mental contents. However, others certainly have explicitly invoked the beetle story as the basis for just such conclusions.

In fairness to Elliott, there is a long tradition of reading the beetle story as a compressed parable from which a whole philosophy of mind and language, with far-reaching consequences for traditional "Cartesian" and "behaviourist" theories of mind, can be rapidly unpacked. For instance, Judith Genova reads the beetle story much more ambitiously, as the culmination of an argument designed to show that

> Words do not mean by referring to either objects or ideas. Reference or denotation is irrelevant for determining meaning. Rather, meaning is a function of a) a word's place in the language and b) its use by speakers. Thus, to show that not even sensation words mean by referring is to clinch the more general argument about how words mean. (Genova 1995, 177–8)

Indeed, this style of broad-brushed pedagogy with the beetle-box story was already well established thirty years ago. The second issue of *Teaching Philosophy* included an article by Bruce Russell on "Beetle Boxes: Demonstrating the Logic of P-predicates." It tells instructors how to "facilitate an understanding of the role played by 'inner' and 'outer' data" (Russell 1975, 153) by means of an in-class "demonstration" of the beetle-box scenario, using envelopes, one for each student: most of them are to contain suitable small objects, while some are left empty. He even proposes a pair of sequels: on a second day, one can redistribute the envelopes to their original owners (to consider memory issues), and a new set of transparent envelopes (to consider the case where others can see inside the box). Russell is considerably more careful than the expositors we have just considered, and at one point explicitly states the conditional conclusion that eludes Cohen and Elliott, namely:

> An intersubjective language is impossible if mental predicates refer to private "contents" or events from which they derive their meaning. (Russell 1975, 154)

However, like Elliott, and many other readers, he takes the beetle-box scenario to provide the basis for far-reaching conclusions. Yet, in drawing out his further conclusions about the nature of mind and language, Russell actually provides an excellent illustration of Cohen's principal criticism of the misuse of the beetle story. For in doing so, Russell has to introduce extra premises concerning such matters as the nature of criteria and privacy, the reliability of memory and the numerical identity of non-continuously observed particulars, so that the supposedly self-contained "demonstration" becomes nothing more than a convenient pedagogical point of departure for a wide-ranging discussion of the logic of P-predicates, and of a Strawsonian descriptive metaphysics.

V   Hacker's and Baker's Interpretations of the Beetle Story

The readings of the beetle story we have met so far make use of Wittgenstein's story in order to advance a variety of different philosophical programs, and do so in a wide variety of ways. The more careful readings identify a strand in the argument that seems promising, and defend it by articulating a sophisticated philosophical theory that is supposedly implicit in Wittgenstein's conversational exposition. The less careful readings simply identify a promising conclusion, and claim that it follows from the passage in question. How should we move beyond this impasse?

A natural response to this diverse assortment of interpretations would be to look more carefully at the text, not only at §293, but also at the *Philosophical Investigations* as a whole and Wittgenstein's writings on private language for further clues as to how best to understand the deceptively simple dialogue we find in §293. Instead of reading our own preconceptions into the gaps we find in Wittgenstein's telling of the beetle story, we might reread the passage in question with an eye to detail, and look to the broader context for further clarification. Even a minimal application of this strategy will certainly suffice to eliminate most of the readings we have considered so far. The interpretations we considered in section 4, while representative of much of what passes for exposition of the beetle story, do not even take into account the paragraphs that immediately precede and follow that story. The readings we considered in sections 2 and 3 are far more painstaking and thorough in their attempts to articulate a coherent train of argumentation. Nevertheless, they all import assumptions and commitments that turn Wittgenstein's story into a compressed, and potentially question-begging, exposition of a number of systematic commitments, each requiring further defense in turn.

Wittgenstein's writing, composed of dialogues without clearly identified voices, certainly calls for a reconstructive engagement with the text. As the reader works to identify the positions being attacked and defended, he or she inevitably finds his or her own concerns being addressed there. As a result, each generation of readers has discovered a Wittgenstein who seems to have anticipated their own philosophical concerns with remarkable farsightedness.[13] This is not to deny the value of the pathbreaking interpretations we considered from the 1950s and 1960s. While none of them is entirely successful, they all help us to see interpretive avenues that might well not be apparent otherwise.

However, if we are to make any progress, we need to distinguish the well-established practice of making use of Wittgenstein's writings in pursuit of one's own philosophical goals from the question of how best to understand Wittgenstein's use of the beetle story in the *Philosophical Investigations*. One approach that naturally presents itself at this point would be to focus narrowly on the text of §293, with the aim of making explicit precisely what Wittgenstein is doing there. Another complementary approach would be to place §293 in a broader context, connecting it with one's reading of the "private language argument" as a whole. These approaches are pursued with extraordinary thoroughness by Peter Hacker, both in *Insight and Illusion* and *Wittgenstein: Meaning and Mind*. The former was published in 1972, when Baker was a student of Hacker's, and published in a revised second edition in 1986, toward the end of their collaboration on a series of joint projects. The latter was written after they had ceased writing together; the two books are among the principal targets of Baker's critical discussion of previous work on "the private language argument."

As we have already seen, Hacker identifies the target of the beetle story as a form of semi-solipsism: the view that each of us "knows what 'pain' means only from one's own case, for it seems that it is the sensation one *has* that gives the word its meaning" (Hacker 1990a, 110–111). This then leads to the problem of how I know what others mean by "pain," for on this view, each of us names our own sensations, "as if they were objects in a peep-show into which only he can peer" (Hacker 1990a, 111). The beetle story then provides an analogy for this supposed epistemic predicament, which allows us to see that semi-solipsism, with its construal of the grammar of expression of sensation on the model of name and object, leads to a dilemma:

On the private-linguist's conception of the relation between a name and the object it refers to, then, *if communication is possible*, the private object allegedly referred to is a piece of idle machinery and plays no part in the mechanism of communication, and conversely *if the private object does play a part*, then communication is impossible. (Hacker 1986, 270)

Or, put more concisely, and without invoking the mechanism-of-communication metaphor:

If what is in the box is relevant to the meaning of 'beetle', then no one else can understand what I mean by 'beetle'; and if 'beetle' is understood by others, it cannot signify what is in each person's private box. (Hacker 1990a, 111)

Both formulations may seem too concise to do justice to the full nature of the argument here. Nevertheless, they do elegantly summarize the nub of the narrator's objection in §293 to the interlocutor's idea that we each know what "pain" means on the basis of identifying a private inner object: it cannot connect up with our public talk of pain. On the other hand, the virtue of such a concise summary is that it identifies the principal claim made by the narrator in §293, while leaving open the question of how best to understand how it might be further defended and articulated.

However, this may well seem to call for further elucidation: what is the narrator's reason for maintaining that 'beetle' cannot be used to refer to what is in each person's box, that 'pain' does not refer to a private object? Here, Hacker relies on his previous exposition of the private language argument, and its conclusion there can be no such thing as a private ostensive definition. On Hacker's reading of the preceding argument, in a supposed private ostensive definition "there is no technique of application, there is no *practice* of applying [the supposed word in question], but only the appearance of a practice" (Hacker 1986, 269). In other words, there is no technique of applying words to private objects "*on the model of applying them to public ones.* There is no *method* of comparing a sample with a private object. . . . nothing has been determined to *count as the same*" (Hacker 1990a, 112). This, in turn, is because without the possibility of a public, independent, check on the private use of a term, no distinction can be established between what seems right to me, and what is right. On Hacker's reading, the argument turns on the point that the distinction is only possible in the public world, where others can, at least in principle, provide an independent check on my usage. Hacker draws the moral that there is no such thing as following 'private' rules, i.e. rules which no one else could in principle understand inasmuch as the rules in question *can have no public expression*. Such putative rules are 'private ostensive definitions', which, since there is no such thing as exhibiting 'private samples', are *essentially* incommunicable. (Hacker 1986, 272)

Furthermore, Hacker claims that idealism and solipsism presuppose the intelligibility of such rule-following, and a further consequence of this train of argument is to cast light on "the deep and ineradicable flaws of these philosophical pictures" (ibid.).

In this way, Hacker's elucidation of the beetle story attempts to combine two very different approaches to the idea that each of us only knows what pain is from one's own case. On the one hand, he insists that the point of the beetle story is that the interlocutor's conception of the meaning of pain is nonsensical, more like a delusion, or a misconception, than a straightforward falsehood. While it appears intelligible, it is actually incoherent. On the other hand, he provides a sophisticated and subtle chain of reasoning about the nature of language, concerning the need for public rules and objective standards of application that is designed to underwrite this very conclusion. In so doing, Hacker claims to have identified a condition for the possibility of successful reference, and shown that private inner objects cannot satisfy that condition. However, this elaboration of a detailed argument in order to underwrite the analogy carries with it the almost irresistible suggestion that the interlocutor's conception of sensation *is* intelligible, that we do know what he was talking about.

Baker observes that on Hacker's approach, "Wittgenstein offers the hypothesis of a private language as something subtle and important which is worthy of thorough and detailed investigation. Consequently, he is taken not to think that this hypothesis, once it is made explicit, is *manifestly* absurd (without further argument)" (Baker 1998, 328). Baker's response to Hacker amounts to a spirited defense of the latter strategy, and a resolute rejection of the former approach. Baker argues that the traditional "PLA-interpreter," the reader who attempts to reconstruct the "weaker thesis" supposedly underlying the discussion of a private language in the *Philosophical Investigations*, looking for the definitive "arguments which are parts of a consistent chain of reasoning and which jointly constitute a definitive demonstration of the absurdity of the hypothesis" (ibid.), misses the point of the story. Wittgenstein's aim in §293, Baker proposes, is not to provide a subtle proof that it is impossible to answer the question "What does the word 'pain' *name?*," but rather, to get us to see that it is pointless (Baker 1998, 340–341). Elaborating the impossibility claim leads us toward the elaborate anti-Cartesian train of argument that Hacker imputes to Wittgenstein, and away from the bolder, and simpler, construal on which the very idea of referring to a private, inner object is incoherent. In other words, we are to reject the idea that the PLA is a species of transcendental argument, a solution, of sorts, to a traditional problem, and instead approach it as a dissolution, a repudiation of the framework it takes for granted.

In the closing section of his final paper on private language (1998, 346–354; 2004, Ch. 7), Baker provides a wealth of detailed advice designed to help us develop a different framework of interpretation, one that will provide an alternative approach to the "anti-Cartesian" reading that seems almost unavoidable to most readers. He proposes that we take our bearings from the remarks "which open the *Investigations* and set the stage for everything that follows" (1998, 348). Baker reads those opening remarks as a criticism of "Augustine's picture of language" (1998, 347), a "set of very general ideas that affects almost everyone who reflects on the meaning of words" (1998, 348). This, to my mind, is still too Hackerian a way of reading those opening sections, which I believe are better read as taking on a much less monolithic target.[14] But Baker is right to stress the deep continuities between the discussion of misunderstandings about reference to outer objects, and ostensive definition, in the opening sections, and the discussion of misunderstandings about reference to inner objects, and private ostensive definition in the remarks that follow §243, and to propose that we explore these continuities in seeking new bearings in understanding Wittgenstein on private language. The methods introduced in the opening sections of the book – and especially the "method of §2," with the associated technique of articulating a language-game that seems to give the interlocutor what he says he wants, are also the methods that Wittgenstein employs in the subsequent discussion of private language.

Baker also suggests that we will find it easier to give up the idea that §243ff. must be addressed toward sophisticated philosophical theories (such as Cartesianism, solipsism, or idealism), positions that supposedly underlie the interlocutor's naïve and fragmentary contributions, if we think of the discussion in the book as directed toward the audience Wittgenstein actually engaged with while writing and teaching: his students, and his own earlier self. Here Baker suggests we think of the interlocutory voice as Francis Skinner, or another student in Wittgenstein's classes, not a veteran philosopher who is implacably committed to some quite specific

"Cartesian" theory. He proposes that we approach the dialogue in the *Philosophical Investigations* as much more exploratory and open-ended, and much less like a sustained debate between well-worked out philosophical positions. I agree that much of the material presented in these fragmentary snatches of discussion does have the conversational and piecemeal character of classroom discussion, and no doubt emerged out of Wittgenstein's engagement with both his students' ideas, and his own earlier writing. However, in the carefully revised and artfully constructed form that it takes in the finished text of the *Philosophical Investigations*, we should also think of it as akin to Socrates' relationship to his interlocutors in the Socratic dialogues. While it may well have been composed as a record, or reconstruction, of an informal discussion, its final polished form is that of a distinctly literary achievement that invites the reader to take part in the debate it presents.

With this guidance in mind, let us return to Hacker's exposition of the beetle story, and reconsider how best to further elucidate Hacker's construal of its basic point – namely that if "beetle" has a private meaning, it is incommunicable, and if it has a public meaning, it has no connection with what is in the box, and so such an object cannot connect up with our public talk. If we follow Baker's advice, that further elucidation cannot consist in elaborating the presupposed argument against the possibility of a private language that we find in Hacker's exposition. Rather, we need to find a way of reading the passage on which nothing is hidden, so that the beetle story's point is no more than the dissolution of the interlocutor's conviction that everyone "knows what pain is only from his own case!" (§293b1). Even if we agree with Baker that the overall aim of the passage is to convince us that this conviction is "*manifestly* absurd" (Baker 1998, 328), we ought to be able to say more about how it does this.

First, we should note that the vast majority of §293 is in the narrator's voice, not the interlocutor's. The narrator is in charge of the discussion, working to provide an analogy that will come as close as possible to giving the interlocutor what he says he wants. While §293a discusses the interlocutor's views about the meaning of pain, it is the narrator who speaks, pointing out that the interlocutor must generalize his view about his knowledge of the meaning of 'pain' to others. Apart from the first sentence of §293b, where the interlocutor accepts this point, thus provoking the narrator to outline the beetle scenario (§293b2–3), the interlocutor only speaks to reply to the narrator's suggestion that it would be quite possible for everyone to have something different in their box, or for it to be constantly changing (§293b4–5), namely "– But suppose the word 'beetle' had a use in these people's language? –" (§293b6). The narrator responds that "beetle" couldn't function as the name of a thing – the language-game has been set up in such a way that the word could make no connection with the thing in the box, so that even if it were empty it would make no difference. In other words, even if we assume for the sake of argument that the word does have a use, it couldn't do what the interlocutor wants.

In conversation, J. L. Austin claimed Wittgenstein was simply contradicting himself here. "First he says, there definitely is a beetle in the box, and then he says there might be nothing in the box, a plain contradiction" (Searle 2001, 226). But that beautifully concise and pointed objection misses the point of the contradiction. Wittgenstein's narrator has told us a story in which a term – "beetle" – is supposedly introduced. But the moral of the story is that no introduction has occurred, at least if one conceives of the word as naming its object. The initial ceremony is entirely unconnected with the rest of our language, and *that* is why everyone could have something different in his or her box, or the item in the box could be constantly changing, or it could even be empty.[15] The person who supposedly "has" a beetle is in the same position as those friends of Wittgenstein's to whom he would "give" trees while out on a walk together – on condition they didn't do anything with their "gifts," or prevent the previous owners from doing anything with them (Malcolm 1984, 29).

The contradiction here is comparable to that which arises at the end of §2, when we are told to conceive of the builders' language-game as "a complete primitive language." That game is offered to the reader as a way of giving the interlocutor what he says he wants: an example of a use of language in which words do get their meaning by standing for objects. Similarly, the beetle story is a way of giving the interlocutor what he says he wants: a use of language in which words get their meaning by standing for private objects. However, one crucial moral that emerges from the discussion of that example is that we cannot do what the interlocutor wants, that we cannot really conceive of such a language. Instead, we are led to see that the best we can do is to come up with a limited example that serves its purpose when we see just how limited it is. In both §2 and §293, the narrator attempts to provide the interlocutor with an imaginary language-game that best approximates the relationship between language and the world that the interlocutor imagines. Yet in trying to think through how that scenario might be realized, we come to see that nothing we could do would satisfy the interlocutor's contradictory demands.

However, perhaps the closest anticipation of the strategy of §293 is not the method of §2, but the story of the grocer which concludes §1. For the 'beetle' story provides a physical, "outer" analogy for the interlocutor's inner peep show, much as the "grocer" story in the opening remark of the *Philosophical Investigations* provides a comparable physical analogy for the mental operations that supposedly go on in our minds when we identify five red apples. As long as we imagine these processes occurring within us, we think of them as animating our ordinary use of words; but once we bring them out into the open, by imagining a comparable public procedure, they seem both lifeless and bizarre.[16] While those processes seemed natural and necessary, as long as they were going on in the mysterious medium of the mind, they lose their magic in the light of day.

Wittgenstein's beetle has been used by most of his interpreters as an opportunity to articulate the arguments that underlie his theory of the nature of sensation; it would be closer to the truth to say that it is an excellent illustration of his attack on the intuitions that feed such theories. But perhaps, like Gordon Baker, we can only fully appreciate the nature of Wittgenstein's attack after working our way through the arguments his interpreters have offered on his behalf.

Notes

1 I have used Anscombe's translation, but have incorporated two improvements recommended by Hacker (1990a, 112): "Well, everyone" (293b1) for "Now someone," and "name" for "designation" (293c).

2 From an MA exam paper on Wittgenstein, given at the University of London in May 2000. www.london.ac.uk/fileadmin/documents/students/philosophy/ma_examination_papers/wittgenstein_ma_old2000.pdf.

3 Baker (1998, 353); cf. Baker (2004, 139).

4 I follow the convention of using letters in alphabetical order to identify specific paragraphs within a numbered remark in the *Philosophical Investigations*, and numbers to identify sentences, when needed. Thus §293c refers to the third and final paragraph of §293.

5 While the word "then" does not occur in the English translation, the corresponding German word "dann" does occur in the German text. Following Gordon Baker's example, I use bold, not italics, to indicate my emphasis in the context of quotations.

6   Cf. Conant (2004) on irresolute private language arguments, which discusses a parallel problem concerning the status of the grammatical rules that underwrite such arguments: in both cases, interpreters are driven to hold that what is important to the argument cannot be said, but can only be shown.

7   Wittgenstein uses this expression in MS 165, p. 150; Hacker (1990a, 111) uses the term in his discussion of §293's target.

8   For further discussion, see Stern (1995, 5.2–5.4).

9   Although "the interlocutor" is not a term that is ever used by Wittgenstein, it has become a standard term of art for identifying those passages which express views clearly at odds with the principal voice in the *Philosophical Investigations*, which is usually taken to express Wittgenstein's own views. For further discussion of questions concerning the identification of voices in the *Philosophical Investigations*, see Stern (2004, 3–5, 21–26).

10 Cohen quotes *Philosophical Investigations* §293b2–8 on p. 87 of Cohen (2005); his discussion of the beetle story is on pp. 87–89 and pp. 106–110.

11 From   www.bioethicsprint.bioethics.gov/transcripts/sep02/session4.html, accessed on July 11, 2006. Quoted, in a slightly different form, in Cohen (2005, 107). Elliott gives a somewhat more detailed account of the beetle story, but draws the same conclusions, in Elliott (2003, 188–190).

12 Elliott (2003, 189).

13 For further discussion of these interpretive issues, see Stern (2004), esp. Ch. 2.

14 For an alternative approach to reading the opening of the *Philosophical Investigations* as an attack on the "Augustinian picture", see Stern (2004, Ch. 4). Oddly, while Baker became such an acute critic of the idea that the remarks following §243 are directed at a single, overarching set of ideas, he continued to read the remarks that open the book along remarkably similar lines.

15 Of course, if we change the setup of the beetle scenario so that people are allowed to talk about what is in their boxes, say, by comparing them to what they see around them, as Cohen (2005, 89) suggests, then we would be able to tell each other about what our "beetles" are like.

16 For further discussion of the grocer story, see Stern (2004, 83–86).

Chapter 11

Bourgeois, Bolshevist or Anarchist? The Reception of Wittgenstein's Philosophy of Mathematics[1]

Ray Monk

I   Some Personal Prefatory Remarks

It was Wittgenstein's philosophy of mathematics – or, more precisely, its reception among Anglophone philosophers – that got me into biography. And, among the people I discussed it with before I started writing my biography of Wittgenstein, it was Gordon Baker who best understood the connection between the two.

When I was a postgraduate student at Oxford in the early 1980s, all the talk was of Dummett and Davidson, anti-realism and truth-functional semantics. An interest in Wittgenstein was considered slightly old-fashioned. The famous seminars conducted by Baker and Hacker, always challenging, reliably entertaining and fiercely combative, attracted a good audience and inspired fervent and passionately partisan debate, but, in their attacks on the views that were then establishing themselves as ortho-doxies at Oxford, they were considered by most postgraduate students to be a rearguard action by exponents – albeit extremely able and even for-midable exponents – of an outmoded way of doing philosophy.

Perhaps somewhat perversely, my own philosophical views became increasingly Wittgensteinian during my time at Oxford and, still more perversely, I chose to write my dissertation on that most neglected and maligned aspect of his work: his philosophy of mathematics. I soon dis-covered what a lonely world it was for a Wittgensteinian philosopher of mathematics. There were, in those days, very few philosophers of mathematics at Oxford of any kind. My supervision was divided between Wittgensteinians in the sub-Faculty of Philosophy who knew little about the philosophy of mathematics and mathematicians who knew little (and cared less) about Wittgenstein.

What was worse for an enthusiastic advocate of Baker and Hacker (as I had then become) was that the literature on Wittgenstein's philosophy of mathematics, such as it then was, was dominated by none other than Michael Dummett, whose 1959 article (reprinted in Shanker, 1986, 121–137) was far and away the most influential discussion of the subject. So influential was it that, around this time, Crispin Wright could publish a book entitled *Wittgenstein on the Foundations of Mathematics* (Wright 1980) that was as much about Dummett as it was about Wittgenstein.

My own feelings about Dummett's article were those most trenchantly expressed years later by Gordon Baker in *Wittgenstein, Frege and the Vienna Circle*:

> [It] has served as the focal point of most subsequent thought and writing about Wittgenstein's philosophy of mathematics. It presents conventionalism as a philosophical theory addressed to the questions what makes an arithmetical equation true and how we apprehend these truths; it categorizes Wittgenstein as a conventionalist; it compares his conventionalism with the theory advocated in the Vienna Circle; and it introduces the concept of full-blooded conventionalism. In all these respects its influence has been catastrophic for understanding Wittgenstein's ideas. (Baker, 1988, 259)

What came to preoccupy me more and more was the thought that Dummett's misunderstanding of Wittgenstein's philosophy of mathematics was part of a more general problem, a failure on the part of English-speaking philosophers to understand the *spirit* in which Wittgenstein wrote, or, to put it another way, a failure to understand Wittgenstein *himself*. Maurice Drury, in explaining why he published his notes of conversations with Wittgenstein, wrote that it was to counteract the effect of 'well-meaning commentators' who 'make it appear that his writings were now easily assimilable into the very intellectual milieu they were largely a warning against' (Rhees, 1984, 101). If we had access to some of Wittgenstein's *private* conversations, Drury clearly felt, we would be better placed to understand the spirit of his philosophical work. Or at least, we would be less tempted to embrace certain prevalent misunderstandings of it. Chief among those, I felt, were the misunderstandings of Wittgenstein's philosophy of mathematics that dominated the literature in the early

1980s. It was that conviction that persuaded me to write a biography of Wittgenstein.

First, however, I had to write my dissertation. It was called 'Seeing Perceptions: The Perceptual Aspects of Wittgenstein's Philosophy of Mathematics' and emphasised three things: 1. the connections between Wittgenstein's work on mathematics and his work on language and psychology; 2. the cultural and spiritual attitudes that informed Wittgenstein's philosophy of mathematics; and 3. the gulf that separated Wittgenstein's thinking about mathematics from that of most mathematicians and philosophers of mathematics. It was in many ways a crude piece of work, but it was written with great fervour and conviction and I had the good fortune to be examined by Brian McGuinness and Gordon Baker, both of whom appreciated the fervour and turned a blind eye to the crudities. Gordon was especially sympathetic, telling me that he was convinced that, wherever I might have erred on this or that detailed point, my general *tendency* was right.

It was only after reading the various essays contained in the posthumously published collection, *Wittgenstein's Method: Neglected Aspects* (Baker, 2004) that I fully understood what he meant. Charles Chihara, in his review of Crispin Wright's book (Chihara, 1982), distinguished 'left-wing' from 'right-wing' interpretations of Wittgenstein as follows:

> Left-wing interpretations emphasize Wittgenstein's radical views about the nature of philosophy; they stress the ideas that philosophical problems arise from misconceptions about grammar and meaning and that these problems should be resolved by a kind of therapy in which the therapist puts forward no theses, explanations, or theories of any kind. Right-wing interpretations emphasize Wittgensteinian *doctrines*. (Chihara, 1982, 105)

As Chihara rightly says, on that classification, Crispin Wright is a right-wing interpreter, as are most of the people who have written on Wittgenstein's philosophy of mathematics, including Dummett. On the other hand, to name but a few, Gordon Baker, Peter Hacker, and the 'New Wittgensteinians' led by Cora Diamond and James Conant are left-wingers. As that list illustrates, however, there are many different ways of being, in this sense, left-wing.

Katherine Morris, in her introduction to *Wittgenstein's Method: Neglected Aspects*, distinguishes three phases in Gordon Baker's career. The 'early Baker', astonishingly, would, on Chihara's classification, be categorised as a right-winger, one who saw in the later Wittgenstein a theory of meaning that might provide, as the title of Baker's DPhil thesis put it, 'A New Foundation for Semantics'. The 'Middle Baker', the one known to generations of students as the co-author with Peter Hacker of standard and seminal texts of Wittgenstein commentary, 'roundly rejected', in Morris's words, 'the idea that the later Wittgenstein would develop a "theory of meaning" or a "foundation for semantics"' and considered that: 'The true task of philosophy, rather, was to police the borders between sense and nonsense, issuing tickets to those philosophers, psychologists and linguists who transgressed the bounds of sense' (Baker, 2004, 1).

The 'Middle Baker', then, was certainly no right-winger. There was, however, it turned out, plenty of room for a sharp turn to the left. The later Baker, as Katherine Morris summarises him, saw Wittgenstein, not as a policeman but as a therapist: 'his tools were less "factual" descriptions of grammar than pictures and analogies; his aim was not to get others to toe the line of sense as opposed to nonsense but to free them from their intellectual torment by enabling them to see new aspects' (Baker, 2004, 2). In these words, Morris has summarised perfectly the Wittgenstein I tried to present in my dissertation on the philosophy of mathematics and in my biography.

Much to my disappointment and to the detriment of both Wittgenstein studies and philosophy, Gordon Baker never wrote much on the philosophy of mathematics. In his last essays, however, he presented a vision of Wittgenstein's later work, a vision faithful to the spirit of the man, that is the ideal starting point for anyone who cares to understand, not just *what* Wittgenstein said about mathematics but also *why* he said it. The task of expounding Wittgenstein's philosophy of mathematics in the light of that vision is a tough one; it requires a detailed understanding of Wittgenstein's own work, an awareness of the mathematical and philosophical context within which Wittgenstein was writing, and a willingness and an ability to engage with – while remaining intellectually independent of – a secondary literature imbued with the very attitudes against which Wittgenstein's work was addressed.

Some of these qualities are present in the best recent work on Wittgenstein's philosophy of mathematics. Unfortunately, however, almost all of this work belongs to, in Chihara's sense, the right wing. Though 'left-wing' interpretations of Wittgenstein's work have gained ascendancy in the discussion of his later philosophy of language, his later philosophy of mind and even the *Tractatus Logico-Philosophicus*, the discussion of his later philosophy of mathematics remains dominated by right-wingers. In my view, however, his later philosophy of mathematics will only be seen in the correct light when a 'left-winger' with the appropriate knowledge and skills steps forward to show how Wittgenstein's emphasis on pictures, analogies and seeing aspects lies at its very heart. In other words, the secondary literature on Wittgenstein's philosophy of mathematics desperately needs, and still awaits, its Gordon Baker.

II   Introduction: Wittgenstein's Chief Contribution?

'Wittgenstein's chief contribution has been in the philosophy of mathematics' (Monk, 1990, 466).[2] This, it seems, was Wittgenstein's own judgment on himself. In the spring of 1944, when Wittgenstein was living in Swansea and seeing Rhees almost every day, he received from John Wisdom a short biographical paragraph that Wisdom had written on Wittgenstein for inclusion in a biographical dictionary. Wisdom wanted to know if Wittgenstein wanted to make any corrections to the piece. The only change Wittgenstein insisted on was the inclusion of the above sentence.

Such, anyway, was the story I heard from Rush Rhees when I was researching my biography. Wisdom himself had no recollection of the event, but Rhees was adamant that his memory was accurate. If the story is true, it shows that Wittgenstein's own assessment of the importance of his work was radically out of step with that of the rest of the scholarly community. For, whereas his philosophy of language, his philosophy of mind and his conception of philosophy itself have all had a decisive influence on the way philosophy has developed in the half-century since his death, his philosophy of mathematics – far from being regarded as his 'chief contribution' – has been met with a mixture of bewilderment, disdain, disappointment and even anger and has had very little influence either among mathematicians or among philosophers of mathematics.

That this is so is partly to do with the unfinished state in which Wittgenstein left his major statement of his later philosophy, *Philosophical Investigations*. If, as he had originally planned, Part II of the *Investigations* had contained his remarks on the foundations of mathematics, it would at least have been obvious that he himself regarded those remarks as central to his project and they would not have been marginalised in the way that they have been. The separate publication of *Remarks on the Foundations of Mathematics* has created the impression that Wittgenstein, in addition to his main work on language and mind, also wrote about mathematics, but that this aspect of his work is peripheral and can safely be left alone by all but the small minority of philosophers actively pursuing questions in the philosophy of mathematics. If Wittgenstein's writing on mathematics had been included in the *Investigations* more people would have studied it, but also, I believe, they would have studied it in a different way. Instead of reading it as a contribution to a highly technical, esoteric and specialist subdiscipline of philosophy, they might have read it as an integral part of Wittgenstein's later project, seeing straight away the close connections that exist between what Wittgenstein has to say about mathematics and what he has to say about psychology.

Related to the relative neglect of Wittgenstein's work on mathematics is the widespread misunderstanding of it, which is reflected in repeated attempts to place it in a hole into which it will not fit. Generation after generation of commentators have attempted to see in Wittgenstein's work on mathematics the very views that he was campaigning against. If there is a common thread in these misinterpretations, I would locate it in the reluctance of commentators to admit how *radical* Wittgenstein's views on mathematics are, how at odds they are with the views and attitudes that prevail among mathematicians and philosophers of mathematics.

In this respect, I think, there is a connection, between Wittgenstein's evaluation of the importance of his philosophy of mathematics and his feelings, expressed repeatedly over the last twenty years of his life, that there was a gulf between the attitudes that informed his thought and those which prevailed in our civilisation, that he was (therefore) misunderstood, that he did not belong in academic life, that he was swimming against the tide, etc., etc. I think Wittgenstein felt that it was *especially* in the philosophy of mathematics that he was out of kilter with the times and that this was precisely why his work in that area mattered so much to him.

Ironically, many of Wittgenstein's detractors have grasped this better than some of his sympathisers. For the latter, trying to present Wittgenstein's views in a so-called "sympathetic" light, have sought to smooth over the cracks and to lessen the distance between his views on mathematics and those of the late-twentieth century mainstream. The Wittgenstein they thus produced may be one more acceptable to today's mathematicians and philosophers, but he is not recognisable as the man who declared that: 'There is no religious denomination in which the misuse of metaphysical expressions has been responsible for so much sin as it has in mathematics' (CV, 1) and announced: 'It is all one to me whether or not the typical western scientist understands or appreciates my work, since he will not in any case understand the spirit in which I write' (CV, 7).

The challenge facing the sympathetic interpreter of Wittgenstein's philosophy of mathematics is to understand his writings on mathematics *in the spirit in which he intended them to be understood*, and also to show why, thus understood, those writings deserve serious consideration, why they might even have been regarded as Wittgenstein's 'chief contribution' to philosophy. It is a challenge that few have even attempted, either during Wittgenstein's lifetime or since.

III The Reception of Wittgenstein's Philosophy of Mathematics in His Own Lifetime

When Wittgenstein returned to Cambridge in 1929, he did so precisely to work on the philosophy of logic and mathematics as, ostensibly at least, a postgraduate student, with Frank Ramsey as his supervisor. Ramsey was to die just a year after Wittgenstein's return, but during that year the two spent many hours discussing philosophy, primarily, one assumes, the philosophy of mathematics. So intense were these discussions that Wittgenstein, in the preface to *Philosophical Investigations*, mistakenly says that they were in discussion for the last *two* years of Ramsey's life.

In that preface, Wittgenstein acknowledges the force of Ramsey's criticisms of the views Wittgenstein had held in *Tractatus Logico-Philosophicus*, saying that it was those criticisms that helped him to see how mistaken his earlier views were. Evidently, the discussions had a large impact on Ramsey as well, for during the last year of his life, he underwent a far-reaching and fundamental change in his philosophical outlook. Until his last year, Ramsey had been a Platonist and a logicist, announcing in his important article 'The Foundations of Mathematics' his hope of rebuilding the Frege-Russell class theory of arithmetic so as to, as he put it, save mathematics from the 'Bolshevik menace of [the intuitionists] Brouwer and Weyl' (Ramsey, 1978, 207).

The political metaphor here was picked up by Wittgenstein in an unflattering description of Ramsey that was included in the collection of remarks, *Culture and Value*:

> Ramsey was a bourgeois thinker. I.e. he thought with the aim of clearing up the affairs of some particular community. He did not reflect on the essence of the state – or at least did not like doing so – but on how *this* state might reasonably be organised. The idea that this state might not be the only possible one in part disquieted him and in part bored him. He

wanted to get down as quickly as possible to reflecting on the foundations of this state. This is what really interested him; whereas real philosophical reflection disturbed him until he put its result (if it had one) to one side and declared it trivial. (CV, 17)

This was written after Ramsey's death, but it ties in with a remark that Wittgenstein made in his notebooks at the time of his discussions with Ramsey to the effect that Ramsey's objections to his work were fundamentally shallow, directed, not at the root of the problem, but at the periphery (see Monk, 1990, 259). He compared them to knots in the trunk of a tree around which the tree has to grow.

Despite these rather harsh descriptions, however, Ramsey *was* apparently prepared to attack at least his own ideas, if not Wittgenstein's, at their root. For in his last year, seemingly under the influence of Wittgenstein, he abandoned his earlier logicism and embraced a finitist view of mathematics, closer to the Bolsheviks Brouwer and Weyl than to the more establishment views of Frege and Russell.

The relationship between Wittgenstein and Ramsey, then, raises the question that dominates the contemporary secondary literature on Wittgenstein's philosophy of mathematics and which has dogged the reception of Wittgenstein's work in this area ever since his return to philosophy in 1929: namely, the extent to which his philosophy of mathematics is correctly labelled 'finitism'. For one might think that the conclusion to draw from the preceding story is that Wittgenstein arrived in Cambridge in 1929 – inspired, perhaps, by hearing Brouwer lecture on mathematics in Vienna the previous year – already converted to a finitist view of mathematics, to which he then converted Ramsey. The problem with this, however, is that, in his manuscripts, his lectures and his private conversations, Wittgenstein repeatedly denied being either a finitist or an intuitionist, upon both of which he poured the utmost scorn.

One way of understanding this situation – a way favoured by many of the best contemporary commentators on Wittgenstein's philosophy of mathematics – is to distinguish sharply between the 'middle Wittgenstein' (1929 to, say, 1935) and the 'late Wittgenstein' (c. 1936–51), seeing the former as advocating a finitism which the latter came to reject.

Another way – and my own preference – is to see Wittgenstein's thought during the so-called 'middle period' as consistent with his repeated denials that he was offering a thesis or a theory of mathematics and thus to resist the temptation to label him a finitist. Of course, much here will depend on what the word 'finitist' is taken to mean. If a rejection of the actual infinite is sufficient to be labelled a finitist, then it is surely correct to call Wittgenstein, at least at the time of *Philosophical Remarks*, a finitist. In a passage in *Philosophical Remarks* in which he recounts his conversations with Ramsey, he tells us: 'I once said there was no extensional infinity' (PR, 304). A few paragraphs later he speaks of 'the strange mistake of denying a fact, instead of denying that a particular proposition makes sense' (PR, 306).

There are, then, at least two ways of rejecting the actual infinite and the difference between them was something upon which Wittgenstein laid great stress. The first is to deny that the actual infinite exists; the second is to insist that the assertion (and, crucially, therefore, the denial) of the existence of the actual infinite makes no sense. In *Philosophical Remarks* section XII, Wittgenstein says:

> The infinite number series is only the infinite possibility of finite series of numbers. It is senseless to speak of the *whole* infinite number-series, as if it, too, were an extension. (PR, 144)

If somebody who denies that it makes sense to speak of an infinite series in extension is a finitist, then, to be sure, the 'middle Wittgenstein' was a finitist.

However, I think that the term is more likely to mislead than to shed light on Wittgenstein's position. For the word 'finitism' is generally used to characterise, not just the above general view about the meaninglessness of statements of the existence of infinity in extension, nor the importantly different *denial* of the existence of infinity in extension, but also a view about the consequences this rejection of the actual infinite has for mathematics itself. What aroused Ramsey to call Brouwer and Weyl a 'Bolshevik menace' was not that they thought (philosophical) statements about the existence of infinite quantities to be nonsense, but that they inferred from that certain restrictions on what a mathematician can do in a mathematical proof: namely, that a proof must be constructive and that it cannot apply the law of excluded middle to statements about infinite collections. In the light of these restrictions, they urged, large sections of mathematics needed to be, so to speak, pulled down and rebuilt on new principles – hence the appropriateness of Ramsey's accusation of 'Bolshevism'.

Wittgenstein was never a 'Bolshevik' in this sense. He had no wish to lay down the law about correct method in mathematics. And, whatever other differences there may or may not be between the 'middle' and the 'late' Wittgenstein, his adherence to a strict separation between philosophical questions and mathematical ones was surely constant. In *Philosophical Grammar*, Wittgenstein says:

> In mathematics there can only be mathematical troubles, there can't be philosophical ones. (PG, 369)

> Philosophy does not examine the calculi of mathematics, but only what mathematicians say about these calculi. (PG, 396)

However, he also says: 'Philosophical clarity will have the same effect on the growth of mathematics as sunlight has on the growth of potato shoots' (PG, 381), which suggests *some* influence of philosophy upon mathematics!

Understanding the nature of that desired influence is, I think, the key to understanding, not only the extent to which Wittgenstein was or was not a finitist, but also Wittgenstein's later philosophy of mathematics *tout court*.

Wittgenstein did *not* want to restrict mathematicians to finitistic proofs – he did not want to legislate for mathematical practice any more than he wanted to legislate for method in psychology – but he certainly wanted to examine critically what mathematicians *said* about their proofs, and thus to raise doubts about the *meaning* of those proofs. And he clearly thought that this *philosophical* investigation would, if it were successful, have very drastic consequences, not *within* mathematics – establishing legitimate principles for mathematical proof – but *for* mathematics, since various branches of mathematics (set theory pre-eminently among them) would lose their interest and thus shrink like potato roots exposed to sunlight.

The crucial thing in evaluating the extent to which Wittgenstein's philosophy is 'revisionist' is to understand his *attitude* and here, I think, reflection on his remark about Ramsey might be helpful. Ramsey was bourgeois, according to Wittgenstein, not because he was a logicist rather than a finitist, or a Platonist rather than a constructivist, but because he was concerned with 'how *this* state might reasonably be organised', logicism and finitism being two rival views as to how the state (mathematics) might be organised. Wittgenstein, on the other hand, was interested neither in repairing the holes in Russell's foundation for mathematics, nor in seeking in intuitionism or finitism a new foundation. Rather, using (as the 'later Baker' emphasises) pictures and analogies, he wanted to 'change the aspect' under which we look at mathematics, so that we no longer see it as something that *needs* foundations. In this respect, Michael Dummett might have been right when he suggested that Wittgenstein should be regarded neither as a bourgeois nor as a Bolshevik, but as an anarchist (Shanker, 1986, 113). It might, then, be true that his discussions with Wittgenstein contributed to Ramsey's rejection of Platonism, but it might equally be that, in adopting finitism, Ramsey became no less 'bourgeois' in Wittgenstein's eyes than he had been before.

The problem of trying to 'place' Wittgenstein's later philosophy of mathematics among the competing 'isms' that fought each other in the inter-war years – in particular, the question of whether, and, if so, to what extent, he might correctly be labelled a 'finitist' – is one that raised itself from the very beginning of anything that one can call the 'reception' of his work on mathematics. Apart from Ramsey, the first person to be called upon to comment on Wittgenstein's post-1929 work was Bertrand Russell, who was asked in 1930 to write a report on Wittgenstein's work for Trinity College. In his report, Russell felt obliged to point out that Wittgenstein's 'stuff about infinity' was 'always in danger of becoming what Brouwer has said' (Monk, 1990, 293).

Wittgenstein, one imagines, would have been horrified to think that his work could be regarded as simply a restatement of Brouwer's, and perhaps it was partly in order to put some distance between his own view and intuitionism that he agreed to present (albeit indirectly through Friedrich Waismann) a paper on his philosophy of mathematics at the Königsberg conference in the summer of 1930. The paper Waismann delivered, 'The Nature of Mathematics: Wittgenstein's Standpoint' was one of four, the other three presenting, respectively, the logicist, the intuitionist and the formalist "standpoints." The implication, surely, was that Wittgenstein's view was quite distinct from *all* the other three, and therefore *not* simply a variant of intuitionism.

The full text of Waismann's paper has not survived. Unlike the other three, it was not published in *Erkenntnis* in 1931, presumably because Wittgenstein was dissatisfied with it as an expression of his thoughts, which were developing quickly and radically at that time. A small fragment of it survived and was published in German in Waismann's *Lectures on the Philosophy of Mathematics* (Waismann, 1982) and in English in Volume Three of *Ludwig Wittgenstein: Critical Assessments* (Shanker, 1986). From this fragment, we learn that it was divided into four sections: 1. the nature of numbers; 2. the idea of infinity; 3. the concept of set; and 4. the principle of complete induction. The surviving fragment is concerned only with the first of these four sections and is taken up largely with an attack on the Russellian definition of numbers as classes of classes, a definition, it is alleged, that makes the mistake of treating numbers as if they were part of a *totality* rather than recognising them to be what they are, namely parts of a *system*. The paper (what survives of it, at any rate) puts great stress on the difference between a totality and a system, emphasising, among other differences, that a totality is something that is discovered, while a system is something that is constructed.

If the intention of Waismann's paper was to promote a distinctly Wittgensteinian approach to the philosophy of mathematics as a rival to the schools of formalism, logicism and intuitionism, then it was, for a number of reasons, a failure. Firstly, there was, at that time, no settled Wittgensteinian position; his thoughts were in flux and his thinking, on mathematics as on much else, in a 'transitional' stage. Secondly, and relatedly, the paper fails to spell out very clearly exactly what it is that distinguishes Wittgenstein's approach from Brouwer's finitism. Formalism is attacked directly, as is logicism, but, in the surviving fragment at least, Wittgenstein does not directly address the question of how his thought differs from that of intuitionism and finitism. To be sure, the *emphasis* of what Waismann presents as 'Wittgenstein's standpoint' differs sharply from that of Brouwer and Weyl. There is little talk of the law of excluded middle, or of the necessity of constructivist proofs, and the Brouwerian appeal to 'basal intuitions' as the foundation for mathematics clearly belongs to a completely different philosophical approach. But, the two principles that Waismann presents as constitutive of Wittgenstein's 'method' – 1. 'in order to ascertain the meaning of a mathematical concept, one must pay attention to the *use* that is made of it'; and 2. 'in order to visualise the significance of a mathematical proposition one must make clear how it is *verified*' (Shanker, 1986, 61) – are not, in any obvious way, inconsistent with intuitionism or finitism.

One's lasting impression from reading the surviving fragment of the paper is that 1930 was simply *too early* for Wittgenstein to be announcing his 'standpoint' to the world. As Waismann was to discover to his cost, Wittgenstein's views were changing rapidly during this period. For some years after the Königsberg conference, Waismann was involved in several attempts to present Wittgenstein's thought.[3] The original idea (the details of which underwent several changes over the years) was announced in the journal *Erkenntnis* in 1930 and involved Waismann writing a book under the title *Logik, Sprache, Philosophie*, which would be a systematic presentation of Wittgenstein's thought. After this idea was finally abandoned, Waismann published his own book, *Einführung in das mathematische Denken* (Waismann, 1936), which, despite being described by none other than Gordon Baker as 'the first comprehensive overview of the nature of mathematics along Wittgensteinian lines' (VW, xx), has attracted very little attention.

Despite Waismann's efforts, the publication widely regarded – in the English-speaking world at least – as the first public statement of Wittgenstein's later philosophy of mathematics was Alice Ambrose's 1935 *Mind* article, 'Finitism in Mathematics' (Ambrose, 1935). The article was published in two parts. In the first part, Ambrose writes:

> The view presented is guided throughout by certain suggestions made by Dr. L. Wittgenstein in lectures delivered at Cambridge in 1932–35. (Ambrose, 1935, 188)

This was generally understood to mean that Ambrose was presenting Wittgenstein's views, and Bertrand Russell, for one, felt confident that, in responding to Ambrose's article – as he did in 'The Limits of Empiricism' (Russell, 1936) – he was responding to Wittgenstein himself. Wittgenstein, however, was furious about the article and attempted to persuade both Ambrose and Moore (in his capacity as editor of *Mind*) to withdraw it, insisting that it was a *mis*representation of his views. By this time, Wittgenstein had acquired a reputation of objecting to *any* representation of his views – two years earlier he had published in *Mind* a letter accusing Richard Braithwaite of misrepresenting him in an article Braithwaite had contributed to a collection called *Cambridge University Studies*; he also elicited from Braithwaite a public apology – and Ambrose's repeated insistence that she had *not* misrepresented Wittgenstein has been widely accepted. In the second part of her article, she took the precaution of qualifying her earlier statement about having been 'guided' by Wittgenstein:

> In stating on p. 188 of my last article that my views were so guided . . . I did not intend to claim either that I had understood him correctly or that inferences which I drew from what I understood him to mean would follow from his actual views. Any reader who finds mistakes or absurdities in my views must not suppose that he is responsible for them. Even where, as on p. 197 in my last article, I cite an example actually given by him, it must not be assumed that the use which I make of such an example is that which he intended to make. (Ambrose, 1935, 319)

But these qualifications did nothing, either to assuage Wittgenstein's displeasure or to dispel the impression that the thoughts she was publishing were Wittgenstein's thoughts.

Ambrose's article has had a great influence on the reception of Wittgenstein's philosophy of mathematics, helping to establish the common view that it is correctly to be called 'finitism'. On Ambrose's account, finitism – or, at least, the Wittgensteinian variant of it – is a direct application to mathematics of the verification principle. 'The finitist', she writes, 'demands that we should be certain of being able to verify or to prove false a verbal form before we hold it to be either true or false' (Ambrose, 1935, 189). She speaks of 'verbal forms' rather than of propositions because she wants to restrict the term 'proposition' to a 'verbal form' that has a meaning, i.e. a method of verification. All propositions, therefore, on her account have a truth value, and the law of excluded middle applies to them. The law of excluded middle does not, however, apply to 'verbal forms' that purport to refer to infinite totalities, precisely because those 'verbal forms', lacking a method of verification, lack meaning and are therefore *not* propositions. Ambrose draws from this direct lessons for mathematics itself, and ends the second part of her article with an examination of 'the actual consequences of the finitist position in analysis and other branches of mathematics' (Ambrose, 1935, 335), these being, by and large, the very consequences that Ramsey had denounced as Bolshevism.

Despite the widespread acceptance of Ambrose's claim to have represented faithfully what Wittgenstein had said in his lectures, there are at least two respects in which what she calls 'finitism' is quite clearly *not* Wittgenstein's view. The first concerns the strict separation mentioned earlier that Wittgenstein insisted on maintaining between mathematical questions and philosophical ones. Philosophical clarity could have drastic results on certain branches of mathematics, Wittgenstein believed, *not* because philosophy could legislate on the methods of proof used within those branches of the subject, but because the motivation for studying them in the first place (Wittgenstein has in mind here set theory and transfinite arithmetic) rests on a philosophical confusion. Ambrose's talk about the *mathematical* consequences of 'finitism' is pitched at a very different level, concerned not with the *motivation* for studying, e.g. set theory, but the meaningfulness or otherwise of its axioms and theorems, and, therefore, the legitimacy or otherwise of its proofs. All this is quite clearly and radically *non*-Wittgensteinian.

The second respect in which her view runs counter to what Wittgenstein was saying in his lectures and writing in his manuscripts (the ones that became *Philosophical Remarks* and *Philosophical Grammar*) is in her application of the verification principle to the 'verbal forms' of mathematics in order to distinguish the genuine propositions – to which the law of excluded middle can legitimately be applied – from nonsense. This is, in a crucial respect, the *exact opposite* of the view that Wittgenstein had been developing. Far from regarding mathematics as a body of propositions, the proofs of which established their method of verification and therefore their meaning, Wittgenstein had, since *Philosophical Remarks*, been advocating a *non-propositional* view of mathematics, warning against the philosophical confusions that result from what he describes as 'the analogy between "mathematical proposition" and the other things we call propositions' (PG, 366). 'The essential point in all these cases [Euclidean geometry, Russellian proofs, etc.]', he writes, 'is that what is demonstrated can't be expressed by a proposition' (PR, 131).

There are signs that the publication of Ambrose's article stung Wittgenstein into trying to get his own version of his views into the public domain and to make sure those views were correctly understood. In the immediate aftermath of the article, he redoubled his efforts on two fronts: 1. he made efforts to prepare his work for publication so that the public could see for themselves where his work differed from the views attributed to him by Braithwaite and Ambrose; and 2. in his written work and in his lectures he tried to spell out as clearly and as unambiguously as possible what he thought he was up to, using simpler, more direct language than he had used hitherto.

By the summer of 1938, Wittgenstein had prepared a typescript of *Philosophical Investigations*, together with a preface in which he alluded to the fact that versions of his ideas written by others had already been published. This version of the book gave due prominence to his writings on mathematics; the second half of the book, Part II, was made up of what we now know as Part I of *Remarks on the Foundations of Mathematics*. It is in the first half, Part I, however, that Wittgenstein makes clear where he thinks his philosophical remarks are to be placed vis-à-vis mathematics:

> Philosophy may in no way interfere with the actual use of language; it can in the end only describe it.
> For it cannot give it any foundation either.
> It leaves everything as it is.
> It also leaves mathematics as it is, and no mathematical discovery can advance it. A "leading problem of mathematical logic" is for us a problem of mathematics like any other. (PI, §124)

In the above quotation, Wittgenstein is surely going out of his way to make it clear that arguing for Ambrose's version of finitism was *not* what he thought he was up to.

As the previously quoted remark from *Philosophical Grammar* about the effect of philosophical clarity on the growth of mathematics indicates, however, one has to be very careful about describing Wittgenstein as a 'non-revisionist' with regard to mathematics. Wittgenstein's philosophy of mathematics 'leaves mathematics as it is' in the sense that it does not, like Brouwer's intuitionism and the kind of finitism Ambrose describes, seek to regulate mathematical practice. On the other hand, it is quite clearly Wittgenstein's aim to affect mathematics in *some* sense. He evidently wanted to put certain branches of mathematics – transfinite set theory, for example – out of business. In fact, in this respect he was *more* radical than the people Ramsey had called 'Bolsheviks', but he was radical in a *very* different way, a way that has proved extremely difficult to describe and to defend.

Wittgenstein himself outlined his strategy for shedding philosophical light on the branches of mathematics that grew in the dark in his 1938 lectures on (of all things) Aesthetics, when, in discussing the "charm" of Cantor's Diagonal Proof, he told his audience:

> I would do my utmost to show the effects of this charm, and of the associations of "Mathematics." Being Mathematics . . . it looks incontrovertible and this gives it a still greater charm. If we explain the surrounding of the expression we see that the things could have been expressed in an entirely different way. I can put it in a way in which it will lose its charm for a great number of people and certainly will lose its charm for me. (LC, 28)

Hilbert, famously, had said: 'No one is going to turn us out of the paradise which Cantor has created'. 'I would say', Wittgenstein told his class:

> I wouldn't dream of trying to drive anyone out of this paradise. I would do something quite different: I would try to show you that it is not a paradise – so that you'll leave of your own accord. I would say, 'You're welcome to this; just look about you.' (LC, 28)

Thus, his aim was not, like the intuitionists, to persuade mathematicians that some of the techniques they were using were illegitimate, nor was it his aim to argue for or against any particular metaphysical or epistemological view concerning mathematics. He was not, for example, arguing that

Cantor's transfinite arithmetic was *false*, nor, more generally, that Platonism was false.

'What a mathematician is inclined to say about the objectivity and reality of mathematical facts', Wittgenstein says in the *Investigations*, 'is not a philosophy of mathematics, but something for philosophical *treatment*' (PI, §254). In that respect, as Steve Gerrard has argued in his perceptive article, 'Wittgenstein's Philosophies of Mathematics' (Gerrard, 1991), what mathematicians are inclined to say about the objectivity and reality of mathematical facts is analogous to what St. Augustine, as quoted at the beginning of *Philosophical Investigations*, is inclined to say about how he learned to speak. St. Augustine, in that passage, is not articulating a *theory* about language and what follows that passage is not an attempt by Wittgenstein to *refute* a theory. The point of opening the book with that quotation, rather, is that it gives a perfect example of the kind of pre-philosophical *picture* of the relation between words and objects that Wittgenstein believes gives rise to philosophical *ideas* and *theories* and, therefore, to confusion. Wittgenstein's task, then, is not to argue against an idea or a theory; it is to locate the source of the Augustinian picture and to try to replace it with another picture, one that does *not* give rise to the relevant philosophical confusions. This task, as both the 'later Baker' and Wittgenstein himself have pointed out, has more in common with Freudian psychoanalysis than it does with traditional philosophical argumentation, and, as the later Baker came to see, is importantly different from the policing of the bounds of sense.

Analogously, Gerrard points out, we should regard the target of Wittgenstein's philosophy of mathematics, not as a *theory* about mathematics, but a pre-philosophical *picture* (what Gerrard calls the 'Hardyian Picture'). Wittgenstein's aim, then, is not to argue for the falsity of a particular theory or view of mathematics – still less to argue for (or against) a particular way of doing mathematics – but to "redescribe" mathematics so as to dispel the 'Hardyian Picture'. In other words, his aim is to get us to *see* mathematics differently, to see it under a different aspect. This will 'leave mathematics as it is' in the sense that switching from seeing the duck to seeing the rabbit leaves the picture as it is. In another sense, though, it will have a radical effect, since, Wittgenstein believes, the "charm" of, for example, Cantor's Diagonal Proof, *depends* upon seeing mathematics in a particular way. Once the Hardyian Picture is abandoned, that charm disappears and, with it, so Wittgenstein believed, the motivation for pursuing whole subdisciplines of mathematics, such as transfinite set theory.

A year after his lectures on Aesthetics, Wittgenstein gave a series of lectures on the foundations of mathematics, in which – perhaps with Ambrose's article in mind – he dealt head-on with the question of whether he was or was not advocating 'finitism in mathematics':

> Finitism and behaviourism are as alike as two eggs. The same absurdities, and the same kind of answers. Both sides of such disputes are based on a particular kind of misunderstanding – which arises from gazing at a form of words and forgetting to ask yourself what's done with it. (LFM, 111)

> If you say that mathematical propositions are about a mathematical reality – although this is quite vague, it has very definite consequences. And if you deny it, there are also queer consequences – for example, one may be led to finitism. Both would be quite wrong. There is a muddle at present, an unclarity. But this doesn't mean that certain mathematical propositions are wrong, but that we think their interest lies in something in which it does not lie. I am not saying that transfinite propositions are false, but that the wrong pictures go with them. And when you see this the result may be that you lose your interest. It may have enormous consequences but not mathematical consequences, not the consequences which the finitists expect. (LFM, 141)

Wittgenstein most emphatically did *not*, then, see himself as a finitist. He saw himself as wrestling, not with false – nor even with nonsensical – propositions, but with 'wrong pictures'. These 1939 lectures are fascinating for showing how a very able mathematical logician – one in the grip of precisely the picture of mathematics that Wittgenstein was opposing – might react to Wittgenstein's attempts to 'change the aspect' under which he looked at his own discipline when no less a logician than Alan Turing began attending and raising questions.

Of course, Turing's opposition came as no surprise to Wittgenstein. 'A mathematician is bound to be horrified by my mathematical comments', he had written in what became *Philosophical Grammar* (PG, 381), 'since he has always been trained to avoid indulging in thoughts and doubts of the kind I develop'. Indeed, this, I think, is a case in point where one can say that Turing's horror at what Wittgenstein was saying shows a better understanding than Alice Ambrose's sympathetic exposition.

What particularly shocked Turing – and what would shock many mathematicians later when Wittgenstein's philosophy of mathematics was finally published in the 1950s – was Wittgenstein's attitude to contradiction. In his manuscripts Wittgenstein had spoken of 'the superstitious dread and veneration by mathematicians in face of contradiction' (RFM, Appendix III, 17), prompting an early reviewer of the *Remarks*, Alan Ross Anderson, to retort that one may as well speak of the 'superstitious dread and awe of chess players in the face of checkmate' (Benacerraf and Putnam, 1964, 489).

Wittgenstein's casual way with contradiction in mathematics is but one consequence – perhaps the most startling consequence – of his "redescription" of mathematics, of his attempt to get us to *see* mathematics in a different way to that which predominates among mathematicians and philosophers of mathematics, and one of the things it illustrates is *how* differently mathematics looks when viewed in the light he wants to shine upon it.

There are two crucial aspects to this that are often missed by commentators – both sympathisers and detractors – which I think are important in order to understand how he could possibly take contradiction so lightly.

1. The first is that when Wittgenstein talks about "mathematics" he does not primarily mean what almost everybody else who discusses the philosophy of mathematics primarily means – namely, the subject studied by mathematicians. 'It is the use outside mathematics', he writes, 'and so the *meaning* of the signs, that makes the sign-game into mathematics' (RFM, V2). Mathematics is, for Wittgenstein, first and foremost the motley of techniques and practices we employ that use mathematical signs; we count out the money we give to the bus driver, we calculate how much money we will need to save to afford a holiday, we estimate how fast a car was travelling when it hit a pedestrian, etc., etc. *These* are the primary uses of mathematical signs that, for Wittgenstein, are the subject matter of the philosophy of mathematics; things like the use of the system of *Principia Mathematica* to prove the incompleteness of arithmetic or the use of set theory to prove the non-denumerability of the real numbers are called 'mathematics' only because of their connections with the more paradigmatic cases.

2. The second – related to the first – is that what we call a "proof" in mathematics is better, more clearly, seen as a *picture* designed to establish the usefulness of a technique than as a series of propositions designed to establish the truth of a theorem. Wittgenstein's paradigm of a mathematical proof was something like the following:

Proof that $4 \times 3 = 12$.

O   O   O
O   O   O
O   O   O
O   O   O
(PG, 350)

Using this sort of thing as a paradigm, mathematics no longer looks like – or could possibly be confused with – a body of truth. Donald Gillies, in his article 'Wittgenstein and Revisionism' (Gillies, 1982), finds it hard to believe that Wittgenstein could have adopted a view so transparently silly as the one attributed to him by Crispin Wright, namely (what Gillies calls) the 'rejection of mathematical truth theory' (Gillies, 1982, 430). 'Ordinary, standard mathematics', Gillies says, 'depends crucially on the assumption that we can apply the concepts of truth and falsehood to most mathematical propositions':

> In any standard proof of a theorem, the conclusion will be derived from the premises using ordinary two-valued logic, and anyone applying such a logic is implicitly assuming that the propositions involved are either true or false.

'A great deal of mathematics', Gillies goes on, 'consists in deducing conclusions from premises using two-valued logic. I do not see how anyone could understand and carry out such deductions without having grasped the concepts of proposition, of truth-value of a proposition, of one proposition following logically from others, etc.' In short: 'Rejection of the notion of mathematical truth would actually be more revisionist than intuitionism' (Gillies, 1982, 430–1).

Gillies has a point, of course, except that what is going on here – and Gillies is certainly not alone in not spotting this – is not a *revision* of mathematics, but a wholesale redescription of it. Wittgenstein urges us to abandon the 'Hardyian Picture' which sees mathematical formulae as true or false propositions. In that sense, he urges us to reject mathematical truth. But he does *not* have a 'rejection of mathematical truth *theory*'.

IV   The Post 1956 Reaction

The version of *Philosophical Investigations* that Wittgenstein prepared in 1938 never saw the light of day. Instead, the version we now have – with the section on the philosophy of mathematics removed – was published posthumously in 1953 and just three years later, in 1956, the typescript that had been Part II of the 1938 version of the *Investigations* was published, together with other manuscripts that Wittgenstein produced during the Second World War, as *Remarks on the Foundations of Mathematics*.

The receptions given these two publications were – especially when one considers that they are, essentially, two parts of the same book – extraordinarily different. Whereas the *Investigations* was immediately hailed as one of the most important philosophical works of the twentieth century, the *Remarks* was greeted with almost unanimous disdain. Alan Ross Anderson, in *The Review of Metaphysics*, wrote: 'it is very doubtful whether this application of his [Wittgenstein's] method to questions in the foundations of mathematics will contribute substantially to his reputation as a philosopher' (reprinted in Benacerraf and Putnam, 1964, 490) and: 'It is hard to avoid the conclusion that Wittgenstein failed to understand clearly the problems with which workers in the foundations have been concerned' (Benacerraf and Putnam, 1964, 489). Paul Bernays, reviewing it for *Ratio*, attributed to Wittgenstein behaviourism, constructivism and strict finitism and explained at length why he found Wittgenstein's general position and his discussions of particular issues – such as Cantor's Diagonal Proof and Gödel's Incompleteness Result – unconvincing. Still more critical than either Anderson or Bernays was Georg Kreisel, who wrote: 'Wittgenstein's views on mathematical logic are not worth much because he knew very little and what he knew was confined to the Frege-Russell line of goods' (Kreisel, 1958, 143–144).

Michael Dummett's aforementioned article, 'Wittgenstein's Philosophy of Mathematics', was an attempt to present a more sympathetic view of the *Remarks* than those quoted above. He begins, however, on a similar note to that struck by Anderson, Bernays and Kreisel, describing how 'disappointing' the *Remarks* are:

> Many of the thoughts are expressed in a manner which the author recognized as inaccurate or obscure; some passages contradict others; some are quite inconclusive; some raise objections to ideas which Wittgenstein held or had held which are not themselves stated clearly in the volume; other passages again, particularly those on consistency and on Gödel's theorem, are of poor quality or contain definite errors. (Benacerraf and Putnam, 1964, 491)

Seeking to give a general characterisation of Wittgenstein's position, Dummett hits upon what he calls 'full-blooded conventionalism', which he describes as the view that:

> . . . there is nothing which forces us to accept [a mathematical] proof. If we accept the proof we confer necessity on the theorem proved . . . In doing this we are making a new decision, and not merely making explicit a decision we had already made implicitly. (496)

That this characterisation of Wittgenstein's position should have gained such wide currency is, on the face of it, extremely odd. It gives a completely misleading impression of which *questions* Wittgenstein was dealing with in his work on mathematics; it gets Wittgenstein completely wrong on the nature of mathematical proof; and it attributes to Wittgenstein a view that he, in his lectures of 1939, explicitly rejects on more than one occasion:

> We might as well say that we need, not an intuition at each step, but a *decision* – Actually there is neither. You don't make a decision: you simply do a certain thing. It is a question of a certain practice. (LFM, 237)

> Suppose that I tell you to multiply 418 by 563. Do you *decide* how to apply the rule for multiplication? No: you just multiply . . . It is not a decision. (LFM, 238)

Admittedly, these lecture notes were not published until 1976, but, when they were published, Dummett wrote a review of them for *Encounter* (Shanker, 1986, 111–120), and, though he restated his view that 'Wittgenstein's vision of mathematics cannot . . . be sustained; it was a radically faulty vision' (119), he did not take the opportunity to correct his earlier characterisation of that 'faulty vision'.

During the twenty years that separated the publication of the *Remarks* and that of the *Lectures*, there was very little written on Wittgenstein's philosophy of mathematics. The reviews of the *Remarks* by Anderson, Bernays and Dummett were reprinted – along with selections from the *Remarks* itself – in the first edition of Benacerraf and Putnam's widely used anthology, *Philosophy of Mathematics: Selected Readings*, prompting Morris Engel in his article 'Wittgenstein's "Foundations" and its Reception' to remark: 'one may wonder what led the editors to devote almost a fourth of their text to Wittgenstein . . . since the present reviews tend to throw the value of the excerpts into doubt, what justification remains for including them in the first place?' (Shanker, 1986, 148). In subsequent editions, the section on Wittgenstein was dropped.

As far as I am aware, just two book length studies of Wittgenstein's philosophy of mathematics were published in the 1970s, Charles F. Kielkopf's *Strict Finitism: An Examination of Ludwig Wittgenstein's*

Remarks on the Foundations of Mathematics, and Virginia Klenk's *Witt-genstein's Philosophy of Mathematics*. Both have sunk almost without trace. Kielkopf's book is the subject of a short, dismissive footnote by Crispin Wright (1980, 82), which is one of the very few acknowledgements of its existence that one can find in print. A similar indifference has greeted Klenk's book, which, in my opinion, deserves to be better known, particularly for its clear and persuasive statements of why Wittgenstein should *not* be regarded as an intuitionist, a strict finitist or as a conventionalist (see Klenk 1976, 18–24, 92–123).

Things warmed up a little in the 1980s, beginning with the publication of Crispin Wright's widely-read study, *Wittgenstein on the Foundations of Mathematics*. Wright's book shows almost no interest in defending Wittgenstein against the charge that he had misunderstood, e.g. Gödel's Incompleteness Theorem or Cantor's Diagonal Proof, and he has no truck whatsoever with the notion that Wittgenstein's remarks on mathematics are aimed at a pre-philosophical, non-theoretical level. What interests him primarily is the debate between realism and anti-realism as that debate had been characterised by Dummett, and indeed for page after page both Wittgenstein and mathematics get forgotten while Wright considers in great detail objections and counter-objections to Dummett's philosophy of logic. When Cora Diamond remarked in her review: 'Wright's Wittgenstein is too far from Wittgenstein' (Shanker, 1986, 361), she summed up the feeling that many of us had about what was wrong with Wright's book.

Arguably closer to Wittgenstein, and written both as a corrective to the Dummett/Wright conception of Wittgenstein's philosophy of mathematics and as an attempt to rebut earlier charges of technical mistakes on Wittgenstein's part, is Stuart Shanker's 1987 book, *Wittgenstein and the Turning-point in the Philosophy of Mathematics*, perhaps the first 'left-wing' (in Chihara's sense) discussion of Wittgenstein's philosophy of mathematics to appear in print. A year later, Shanker published a long article entitled 'Wittgenstein's Remarks on the Significance of Gödel's Theorem', which attempted to defend Wittgenstein's discussion of the theorem from the widespread criticism it had received. Shanker's article was published in a collection called *Gödel's Theorem in Focus*, another contribution to which – John Dawson's 'The Reception of Gödel's Incompleteness Theorems' – revealed that, in a letter to Abraham Robinson, Gödel himself had dismissed Wittgenstein's remarks on the Incompleteness Theorem as 'a completely trivial and uninteresting misinterpretation' (Shanker, 1988, 89).

Shanker's article has done little or nothing to persuade logicians that Gödel was wrong about Wittgenstein's remarks and despite an interesting article by Juliet Floyd and Hilary Putnam (Floyd and Putnam, 2000) in which – without going so far as to defend everything Wittgenstein says about Gödel's Theorem – they attempt to rescue *something* of philosophical interest from those 'notorious' remarks, it is probably now a lost cause, if only because the logicians have stopped listening. What Shanker's book has achieved, however (and in this respect it signals an advance on Klenk's worthwhile but neglected book), is to show that Wittgenstein's writings on mathematics can profitably be read as an integral part of his later work and can be understood *without* attributing to him either conventionalism or finitism.

The debate about whether Wittgenstein should or should not be described as a finitist continues in the excellent work that has been produced in the last ten years or so by the three commentators who have established themselves as the leaders in the field: Pasquale Frascolla, Mathieu Marion and Juliet Floyd. All three bring to their work a genuinely sympathetic attitude to Wittgenstein, a detailed scholarly grasp of his *Nachlass* and of the secondary literature, a sophisticated understanding of the issues in the philosophy of mathematics that Wittgenstein was interested in, and a detailed knowledge of the history of the field.

Despite the extraordinarily high quality of their work, however, they are unlikely to succeed in gaining widespread acceptance of Wittgenstein's own assessment that his 'chief contribution' was in the philosophy of mathematics, mainly because their work will not be read by anyone except specialists working in what has now become a scholarly field of its own. *In* that field, all three have had a large impact: Frascolla has persuaded commentators that Wittgenstein's 'middle period' expresses a view of mathematics significantly different from either that expressed in the *Tractatus* or that expressed in the *Remarks*, a view, he claims, that holds onto the notion that mathematical formulae *are* propositions. Marion, though he resists the 'full-blooded conventionalism' of Dummett and the 'strict finitism' of Wright, presents the later Wittgenstein as a finitist and a constructivist, aligning his views with those of his 'supervisor' Frank Ramsey and his student, R. L. Goodstein. As will be apparent, both Frascolla and Marion are unashamedly 'right-wing' commentators. With regard to what he dismissively describes as the 'oxymoron of the "no-position position"', Marion remarks that he has 'little inclination for the endless subtleties needed to make sense of [it]' (Marion, 1998, xii).

Juliet Floyd is more 'left-wing', but, up to now, with the notable exception of her contribution to *The Oxford Handbook of Philosophy of Mathematics and Logic* (Floyd, 2005), her publications have attempted to shed light on particular details of Wittgenstein's writings on mathematics rather than to present a vision of the whole of them. She is known to be working on a book and it seems just possible that, in her, Wittgenstein's philosophy of mathematics might at last find its 'later Baker'. The aforementioned contribution to *The Oxford Handbook*, with its emphasis on the role of pictures in Wittgenstein's later philosophy of mathematics, promises much in that respect.

When it appears, Floyd's book will enter a small, but surprisingly crowded field. There is more being written on Wittgenstein's philosophy of mathematics now than there has ever been, and much of it is of an extremely high standard. However, as the conference at the University of Kent held in January 2006 illustrates, something odd, peculiar and unexpected has happened: Wittgenstein's philosophy of mathematics has now become a specialist scholarly field in its own right. Researchers in this field are now writing, not for logicians or mathematicians, nor even for philosophers of mathematics. They cannot even assume they will be read by other, more general Wittgenstein scholars. The *only* people they can assume will read their work are other researchers working on Wittgenstein's philosophy of mathematics. Wittgenstein hoped that his work on mathematics would have a cultural impact, that it would threaten the attitudes that prevail in logic, mathematics and the philosophies of them. On this measure, it has been a spectacular failure. What, were he alive, might cause Wittgenstein to despair even more is that where his work on mathematics has been successful is in creating a new field of professional academic enquiry.

Notes

1 In this paper I shall be concerned only with Wittgenstein's *later* (i.e. post-*Tractatus*) philosophy of mathematics. The reception of the philosophy of mathematics in *Tractatus Logico-Philosophicus* is something of a non-story. In so far as it differs from logicism, it has largely been ignored. For a rare detailed discussion of it, see chap. 1 of Frascolla (1994).

2 For an alternative version of this story, see Nedo (1993, 57). According to Nedo's version, Wittgenstein wrote: 'He has concerned himself principally

with questions about the foundations of mathematics', which, though signifi-cantly different and rather more modest, still raises, in some form, the issue of the discrepancy between Wittgenstein's 'chief contribution' or 'principal concern' as he himself saw it and the way his work has been received by others.

3   These efforts of Waismann's have been studied in great detail by Gordon Baker (see, especially, Baker 1979 and 2003 and Waismann 1976).

Chapter 12

Wittgenstein and Ethical Naturalism

Alice Crary

1. The idea of a satisfactory ethical naturalism, long out of favor, is enjoying something of a renaissance. A significant number of moral philosophers now describe themselves as championing naturalistic approaches in ethics. This new trend toward ethical naturalism does not, however, signal an unqualified return to previously disparaged modes of thought. Many of the moral philosophers participating in it are concerned to challenge traditional assumptions about what naturalism in ethics is like.

As it is traditionally understood, ethical naturalism is a doctrine about moral judgments that has a straightforwardly *reductive* character. The traditional ethical naturalist represents moral judgments as grounded in facts that are 'natural' in that they fall within the purview of the natural sciences, and she thus in effect takes for granted the possibility of specifying the normative qualities with which moral judgments are concerned, in what gets described as a reductive manner, in terms of non-normative, natural-scientific facts. Moreover, the reductive character of her project is a key source of its appeal. The project owes its interest largely to the fact that it appears to license us to depict moral judgments as objectively authoritative, and it is insofar as it calls for a reduction from the normative qualities in which moral judgments deal to certain non-normative and objective facts that it enjoys this appearance. At the same time, it is also insofar as the project calls for such a reduction that it seems most vulnerable to criticism. Critics often speak of a 'naturalistic fallacy in ethics' in reference to the envisioned reductive strategy.[1]

This classic charge, however threatening to traditional ethical naturalisms, has no bearing on the work of many of the philosophers who today call themselves 'ethical naturalists'. This is because many who do so renounce the reductive ambitions that draw the charge. The philosophers in question undertake projects in ethics that resemble traditional ethical naturalisms in focusing on moral judgments and treating them as essentially a matter of sensitivity to how things are in the real – or 'natural' – world. But where traditional ethical naturalists talk about such sensitivity in connection with non-normative, natural-scientific facts, these philosophers talk about it in connection with features of the world that are only properly conceived in normative terms. To be sure, they follow in the footsteps of traditional ethical naturalists both in portraying the features of the world to which they take moral judgments to be responsible as objective and in assuming that this portrayal licenses them to depict moral judgments as objectively authoritative. Furthermore, their willingness thus to mirror the efforts of traditional ethical naturalists is directly connected to the philosophically most contentious aspect of their work. It leads them to treat some features of the world as simultaneously normative and objective and, by the same token, also to embrace a philosophically heterodox understanding of the objective realm as broad enough to include the normative. But, setting aside for the moment this observation about what is controversial about their work,[2] the point here is simply that, to the extent that some self-avowed ethical naturalists represent moral judgments as based in normative features of the world, it would be wrong to describe them as harboring reductive aspirations. It would be more accurate to speak in reference to their endeavors of the emergence of a set of naturalistic positions in ethics that are decidedly *non-reductive*.[3]

I am generally sympathetic to this philosophical trend,[4] and, in this paper, I say something both about its appeal and about the kind of defense it admits. My goal in doing so is to bring out some of the more striking implications of a non-reductively naturalistic account of moral judgments for how we conceive of the nature and difficulty of moral thought. I proceed by following up on the case for such an account that Philippa Foot presents in her 2001 monograph *Natural Goodness*. One of my auxiliary aims is to show that, while Foot's book expresses her characteristic moral and philosophical intelligence, and while in the book Foot makes a perceptive contribution to conversations about ethical naturalism, she nevertheless fails to register some of the more important implications of her preferred account of moral judgments for how we think about challenges of moral reflection. In pursuing this aim, I attempt to demonstrate – and this is a second auxiliary aim – that there is a sense in which the question Foot raises about the prospects for a satisfactory non-reductive ethical naturalism gets raised in ongoing conversations about the bearing of Wittgenstein's later philosophy on ethics. I use an argument from Wittgenstein's later philosophy to underwrite a portion of Foot's position that she herself leaves undefended, and I observe that, within conversations about Wittgenstein and ethics, this argument is taken to fund an account of moral judgments that, while only infrequently described as 'naturalistic', is fundamentally similar to Foot's. Having made this observation, I point out both that the Wittgensteinian argument has consequences for our understanding of moral thought that take us beyond the account in question and that these consequences, which have no analogues in Foot's thought, are overlooked by many readers of Wittgenstein who are explicitly concerned with the argument's ethical significance. Finally, I claim that Wittgenstein, far from merely providing us with resources to develop the relevant consequences, also lays claim to them, and that it is thus possible to capture the basic significance of his later writings for ethics by saying that they contain a model for a satisfying non-reductive ethical naturalism. The particular moments in Wittgenstein's thought that I consider along the way are aptly thought of as what Gordon Baker calls "neglected aspects" of Wittgenstein's philosophy (Baker, 2004), and, although in discussing them I do not undertake the kind of rigorously detailed textual investigation that is Baker's signature, I hope that my reflections here celebrate the spirit of his work.

2. When Foot (2001) turns to sketching her preferred ethical outlook, she invites us to regard it as naturalistic in two distinct respects. It is naturalistic both in that it contains an account of moral judgments as grounded in "facts about human life" (Foot, 2001, 24) and in that it tries to get us to see what speaks for this account by urging us to think of human beings as belonging to the natural world. Now, for the purposes of this paper, I am primarily concerned with the first of these two respects in which Foot's ethical position is naturalistic. Most of my remarks about her work are about her naturalistic account of moral judgments and, more specifically, about the sense in which this account qualifies as a non-reductive one. Toward the end of this section, I attempt to justify this selective focus by suggesting that the account is separable from the – independently naturalistic – argument for it Foot presents and that it is possible to defend the account without relying on the argument. But before I can explain what speaks for this suggestion, I need to describe the structure of the argument and discuss how Foot uses it to motivate the account she favors.

   The point of the argument is to show that the naturalistic account of moral judgments Foot prefers is at home within a unified theory of 'natural goodness'. Drawing on the assumption that species-relative assessments of plants and animals are special in that they are concerned with a kind of goodness that has "nothing to do with the needs or wants of the members of any other species or living thing" (Foot, 2001, 26), Foot attempts to bring out the appeal of the account by showing that it allows us to see moral judgments as exactly analogous to these assessments and, more specifically, that it allows us to see that, just as we appeal to facts about the life-form to which a plant or animal belongs in making the assessments, we appeal to 'facts about human life' in making moral judgments.[5] In developing this analogy, Foot takes her cue from Michael Thompson (1995), crediting him with an accurate analysis of species-relative assessments of non-human organisms. So it makes sense to begin here with an overview of relevant portions of Thompson's work.

Thompson starts from the observation that some statements we make about the life-forms to which organisms belong are characterized by a form of generality that isn't a matter of statistical accuracy. Consider in this connection, to take one example of Thompson's that Foot discusses, the statement "the domestic cat has four legs" (Thompson, 1995, 281–282; see Foot, 2001, 28). While this statement does not refer to a particular cat, it also does not predicate something of every cat. Moreover, the point is not merely that the truth of the statement is unaffected by the fact that an individual cat – say, Tibbles – "may only have three [legs]" (Foot, 2001, 28). The larger point is that true statements of its type need not do justice to the actual character of even a significant proportion of members of the species in question[6] and, further, that by conjoining a number of such statements about a given species we could, in all likelihood, therefore arrive at a compound statement that, while true, does not do justice to the actual character of even one member of the species (Thompson, 1995, 287–288). So there can be no question of treating the statements as matters of statistical generalization. Instead, we understand their provenance when we see that they have a significant *teleological* dimension (Foot, 2001, 31 also 32–33). The idea is that the statements contain a reference to the characteristic life of the members of a species – something that, in the case of non-human organisms, can be spelled out at least roughly in terms of self-maintenance and reproduction (Foot, 2001, 31) – and, further, that we arrive at them by recognizing that some operation or feature of an organism (say, the legs of a cat) has a function within that life. This recognition is, Thompson tells us, what is expressed in the relevant sorts of statements about how creatures of a given kind live – statements that, insofar as they form part of a "natural-history account" of the kind, are aptly thought of as "natural-history statements" (Thompson, 1995, 288ff).

It is a very short step from here to Thompson's analysis of species-relative assessments of non-human organisms. When Thompson isolates natural-history statements, he at the same time underlines the way in which they ground these assessments. He points out that an individual organism is defective when it fails to conform to true natural-history statements about its kind and, more specifically, that what such non-conformity reveals is that some feature or operation of the organism is unsuited to make its proper, species-specific contribution to self-maintenance or reproduction.[7]

While this analysis of species-relative assessments of non-human organisms possesses independent interest, what concerns me here is simply how Foot draws on it in describing the analogy central to her larger naturalistic project in ethics. She is referring to the analysis when she declares that moral judgments are grounded in 'facts about human life' in just the same way that species-relative assessments of non-human organisms of a certain kind are grounded in facts about the life-form of that kind (Foot, 2001, 4–5, 24, 25–26 and 39). So, what are we to make of her declaration? One potential misinterpretation needs to be dispensed with right away. While it might at first blush seem reasonable to interpret Foot's insistence on an analogy between moral judgments and species-relative assessments of non-human organisms as suggesting an interest in grounding moral judgments, reductively, in facts of human biology, nothing could be clearer than Foot's hostility to this sort of 'biologism'. She repeatedly rejects it, telling us that she has no interest in treating deviations from biological norms as grounds for moral censure.[8]

The point here is not that Foot thinks her analogy between moral judgments and species-relative assessments of non-human organisms is an inexact one. The point is, rather, that, while she thinks the analogy is exact, she also thinks that, if we are to develop it correctly, we need to appreciate how very different the natural-history account of human beings is from the natural-history accounts of non-human creatures. To begin with, there can be no question of specifying the sort of 'characteristic life' to which our natural-history statements about humans need to refer in terms of things like self-maintenance and reproduction or, in Foot's words, no question of specifying it in terms of "merely animal life" (Foot, 2001, 41). This is because, as Rosalind Hursthouse puts it, nature is not "normative with respect to us" (Hursthouse, 1999, 220), and because we rightly recognize as legitimate an indefinitely rich range of different human life-projects and purposes (Foot, 2001, 37). The correct conclusion to draw at this point is not, however, that there is no such thing as a characteristic human life. We can see that we are entitled to speak of such a life if we recognize that (as Foot believes) human beings are essentially possessed of reason and that a characteristic human life is therefore one that is guided by reason's practical exercise. This is significant because, once we see this, we can also see that (again, as Foot believes) our assessments of human actions with respect to "rational will" are analogous to our assessments of different features and operations of plants and animals with respect to their characteristic forms of self-maintenance and reproduction (Foot, 2001, 66; also 16–17 and 41–42).[9]

I just observed that, when Foot develops her naturalistic analogy, she is attempting to motivate an account of moral judgments on which they are assessments of a human being's practical reason.[10] I should add that this account, while not unattractively 'biologistic', is nevertheless relatively thin and undistinguished and that it does not by itself qualify as a naturalistic one. Indeed, if Foot had nothing more to say about the analogy, it would be difficult to understand why she thinks she is entitled to represent her remarks about it as motivating a naturalistic account of moral judgments. But Foot does have more to say about the analogy. She dedicates the opening chapter of her book to a philosophically distinctive view of practical reason, and what deserves emphasis is that it is impossible to understand how she thinks her analogy speaks for a naturalistic account of moral judgments apart from an appreciation of how she draws on this view in developing it.[11]

When Foot talks about practical reason, her main concern is criticizing Humean views and distancing herself from the way in which they are brought to bear on discussions of moral judgment in non-cognitivist theories of ethics.[12] In addition to disputing the Humean contention that beliefs by themselves are practically impotent and that any full specification of a reason for acting therefore needs to mention a desire as well as a belief (2001, 10 and 21), she both declares her allegiance to a non-Humean view on which an undistorted or objectively accurate belief may by itself have a direct bearing on action and discusses ramifications of this view for our understanding of moral judgments. While she endorses the thought, cherished by non-cognitivists, that any reasonable account of moral judgments must represent them as intrinsically practical, she repudiates efforts to satisfy this "practicality requirement" in a manner consistent with Humean views of practical reason (2001, 9). She claims that, in opposition to what non-cognitivists would have us think, the recognition that moral judgments are intrinsically practical does not prevent us from representing them as essentially in the business of expressing beliefs that are open to objective assessment. Moreover, when Foot advances this claim, she is not suggesting that moral judgments are governed by the sort of "abstract" or formal ideal of objectivity that Kantian moral philosophers take themselves to have identified (2001, 14). Rather, she is maintaining that they are governed by our ordinary, substantive ideal of objectivity and that, as she puts it, they are essentially a matter of sensitivity to certain "facts of human life" (2001, 18; also 24 and 45). We might accordingly summarize her view of the practical exercise of reason by saying that it allows her to treat moral judgments as, in a distinctive substantive sense, "part of practical rationality" (2001, 9).[13]

It is worth pausing to note that Foot for the most part simply presents this view without arguing for it. Thus, for instance, while she gestures at a couple of strategies for combatting Humean views of practical reason,[14] she never develops these strategies in a manner that an advocate of a Humean view would find persuasive. Additionally, there is an even more striking respect in which Foot leaves her preferred view of practical reason undefended. When Foot represents moral judgments as both inherently practical and essentially a matter of sensitivity to what she calls certain 'facts of human life', she tacitly commits herself to an understanding of the relevant 'facts' as intrinsically normative in the sense of having a direct bearing on what we have reason to do.[15] Although it would be difficult to exaggerate how philosophically contentious the idea of such 'intrinsically normative facts' is in contemporary moral philosophy, Foot neither defends nor, for that matter, even explicitly acknowledges her interest in this idea.[16] I will have more to say on this topic below. Right now I simply want to make two observations. First, once we notice that Foot is both taking for granted a certain idea of 'intrinsically normative facts' and representing moral judgments as essentially concerned with such facts, we can see that she is from the outset preoccupied with an account of moral judgments that proceeds along non-reductively naturalistic lines. Second, once we notice that Foot nowhere defends the idea of 'intrinsically normative facts' on which the account of moral judgments she champions rests, we can see that she does not provide a compelling explanation of what initially speaks for taking the account seriously.

These observations are apposite because Foot draws on her preferred account of moral judgments, together with the view of practical reason in which it is at home, in developing her central, naturalistic analogy. If we are to appreciate how she draws on these elements of her thought, we need to bear in mind that, as we already saw, she takes the characteristic life for a human being to be one that is governed by practical reason and, further, that, when she insists on an analogy between moral judgments and species-relative assessments of non-human organisms, one thing she is claiming is that moral judgments are assessments of our practical reason. Bearing these things in mind, we can now see that, when she insists on this analogy, she is also making a more far-reaching claim. She is at the same time claiming that moral judgments – which she takes to be both essentially concerned with certain 'facts of human life' and integral to practical reason – are grounded in facts about the characteristic life for human beings in just the same way that species-relative assessments of non-human organisms of a given kind are grounded in facts about the characteristic life of that kind.[17]

Now we have before us a description of how Foot uses a naturalistic analogy to motivate a non-reductively naturalistic account of moral judgments. The description reveals that Foot's strategy for developing her analogy involves starting from the very account of moral judgments that the analogy is designed to motivate, and it accordingly suggests that any discussion of the analogy that, like hers, lacks a substantial story about what speaks for taking the account seriously in the first place will in an important sense be incomplete. This brings me to one of my central preoccupations in this paper. Setting aside the question of whether we should accept Foot's analogy or treat it as significant for ethics,[18] I am going to argue that, despite the fact that Foot herself fails to tell a story of the relevant kind, it *is* in fact possible to tell a persuasive story about the original interest of the account of moral judgments that her analogy is intended to reinforce.

The argument that I present takes its cue from the following familiar reflections about what underlies resistance to accepting the sort of non-reductively naturalistic account of moral judgments Foot favors as a candidate for serious philosophical reflection. Central to the reflections is the recognition of a general consensus among moral philosophers about how, abstracting from the question of the intuitive appeal of such an account,[19] there are insurmountable obstacles to representing moral judgments, in the style of the account, as both essentially concerned with objective reality and intrinsically practical. What underlies this consensus is, at the most fundamental level, an enormously influential metaphysical assumption about how there can be no such thing as objective and intrinsically practical features of the world. Now, we have already seen that, while Foot does not acknowledge her reliance on the idea of such features, she tacitly

takes it for granted in presenting her preferred account of moral judgments. (Or, to return to the terms I used in discussing her work, we have
already seen that Foot here tacitly takes for granted a certain idea of
'intrinsically normative facts'.) What deserves emphasis at this juncture is
that it is widely assumed that, if we attempted to accommodate such features, we could not help but take for granted a category of metaphysically
odd (or unnatural) qualities. The result appears to be that any ethical
position that straightforwardly depicts moral judgments as both essentially
world-guided and intrinsically practical – i.e. any ethical position that has
the distinctive characteristics of Foot's non-reductively naturalistic account
of moral judgments – needs to be relinquished as unacceptable.

This is the appearance we need to challenge if, going beyond Foot's
own handling of these matters, we are to demonstrate our entitlement to
seriously consider such an account, and the argument that I present in
the next section directly challenges it. This argument is intended to show
that the idea of objective and intrinsically practical features of the world
is philosophically quite innocent, and, one of my goals in presenting it is
simply to use this idea to reinforce Foot's case for a non-reductively naturalistic account of moral judgments. A second goal is to criticize her larger
ethical position by showing that an appreciation of the kinds of philosophical considerations required to underwrite the idea puts us in a position to recognize that there is good reason, not only to accept the
account, but also to revise the overarching ethical view in which she situ-
ates it. But, before I can advance these projects, I need to describe an
argument for the idea of objective and intrinsically practical features of
the world.

3. Let me preface my description of the argument with a few words
about why philosophers tend to exclude this idea. To begin with, I should
note that I here assume that, in speaking of features of the world that are
intrinsically practical, we are speaking of features that are internally related
to attitudes in roughly this sense. They are features such that a person
fails to possess a fully adequate conception of what it is for something to
possess them if she does not conceive whatever is in question as something
that, in appropriate conditions, merits certain attitudes or forms of treatment. If we refer to such intrinsically normative features of the world as
meanings, and if we bear in mind that what interests us is philosophers'
tendency to exclude the idea of what we can now call *objective meanings*,
we can say that classic cases for this exclusion begin from the following,
initially plausible thought: namely, that our subjective (i.e. perceptual and

affective) responses have an essential tendency to obstruct our view of how things are, and that we accordingly need to distance ourselves from such responses if we are to be justified in our confidence that we have our minds around more than mere appearance. The most familiar expression of this thought is a requirement to look upon the world from a maximally abstract standpoint, and the point here is that, thus expressed, the thought seems to underwrite a conception of objectivity hostile to meanings. For our willingness to insist on a requirement to inspect the world from an abstract standpoint commits us to holding that we approach an accurate view of how things objectively are by progressively eliminating all those features of the world that, like meanings, have an essential reference to subjectivity.

Notice that where a conception of objectivity that excludes meanings is thus explained in terms of an abstract epistemological requirement[20] – or, as I will put it, an *abstraction requirement* – it appears to have important consequences for how we understand our practices with concepts. It appears to follow from the idea of an abstraction requirement that the regularities constitutive of a sound conceptual practice need to transcend it in the sense of being open to view in a manner that does not presuppose any subjective responses characteristic of us as participants in the practice.

The argument against excluding meanings from objectivity that I want to consider in this section turns on the question of whether we are right to understand our conceptual practices as thus governed by an abstraction requirement. The particular argument I have in mind is one that is inspired by a central line of thought in Wittgenstein's *Investigations* and that, in its fundamentals, was introduced into conversations about how to conceive of objectivity by Stanley Cavell (1969 and 1979) and John McDowell (1994, 1998a and 1998c). This argument gets presented in a variety of different versions, and, without regard to which version is in question, it is often interpreted, not – in what would in fact be an appropriate fashion – as an attempt to arrive at a more faithful image of our ideal of objectivity, but rather – wrongly – as a skeptical attack on this ideal. While it would therefore not be unreasonable to carefully revisit the argument, clarifying its most frequently misunderstood points, this is not the project to which this section is dedicated.[21] What primarily interests me here is rehearsing some of the argument's basic steps with an eye to eventually noting both (i) that, in addition to underwriting Foot's non-reductively naturalistic account of moral judgments, the argument has significant implications for our understanding of moral thought that go beyond the account and (ii) that, although some readers of Wittgenstein use the argument to defend an account of moral judgments fundamentally similar to Foot's, even these readers rarely discuss the relevant implications.

Wittgenstein's hostility to an understanding of our conceptual practices as governed by (what I am calling) an abstraction requirement receives one of its clearest and most famous expressions in the part of the *Investigations* in which he presents us with the image of an infinitely long and ideally rigid rail (§218). We can capture the fundamental interest of the image with the following observation: If a person's grasp of a practice satisfied an abstraction requirement, it would produce correct behavior in a manner that didn't depend on her possession of any subjective responses, just as a mechanical rail to which she hitched herself would pull her along. Now, although Wittgenstein introduces his rail-imagery with an eye to questioning its applicability to our conceptual practices, he recognizes that it may strike us as a straightforward matter to describe a case of conceptual mastery that calls for the imagery, and in *Investigations* §185 he invites us to try describing in these terms the capacity of a student who, having learned various simple mathematical series, now masters the series of even natural numbers. The idea, which at first glance seems entirely innocent, is that this student's grasp of the command "add two" is something from which correct behavior emanates in a mechanical manner, allowing her to 'run along the rails'.

At second glance, however, this idea no longer seems so innocent. The problem is that, once we are captivated by the pertinent image of conceptual mastery, it is no longer clear what would warrant us in attributing such mastery. Having excluded the possibility that any sensitivity to the learning situation our student exhibits (say, a sensitivity she exhibits by saying "see, I went on and added two each time") could count as manifesting understanding, we are obliged to limit ourselves to recording her production of bare correct behavior. This is a problem because no stretch of bare behavior we witness, however prolonged, could constitute a 'complete demonstration' of the indefinitely extended behavior that the student's understanding is capable of producing. Since any stretch of bare behavior will be consistent with incorrect behavior later on, no such stretch can justify us in introducing talk of mastery. This is the basic thought that Wittgenstein illustrates, in §185, with his now notorious description of a student who, after completing the series of even natural numbers up to 1000, continues like this: 1004, 1008, 1012 . . . The lesson we are supposed to take from the illustration is that, as long as we take our cue from the image of rules-as-rails, nothing could warrant us in speaking of conceptual mastery and, further, that, despite what we are inclined to think, we ourselves therefore have no clear idea of what would satisfy the demands we are inclined to place on an appropriate display of understanding.

While readers of the *Investigations* generally agree that it contains a line of reasoning that proceeds (at least roughly) in this manner, there is significant disagreement about how to interpret the line in question. It is traditionally (mis)interpreted as suggesting a form of skepticism about objectivity and, although I cannot here enter into the pertinent exegetical disputes, I want to make one comment about why this interpretation ought to strike us as suspicious. The trouble is that the impetus to a skeptical conclusion is provided by the very mode of thought that the line of reasoning aims to discredit. The moral of the pertinent sections of the *Investigations* is that it is not clear what it would be for a conceptual practice to satisfy an abstraction requirement, and this moral will only strike us as inseparable from a form of skepticism about objectivity if we insist on formulating our ideal of objectivity in terms of such a requirement. But, once the requirement has come into question, the more appropriate conclusion to draw is surely, not that its inaccessibility somehow threatens to cut us off from basic logical ideals like objectivity, but rather that we should free ourselves from renderings of these ideals that are formulated in its abstract terms.

This conclusion has a direct bearing on the assessment of a conception of objectivity – of the sort at issue in this section – that excludes all qualities, such as meanings, with an essential reference to subjectivity. As it is classically understood, this conception encodes an abstraction requirement, and the conclusion indicates the need to reformulate our image of objectivity so that it no longer refers to such a requirement. Now there is no question of an abstract standpoint from which to make the *a priori* determination that everything subjective is excluded from objectivity. This means that, in our efforts to determine the status of qualities with an essential reference to subjectivity, we are obliged to rely on our ordinary, non-metaphysical ways of finding things out and, further, that in particular cases we may well find that the attribution of such a quality figures in the best, objectively most accurate account of the world. The result is the emergence of a conception of objectivity that is capacious enough to incorporate some qualities that, like meanings, are only adequately conceived in subjective terms.

The case I just made for such a conception is bound to raise many questions, but I am not going to discuss questions about its merits further here. Instead I want to consider an objection that, taking its merits for granted, it might seem reasonable to make to my suggestion that a conception of objectivity broad enough to include some subjective qualities should be understood as including those that I am calling meanings. What may seem to license this objection is the thought that the class of subjective qualities is far from uniform and that meanings differ in significant respects from some of its other members. Consider, for instance, the case of perceptual qualities like colors. Where colors are the kinds of things that merely cause appropriate perceptual experiences, meanings as I am speaking of them here, are the kinds of things that *merit* appropriate attitudes.[22] And, insofar as the question of whether something merits a certain attitude is itself a question about meanings, it follows that the standards that govern our talk about meanings are themselves informed by our substantive views about meanings. We might summarize these reflections by saying that modes of discourse that concern meanings are characterized by a certain form of *circularity*, and the point here is that many philosophers take the presence of such circularity by itself to show that, even allowing for a conception of objectivity that incorporates some subjective qualities, it would be wrong to represent these modes of discourse as giving us a window on how things objectively are.

However plausible they initially seem, these reflections ought to raise serious suspicions. In order to demonstrate our entitlement to conceive the very presence of circularity as a sign of epistemic limitation, we would need to have an at least minimally coherent grasp of the idea of a contrasting, non-circular mode of discourse, and, while it is not difficult to find philosophical treatments of different discursive practices that are intended to show that they are non-circular in the relevant sense, it is to the point here to observe that any practice that qualified as non-circular would, by the same token, qualify as satisfying an abstraction-requirement. For it would be a practice in which the standards on which we relied in applying concepts were not informed by the substantive body of beliefs to which the practice contributes, and in which those standards were therefore 'abstract' in the sense of being free from the influence of any sensitivities we acquired in arriving at the relevant body of beliefs.

Consider this result in the light of the above case against the idea of an abstraction requirement. What emerges is that if, following up on the case, we relinquish the idea of such a requirement, we at the same time relinquish the idea of a discursive practice that qualifies as ideally non-circular. This is noteworthy because in relinquishing the latter idea we deprive ourselves of a position from which to insist that the circular character of a discursive practice – say, a practice concerned with meanings – by itself disqualifies it from having an essential concern with how things objectively are. The upshot is that the transition to a conception of objectivity no longer governed by an abstraction requirement justifies us in dismissing what might aptly be thought of as the most fundamental philosophical objection to an objectivist interpretation of meanings.

I just sketched the Wittgensteinian argument for an objectivist interpretation of meanings that was this section's main objective. I presented the argument with an eye to filling in what in the last section I described as a significant gap in Foot's case for her non-reductively naturalistic account of moral judgments. In discussing this account, I observed that it is distinguished by an understanding of moral judgments as concerned with features of the world that, while objective, are also intrinsically practical and that thus qualify as 'meanings' in my sense. I also observed that, although Foot thus in effect helps herself to an idea of 'objective meanings', she never undertakes to defend it and, further, that she therefore leaves her account of moral judgments exposed to one of the most fundamental criticisms that it can be expected to encounter. What I now hope to have shown is there is good reason to think that fans of Foot's account can answer the pertinent criticism.

The point I just made about how a Wittgensteinian argument underwrites Foot's preferred account of moral judgments is one that also gets made, albeit in somewhat different terms, in conversations about the bearing of Wittgenstein's later philosophy on ethics. A number of readers of Wittgenstein have claimed that an argument on these basic lines makes room for an account that, like Foot's, represents moral judgments as, in an entirely unqualified manner, both essentially concerned with how things are in the world and intrinsically practical. Admittedly, these philosophers often highlight features of the account that Foot neglects. They typically point out that what is in question is an account on which the concepts that moral judgments apply pick out features of the world that, while they need to be understood in terms of our attitudes (and while they thus qualify as 'meanings' in my sense), are nevertheless fully objective. Further, they typically tell us that the objective regularities that, according to the account, our moral concepts trace out are revealed by the non-neutral considerations that speak in favor of applying them. Their suggestion is that here there can be no question of regarding the person who lacks an (even imaginative) appreciation of the attitudes in terms of which a given moral concept makes sense as capable of authoritatively determining whether an application of it is correct or incorrect.[23] They thus draw attention to their interest in an account of moral judgments on which projecting a moral concept is a matter of tracing out patterns, not in an indifferently accessible region of fact, but rather – as we might put it – in an already moralized vision of the world.[24]

4. Having just discussed how a Wittgensteinian strategy equips us to defend the sort of non-reductively naturalistic account of moral thought Foot favors, I now want to show that the strategy has implications for our understanding of moral thought that take us beyond this account – implications overlooked, not only by Foot, but also by many commentators on Wittgenstein who use the strategy to defend accounts of moral judgments that in essentials resemble hers. The strategy starts from a view of language, one distinguished by its repudiation of the very idea of an abstraction requirement, that both rejects conditions that an abstraction requirement seems to place on the use of concepts and represents our capacity to identify the regularities internal to a sound conceptual practice as inseparable from the possession of sensitivities acquired in learning the practice. To the extent that the view thus asks us to understand linguistic competence as an essentially practical ability, it might aptly be described as a *pragmatic* one,[25] and my aim in this section is to show that this pragmatic view calls on us to challenge a deeply engrained philosophical understanding of moral reflection – one that informs both Foot's writings and the writings of many philosophers concerned with implications of Wittgenstein's philosophy for ethics – on which moral reflection is taken to be exclusively composed of *moral judgments* (i.e. judgments that apply members of one or another set of specifically moral concepts).

My comments here will of necessity be very condensed.[26] But even a schematic description of how a pragmatic, Wittgensteinian view of language calls on us to rethink moral philosophers' traditional fixation on moral judgments suffices to draw attention to ways in which, in the interest of consistency, Foot needs to revise her larger naturalistic project in ethics. Further, even such a schematic description suffices to set up the remark I want to make, in the next and final section, about the appropriateness of representing Wittgenstein as providing a model of a satisfactory non-reductive ethical naturalism.

Let me start with a description of what it amounts to, within the pragmatic view of language under consideration here, to characterize the mastery of a concept as a practical accomplishment. The basic idea is that we master a concept when we develop a sensitivity to the importance of similarities and differences among its different uses. But it is here important to add that, when we talk about such a sensitivity, we are not concerned with a fixed linguistic competence. Within the context of the pertinent pragmatic view, there is no question of surveying the extension of a concept in a purely abstract manner, and hence no question of determining, in advance of efforts to develop the concept, what shape the sensitivity needs to take in order to warrant us in speaking of conceptual mastery. Moreover, even where we are clearly warranted in speaking of such mastery, there is still no question of a rigidly circumscribed linguistic competence. For it is invariably possible for the sensitivity internal to mastery to grow, giving a speaker access to new uses.

One thing this means is that individuals who have mastered a given concept may have sensitivities to different – and equally real – similarities among its uses. Admittedly, there may be certain core applications of a concept that a mature speaker has to recognize in order to count as having mastered it. But, even taking for granted the demand for a sensitivity to the importance of similarities uniting members of some such 'core' set of a concept's applications, it is always in theory possible for the sensitivity internal to an individual's mastery of a concept to develop and – to use a familiar philosophical idiom – for her grasp of the concept thereby to *deepen*. It follows that the practical capacity that here conceptual mastery represents is a matter of a sensitivity that may vary, not only intrapersonally (i.e. because it may develop as an individual first grasps a concept and as her grasp then deepens), but also interpersonally (i.e. because, with regard to each individual, it may develop in different ways and to different extents as she first grasps the concept and as her grasp then deepens).

It is possible to move directly from these observations about what it comes to, within the context of the pragmatic, Wittgensteinian view of language that I am discussing, to say that the mastery of a particular concept is a practical affair to a set of closely related observations about how, within this same context, mastery of a language is a practical affair. To be sure, we should not forget that the individual speakers of a given natural language master different concepts, and that it would therefore be wrong to equate such a language with a determinate set of concepts. But, without losing sight of these things, we can say that, insofar as language-learning involves the mastery of a range of concepts, it is here rightly understood as involving the development of a range of practical sensitivities that exhibit variation, not only within, but also among individual speakers.

What emerges here is an understanding of mastery of a language as a simultaneously individual and practical matter, and it is a consequence of this understanding that language-learning is inseparable from the adoption of an individual, practical orientation to the world. Wittgenstein himself brings out this consequence when he declares that "to imagine a language means to imagine a life-form" (PI §19; see also §23), and the point he is making takes on a quite striking aspect once we notice that the sort of 'life-form' or practical orientation in question is inseparable from an (at least implicit) view of what matters in life, or of how best to live. Helping ourselves to a characterization of such a view as a moral view, we can say that there is an important sense in which, according to the pragmatic view of language under consideration, language is as such a moral acquisition.

This philosophically striking, moral image of language has important implications for how we understand moral reflection. We can see this if we first observe that the image is not informed by any assumptions about the presence of moral concepts. What distinguishes it is a thought about how the competence possessed by individual language-users, when understood as having a certain practical character, is directly tied to a moral view, and this thought has a straightforward bearing on the case of speakers who, for whatever reason, manage with few (or no) moral concepts. This is significant because, in making room for an image of language on which it has a moral dimension that is not a function of the presence of moral concepts, we thereby make room for the possibility that a stretch of thought that does not employ moral concepts, and that is accordingly not composed of moral judgments, may nevertheless play the sort of role in expressing an individual's moral outlook that establishes it as moral reflection.

To see this, notice that, within the context of the pragmatic view of language that is in question, a person's mastery of any (moral or nonmoral) concept necessarily presupposes a sensitivity to similarities and differences uniting some set of its uses and, further, that, since here this sensitivity is taken to be part of a practical stance that embodies a moral outlook, it cannot help but play a more or less significant role in expressing such an outlook. What these observations reveal is that a person may rightly be characterized as engaged in moral reflection when, without regard to whether she is using moral concepts or discoursing about (what we may be inclined to think of as) 'moral topics', she is, in her conceptual activity, drawing on a sense of importance that figures centrally her moral outlook. It follows that, where the connections of thought a person is making substantively depend for their (at least apparent) integrity on her view of what matters most in life, we will be correct to classify her thought as moral without regard to its subject-matter. Moral thought, as it is here conceived, is characterized by an indifference to subject-matter that allows it to address in principle any topic (e.g. the role of chance in human life, the way sibling rivalries and relations of admiration and envy affect our chosen paths in life, the circumstances in which people do and do not fall in love, the different ways in which humans interact with animals, the imaginative games that children play, etc.). This is what it comes to to say that, within the context of Wittgenstein's pragmatic view of language, moral reflections need not take the form of moral judgments, and I should add that I am inclined to think that, once we achieve a certain distance from the setting of contemporary moral philosophy, where a fixation on moral judgments is treated as something like an unquestionable disciplinary requirement, this expansive understanding of moral thought is likely to strike us as anything but unnatural.

Moreover, the envisioned expansion, far from representing a mere addition to our inventory of forms of moral thought, amounts to a substantive shift in our conception of the demands of such thought. We can see this if we consider implications of the expansion for what moral differences are like. Moral philosophers traditionally assume that moral differences take the form either of disagreements about whether to apply a given moral concept or, perhaps, disagreements about whether some moral concept (or set of such concepts) is one we ought to employ in the first place. In contrast, within the framework of this broader understanding of moral thought, it is possible to speak of moral differences even where there is no question of a disagreement of either of these types, in reference to certain circumstances involving individuals with very different ways of thinking and speaking about the world. For the view of language that underwrites the understanding asks us to regard even those of an individual's modes of thought and speech that are free from the use of moral concepts as expressive of a sensibility that contributes internally to her moral outlook, and it thus accommodates the possibility of moral differences that are not a matter of disagreements about how (or whether) to apply particular moral concepts. Consideration of these alternative kinds of moral differences suggests that, if we are to cope responsibly with demands of moral conversation, we need an ethical practice that urges attention, not only to moral judgments that individuals produce, but also to even those of their modes of thought and speech that do not involve the use of moral concepts and to ways in which the sensibility internal to these modes of thought and speech shapes their moral outlooks. It is in this way that the expansive understanding of moral thought at issue in this section winds up calling on us to reconceive challenges of such thought.

These remarks apply directly to my discussion, above in section 2, of Foot's naturalistic project in ethics. Where in section 3 I argued that Foot's non-reductively naturalistic account of moral judgments commits her to rejecting the idea of an abstraction requirement and embracing the sort of pragmatic view of language that is consequent on its rejection, in this section I have been arguing that this pragmatic view of language is inseparable from an understanding of moral thought – one with significant implications for our conception of challenges of such thought – on which it includes more than moral judgments. Considered together, these two lines of argument suggest that Foot's exclusive focus on moral judgments is inappropriate by the lights of her own naturalistic position in ethics and that she herself is obliged to admit that attention in ethics needs to be directed, beyond moral judgments, to moral thought that comes in other forms.

We can summarize these reflections by observing that there is something amiss with the terms Foot uses to gloss her overarching naturalistic position in ethics. Because Foot assumes that moral thought is limited to moral judgments, it strikes her as natural to move from the observation that her non-reductively naturalistic account of moral judgments represents these judgments as exercises of practical rationality to the conclusion that "morality is part of practical rationality" (2001, 9). But this slogan expresses a limited understanding of the account's significance. Accepting the sort of non-reductively naturalistic account of moral judgments that Foot espouses is tantamount to admitting that moral thought, instead of being limited to moral judgments, can in theory range over any subject-matter, and, once we see this, it becomes apparent that the slogan is misleading. Since there can be no question of regarding *all* the bits of thought that we are now willing to count as moral as having the kind of direct bearing on action that Foot (quite plausibly) takes moral judgments to have, it would be inappropriate to speak in this connection of grounding morality in practical reason.

If we wanted a more fitting slogan for the expansive understanding of moral thought that Foot is tacitly committed to developing, as well as for the conception of challenges of such thought that is its counterpart, we might note that this understanding represents moral thought, not as restricted to moral judgments, but rather as capacious enough to in principle encompass any mode of thought and talk without regard to the subject-matter in which it deals. And we might say that, far from asking us to conceive morality as grounded in a specifically *practical* reason, this understanding accordingly asks us to conceive it as grounded in reason simpliciter.

5. The slogan I just proposed for Foot's naturalistic project in ethics (viz. 'ethics is grounded in reason') is equally well suited to conversations about 'Wittgenstein and ethics'. It follows from the last section's main line of reasoning that readers of Wittgenstein who recognize that elements of his thought can be used to defend what I am here calling a non-reductively naturalistic account of moral judgments are, despite the fact that they tend to focus more or less exclusively on what Wittgenstein equips us to say about moral judgments, tacitly committed to representing him as endorsing a more expansive understanding of moral thought.[27] What I want to suggest by way of concluding this paper is that it is possible to reinforce this conclusion by observing that Wittgenstein himself explicitly endorses the pertinent understanding.

Wittgenstein's remarks on 'ethical themes' are scattered throughout his later writings, and, within these remarks, it is possible to find various characteristic expressions of the idea that ethics is distinguished by a concern, not with a particular region of discourse (say, what we might be inclined to think of as the 'region' composed of moral judgments), but rather with a dimension of all of discourse. Thus, in a number of remarks Wittgenstein tells us – in a manner that tacitly draws on his (in my terms) pragmatic view of language – that all thought calls for an active or spontaneous contribution and that it is therefore inseparable from forms of self-mastery. ("No one *can* speak the truth," he writes, "if he has still not mastered himself.")[28] And in a number of other remarks he tells us that all thought imposes an ethical demand. ("[H]ow does one pay for thoughts? The answer, I think, is: with courage.")[29] What gives these remarks particular significance here is the fact that Wittgenstein, in addition to thus giving expression to the expansive understanding of the concerns of ethics to which advocates of the basic account of moral judgments I have been discussing are at least tacitly committed, also – as we saw – presents us with the basic view of language that the account takes for granted. Since the account in question is aptly described as a non-reductively naturalistic one, we might summarize the interest of this observation by saying that, in our efforts to formulate an internally consistent non-reductive ethical naturalism, Wittgenstein is a true and faithful guide.[30]

Notes

1   For a helpful discussion of the tenets of traditional – reductive – ethical naturalisms as well as of some of the central criticisms directed at them, see Pigden (1991).

2   I touch on this topic in section 2 and address it in all of section 3, below.

3   For a useful outline of the sorts of non-reductive ethical naturalisms in question here, see Stroud (2004, 30–35).

4   A list of significant contributions by some of the most notable participants in this trend should include, in addition to Foot (2001) (which I discuss at length below), Annas (2005), Hursthouse (1999, chapters 9 and 10), McDowell (1998b) and Thompson (1995, 2003 and 2004). These different works are united by the thought that efforts to articulate a non-reductively naturalistic position in ethics have Aristotelian roots. Although I am inclined to accept this thought, I do not discuss it further in what follows.

5   Hursthouse (1999, chapters 9 and 10) follows Foot in adopting this basic approach to defending her own preferred (non-reductively) naturalistic account of moral judgments. For a comment on how Hursthouse's project ultimately diverges from Foot's, see note 9, below.

6   Since most domestic cats do have four legs, we might turn here to a different example of Thompson's. We might note that a statement about how a certain jellyfish reproduces may be true even though only a tiny fraction of such jellyfish ever survive to reproduce in the stated manner (2004, 50–51).

7   Thompson thinks that in order to appreciate what speaks for this account of species-based assessments of non-human organisms we need to recognize that descriptions we give of the features and operations of such organisms – or, in his terms, "vital descriptions" (Thompson, 1995, 274ff. and 2004, 51) – have an essential reference to natural-history statements about their kind. We can appreciate what Thompson has in mind if we imagine a case in which we describe an individual organism as, for instance, eating (Thompson, 1995, 272–273). The idea, brought to bear on this case, is that whatever "flat physicalistic" process we take to underwrite our description will necessarily be one that, while it may serve the maintenance of tissue in one life-form, and while it may indeed license talk about eating in a particular case, may – say, because it now serves a defensive purpose, or no purpose at all – fail to license such talk in another. This is what it comes to, for Thompson, to claim that the ('vital') description of an organism as eating contains an essential

reference to a ('natural-history') statement about how creatures of the relevant kind nourish themselves, and, more generally, that vital descriptions contain an essential reference to natural-history statements. (For Foot's treatment of this part of Thompson's thought, see 2001, 28–29.)

8   See, for example, her remarks on attempts to use merely biological observations about human life to criticize specific sexual practices (2001, 3 and 109) or attitudes toward childbearing (2001, 42). A number of readers have overlooked or downplayed the significance of passages like these in which Foot expresses hostility to a 'biologistic' program in ethics. Here I should emphasize that, while I believe that these readers misrepresent Foot's guiding concerns, I also believe that some of their reflections about the prospects for such a program are interesting on their own terms. This includes Andreou (2006) and Slote (2003). It also includes McDowell (1998b) who, however, differs from these two authors in that he penned his remarks on Foot's alleged biologism years before the full text of Foot (2001) was available.

9   For a helpful discussion of Foot's claim that moral assessments are assessments of human actions with respect to 'rational will', see Annas (2005, esp. 14–16) and Copp and Sobel (2004, esp. 538–539). The elements of Foot's thought that lead up to this claim are clearly brought out in Thompson's treatments of Foot's ethical project. Thompson (2003) places particular emphasis on pertinent points, though his concerns are prefigured in Thompson (1995, esp. 250–251) and taken up again in Thompson (2004, esp. 62–63). Hursthouse (1999) presents herself inheriting Foot's claim that the characteristic human life is one lived in accordance with reason, but she also wrongly attempts to combine this claim with an understanding of moral judgments, foreign to Foot's work, as assessments of human beings with respect to ends such as individual survival and the continuance of the species. (For a criticism of this moment in Hursthouse's work, see Copp and Sobel, 2004, 540ff.)

10   To be sure, Foot is not associating *all* defects in the practical reason of human beings (say, those stemming from mental retardation) with moral limitations. Rather she is drawing attention to the particular defects we suffer from when, while possessing the capacity to reason practically, we fail to recognize considerations in favor of acting in a certain way or when, while in fact recognizing that we should act in a certain way, we either do not act in that way or, if we do, nevertheless take as our operative reason something apart from the recognition that it is correct (Foot, 2001, chapter 4).

11   In an otherwise insightful critical discussion of Foot's work, Copp and Sobel somehow manage to miss this decisive point. Their ultimate verdict on Foot's position is that it is too "bare" for authoritative assessment (2004, 542), but it would be more accurate to say that what they perceive as its 'bareness' is at bottom a reflection of their own failure to engage with some of its fundamental tenets.

12   Foot's insistence on attacking Humean views is noteworthy in part because Foot herself was once a staunch advocate of such a view. See Foot (1978b and 1978c).

13   There are fundamental similarities between the account of moral judgments that Foot defends here and the account she defends in Foot (1978a). However, since Foot's recent work departs significantly from many of her early essays on ethics, I am for the most part restricting my discussion in this paper to material included in Foot (2001). For the two additional places in this paper at which I relax this restriction, see note 12, above and note 24, below.

14   Foot declares that an investigation of our habits of practical reflection reveals that Humean views of practical reason are phenomenologically flawed (2001, 10f.), and she also claims that advocates of the views are, in her words, seduced by a "mechanical or hydraulic picture of the psychological determinants of action" (Foot, 2001, 21). But she never defends this claim or attempts to show that it licenses us to treat what she sees as the phenomenological limitations of Humean views as grounds for serious criticism.

15   Given that philosophers often speak of 'facts' exclusively in reference to the sorts of (non-normative and non-practical) states of affairs at issue in the natural sciences, it would not be unreasonable to complain that Foot's willingness to speak of 'facts' in this connection is misleading. By the same token, it would not be unreasonable to complain that, because she herself never underlines the idiosyncratic character of her terminology, she is herself partly responsible for the misunderstandings of those who – assuming that she is speaking of facts in a philosophically more familiar manner – take her to be trying to ground moral judgments in facts about human biology. (In this connection, see note 8, above.)

16   See Hursthouse's remarks on how an ethical naturalism of the sort Foot espouses requires an idea of 'intrinsically normative facts' (1999, esp. 20–21 and 189–190). Interestingly, while Hursthouse explicitly underlines the need for an idea of such facts, and while she also follows Foot in endorsing the kind of non-reductively naturalistic account of moral judgments that by her own lights requires it, she nevertheless does not attempt to defend it.

17   Foot sometimes glosses this claim by saying that she conceives vice as "a kind of natural defect" (2001, 5). When she speaks of vice here, she is thinking of the person who, instead of consistently acting in accordance with accurate moral judgments and doing so because she recognizes them as correct, tends to fall short of this ideal of conduct in certain kinds of cases. (See note 10, above.) Her thought is that the person who is in this sense possessed of some vice departs from the characteristic life of human beings and is thus rightly understood as naturally defective in just the same way that a cat with three legs, or a bird that can't fly, is naturally defective.

18   It is helpful to see that there are in fact two separate questions here: (i) the question of whether the analogy is in fact a good one and (ii) the question of whether, even taking for granted its soundness, it ought to be treated as significant for ethics. (For a discussion of one way in which these two questions come apart, see Copp and Sobel, 2004, 534ff.) It is partly out of respect for the complexity of the different issues involved here that, having outlined the case Foot makes for her analogy and having discussed how a study of it confirms that she is concerned with a naturalistic account of moral judgments that has a decidedly non-reductive character, I am now entirely setting aside the project of assessing it.

19   Such an account is rightly characterized as intuitively appealing in that it invites us to take at face value a couple of very fundamental features of our intuitive understanding of such judgments. First, as Foot herself notes, it invites us to take at face value the fact that such judgments ordinarily strike us as having a direct bearing on what we have reason to do. (See Foot's remarks on a 'practicality requirement', touched on above in the text, at Foot, 2001, 9.) Second, insofar as it represents moral judgments as grounded in certain 'natural facts', it also invites us to take at face value the fact that such judgments ordinarily strike us as a matter of sensitivity to how things are. (Thus, for example, it ordinarily strikes us as natural to regard a statement to the effect that a given person is "cowardly" or that a given action is "wrong" as expressing claims that we evaluate by attending to what the pertinent person or action is like.)

20   There are some defenses of the pertinent conception of objectivity that aim to avoid any appeal to such a requirement. Although I am inclined to think that such defenses invariably wind up tacitly invoking the very sort of abstract epistemological requirement that they aim to avoid, and although I attempt to show this elsewhere (for a reference, see the next note), I will not here further discuss this issue.

21   I undertake this project elsewhere. See Crary (2007, chapter 1, §§1.2–1.3).

22   This observation is frequently made in reference to what gets described as a disanalogy between secondary qualities and values, where the latter are understood as a proper subclass of what I am calling meanings.

23   Moral philosophers often speak of "thickness" in connection with an understanding of moral concepts as thus tracing out patterns that are not indifferently available. I avoid this terminology because it fails to discriminate between the views of moral philosophers who assume that this understanding commits us to a subjectivist interpretation of moral concepts and those who believe – rightly, in my view – that it is consistent with an objectivist interpretation.

24   A list of the most prominent readers of Wittgenstein to present accounts of moral judgments that proceed along these basic lines would need to include

Sabina Lovibond (1983 and 2002), McDowell (1998a and 1998c) and David Wiggins (1998). Such a list should also include Cora Diamond (esp. 1996) and Murdoch (esp. 1970 and 1997, chapter 5), though the larger emphases of these two philosophers' attempts to inherit Wittgenstein's philosophy for ethics are in certain respects distinctive. (For an explanation of the last comment, see note 27, below, and the associated text.) Here it is worth noting that Murdoch was a close friend and philosophical associate of Foot's and that the influence of Murdoch's thought is evident in Foot (1978b)'s description of an account of moral judgment-making as an objectively legitimate affair involving the application of concepts with inseparably intertwined descriptive and prescriptive components. This early hint of Murdoch's influence is noteworthy in part because at the time Foot championed a subjectivist or Humean account of moral motivation that was in tension with such an account of moral judgments. (See note 12, above.) Indeed, there is real irony in the fact that Foot seemed more interested in discussing a roughly Murdochian account of moral judgments at a time at which it figured anomalously in her thought than she is now that her overarching ethical position has shifted in ways that allow her to accommodate it.

25 The view counts as 'pragmatic' in a sense that distinguishes it from the pragmatic projects of most philosophers of language. Where contemporary – analytic – philosophers of language tend to speak of pragmatic dimensions of language in reference to questions about how we use words that are presumed to be separable from those aspects of the relations between words and the world that determine truth and falsity, what is at issue here is a view that counts as pragmatic insofar as it treats sensitivities that we acquire in learning to use words – i.e., sensitivities that qualify as 'pragmatic' by any standard – as making internal contributions to all our linguistic capacities, including those we exercise in formulating claims about the world that are evaluable with regard to truth and falsity.

26 For a more expansive treatment of the points developed in this section, see Crary (2007, esp. chapter 1, §§1.4–1.5 and chapters 3, 4 and 6).

27 There are some readers of Wittgenstein who *explicitly* represent him as advocating the expansive understanding of moral thought just presented, and who might in this respect be described as allies for this paper's larger project. A list of the most interesting and original of these commentators would need to include Cavell (esp. 1989, lecture I), Diamond (esp. 1996) and Murdoch (esp. 1997, chapter 5).

28 *CV*, 35; see also, e.g., 33, 34 and 45.

29 *CV*, 52; see also, e.g., 35 and 38.

30 I would like to thank Akeel Bilgrami, Cora Diamond and Elijah Millgram for helpful correspondence and conversation about these matters, and Benjamin Olson for valuable assistance with research.

Bibliography

Adorno, T. W. *Against Epistemology*, trans. Willis Domingo. Cambridge, MA: MIT Press, 1982.

Affeldt, Steven G. "The Ground of Mutuality: Criteria, Judgement, and Intelligibility in Stanley Cavell and Stephen Mulhall." *European Journal of Philosophy*, 6:1 (1998): 1–31.

Albritton, R. "On Wittgenstein's Use of the Term Criterion." *Journal of Philosophy*, 56 (1959): 845–857. Reprinted in Pitcher ed. 1968, pp. 231–250.

Ambrose, Alice. "Finitism in Mathematics." *Mind*, 44 (1935): 186–203 and 317–340.

Ambrose, Alice. "Wittgenstein on Some Questions in Foundations of Mathematics." *Journal of Philosophy*, 52 (1955): 197–213. Reprinted in Shanker ed. 1986, pp. 203–216.

Ambrose, Alice. *Essays in Analysis*. London: George Allen & Unwin, 1966.

Ammereller, Erich and Fischer, Eugen, eds. *Wittgenstein at Work: Method in the Philosophical Investigations*. New York: Routledge, 2004.

Andreou, Chrisoula. "Getting On in a Varied World." *Social Theory and Practice*, 32 (2006): 61–73.

Annas, Julia. "Virtue Ethics: What Kind of Naturalism?" In *Virtue Ethics, Old and New*, ed. Stephen M. Gardiner, pp. 11–29. Ithaca, NY: Cornell University Press, 2005.

Anscombe, Elisabeth. *An Introduction to Wittgenstein's Tractatus*. London: Hutchinson University Library, 1959.

Anscombe, Elisabeth. "The Question of Linguistic Idealism." In *From Parmenides to Wittgenstein: Collected Philosophical Papers* Vol. 1, pp. 112–133. Oxford: Blackwell, 1981.

Anscombe, Elisabeth. *The Collected Philosophical Papers of G. E. M. Anscombe*, Vol. 3, *Ethics, Religion and Politics*. Oxford: Blackwell, 1981.

Anscombe, Elisabeth. "Wittgenstein on Rules and Private Language." *Ethics*, 95 (1985): 342–352.

Anscombe, Elisabeth. *Intention*, 2nd edition. Cambridge, MA: Harvard University Press, 2000. (Originally published by Blackwell, 1957.)

Apel, Karl-Otto. *Transformation der Philosophie*, Vols. 1 and 2. Frankfurt am Main: Suhrkamp, 1973.

Apel, Karl-Otto. *Towards the Transformation of Philosophy*. London: Routledge & Kegan Paul, 1980.

Apel, Karl-Otto. "Wittgenstein and Heidegger: Language Games and Life Forms. A Critical Comparison." In *Martin Heidegger: Critical Assessments*, Vol. 3, ed. C. Macann, pp. 341–374. London: Routledge, 1992.

Arrington, R. L. "Representation in Wittgenstein's *Tractatus* and Middle Writings." *Synthese*, 56 (1983): 181–198.

Arrington, R. L. *Rationalism, Realism, and Relativism: Perspectives in Contemporary Moral Epistemology*. Ithaca, NY: Cornell University Press, 1989.

Austin, J. L. *Sense and Sensibilia*. Oxford: Oxford University Press, 1962.

Austin, J. L. "Intelligent Behaviour: A Critical Review of *The Concept of Mind*." In *Ryle: A Collection of Critical Essays*, ed. O. P. Woods and G. Pitcher, pp. 45–51. New York: Anchor Books, Doubleday, 1970.

Ayer, A. J. *Language, Truth and Logic*. London: Victor Gollancz, 1936.

Ayer, A. J. "Can There Be a Private Language?" *Proceedings of the Aristotelian Society*, Supplementary Vol. 28 (1954): 63–74. Reprinted in Pitcher ed. 1968, pp. 251–266.

Ayer, A. J. *Part of My Life*. Oxford: Oxford University Press, 1977.

Baker, Gordon. "Defeasibility and Meaning." In *Law, Morality and Society*, ed. P. M. S. Hacker and J. Raz, pp. 26–57. Oxford: Clarendon Press, 1977.

Baker, Gordon. "Verehrung und Verkehrung: Waismann and Wittgenstein." In *Wittgenstein: Sources and Perspectives*, ed. C. G. Luckhardt, pp. 243–285. Hassocks: Harvester Press, 1979.

Baker, Gordon. "Criteria: A New Foundation for Semantics." In *The Philosophy of Wittgenstein*, Vol. 7, *Criteria*, ed. John V. Canfield, pp. 234–268. New York: Garland Publishing, 1986. (Originally *Ratio* 16 (1974): 156–189.)

Baker, Gordon. *Wittgenstein, Frege and the Vienna Circle*. Oxford: Blackwell, 1988.

Baker, Gordon. "Preface to the Second Edition." In *The Principles of Linguistic Philosophy*, ed. Rom Harré, pp. xi–xxiii. Basingstoke: Macmillan, 1997.

Baker, Gordon. "The Private Language Argument." *Language & Communication*, 18 (1998): 325–356. Section 4 (pp. 346–354). Reprinted as Chapter 7 of Baker 2004.

Baker, Gordon. "Preface." In *The Voices of Wittgenstein: The Vienna Circle*, ed. G. P. Baker, pp. xvi–xlviii. London: Routledge, 2003.

Baker, Gordon. "Friedrich Waismann: How I See Philosophy." *Philosophy*, 78 (2003): 163–179. (2003a)

Baker, Gordon. *Wittgenstein's Method, Neglected Aspects*, ed. K. Morris. Oxford: Blackwell, 2004.

Baker, Gordon and Hacker P. M. S. "Critical Notice, Philosophical Grammar." *Mind*, 85 (1976): 269–294. Reprinted in Shanker ed. 1986 Vol. 1, pp. 323–351.

Baker, Gordon and Hacker P. M. S. *Wittgenstein: Understanding and Meaning: An Analytical Commentary on the Philosophical Investigations*. Oxford: Blackwell, 1980.

Baker, Gordon and Hacker P. M. S. *Wittgenstein: Meaning and Understanding: Essays on the Philosophical Investigations*, Vol. 1. Oxford: Blackwell, 1983.

Baker, Gordon and Hacker P. M. S. *Scepticism, Rules and Language*. Oxford: Blackwell, 1984.

Baker, Gordon and Hacker P. M. S. *Language, Sense and Nonsense*. Oxford: Blackwell, 1984.

Baker, Gordon and Hacker P. M. S. *Wittgenstein, Rules, Grammar and Necessity: An Analytical Commentary on the Philosophical Investigations*, Vol. 2. Oxford: Blackwell, 1985.

Baker, Gordon and Hacker P. M. S. "Malcolm on Language and Rules." In *Connections and Controversies*, pp. 310–332. Oxford: Clarendon Press, Oxford University Press, 2001.

Baker, Gordon and Hacker P. M. S. *Wittgenstein: Understanding and Meaning*, 2nd edition. Oxford: Blackwell, 2005.

Bambrough, J. R. "Universals and Family Resemblances." *Proceedings of the Aristotelian Society*, 61 (1961/62): 207–222.

Bartley, W. W. *Wittgenstein*. La Salle: Open Court, 1985. (1st edition, 1973.)

Baum, W. "Nachwort zur Edition." In *Wittgenstein: Geheime Tagebücher*, ed. W. Baum, pp. 159–186. Vienna: Turia & Kant, 1991.

Benancerraf, Paul and Putnam, Hilary, eds. *Philosophy of Mathematics: Selected Readings*. Englewood Cilffs, NJ: Prentice-Hall, 1964.

Benancerraf, Paul and Putnam, Hilary, eds. *Philosophy of Mathematics: Selected Readings*, 2nd edition. Cambridge: Cambridge University Press, 1983.

Bennett, M. R. and Hacker, P. M. S. *The Philosophical Foundations of Neuroscience*. Oxford: Blackwell, 2003.

Biggs, Michael and Pichler, Alois. *Wittgenstein: Two Source Catalogues and a Bibliography*. Working Papers from the Wittgenstein Archives at the University of Bergen No. 7, 1993.

Biggs, Michael. "Graphical Problems in Wittgenstein's *Nachlaß*." In *Culture and Value*, ed. K. S. Johannessen and Tore Nordenstam, pp. 751–761. Kirchberg a. W.: ALWS, 1995.

Bilezki, Anat. *(Over)Interpreting Wittgenstein*. Dordrecht: Kluwer Academic Publishers, 2003.

Binkley, Timothy. *Wittgenstein's Language*. The Hague: Nijhoff, 1973.

Black, Max. *A Companion to Wittgenstein's Tractatus*. Ithaca, NY: Cornell University Press, 1964.

Blackburn, Simon. "Rule-Following and Moral Realism." In *Wittgenstein: To Follow a Rule*, ed. Steven H. Holtzman and Christopher M. Leich, pp. 163–187. London: Routledge, 1981.

Blackburn, Simon. "The Individual Strikes Back." *Synthese*, 58 (1984): 281–301.

Blackburn, Simon. "Wittgenstein's Irrealism." In *Wittgenstein: Towards a Reevaluation / Eine Neubewertung, Proceedings of the 14th International Wittgenstein-symposium*, Vol. 2, ed. J. Brandl and R. Haller, pp. 13–26. Vienna: Holder-Richler-Temsky, 1990.

Blackburn, Simon. "Wittgenstein and Minimalism." *Themes From Wittgenstein*, Working Papers in Philosophy, No. 4, ed. B. Garrett and K. Mulligan (1993): 1–14.

Blackburn, Simon. *Essays in Quasi-Realism*. Oxford: Oxford University Press, 1993. (1993a)

Block, Irvin ed. *Perspectives on the Philosophy of Wittgenstein*. Oxford: Blackwell, 1981.

Bloor, David. *Wittgenstein: A Social Theory of Knowledge*. London: Macmillan, 1983.

Bloor, David. "Left and Right Wittgensteinians." In *Science as Practice and Culture*, ed. A. Pickering, pp. 266–282. Chicago: University of Chicago Press, 1992.

Bloor, David. "The Question of Linguistic Idealism Revisited." In Sluga and Stern eds. 1996, pp. 354–382.

Bogen, James. *Wittgenstein's Philosophy of Language: Some Aspects of Its Development*. New York: Humanities Press, 1972.

Boghossian, Paul A. "The Rule-Following Considerations." *Mind*, 98 (1989): 507–549.

Bolton, Derek. "Life-form and Idealism." In *Idealism Past and Present*, ed. Godfrey Vesey, pp. 269–284. Cambridge: Cambridge University Press, 1982.

Bourdieu, Pierre. "Fieldwork in Philosophy." Interview with A. Honneth, H. Kocyba and B. Scwibs, Paris, 1985. In *In Other Words: Essays Towards a Reflexive Sociology*, pp. 3–33. Stanford: Stanford University Press, 1990.

Bouveresse, Jacques. *Le Mythe de l'intériorité: experience, signification et langage privé chez Wittgenstein*. Paris: Minuit, 1987.

Bouveresse, Jacques. *Wittgenstein Reads Freud: The Myth of the Unconscious*. Princeton, NJ: Princeton University Press, 1995.

Bouwsma, O. K. "The Blue Book." *Journal of Philosophy*, 58 (1961), pp. 141–62. Reprinted in John V. Canfield, ed., *The Philosophy of Wittgenstein*, Vol. 4, *The Later Philosophy – Views and Reviews*, pp. 121–142. New York: Garland Publishing, 1986.

Brandom, Robert. *Making it Explicit*. Cambridge, MA: Harvard University Press, 1994.

Budd, Malcolm. *Wittgenstein's Philosophy of Psychology*. London: Routledge, 1989.

Canfield, John V., ed. *The Philosophy of Wittgenstein*, Vol. 11, *Philosophy of Mathematics*. New York: Garland Publishing, 1986.

Canfield, John V. "The Community View." *Philosophical Review*, 105 (1996): 469–488.

Cassam, Quassim. "Necessity and Externality." *Mind*, 95 (1986): 446–464.

Cavell, Stanley. "The Availability of Wittgenstein's Later Philosophy." *Philosophical Review*, 71 (1962): 67–93. Reprinted in Cavell 1969, pp. 44–72. (1969a)

Cavell, Stanley. *Must We Mean What We Say? A Book of Essays*. Charles Scribner's Sons, 1969/Cambridge: Cambridge University Press, 1976.

Cavell, Stanley. *The World Viewed: Reflections on the Ontology of Film*. New York: Viking Press, 1977.

Cavell, Stanley. *Pursuits of Happiness: The Hollywood Comedy of Remarriage*. Cambridge, MA: Harvard University Press, 1981.

Cavell, Stanley. *The Claim of Reason: Wittgenstein, Scepticism, Morality and Tragedy*. New York: Oxford University Press, 1982. (Originally published 1979.)

Cavell, Stanley. *Disowning Knowledge in Six Plays of Shakespeare*. Cambridge: Cambridge University Press, 1987.

Cavell, Stanley. *Themes Out of School: Cause and Effect*. Chicago: University of Chicago Press, 1988.

Cavell, Stanley. *This New Yet Unapproachable America*. Albuquerque: Living Batch Press, 1989.

Cavell, Stanley. *Conditions Handsome and Unhandsome: The Constitution of Emersonian Perfectionism: The Carus Lectures, 1988*. Chicago: University of Chicago Press, 1990.

Cavell, Stanley. *A Pitch of Philosophy: Autobiographical Exercises*. Cambridge, MA: Harvard University Press, 1994.

Cavell, Stanley. "Notes and Afterthoughts on the Opening of Wittgenstein's *Investigations*." In Cavell 1995, pp. 124–186. Reprinted in Sluga and Stern eds. 1996, pp. 261–295.

Cavell, Stanley. *Philosophical Passages: Wittgenstein, Emerson, Austin, Derrida*. Oxford: Blackwell, 1995.

Cavell, Stanley. "Epilogue: The *Investigations'* Everyday Aesthetics of Itself." In Mulhall ed. 1996, pp. 369–389.

Cavell, Stanley. "The *Investigations'* Everyday Aesthetics of Itself." In McCarthy and Stidd eds. 2001, pp. 250–266.

Cavell, Stanley. *Philosophy the Day After Tomorrow*. Cambridge, MA: Belknap, Harvard University Press, 2005.

Chihara, Charles. "Wittgenstein and Logical Compulsion." *Analysis*, 21 (1961): 136–140.

Chihara, Charles. "Mathematical Discovery and Concept Formation." *Philosophical Review*, 72 (1963): 17–34. Reprinted in Shanker ed. 1986, pp. 264–276.

Chihara, Charles. "Wittgenstein's Analysis of the Paradoxes in his Lectures on the Foundations of Mathematics." *Philosophical Review*, 86 (1977): 365–381. Reprinted in Shanker ed. 1986, pp. 325–337.

Chihara, Charles. "The Wright-Wing Defense of Wittgenstein's Philosophy of Logic." *Philosophical Review*, 9 (1982): 99–108.

Cioffi, Frank. "Wittgenstein's Freud." In *Studies in the Philosophy of Wittgenstein*, ed. Peter Winch, pp. 184–210. London: Routledge & Kegan Paul, 1969.

Cioffi, Frank. *Wittgenstein on Freud and Frazer*. Cambridge: Cambridge University Press, 1998.

Cohen, J. L. *The Dialogue of Reason*. Oxford: Clarendon Press, 1986.

Cohen, Martin. *Wittgenstein's Beetle and Other Classic Thought Experiments*. Oxford: Blackwell, 2005.

Collins, R. *The Sociology of Philosophies*. Cambridge, MA: Harvard University Press, 1998.

Conant, James. "Throwing Away the Top of the Ladder." *Yale Review*, 79 (1990): 328–364.

Conant, James. "Search for Logically Alien Thought: Descartes, Kant, Frege and the *Tractatus*." *Philosophical Topics*, 20 (1991): 115–180.

Conant, James. "Kierkegaard, Wittgenstein and Nonsense." In *Pursuits of Reason*, ed. T. Cohen, P. Guyer and H. Putnam, pp. 195–224. Lubbock: Texas Tech University Press, 1992.

Conant, James. "Elucidation and Nonsense in Frege and Early Wittgenstein." In Crary and Read eds. 2000, pp. 174–217.

Conant, James. "Two Conceptions of Die Überwindung der Metaphysik: Carnap and Early Wittgenstein." In McCarthy and Stidd eds. 2001, pp. 13–61.

Conant, James. "The Method of the *Tractatus*." In Reck ed. 2002, pp. 374–462.

Conant, James. "Why Worry about the *Tractatus*?" In Stocker 2004, pp. 167–192.

Conant, James. "What 'Ethics' in the *Tractatus* is Not." In *Religion and Wittgenstein's Legacy*, ed. D. Z. Phillips and Mario Von Der Ruhr, pp. 39–88. Aldershot: Ashgate, 2005.

Conant, James. "Mild Mono Wittgensteinianism." In *Wittgenstein and the Moral Life: Essays in Honor of Cora Diamond*, ed. Alice Crary. Cambridge, MA: MIT Press, 2007.

Conant, James and Diamond, Cora. "On Reading the *Tractatus* Resolutely: Reply to Meredith Williams and Peter Sullivan." In Kölbel and Weiss eds. 2004, pp. 46–99.

Cook, John, W. "Wittgenstein on Privacy." *Philosophical Review*, 73 (1965): 281–314. Reprinted in Pitcher 1968, pp. 286–323.

Cook, John W. "Wittgenstein and Religious Belief." *Philosophy*, 63 (1988): 427–452.

Cook, John, W. *Wittgenstein's Metaphysics.* Cambridge: Cambridge University Press, 1994.

Cook, John, W. *Wittgenstein, Empiricism, and Language.* New York: Oxford University Press, 1999.

Cook, John, W. *The Undiscovered Wittgenstein: The Twentieth Century's Most Misunderstood Philosopher.* New York: Humanity Books, 2005.

Copi, Irving and Beard, Robert, eds. *Essays on Wittgenstein's Tractatus.* New York: Macmillar, 1966.

Copp, David and Sobel, David. "Morality and Virtue: An Assessment of Some Recent Work in Virtue Ethics." *Ethics,* 114 (2004): 524–554.

Crary, Alice. "Introduction." In Crary and Read eds. 2000, pp. 1–18.

Crary, Alice. "Wittgenstein and Political Thought." In Crary and Read eds. 2000, pp. 118–145. (2000a)

Crary, Alice. *Beyond Moral Judgement.* Cambridge, MA: Harvard University Press, 2007.

Crary, Alice and Read, Rupert, eds. *The New Wittgenstein.* London: Routledge, 2000.

Creegan, Charles L. *Wittgenstein and Kierkegaard: Religion, Individuality and Philosophical Method.* London: Routledge, 1989.

Davidson, Donald. "On the Very Idea of a Conceptual Scheme." In *Inquiries into Truth and Interpretation*, pp. 183–198. Oxford: Oxford University Press, 1984.

Dawson, John. "The Reception of Gödel's Incompleteness Theorems." In *Gödel's Theorem in Focus,* ed. S. Shanker, pp. 1–16. London: Routledge, 1989.

Derrida, Jacques. "Response to Mulhall." In *Arguing with Derrida,* ed. Simon Glendinning, pp. 116–120. Oxford: Blackwell, 2001.

Descartes, René. *Principles of Philosophy.* In *The Philosophical Writings of Descartes,* Vol. 1, trans. John Cottingham, Robert Stoothoff and Dugald Murdoch, pp. 177–292. Cambridge: Cambridge University Press, 1985.

Diamond, Cora. "Critical Study: Wright's Wittgenstein." *Philosophical Quarterly,* 31 (1981): 352–366. Reprinted in Shanker ed. 1986, pp. 360–377.

Diamond, Cora. "Throwing Away the Ladder: How to Read the *Tractatus.*" *Philosophy,* 63 (1988): 5–27. Reprinted in Diamond 1991, pp. 179–204.

Diamond, Cora. *The Realistic Spirit.* Cambridge, MA: MIT Press, 1991.

Diamond, Cora. "'We are Perpetually Moralists': Iris Murdoch, Fact and Value." In *Iris Murdoch and the Search for Human Goodness,* ed. Maria Antonaccio and William Schweiker, pp. 79–109. Chicago: University of Chicago Press, 1996.

Diamond, Cora. "Ethics, Imagination and the Method of Wittgenstein's *Tractatus.*" In Crary and Read eds. 2000, pp. 149–173.

Diamond, Cora. "Criss Cross Philosophy." In Ammereller and Fischer eds. 2004, pp. 201–220.

Diamond, Cora. "Peter Winch on the *Tractatus* and the Unity of Wittgenstein's Philosophy." In Pichler and Säätelä eds. 2005, pp. 133–163.

Dilman, Ilham. "Universals: Bambrough on Wittgenstein." *Aristotelian Society Proceedings*, 79 (1978): 35–58. Reprinted in John V. Canfield, ed., *The Philosophy of Wittgenstein*, Vol. 5, *Method and Essence*, pp. 305–328. New York: Garland Publishing, 1986.

Donagan, Alan. "Wittgenstein on Sensation." In Pitcher ed. 1968, pp. 323–351.

Dummett, Michael. "Wittgenstein's Philosophy of Mathematics." *Philosophical Review*, 68 (1959): 324–348. Reprinted in Benancerraf and Putnam eds. 1964, pp. 491–509; Dummett 1978, pp. 166–185; Shanker ed. 1986, pp. 121–137; Canfield ed. 1986, pp. 110–134.

Dummett, Michael. "What is a Theory of Meaning? (II)." In *Truth and Meaning: Essays in Semantics*, ed. G. Evans and J. McDowell, pp. 67–137. Oxford: Clarendon Press, 1976.

Dummett, Michael. *Truth and Other Enigmas*. London: Duckworth, 1978.

Dummett, Michael. "Can Analytic Philosophy Be Systematic and Ought it to Be?" In Dummett 1978, pp. 437–458. (1978a)

Dummett, Michael. "Reckonings: Wittgenstein on Mathematics." *Encounter*, 50 (1978): 63–68. Reprinted in Shanker ed. 1986, pp. 111–120; Canfield ed. 1986, pp. 303–305.

Dummett, Michael. "Wittgenstein on Philosophy and Mathematics." *Journal of Philosophy*, 94 (1997): 359–374.

Elliott, Carl. "Does Your Patient Have a Beetle in His Box? Language-Games and the Spread of Psychopathology." In *Wittgenstein and Political Philosophy*, ed. Cressida J. Heyes, pp. 186–201. Ithaca, NY: Cornell University Press, 2003.

Engel, M. S. "Wittgenstein's 'Foundations' and its Reception." *American Philosophical Quarterly*, 4 (1967): 257–268. Reprinted in Shanker ed. 1986, pp. 146–164.

Fann, K. T. *Wittgenstein's Conception of Philosophy*. Berkeley: University of California Press, 1969.

Feyerabend, Paul "Wittgenstein's Philosophical Investigations." *Philosophical Review*, 64 (1955): 449–483. Reprinted in Pitcher ed. 1968, pp. 104–150.

Findlay, J. N. *Wittgenstein: A Critique*. London: Routledge, 1984.

Fischer, Eugen. "Philosophical Pictures." *Synthese*, 148 (2006): 469–501.

Flew, Anthony. *Hume's Philosophy of Belief*. London: Routledge & Kegan Paul, 1961.

Floyd, Juliet. "Wittgenstein on 2,2,2 . . . The Opening of Remarks on the Foundations of Mathematics." *Synthese*, 87 (1991): 143–180.

Floyd, Juliet. "On Saying What You Really Want to Say: Wittgenstein, Gödel, and the Trisection of the Angle." In *From Dedekind to Gödel*, ed. J. Hintikka, pp. 373–426. Dordrecht: Kluwer, 1995.

Floyd, Juliet. "Wittgenstein, Mathematics and Philosophy." In Crary and Read eds. 2000, pp. 232–261.

Floyd, Juliet. "Number and Ascriptions of Number in Wittgenstein's *Tractatus*." In Reck ed. 2002, pp. 308–352.

Floyd, Juliet. "Wittgenstein on Philosophy of Logic and Mathematics." In *The Oxford Handbook of Philosophy of Mathematics and Logic*, ed. Stewart Shapiro, pp. 75–128. Oxford: Oxford University Press, 2005.

Floyd, Juliet and Putnam, Hilary. "A Note on Wittgenstein's 'Notorious Paragraph' about the Gödel Theorem." *Journal of Philosophy*, 97 (2000): 624–632.

Fogelin, Robert F. *Wittgenstein*. London: Routledge, 1987. (First published 1976.)

Føllesdal, D. "Analytic Philosophy: What Is It, and Why Should One Engage in It?' In Glock ed. 1997, pp. 1–16.

Foot, Philippa. "Moral Beliefs." In *Virtues and Vices and Other Essays in Moral Philosophy*, pp. 110–131. Oxford: Blackwell, 1978a.

Foot, Philippa. "Morality as a System of Hypothetical Imperatives." In *Virtues and Vices and Other Essays in Moral Philosophy*, pp. 157–173. Oxford: Blackwell, 1978b.

Foot, Philippa. "Reasons for Acting and Desires." In *Virtues and Vices and Other Essays in Moral Philosophy*, pp. 148–156. Oxford: Blackwell, 1978c.

Foot, Philippa. *Natural Goodness*. Oxford: Oxford University Press, 2001.

Forster, Michael, N. *Wittgenstein on the Arbitrariness of Grammar*. Princeton, NJ: Princeton University Press, 2004.

Frascolla, Pasquale. *Wittgenstein's Philosophy of Mathematics*. London: Routledge, 1994.

Frascolla, Pasquale. "The Constructivist Model in Wittgenstein's Philosophy of Mathematics." *Revista Filosofia*, 71 (1980): 297–306. Reprinted in Shanker ed. 1986, pp. 242–249.

Frege, Gottlob. *The Foundations of Arithmetic*. Translated by J. L. Austin. Oxford: Blackwell, 1980.

Frongia, Guido and McGuinness, Brian, eds. *Wittgenstein, A Bibliographical Guide*. Oxford: Blackwell, 1990.

Gaita, Raimond. *Common Humanity: Thinking about Love, Truth and Justice*. London: Routledge, 1998.

Gaita, Raimond. *Good and Evil, An Absolute Conception*, 2nd edition. London: Routledge, 2004.

Garver, Newton. *This Complicated Form of Life: Essay on Wittgenstein*. Chicago: Open Court, 1994.

Garver, Newton. "Philosophy as Grammar." In Sluga and Stern eds. 1996, pp. 139–170.

Genova, Judith. *Wittgenstein: A Way of Seeing*. New York: Routledge, 1995.

Gerrard, Steven. "Wittgenstein's Philosophies of Mathematics." *Synthese*, April (1991): 125–142.

Gerrard, Steven. "One Wittgenstein?" In Reck ed. 2002, pp. 52–71.

Gibson, John and Huemer, Wolfgang, eds. *The Literary Wittgenstein*. London: Routledge, 2004.

Gillies, D. A. "Wittgenstein and Revisionism." *British Journal for the Philosophy of Science*, 33 (1982): 422–433.

Glendinning, Simon. *On Being With Others: Heidegger, Derrida, Wittgenstein*. London: Routledge, 1998.

Glock, Hans-Johan. "*Philosophical Investigations*: Principles of Interpretation." In *Wittgenstein – A Re-evaluation*, ed. Johannes Brandl and Rudolf Haller, pp. 152–162. Vienna: Hölder-Pichler-Tempsky, 1990.

Glock, Hans-Johan. "*Philosophical Investigations* Section 128: 'Theses in Philosophy' and Undogmatic Procedure." In *Wittgenstein's Philosophical Investigations, Text and Context*, ed. R. L. Arrington and H.-J. Glock, pp. 69–88. London: Routledge, 1991.

Glock, Hans-Johan. *A Wittgenstein Dictionary*. Oxford: Blackwell, 1996.

Glock, Hans-Johan. "Necessity and Normativity." In Sluga and Stern eds. 1996, pp. 198–225. (1996a)

Glock, Hans-Johan. "Kant and Wittgenstein: Philosophy, Necessity and Representation." *International Journal of Philosophical Studies*, 5 (1997): 285–305.

Glock Hans-Johan, ed. *The Rise of Analytic Philosophy*. Oxford: Blackwell, 1997.

Glock, Hans-Johan. "The Development of Wittgenstein's Philosophy." In Glock ed. 2001, pp. 1–25.

Glock, Hans-Johan, ed. *Wittgenstein: A Critical Reader*. Oxford: Blackwell, 2001.

Glock, Hans-Johan. "All Kinds of Nonsense." In Ammereller and Fischer eds. 2004, pp. 221–245.

Glock, Hans-Johan. "Was Wittgenstein an Analytic Philosopher?" *Metaphilosophy*, 35:4 (2004): 419–444. (2004a)

Glock, Hans-Johan. "Ramsey and Wittgenstein: Mutual Influences." In *F. P. Ramsey: Critical Assessments*, ed. M. J. Frápolli, pp. 41–69. London: Continuum, 2005.

Glock, Hans-Johan. "Ludwig Wittgenstein: *Tractatus Logico-Philosophicus*." In *Central Works of Philosophy*, Vol. 4, ed. J. Shand, pp. 71–91. Chesham: Acumen, 2006.

Glock, Hans-Johan. *What is Analytic Philosophy?* Cambridge: Cambridge University Press, 2007.

Goldfarb, Warren D. "I Want You to Bring Me a Slab: Remarks on the Opening Sections of the *Philosophical Investigations*." *Synthese*, 56 (1983): 256–282.

Goldfarb, Warren D. "Metaphysics and Nonsense: On Cora Diamond's *The Realistic Spirit*." *Journal of Philosophical Research*, 22 (1997): 57–73.

Goodstein, R. L. "Wittgenstein's Philosophy of Mathematics." In *Ludwig Wittgenstein: Philosophy and Language*, ed. A. Ambrose and M. Lazerowitz, pp. 271–286. London: George Allen & Unwin, 1973.

Griffin, James. *Wittgenstein's Logical Atomism*. Oxford: Clarendon Press, Oxford University Press, 1964.

Griffin, Nicholas. "Wittgenstein, Universals and Family Resemblances." *Canadian Journal of Philosophy*, 3 (1974), pp. 635–652. Reprinted in *The Philosophy of Wittgenstein*, Vol. 5, *Method and Essence*, ed. John V. Canfield, pp. 249–266. New York: Garland Publishing, 1986.

Habermas, Jürgen. *The Theory of Communicative Action*. Boston: Beacon Press, 1984.

Habermas, Jürgen. *On the Logic of the Social Sciences*. Cambridge, MA: MIT Press, 1988. (German original, 1967.)

Habermas, Jürgen. *On the Pragmatics of Communication*. Cambridge, MA: MIT Press, 1998.

Hadot, Pierre. *Philosophy as a Way of Life*. Oxford: Blackwell, 1995.

Hacker, P. M. S. "Laying the Ghost of the *Tractatus*." *Review of Metaphysics*, 29 (1975): 96–116.

Hacker, P. M. S. *Insight and Illusion*. Oxford: Clarendon Press, Oxford University Press, 1972. Revised edition, 1986.

Hacker, P. M. S. *Wittgenstein, Meaning and Mind: An Analytical Commentary of the Philosophical Investigations*, Vol. 3. Oxford: Blackwell, 1990.

Hacker, P. M. S. *Wittgenstein: Meaning and Mind, Volume 3 of an Analytical Commentary on the Philosophical Investigations, Part II: Exegesis*. Oxford: Blackwell, 1990a.

Hacker, P. M. S. *Wittgenstein, Mind and Will. An Analytical Commentary on the Philosophical Investigations*, Vol. 4. Oxford: Blackwell, 1996.

Hacker, P. M. S. *Wittgenstein's Place in Twentieth Century Analytical Philosophy*. Oxford: Blackwell, 1996. (1996a)

Hacker, P. M. S. "Was He Trying to Whistle It?" In Crary and Read eds. 2000, pp. 353–388.

Hacker, P. M. S. "Naming, Thinking, and Meaning in the *Tractatus*." *Philosophical Investigations*, 22 (1999): 119–135. Reprinted in Hacker 2001, pp. 98–140.

Hacker, P. M. S. *Connections and Controversies*. Oxford: Clarendon Press, Oxford University Press, 2001.

Hacker, P. M. S. "Eliminative Materialism." In *Wittgenstein and Contemporary Philosophy of Mind*, ed. Severin Schroeder, pp. 60–84. New York: Palgrave, 2001. (2001a)

Hacker, P. M. S. "Philosophy." In *Wittgenstein: A Critical Reader*, ed. Hans-Johan Glock, pp. 322–347. Oxford: Blackwell, 2001. (2001b)

Hacker, P. M. S. "Wittgenstein, Carnap and the New American Wittgensteinians." *Philosophical Quarterly*, 35 (2004): 1–23.

Hagberg, Garry L. *Meaning and Interpretation: Wittgenstein, Henry James and Literary Knowledge*. Ithaca, NY: Cornell University Press, 1994.

Hagberg, Garry L. *Art as Language: Wittgenstein, Meaning and Aesthetic Theory.* Ithaca, NY: Cornell University Press, 1995.

Hagberg, Garry L. "On Philosophy as Therapy: Wittgenstein, Cavell, and Autobiographical Writing." *Philosophy and Literature*, 27 (2003): 196–210.

Hale, Bob. "Rule-following, Objectivity and Meaning." In *A Companion to the Philosophy of Language*, eds. B. Hale and C. Wright, pp. 369–397. Oxford: Blackwell, 1997.

Haller, Rudolf. *Questions on Wittgenstein.* London: Routledge, 1988.

Hallett, Garth. *Wittgenstein's Definition of Meaning as Use.* New York: Fordham University Press, 1967.

Hallett, Garth. *A Companion to Wittgenstein's Philosophical Investigations.* Ithaca, NY: Cornell University Press, 1977.

Hanfling, Oswald. *Wittgenstein's Later Philosophy.* Basingstoke: Macmillan, 1989.

Hanfling, Oswald. *Philosophy and Ordinary Language.* London: Routledge, 2004.

Heal, Jane. "Wittgenstein and Dialogue." In *Philosophical Dialogues: Plato, Hume, Wittgenstein*, ed. T. Smiley. Dawes Hicks Lectures on Philosophy, Proceedings of the British Academy, 85. Oxford: Oxford University Press, 1995.

Hertzberg, Lars. "The Sense Is Where You Find It." In McCarthy and Stidd eds. 2001, pp. 90–103.

Heyes, Cressida J., ed. *The Grammar of Politics: Wittgenstein and Political Philosophy.* Ithaca, NY: Cornell University Press, 2003.

Hilmy, S. Stephen. *The Later Wittgenstein: The Emergence of a New Philosophical Method.* Oxford: Blackwell, 1987.

Hilmy, S. Stephen. "Wittgenstein and Behaviourism." In *Wittgenstein in Focus – im Brennpunkt: Wittgenstein*, ed. R. Haller and B. McGuinnes, pp. 235–252. Amsterdam: Rodopi, 1991.

Hintikka, Jaakko. "Wittgenstein's Semantical Kantianism." In *Ethics: Foundations, Problems and Applications.* Proceedings of the Fifth International Wittgenstein Symposium, ed. E. Morscher and R. Strazinger, pp. 375–390. Vienna: Hölder-Pichler-Tempsky, 1981.

Hintikka, Jaakko. *Ludwig Wittgenstein: Half-truths and One-and-a-half-truths.* Dordrecht: Kluwer, 1996.

Hintikka, Jaakko and Hintikka, M. B. *Investigating Wittgenstein.* Oxford: Blackwell, 1986.

Hintikka, J. and Hintikka, A. M. "Wittgenstein: The Bewitched Writer." In *Wittgenstein and the Future of Philosophy*, ed. R. Haller and K. Puhl, pp. 131–150. Vienna: öbv & hpt, 2001.

Holtzman, Steven H. and Leich, Christopher M., eds. *Wittgenstein: To Follow a Rule.* London: Routledge, 1981.

Hooker, Brad and Little, Margaret. *Moral Particularism*. New York: Oxford University Press, 2000.

Horwich, Paul. "Wittgenstein's Meta-Philosophical Development." In *From a Deflationary Point of View*, pp. 159–171. Oxford: Oxford University Press, 2005.

Hudson, W. D. *Wittgenstein and Religious Belief*. London: Macmillan, 1975.

Hursthouse, Rosalind. *On Virtue Ethics*. Oxford: Oxford University Press, 1999.

Ishiguro, Hidé. "Use and Reference of Names." In Winch ed. 1969, pp. 20–50.

Ishiguro, Hidé. "The So-called Picture Theory: Language and the World in the *Tractatus Logico-Philosophicus*." In Glock ed. 2001, pp. 26–46.

Janik, A. and Toulmin, S. *Wittgenstein's Vienna*. New York: Simon & Schuster, 1973.

Johnston, Paul. *Wittgenstein and Moral Philosophy*. London: Routledge, 1989.

Johnston, Paul. *Wittgenstein: Rethinking the Inner*. London: Routledge, 1993.

Johnston, Paul. *Contradictions of Modern Moral Philosophy: Ethics After Wittgenstein*. London: Routledge, 1999.

Kannisto, Heikki. *Thoughts and Their Subject: A Study of Wittgenstein's Tractatus*. Helsinki: Acta Philosophica Fennica, Vol. 40, 1986.

Kant, Immanuel. *Critique of Practical Reason*. In *Immanuel Kant, Practical Philosophy*, trans. and ed. Mary J. Gregor, pp. 133–272. Cambridge: Cambridge University Press, 1996.

Kant, Immanuel. *Critique of Pure Reason*, trans. and ed. Paul Guyer and Allen W. Wood. Cambridge: Cambridge University Press, 1998.

Kant, Immanuel. *Critique of the Power of Judgment*, trans. Paul Guyer and Eric Matthews, ed. Paul Guyer. Cambridge: Cambridge University Press, 2000.

Keightley, A. W. *Wittgenstein, Grammar and God*. London: Epworth Press, 1976.

Kenny, Anthony. "Wittgenstein." In *The Encyclopedia of Philosophy*, ed. P. Edwards. New York: Macmillan, 1972.

Kenny, Anthony. *Wittgenstein*. London: Allen Lane, 1973.

Kenny, Anthony. "Cartesian Privacy." In *The Anatomy of the Soul*, pp. 113–128. Oxford: Blackwell, 1973.

Kenny, Anthony. "The Ghost of the *Tractatus*." In *The Legacy of Wittgenstein*, pp. 10–23. Oxford: Blackwell, 1984.

Kenny, Anthony. *The Legacy of Wittgenstein*. Oxford: Blackwell, 1984.

Kenny, Anthony. ' "Philosophy States Only What Everyone Admits." ' In Ammereller and Fischer eds. 2004, pp. 173–182.

Kenny, Anthony. "A Brief History of Wittgenstein Editing." In Pichler and Säätelä eds. 2005, pp. 341–355.

Kenny, Anthony. *Wittgenstein*, 2nd edition. Oxford: Blackwell, 2006.

Kielkopf, Charles F. *Strict Finitism: An Examination of Ludwig Wittgenstein's Remarks on the Foundations of Mathematics*. The Hague: Mouton, 1970.

Kienzler, Wolfgang. *Wittgensteins Wende zu seiner Spätphilosophie 1930–1932.* Frankfurt am Main: Suhrkamp, 1997.

Kitching, Gavin and Pleasants, Nigel, eds. *Marx and Wittgenstein: Knowledge, Morality and Politics.* London: Routledge, 2002.

Klagge, J., ed. *Wittgenstein: Biography and Philosophy.* New York: Cambridge University Press, 2001.

Klenk, Virginia. *Wittgenstein's Philosophy of Mathematics.* The Hague: Nijhoff, 1976.

Kölbel, Max and Weiss, Bernhard, eds. *Wittgenstein's Lasting Significance.* London: Routledge, 2004.

Kreisel, G. "Wittgenstein's Remarks on the Foundations of Mathematics." *British Journal for the Philosophy of Science,* 9 (1958): 135–158.

Kreisel, G. "Wittgenstein's Lectures on the Foundations of Mathematics." *Bulletin of the American Mathematical Society,* 84 (1978): 79–90. Reprinted in Shanker ed. 1986, pp. 98–110.

Kremer, Michael. "Contextualism and Holism in the Early Wittgenstein: From *Prototractatus* to *Tractatus.*" *Philosophical Topics,* 25 (1997): 87–120.

Kremer, Michael. "The Purpose of Tractarian Nonsense." *Noûs,* 35 (2001): 39–73.

Kripke, Saul. *Wittgenstein on Rules and Private Language.* Oxford: Blackwell, 1982.

Kuusela, Oskari. "From Metaphysics and Philosophical Theses to Grammar: Wittgenstein's Turn." *Philosophical Investigations,* 28 (2005): 95–133.

Lackey, D. "What are the Modern Classics? The Baruch Poll of Great Philosophy in the Twentieth Century." *Philosophical Forum,* 4 (1999): 329–346.

Lazerowitz, Morris. *Studies in Metaphilosophy.* London: Routledge, 2004.

Lear, Jonathan. "The Disappearing We." *Proceedings of Aristotelian Society,* Supplementary Vol. 58 (1984): 219–242.

Lear, Jonathan. "Transcendental Anthropology." In *Subject, Thought, and Context,* ed. Philip Pettit and John McDowell. Oxford: Oxford University Press, 1986.

Lewis, Peter B., ed. *Wittgenstein, Aesthetics and Philosophy.* Aldershot: Ashgate, 2004.

Lovibond, Sabina. *Realism and Imagination in Ethics.* Oxford: Blackwell, 1983.

Lovibond, Sabina. *Ethical Formation.* Cambridge, MA: Harvard University Press, 2002.

Lyotard, Jean-François. *The Post-Modern Condition: A Report on Knowledge.* Minneapolis: University of Minnesota Press, 1984.

Lyotard, Jean-François. *The Differend: Phrases in Dispute,* trans. Georges Van Den Abbeele. Minneapolis: University of Minnesota Press, 1988.

Lyotard, Jean-François. "Wittgenstein 'After'." In *Political Writings,* ed. Bill Readings and Kevin Paul Geiman, pp. 19–22. Minneapolis: University of Minnesota Press, 1993.

McCarthy, Timothy and Stidd, Sean C. eds. *Wittgenstein in America*. Oxford: Oxford University Press, 2001.

McDonough, Richard M. *The Argument of the Tractatus: Its Relevance to Contemporary Theories of Logic, Language, Mind and Philosophical Truth*. Albany: State University of New York Press, 1986.

McDowell, John. "Criteria, Defeasibility and Knowledge." In *From the Proceedings of the British Academy*, London, 68. Oxford: Oxford University Press, 1982.

McDowell, John. "Wittgenstein on Following a Rule." In *Meaning and Reference*, ed. A. W. Moore, pp. 257–293. Oxford: Oxford University Press, 1993.

McDowell, John. *Mind and World*. Cambridge, MA: Harvard University Press, 1994. (2nd edition 1996.)

McDowell, John. *Mind, Value and Reality*. Cambridge, MA: Harvard University Press, 1998.

McDowell, John. "Non-cognitivism and Rule-following." In *Mind, Value and Reality*, pp. 198–218. (1998a)

McDowell, John. "Two Sorts of Naturalism." In *Mind, Value and Reality*, pp. 167–197. (1998b)

McDowell, John. "Virtue and Reason." In *Mind, Value and Reality*, pp. 50–73. (1998c)

McDowell, John. "Reply to Crispin Wright." In *On Knowing Our Own Minds*, ed. C. McDonald, B. Smith and C. Wright, pp. 47–82. Oxford: Oxford University Press, 1998. (1998d)

McDowell, John. "One Strand in the Private Language Argument." *Grazer Philosophische Studien*, 33/34: 285–303, 1989. In *Mind, Value and Reality*, pp. 279–296. (1998e)

McDowell, John and Evans, Gareth, eds. *Truth and Meaning: Essays in Semantics*. Oxford: Clarendon Press, 1976.

McGinn, Colin. *Wittgenstein on Meaning and Understanding*. Oxford: Blackwell, 1984.

McGinn, Marie. *Wittgenstein and the Philosophical Investigations*. London: Routledge, 1997.

McGinn, Marie. "Saying and Showing and the Continuity of Wittgenstein's Thought." *Harvard Review of Philosophy*, 9 (2001): 24–36.

McGinn, Marie. *Elucidating the Tractatus: Wittgenstein's Early Philosophy of Logic and Language*. Oxford: Oxford University Press, 2006.

McGuinness, Brian. "The So-Called Realism of the *Tractatus*." In Block ed. 1981, pp. 60–73. Reprinted in McGuinness 2002, pp. 82–94.

McGuinness, Brian. *Wittgenstein, a Life: Young Ludwig*. London: Penguin, 1985.

McGuinness, Brian. *Approaches to Wittgenstein: Collected Papers*. London: Routledge, 2002.

McManus, Denis, ed. *Wittgenstein and Scepticism*. London: Routledge, 2004.

McManus, Denis. *The Enchantment of Words: Wittgenstein's Tractatus Logico-Philosophicus*. Oxford: Oxford University Press, 2006.

Malcolm, Norman. "Wittgenstein's Philosophical Investigations." *Philosophical Review*, 63 (1954): 530–559. Revised version in Pitcher ed. 1968, pp. 65–103.

Malcolm, Norman. "Wittgenstein and Idealism." In *Idealism Past and Present*, ed. Godfrey Vesey, pp. 249–267. Cambridge: Cambridge University Press, 1982. Reprinted in Malcolm 1995, pp. 87–108.

Malcolm, Norman. *Wittgenstein, A Memoir, with a Bibliographical Sketch by G. H. von Wright*, 2nd edition. Oxford: Oxford University Press, 1984.

Malcolm, Norman. *Nothing Is Hidden: Wittgenstein's Criticism of his Early Thought*. Oxford: Blackwell, 1986.

Malcolm, Norman. "Language Game (2)." In *Wittgenstein: Attention to Particulars*, ed. D. Z. Phillips and Peter Winch, pp. 35–44. London: Macmillan, 1989.

Malcolm, Norman. *From a Religious Point of View?* London: Routledge, 1993.

Malcolm, Norman. *Wittgensteinian Themes: Essays 1978–1989*. Ed. G. H. von Wright. Ithaca, NY: Cornell University Press, 1995.

Marconi, D. ed. *Guida a Wittgenstein*. Rome: Laterza, 1997.

Marcuse, Herbert. *One-Dimensional Man*. Boston: Beacon Press, 1964.

Marion, Mathieu. *Wittgenstein, Finitism and the Foundations of Mathematics*. Oxford: Oxford University Press, 1998.

Merleau-Ponty, Maurice. *Phenomenology of Perception*, trans. C. Smith. London: Routledge & Kegan Paul, 1962.

Miller, Alexander and Wright, Crispin. *Rule-Following and Meaning*. Chesham: Acumen Publishing, 2002.

Millikan, Ruth G. "Truth Rules, Hoverflies, and the Kripke-Wittgenstein Paradox." *Philosophical Review*, 99 (1990): 323–353.

Minar, Edward. "Wittgenstein and the 'Contingency' of Community." *Pacific Philosophical Quarterly*, 72 (1991): 203–234.

Minar, Edward. "Paradox and Privacy: On §§201–202 of Wittgenstein's *Philosophical Investigations*." *Philosophy and Phenomenological Research*, 54 (1994): 43–76.

Monk, Ray. *Ludwig Wittgenstein: The Duty of Genius*. London: Jonathan Cape, 1990.

Monk, Ray. "Was Russell an Analytic Philosopher?" In Glock ed. 1997, pp. 35–50.

Monk, Ray. "Philosophical Biography: The Very Idea." In Klagge ed. 2001, pp. 3–15.

Moore, A. W. *Points of View*. Oxford: Oxford University Press, 1997.

Moore, A. W. "Ineffability and Nonsense." *Proceedings of the Aristotelian Society*, Supplementary Vol. 77 (2003): 169–193.

Moore, A. W. "Was the Author of the *Tractatus* a Transcendental Idealist?" In *The Tractatus and Its History*, ed. Michael Potter and Peter M. Sullivan, forthcoming.

Moore, G. E. *Philosophical Papers*. London: Allen & Unwin, 1959.

Morris, Katherine. "The 'Context Principle' in the Later Wittgenstein." *Philosophical Quarterly*, 44:1 (1994): 294–310.

Morris, Katherine. "Introduction." In Baker 2004, pp. 1–18.

Mounce, H. O. "Critical Notice of The New Wittgenstein." *Philosophical Investigations*, 24 (2001): 185–192.

Moyal-Scharrock, Danièle. *The Third Wittgenstein*. Aldershot: Ashgate, 2004.

Mulhall, Stephen. *On Being in the World: Wittgenstein and Heidegger on Seeing Aspects*. London: Routledge, 1990.

Mulhall, Stephen, ed. *The Cavell Reader*. Oxford: Blackwell, 1996.

Mulhall, Stephen. *Inheritance and Originality: Wittgenstein, Heidegger, Kierkegaard*. Oxford: Clarendon Press, 2001.

Mulhall, Stephen. "Wittgenstein and Deconstruction." In *Arguing with Derrida*, ed. Simon Glendinning. Oxford: Blackwell, 2001. (2001a)

Murdoch, Iris. *The Sovereignty of Good*. London: ARK Paperbacks, 1970.

Murdoch, Iris. *Existentialists and Mystics: Writings on Philosophy and Literature*. New York: Allen Lane, The Penguin Press, 1997.

Nedo, M. and Ranchetti, M. *Wittgenstein: Sein Leben in Bildern und Texten*. Frankfurt am Main: Suhrkamp, 1983.

Nielsen, Kai. "Wittgensteinian Fideism." *Philosophy*, 42 (1967): 191–209.

Nietzsche, Friedrich. *Thus Spoke Zarathustra, A Book for Everyone and No One*, trans. R. J. Hollingdale. London: Penguin, 1961.

Nietzsche, Friedrich. *Twilight of the Idols*. In *The Portable Nietzsche*, trans. W. Kaufmann. New York: Viking, 1964.

Nietzsche, Friedrich. *The Will to Power*, trans. W. Kaufman and R. J. Hollingdale. New York: Vintage/Random House, 1968.

Nietzsche, Friedrich. *Beyond Good and Evil*, trans. R. J. Hollingdale. London: Penguin, 1973.

Nietzsche, Friedrich. *The Gay Science*, trans. W. Kaufman. New York: Vintage/Random House, 1974.

Nietzsche, Friedrich. *Ecce Homo*, trans. R. J. Hollingdale. London: Penguin, 1979.

Nietzsche, Friedrich. *On the Genealogy of Morals*, trans. D. Smith. Oxford: Oxford University Press, 1996.

Nyíri, J. C. "Wittgenstein's Later Work in Relation to Conservativism." In *Wittgenstein and His Times*, ed. B McGuinness, pp. 44–68. Oxford: Blackwell, 1981.

Ostrow, Matthew B. *Wittgenstein's Tractatus: A Dialectical Interpretation*. Cambridge: Cambridge University Press, 2002.

Pears, David F. "Logical Atomism, Russell and Wittgenstein." In *The Revolution in Philosophy*, ed. A. J. Ayer, pp. 44–55. London: Macmillan, 1956.

Pears, David F. *Wittgenstein*. London: Fontana/Collins, 1971.

Pears, David F. *The False Prison*, Vols. 1 and 2. Oxford: Clarendon Press/Oxford University Press, 1987/1988.

Perloff, Marjorie. *Wittgenstein's Ladder, Poetic Language and the Strangeness of the Ordinary*. Chicago: Chicago University Press, 1996.

Pettit, Phillip. "The Reality of Rule-Following." *Mind*, 99 (1990): 1–21.

Philip, P. *Bibliographie zur Wittgenstein-Literatur*. Bergen: Wittgenstein Archives, 1996.

Phillips, D. Z. *Faith and Philosophical Enquiry*. London: Routledge and Kegan Paul, 1970.

Phillips, D. Z. *Religion Without Explanation*. Oxford: Blackwell, 1976.

Phillips, D. Z. *Belief Change and Forms of Life*. Atlantic Highlands, NJ: Humanities Press, 1986.

Phillips, D. Z. *Interventions in Ethics*. London: Macmillan, 1992.

Phillips, D. Z., ed. *Wittgenstein and Religion*. New York: St. Martin's 1993.

Phillips, D. Z. *Philosophy's Cool Place*. Ithaca, NY: Cornell University Press, 1999.

Phillips, D. Z., ed. *Wittgenstein on Ethics and Religion*. London: Routledge, 2005.

Pichler, Alois. *Untersuchungen zu Wittgensteins Nachlaß*. Working Papers from the Wittgenstein Archives at the University of Bergen, No. 8, 1994.

Pichler, Alois. *Wittgensteins Philosophische Untersuchungen: Zur Textgenese von PU §§1–4*. Bergen: Wittgenstein Archives, 1997.

Pichler, Alois. *Wittgensteins Philosophische Untersuchungen. Vom Buch zum Album*. Amsterdam: Rodopi, 2004.

Pichler, Alois. "Outline of an Argument for a Therapeutic Reading of Wittgenstein's *Philosophical Investigations*." In *Time and History*, ed. Friedrich Stadler and Michael Stöltzner, pp. 235–237. Kirchberg a.W.: ALWS, 2005.

Pichler, Alois and Simo, Säätelä, eds. *Wittgenstein: The Philosopher and His Works*. Working Papers from the Wittgenstein Archives at the University of Bergen, No. 17, 2005.

Pigden, Charles. "Naturalism." In *A Companion to Ethics*, ed. Peter Singer, pp. 421–431. Oxford: Blackwell, 1991.

Pitcher, George. *The Philosophy of Wittgenstein*. Englewood Cliffs, NJ: Prentice-Hall, 1964.

Pitcher, George, ed. *Wittgenstein: The Philosophical Investigations*. Garden City, NY: Doubleday, 1966; London: Macmillan, 1968.

Pitkin, Hanna. *Wittgenstein and Justice: On the Significance of Ludwig Wittgenstein for Social and Political Thought*. Berkeley: University of California Press, 1972.

Pole, David. *The Later Philosophy of Wittgenstein: A Short Introduction with an Epilogue on John Wisdom*. London: University of London/Athlone Press, 1958.

Popper, K. R. *The Logic of Scientific Discovery.* London: Hutchinson, 1959. (*Logik der Forschung.* Vienna: Julius Springer, 1934.)

Proops, I. "The New Wittgenstein: A Critique." *European Journal of Philosophy*, 3 (2001): 375–404.

Puhl, K., ed. *Wittgenstein's Philosophy of Mathematics.* Vienna: Hölder-Pichler-Tempsky, 1993.

Putnam, Hilary. *Renewing Philosophy.* Cambridge, MA: Harvard University Press, 1992.

Putnam, Hilary. *Pragmatism: An Open Question.* Oxford: Blackwell, 1995.

Putnam, Hilary. "Was Wittgenstein Really an Anti-realist about Mathematics?" In McCarthy and Stidd eds. 2001, pp. 140–194.

Raatzsch, Richard. "Warum und wie man Wittgenstein interpretieren sollte." In *Philosophiegeschichte und Hermeneutik*, ed. Volker Caysa and K. D. Eichler, pp. 238–259. Leipzig: Leipziger Universitätsverlag, 1996.

Raatzsch, Richard. *Eigentlich Seltsames: Wittgensteins Philosophische Untersuchungen.* Paderborn: Schöningh, 2003.

Ramsey, Frank P. "Review of 'Tractatus.'" *Mind*, 32 (1923): 465–478. Reprinted in *Essays on Wittgenstein's Tractatus*, ed. Irving Copi and Robert Beard, eds. New York: Macmillan, 1966.

Ramsey, Frank P. "The Foundations of Mathematics." In *Philosophical Papers*, ed. D. H. Mellor, pp. 164–224. Cambridge: Cambridge University Press, 1990. (First published 1925.)

Ramsey, Frank P. *Foundations: Essays in Philosophy, Logic, Mathematics and Economics.* London: Routledge & Kegan Paul, 1978.

Read, Rupert and Deans, Rob. "Nothing Is Shown: A 'Resolute' Response to Mounce, Emiliani, Koethe and Vilhauer." *Philosophical Investigations*, 26 (2003): 239–268.

Read, Rupert and Goodenough, Jerry. *Film as Philosophy: Essays on Cinema After Wittgenstein and Cavell.* New York: Palgrave/Macmillan, 2005.

Reck, E. G., ed. *From Frege to Wittgenstein: Perspectives on Early Analytic Philosophy.* Oxford: Oxford University Press, 2002.

Rhees, Rush. "Can There Be a Private Language?" *Proceedings of the Aristotelian Society*, Supplementary Vol. 28 (1954): 77–94. Reprinted in Pitcher ed. 1968, pp. 267–285.

Rhees, Rush. "The *Tractatus*: Seeds of Some Misunderstandings." *Philosophical Review*, 72 (1963): 213–220. Reprinted in Rhees 1970, pp. 16–22.

Rhees, Rush. "The Philosophy of Wittgenstein." *Ratio*, 8 (1966): 180–193. Reprinted in Rhees 1970, pp. 37–54.

Rhees, Rush. *Without Answers.* London: Routledge & Kegan Paul, 1969.

Rhees, Rush. "'Ontology' and Identity in the *Tractatus*." In Winch ed. 1969, pp. 51–65. Reprinted in Rhees 1970, pp. 23–36. (1969a)

Rhees, Rush. *Discussions of Wittgenstein.* London: Routledge & Kegan Paul, 1970.

Rhees, Rush. "Miss Anscombe on the *Tractatus.*" *Philosophical Quarterly*, 10 (1970): 21–31. Reprinted in Rhees 1970, pp. 1–15.

Rhees, Rush, ed. *Recollections of Wittgenstein*, 2nd edition. Oxford: Oxford University Press, 1984.

Rhees, Rush. *Wittgenstein and the Possibility of Discourse*, ed. D. Z. Phillips. Cambridge: Cambridge University Press, 1998.

Rhees, Rush. *Moral Questions.* New York: Macmillan, 1999.

Richter, Duncan. *Ethics After Anscombe: Post Modern Moral Philosophy.* Dordrecht: Kluwer Academic Publishers, 2000.

Richter, Duncan. *Wittgenstein at His Word.* London: Continuum, Thoemmes Press, 2004.

Ricketts, Thomas. "Pictures, Logic, and the Limits of Sense in Wittgenstein's *Tractatus.*" In Sluga and Stern eds. 1996, pp. 59–99.

Rorty, Richard. *Philosophy and the Mirror of Nature.* Oxford: Blackwell, 1980.

Rorty, Richard. *Consequences of Pragmatism.* Minneapolis: University of Minnesota Press, 1982.

Rossvaer, Viggo. "Wittgenstein, Kant and Perspicious Representation." In *Ethics: Foundations, Problems and Applications, Proceedings of the Fifth International Wittgenstein Symposium*, ed. E. Morscher and R. Strazinger, pp. 414–417. Vienna: Hölder-Pichler-Tempsky, 1981.

Rothhaupt, Josef. "Zur Präzision der Rekonstruktion der Genese der 'Philosophischen Untersuchungen'." In *Metaphysics in the Post-metaphysical Age*, ed. Uwe Meixner and Peter Simons, pp. 196–203. Kirchberg a.W.: ALWS, 1999.

Rundle, Bede. *Wittgenstein and Contemporary Philosophy of Language.* Oxford: Blackwell, 1990.

Russell, Bertrand. "The Philosophy of Logical Atomism." In *Logic and Knowledge: Essays 1901–1950*, ed. R. C. Marsh, pp. 175–281. London: George Allen & Unwin, 1918.

Russell, Bertrand. "The Limits of Empiricism." *Aristotelian Society Proceedings*, 36 (1936): 131–150.

Russell, Bertrand. *My Philosophical Development.* London: George Allen & Unwin, 1985. (First published 1959.)

Russell, Bruce. "Beetle Boxes: Demonstrating the Logic of P-predicates." *Teaching Philosophy*, 1:2 (1975): 153–157.

Ryle, Gilbert. *The Concept of Mind.* London: Hutchinson, 1949.

Ryle, Gilbert. *Dilemmas.* Cambridge: Cambridge University Press, 1954.

Sacks, Mark. *The World We Found: The Limits of Ontological Talk.* London: Duckworth, 1989.

Sacks, Mark. "Transcendental Features and Transcendental Constraints." *International Journal of Philosophical Studies*, 5 (1997): 164–186.

Sartre, Jean-Paul. *Anti-Semite and Jew*, trans. G. J. Becker. New York: Schocken Books, 1948.

Sass, Louis. "Deep Disquietudes: Reflections on Wittgenstein as Antiphilosopher." In *Wittgenstein Philosophy and Biography*, ed. James C. Klagge, pp. 98–155. Cambridge: Cambridge University Press, 2001.

Savickey, Beth. *Wittgenstein's Art of Investigation*. London: Routledge, 1999.

von Savigny, Eike. *Wittgensteins "Philosophische Untersuchungen"*, Vols. 1 and 2. Frankfurt am Main: Vittorio Klostermann, 1988–1989.

von Savigny, Eike. *Wittgensteins "Philosophische Untersuchungen": Ein Kommentar für Leser*, Vols. 1–2, revd. edn. Frankfurt am Main: Klostermann, 1994–1996.

von Savigny, Eike. "'Ich möchte nicht mit meiner Schrift Andern das Denken ersparen.' (PU, Vorwort)." *Wittgenstein Studies*, 2 (1997): www.phil. uni-passau.de/dlwg/ws08/07-2-97.TXT.

Scheman, Naomi and O'Connor, Peg, eds. *Feminist Interpretations of Ludwig Wittgenstein*. University Park: Pennsylvania State University Press, 2002.

Schroeder, Severin. "Private Language and Private Experience." In Glock ed. 2001, pp 174–198.

Schroeder, Severin, ed. *Wittgenstein and Contemporary Philosophy of Mind*. New York: Palgrave, 2001.

Schroeder, Severin. *Wittgenstein: The Way Out of the Fly-Bottle*. Cambridge: Polity Press, 2006.

Schulte, Joachim. "Wittgenstein and Conservatism." *Ratio*, 25 (1983): 69–80.

Schulte, Joachim. *Erlebnis und Ausdruck, Wittgensteins Philosophie der Psychologie*. Munich: Philosophia, 1987.

Schulte, Joachim. *Wittgenstein*. Stuttgart: Reclam, 1989. (German edition of Schulte 1992.)

Schulte, Joachim. "Stilfragen." In *Wittgenstein im Kontext*, ed. J. Schulte, Chor und Gesetz, pp. 59–72. Frankfurt am Main: Suhrkamp, 1990.

Schulte, Joachim. *Wittgenstein: An Introduction*. Albany: State University of New York Press, 1992.

Schulte, Joachim. *Experience and Expression: Wittgenstein's Philosophy of Psychology*. Oxford: Clarendon Press/Oxford University Press, 1993.

Schulte, Joachim. *Ludwig Wittgenstein*. Suhrkamp Basisbiographie. Frankfurt am Main: Suhrkamp, 2005.

Schulte, Joachim. "What is a Work by Wittgenstein?" In Pichler and Säätelä eds. 2005, pp. 356–363. (2005a)

Schulte, Joachim. "The Pneumatic Conception of Thought." *Grazer philosophische Studien*, 71 (2006): 39–55.

Schulte, Joachim. "Phenomenology and Grammar." In Rosa M. Calcaterra, ed., *Le Ragioni del Conoscere e dell'Agire: Scritti in onore di Rosaria Egidi*, pp. 228–240. Milan: Franco Angeli, 2006. (2006a)

Searle, John R. "J. L. Austin (1911–1960)." In *A Companion to Analytic Philosophy*, ed. A. P. Martinich and David Sosa, pp. 218–230. Oxford: Blackwell, 2001.

Shanker, Stuart G., ed. *Ludwig Wittgenstein: Critical Assessments*, Vols. 1–4. London: Croom Helm, 1986.

Shanker, Stuart, G. *Wittgenstein and the Turning Point in the Philosophy of Mathematics*. London: Croom Helm, 1987.

Shanker, Stuart, G. "Wittgenstein's Remarks on the Significance of Gödel's Theorem." In Shanker ed. 1988, pp. 155–256.

Shanker, Stuart G. *Gödel's Theorem in Focus*. London: Croom Helm, 1988/ Routledge, 1989.

Shanker, V. A. and Shanker, S. G. *A Wittgenstein Bibliography*. Beckenham: Croom Helm, 1986.

Slote, Michael. "Review of Philippa Foot, *Natural Goodness* and of Thomas Hurka, *Virtue, Vice and Value*." *Mind*, 112 (2003): 130–139.

Sluga H. and Stern, D., eds. *Cambridge Companion to Wittgenstein*. Cambridge: Cambridge University Press, 1996.

Soames, Scott. *Philosophical Analysis in the Twentieth Century*, Vol. 1: *The Dawn of Analysis*. Princeton, NJ: Princeton University Press, 2003.

Soames, Scott. *Philosophical Analysis in the Twentieth Century*, Vol. 2: *The Age of Meaning*. Princeton, NJ: Princeton University Press, 2003.

Specht, Ernst Konrad. *Die sprachphilosophischen und ontologischen Grundlagen im Spätwerk Ludwig Wittgensteins*. Köln: Kölner Universitäts-Verlag, 1964.

Specht, Ernst Konrad. *The Foundation of Wittgenstein's Late Philosophy*. Manchester: Manchester University Press, 1969.

Staten, Henry. *Wittgenstein and Derrida*. Oxford: Blackwell, 1985.

Stegmüller, Wolfgang. *Hauptströmungen der Gegenwartsphilosophie*. Stuttgart: Kröners Taschenausgabe, 1965.

Stegmüller, Wolfgang. *Main Currents in Contemporary German, British and American Philosophy*. Bloomington: Indiana University Press, 1969.

Stenius, Erik. *Wittgenstein's Tractatus, a Critical Exposition of Its Main Lines of Thought*. Oxford: Blackwell, 1960.

Stern, David. "The 'Middle Wittgenstein': From Logical Atomism to Practical Holism." *Synthese*, 87 (1991): 203–226.

Stern, David. "The Wittgenstein Papers as Text and Hypertext: Cambridge, Bergen, and Beyond." In Wittgenstein and Norway, ed. K. Johannessen, pp. 251–273. Oslo: Solum, 1994.

Stern, David. *Wittgenstein on Mind and Language*. Oxford: Oxford University Press, 1995.

Stern, David. "The Availability of Wittgenstein's Philosophy." In Sluga and Stern eds. 1996, pp. 442–476.

Stern, David. *Wittgenstein's Philosophical Investigations: An Introduction*. Cambridge: Cambridge University Press, 2004.

Stern, David. "How Many Wittgenstein's?" In Pichler and Säätelä eds. 2005, pp. 164–188.

Stocker, Barry. *Post-Analytic Tractatus.* Aldershot: Ashgate, 2004.

Stone, Martin. "Wittgenstein on Deconstruction." In Crary and Read eds. 2000, pp. 83–117.

Strawson, Peter F. "Review of Wittgenstein's *Philosophical Investigations.*" *Mind*, 63 (1954): 70–99. Reprinted in Pitcher ed. 1968, pp. 22–64.

Stroll, Avrum. *Moore and Wittgenstein on Certainty.* Oxford: Oxford University Press, 1994.

Stroud, Barry. "Wittgenstein and Logical Necessity." *The Philosophical Review*, Vol. LXXIV (1965): 504–518.

Stroud, Barry. "The Allure of Idealism." In *Understanding Human Knowledge: Philosophical Essays*, pp. 83–98. Oxford: Oxford University Press, 2000.

Stroud, Barry. "The Charm of Naturalism." In *Naturalism in Question*, ed. Mario de Caro and David Macarthur, pp. 21–35. Cambridge, MA: Harvard University Press, 2004.

Sullivan, Peter M. "The 'Truth' in Solipsism, and Wittgenstein's Rejection of the A Priori." *European Journal of Philosophy*, 4 (1996): 195–219.

Sullivan, Peter M. "On Trying to be Resolute: A Response to Kremer on the *Tractatus.*" *European Journal of Philosophy*, 10 (2002): 43–78.

Sullivan, Peter M. "Ineffability and Nonsense." *Proceedings of the Aristotelian Society*, Supplementary Vol. 77 (2003): 195–223.

Sullivan, Peter M. "What is Squiggle? Ramsey on Wittgenstein's Theory of Judgement." In *Ramsey's Legacy*, ed. H. Lillehammer and D. H. Mellor, pp. 53–71. Oxford: Oxford University Press, 2005.

Taylor, Paul. "Artist's Intention." In *The Routledge Encyclopedia of Philosophy*, ed. E. Craig. London: Routledge, 1998: www.rep.routledge.com/article/M011.

Thompson, Michael. "The Representation of Life." In *Virtues and Reasons: Philippa Foot and Moral Theory*, ed. R. Hursthouse, G. Lawrence, and W. Quinn, pp. 247–296. Oxford: Clarendon Press, 1995.

Thompson, Michael. "Tre Gradi di Bonta Naturale," *Iride*, 38 (2003): 191–197.

Thompson, Michael. "Apprehending Human Form." In *Modern Moral Philosophy*, ed. Anthony O'Hear, pp. 47–74. Cambridge: Cambridge University Press, 2004.

Vlastos, Gregory. *Socrates, Ironist and Moral Philosopher.* Ithaca, NY: Cornell University Press, 1991.

Waismann, Friedrich. *Einführung in das mathematische Denken.* Vienna: Gerold, 1936.

Waismann, Friedrich. "How I See Philosophy." In *How I See Philosophy*, ed. Rom Harré, pp. 1–39. London: Macmillan, 1968. (Abbreviated as HISP.)

Waismann, Friedrich. *Logik, Sprache, Philosophie.* Stuttgart: Reclam, 1976.

Waismann, Friedrich. *Lectures on the Philosophy of Mathematics*, ed. Wolfgang Grassl. Amsterdam: Rodopi, 1982.

Waismann, Friedrich. *The Principles of Linguistic Philosophy*, 2nd edition. London: Macmillan, 1997.

Wallgren, Thomas. *Transformative Philosophy: Socrates, Wittgenstein, and the Democratic Spirit of Philosophy*. Lanham, MD: Lexington Books, 2006.

Weiss, Thomas. *Die Gebrauchstheorie der Bedeutung im Big Typescript – eine neue Perspektive auf Wittgenstein*. Berlin: Tenea, 2004.

Wiggins, David. *Needs, Values, Truth: Essays in the Philosophy of Value*, 3rd edn. Oxford: Clarendon Press, 1998.

Wiggins, David. "Wittgenstein on Ethics and the Riddle of Life." *Philosophy*, 79 (2004): 309–363.

Williams, Bernard. "Wittgenstein and Idealism." In *Moral Luck: Philosophical Papers 1973–1980*, pp. 144–163. Cambridge: Cambridge University Press, 1983.

Williams, Bernard. "What Might Philosophy Become?" In *Philosophy as a Humanistic Discipline*, ed. A. W. Moore, pp. 200–214. Princeton, NJ: Princeton University Press, 2006.

Winch, Peter. *The Idea of a Social Science and its Relation to Philosophy*. London: Routledge & Kegan Paul, 1958.

Winch, Peter. "Introduction: The Unity of Wittgenstein's Philosophy." In Winch ed. 1969, pp. 1–19.

Winch, Peter, ed. *Studies in the Philosophy of Wittgenstein*. London: Routledge & Kegan Paul, 1969.

Winch, Peter. *The Idea of Social Science and Its Relation to Philosophy*. London: Routledge, 1973.

Winch, Peter. "Im Anfang war die Tat." In Block ed. 1981, pp. 159–178.

Winch, Peter. *Trying to Make Sense*. Oxford: Blackwell, 1987.

Winch, Peter. "Language, Thought and World in Wittgenstein's *Tractatus*." In Winch 1987, pp. 3–17. (1987a)

Winch, Peter. "Discussion of Malcolm's Essay." In *Wittgenstein: A Religious Point of View?*, ed. P. Winch, pp. 95–135. London: Routledge, 1993.

Wisdom, John. *Philosophy and Psycho-Analysis*. Oxford: Blackwell, 1953.

Wright, Crispin. *Wittgenstein on the Foundations of Mathematics*. London: Duckworth, 1980.

Wright, Crispin. "Anti-Realist Semantics: The Role of Criteria." In *Idealism: Past and Present*, Royal Institute of Philosophy Lecture Series, 13: Supplement to "Philosophy", ed. Godfrey Vesey, pp. 225–248. Cambridge: Cambridge University Press, 1982.

Wright, Crispin. "Second Thoughts About Criteria." *Synthese*, 58 (1984): 383–405.

Wright, Crispin. *Realism: Meaning and Truth: Collected Papers on Semantic Anti-Realism*. Oxford: Blackwell, 1986.

Wright, Crispin. "Wittgenstein on Mathematical Proof." In *Wittgenstein Centenary Essays*, ed. A. Phillips Griffiths, pp. 79–100. Cambridge: Cambridge University Press, 1991.

Wright, Crispin. "Self-Knowledge: The Wittgensteinian Legacy." In *On Knowing Our Own Minds*, ed. C. McDonald, B. Smith and C. Wright, pp. 13–46. Oxford: Oxford University Press, 1998.

Wright, Crispin. *Rails to Infinity: Essays on Themes from Wittgenstein's Philosophical Investigations*. Cambridge, MA: Harvard University Press, 2001.

von Wright, Georg Henrik. *Wittgenstein*. Oxford: Blackwell, 1982.

von Wright, Georg Henrik. "Wittgenstein and the Twentieth Century." In *The Tree of Knowledge and Other Essays*, pp. 83–102. Leiden: Brill, 1993.

von Wright, Georg Henrik. "The Wittgenstein Papers." In *Ludwig Wittgenstein: Philosophical Occasions 1912–1951*, ed. J. C. Klagge and Alfred Nordmann, pp. 480–515. Indianapolis: Hackett, 1993. (1993a)

von Wright, Georg Henrik. "Remarks on Wittgenstein's Use of the Terms 'Sinn,' 'sinnlos,' 'wahr,' and 'Gedanke' in the *Tractatus*." In Pichler and Säätelä eds. 2005, pp. 90–98.

Wrigley, Michael. "Wittgenstein's Philosophy of Mathematics." *Philosophical Quarterly*, 27:106 (1977): 50–59.

Name Index

Subject Index